Canadian History For Dummies®

A Timeline of Important Events in Canadian History

30,000–10,000 BC	Prehistoric hunters cross over into Canada from Asia
circa 1000 AD	Leif Ericsson leads a Viking expedition to the New World
1451	The Iroquois Confederacy is formed
1497	John Cabot reaches Newfoundland (or perhaps Cape Breton)
1534	Jacques Cartier first explores the St. Lawrence region
1608	Samuel de Champlain establishes a French colony at Québec City
1670	Hudson's Bay Company is formed
1755	Expulsion of the Acadians
1759	Battle of the Plains of Abraham: Québec City is captured
1763	New France is formally ceded to Britain; Pontiac Rebellion erupts
1783	Loyalist refugees begin arriving after the American Revolution
1812–14	War of 1812: U.S. invades Canada
1837–38	Rebellions against British rule in Upper and Lower Canada
1848	Responsible government is won, first in Nova Scotia, then in Canada
1867	Confederation (first four provinces: Québec, Ontario, N.S., and N.B.)
1870	Red River Resistance; province of Manitoba is created
1871, 1873	B.C. and P.E.I. join Canada
1885	North-West Rebellion; the Canadian Pacific Railway is completed
1905	The provinces of Alberta and Saskatchewan are created
1914–18	World War I
1916	Women win the vote in Manitoba, Saskatchewan, and Alberta
1919	The Winnipeg General Strike
1929–39	The Great Depression
1939–45	World War II
1949	Newfoundland joins Canada
1950–53	Korean War
1959	St. Lawrence Seaway (major transportation route) officially opens
1960	Québec's Quiet Revolution begins; Native Canadians given the vote
1967	Canada's 100th birthday; Expo 67 World's Fair in Montréal
1970	October Crisis: political kidnappings, Ottawa suspends civil rights
1976	Summer Olympics take place in Montréal
1980	Québec referendum on "sovereignty-association" defeated 60% to 40%
1982	Constitution comes home — with a Charter of Rights and Freedoms
1987–90	Meech Lake Accord is put forward — and collapses
1988	Winter Olympics are held in Calgary
1992	Charlottetown Accord is rejected by a national referendum
1995	Québec referendum on sovereignty is narrowly defeated
1999	The new Arctic territory of Nunavut is created
2000	Clarity Bill outlines the terms of Québec separation

Canadian History For Dummies®

The Prime Ministers of Canada

1867–73, 1878–91	Sir John A. Macdonald	Conservative
1873–78	Alexander Mackenzie	Liberal
1891–92	Sir John Abbott	Conservative
1892–94	Sir John Thompson	Conservative
1894–96	Sir Mackenzie Bowell	Conservative
1896	Sir Charles Tupper	Conservative
1896–1911	Sir Wilfrid Laurier	Liberal
1911–20	Sir Robert Borden	Conservative/Union
1920–21, 1926	Arthur Meighen	Conservative
1921–26, 1926–30, 1935–48	W. L. Mackenzie King	Liberal
1930–35	R.B. (Richard Bedford) Bennett	Conservative
1948–57	Louis St. Laurent	Liberal
1957–63	John Diefenbaker	Conservative
1963–68	Lester "Mike" Pearson	Liberal
1968–79, 1980–84	Pierre Trudeau	Liberal
1979–80	Joe Clark	Conservative
1984	John Turner	Liberal
1984–93	Brian Mulroney	Conservative
1993	Kim Campbell	Conservative
1993–present	Jean Chrétien	Liberal

Kings and Queens and When They Ruled over Canada

French (1534–1763)	British (1763–present)
Francis I (1515–47)	George III (1760–1820)
Henry II (1547–59)	George IV (1820–30)
Francis II (1559–60)	William IV (1830–37)
Charles IX (1560–74)	Victoria (1837–1901)
Henry III (1574–89)	Edward VII (1901–10)
Henry IV (1589–1610)	George V (1910–36)
Louis XIII (1610–43)	Edward VIII (1936)
Louis XIV (1643–1715)	George VI (1936–52)
Louis XV (1715–74)	Elizabeth II (1952–present)

Provinces and Territories and When They Became Part of Canada

1867	Ontario, Québec, New Brunswick, Nova Scotia
1870	Manitoba
1871	British Columbia
1873	Prince Edward Island
1898	Yukon Territory
1905	Alberta, Saskatchewan
1949	Newfoundland
1999	Nunavut

Copyright © 2000 CDG Books Canada
All rights reserved.

Cheat Sheet $2.95 value. Item 3-19-3.

For more information about CDG Books, call 1-877-963-8830.

CDG BOOKS CANADA

...For Dummies®: Bestselling Book Series for Beginners

Praise for Will Ferguson:

"Eminently readable and entertaining."
— *Vancouver Province*

"Pierre Berton with attitude."
— *Montreal Gazette*

"If Douglas Adams (*Hitchhiker's Guide to the Galaxy*) and P.J. O'Rourke (*Holidays in Hell*) ever had an extraterrestrial Satanic love-child, it would probably write like Will Ferguson. That is, it would be observant, attitudinal, occasionally offensive and funny."
— *Los Angeles Times*

"The Brash Young Writer this country has needed for a long time."
— *Hamilton Spectator*

"Will Ferguson is a talent. He writes refreshingly, provocatively and sometimes eloquently."
— *Ottawa Citizen*

"Ferguson possesses a crafty eye for detail, not to mention a highly developed understanding of the essential folly in what passes for everyday life."
— *Edmonton Journal*

"[Ferguson] is the quintessential Canadian. He's as Canadian as toques and five percent beer. . . . A Canadian's Canadian."
— *January Magazine*

Praise for Why I Hate Canadians:

"An entirely digestible skewering of our national bedrock."
— *Toronto Star*

"Funny and abrasive . . . Ferguson does not try to please everyone, a rather un-Canadian approach, and that's just one of the reasons his book is so much fun to read."
— *Halifax Daily News*

"A wickedly funny book!"
— *Fredericton Daily Gleaner*

"Aggressively patriotic . . . Ferguson shows his love for Canada the way an older brother shows his love for a younger sibling — with a wedgie."
— *Charlottetown Guardian*

"Irreverent, incisive, and informative . . . I give it a resounding five out of five maple leafs."
— *Kingston Whig-Standard*

"A smooth read . . . Ferguson is both insightful and hilarious."
— *Georgia Straight (Vancouver)*

Praise for Bastards & Boneheads: Canada's Glorious Leaders Past and Present:

"Ferguson . . . [gives us] an utterly hilarious tour of our historical contradictions."
— *Calgary Straight*

"Don't be fooled. Beneath the campy rhetoric lies a serious and impressively researched narrative of the pivotal events in Canadian history."
— *National Post*

"Ferguson is Canada's myth-buster extraordinaire . . . . His writing is concise, easily digestible, humourous, dramatic, frank, and sometimes shocking."
— *New Brunswick Telegraph-Journal*

"Lively, knowledgeable, opinionated, disrespectful, debatable and immensely readable."
— *Montreal Gazette*

"A rip-snorting, rib-tickling, white water ride through this country's rich history of outrageous political scandals."
— *See Magazine (Edmonton)*

"Who says Canadian history isn't fun?"
— *Ottawa Citizen*

Canadian History

FOR

DUMMIES®

Canadian History FOR DUMMIES

by Will Ferguson

CDG BOOKS CANADA

CDG Books Canada, Inc.

◆ Toronto, ON ◆

Canadian History For Dummies®

Published by
CDG Books Canada, Inc.
99 Yorkville Avenue
Suite 400
Toronto, ON M5R 3K5
www.cdgbooks.com (CDG Books Canada Web Site)
www.idgbooks.com (IDG Books Worldwide Web Site)
www.dummies.com (Dummies Press Web Site)

Canadian Cataloguing in Publication Data

Ferguson, Will

Canadian history for dummies

Includes index.
ISBN: 1-894413-19-9

1. Canada — History — 19th century. 2. Canada — History — 20th century. I. Title.

FC164.F47 2000   971   C00-931665-5   F1026.F47 2000

Printed in Canada

3 4 5 6 TRI 04 03 02 01

Distributed in Canada by CDG Books Canada, Inc.

For general information on CDG Books, including all IDG Books Worldwide publications, please call our distribution center: HarperCollins Canada at 1-800-387-0117. For reseller information, including discounts and premium sales, please call our Sales department at 1-877-963-8830.

This book is available at special discounts for bulk purchases by your group or organization for resale, premiums, fundraising and seminars. For details, contact CDG Books Canada, Special Sales Department, 99 Yorkville Avenue, Suite 400, Toronto, ON, M5K 3K5; Tel: 416-963-8830; Email: spmarkets@cdgbooks.com.

For press review copies, author interviews, or other publicity information, please contact our Marketing department at 416-963-8830, fax 416-923-4821, or e-mail publicity@cdgbooks.com.

For authorization to photocopy items for corporate, personal, or educational use, please contact Cancopy, The Canadian Copyright Licensing Agency, One Yonge Street, Suite 1900, Toronto, ON, M5E 1E5; Tel: 416-868-1620; Fax: 416-868-1621; www.cancopy.com.

 is a trademark under exclusive license to CDG Books Canada, Inc., from International Data Group, Inc.

About the Author

Will Ferguson was born and raised in the former fur-trapping community of Fort Vermilion, deep in the backwoods of northern Alberta. "Closer to the Arctic Circle than the American border," as he likes to say. Will has lived and worked in almost every region of Canada, from the Okanagan Valley of B.C. to the farmlands of rural Québec, from Saskatoon to southern Ontario, from Manitoba to P.E.I.

He went to South America as a volunteer with Canada World Youth, and later spent five years in Japan. He has travelled across northern China, Korea, Indonesia, and mainland Malaysia — but through it all has remained stubbornly Canadian.

Will has a degree in Fine Arts (Film & Television) from York University in Toronto, and has worked in marketing/publicity, and even — briefly — as a journalist. His debut book, a humorous look at Canadian culture entitled *Why I Hate Canadians*, was a surprise bestseller that allowed him to change careers suddenly in mid-stream. Ever since then, he has been a full-time writer, specializing in travel and Canadiana.

Will is also the author of *The Hitchhiker's Guide to Japan*, a travel guide; *I Was a Teenage Katima-victim!*, a hilarious memoir of his days as a cross-Canada youth volunteer; *Hokkaido Highway Blues*, a travel narrative; and *Bastards & Boneheads: Canada's Glorious Leaders Past and Present*, a frank and funny look at Canada's prime ministers and the history of Canada. He is also the co-author of *The Girlfriend's Guide to Hockey*, a lighthearted and informative guide to Canada's favourite sport.

Although he considers himself an "honorary Maritimer" (his family's roots are in Cape Breton and he lived for several years in the Fundy region of New Brunswick), Will recently returned to his home province of Alberta. He now lives in Calgary with his wife, Terumi, and their three-year-old son, Alex.

ABOUT CDG BOOKS CANADA, INC. AND
IDG BOOKS WORLDWIDE, INC.

Welcome to the world of IDG Books Worldwide and CDG Books Canada.

IDG Books Worldwide, Inc., is a subsidiary of International Data Group, Inc., the world's largest publisher of computer-related information and the leading global provider of information services on information technology. IDG was founded more than 30 years ago and now employs more than 9,000 people worldwide. IDG publishes more than 295 computer publications in over 75 countries (see listing below). More than 90 million people read one or more IDG publications each month.

Launched in 1990, IDG Books Worldwide is today the #1 publisher of best-selling computer books in North America. IDG Books Worldwide is proud to be the recipient of eight awards from the Computer Press Association in recognition of editorial excellence and three from *Computer Currents'* First Annual Readers' Choice Awards. Our best-selling *...For Dummies*® series has more than 55 million copies in print with translations in 31 languages. In record time, IDG Books Worldwide has become the first choice for millions of readers around the world who want to learn how to better manage their businesses.

In 1998, IDG Books Worldwide formally partnered with Macmillan Canada, a subsidiary of Canada Publishing Corporation, to create CDG Books Canada, a dynamic new Canadian publishing company. CDG Books Canada is now Canada's fastest growing publisher, bringing valuable information to Canadians from coast to coast through the introduction of Canadian *...For Dummies*® and *CliffsNotes*™ titles.

Every one of our books is designed to bring extra value and skill-building instructions to the reader. Our books are written by experts who understand and care about our readers. The knowledge base of our editorial staff comes from years of experience in publishing, education, and journalism — experience we use to produce books to carry us into the new millennium. In short, we care about books, so we attract the best people. We devote special attention to details such as audience, interior design, use of icons, and illustrations. And because we use an efficient process of authoring, editing, and desktop publishing our books electronically, we can spend more time ensuring superior content and spend less time on the technicalities of making books.

You can count on our commitment to deliver high-quality books at competitive prices on topics you want to read about. At IDG Books Worldwide and CDG Books Canada, we continue in the IDG tradition of delivering quality for more than 30 years. You can learn more about IDG Books Worldwide and CDG Books Canada by visiting www.idgbooks.com, www.dummies.com, and www.cdgbooks.com.

Eighth Annual Computer Press Awards 1992

Ninth Annual Computer Press Awards 1993

Tenth Annual Computer Press Awards 1994

Eleventh Annual Computer Press Awards 1995

IDG is the world's leading IT media, research and exposition company. Founded in 1964, IDG had 1997 revenues of $2.05 billion and has more than 9,000 employees worldwide. IDG offers the widest range of media options that reach IT buyers in 75 countries representing 95% of worldwide IT spending. IDG's diverse product and services portfolio spans six key areas including print publishing, online publishing, expositions and conferences, market research, education and training, and global marketing services. More than 90 million people read one or more of IDG's 290 magazines and newspapers, including IDG's leading global brands — Computerworld, PC World, Network World, Macworld and the Channel World family of publications. IDG Books Worldwide is one of the fastest-growing computer book publishers in the world, with more than 700 titles in 36 languages. The "...For Dummies®" series alone has more than 50 million copies in print. IDG offers online users the largest network of technology-specific Web sites around the world through IDG.net (http://www.idg.net), which comprises more than 225 targeted Web sites in 55 countries worldwide. International Data Corporation (IDC) is the world's largest provider of information technology data, analysis and consulting, with research centers in over 41 countries and more than 400 research analysts worldwide. IDG World Expo is a leading producer of more than 168 globally branded conferences and expositions in 35 countries including E3 (Electronic Entertainment Expo), Macworld Expo, ComNet, Windows World Expo, ICE (Internet Commerce Expo), Agenda, DEMO, and Spotlight. IDG's training subsidiary, ExecuTrain, is the world's largest computer training company, with more than 230 locations worldwide and 785 training courses. IDG Marketing Services helps industry-leading IT companies build international brand recognition by developing global integrated marketing programs via IDG's print, online and exposition products worldwide. Further information about the company can be found at www.idg.com.   8/24/99

Acknowledgments

First of all, I owe a great big thank you to my editor at CDG, Joan Whitman, who first approached me about writing a . . . *For Dummies* guide to Canadian history and who has supported this project all the way, with great enthusiasm and confidence — even as I was pushing the deadlines to the very edge and tinkering with last-minute changes and additions. Thanks, Joan!

I would also like to thank Amy Black at CDG for her help at the end, and my agent, Carolyn Swayze, for her good cheer and excellent advice. Thanks also to Kirsten Olson, Executive Director of the Legal Archives of Alberta, who first tipped me off about Lizzie Cyr and the *true* story behind the famous Persons Case. Thanks also to historian Harry Sanders, author of an upcoming book on Calgary's Union Cemetery. And to Mark Zuehlke of Victoria, B.C., author of *Ortona: Canada's Epic World War II Battle* and an upcoming Canadian military atlas.

I'd like to thank Pam Stackhouse of Saint John, New Brunswick, as well, who first told me the tale of Madame La Tour and the Acadian Civil War and who helped spark my own long-running fascination with early Maritime history. Thanks also to her husband, Steve, who didn't really teach me anything about history — but he did show me how to parallel park, and that's got to be worth something.

Publisher's Acknowledgments

We're proud of this book; please register your comments through our IDG Books Worldwide Online Registration Form located at http://my2cents.dummies.com.

Some of the people who helped bring this book to market include the following:

Acquisitions and Editorial

Acquisitions Editor: Joan Whitman

Assistant Editors: Melanie Rutledge, Kim Herter

Copy Editor: Lisa Berland

Editorial Assistant: Stella Partheniou

Special Help

Amy Black, Michael Kelly

Production

Production Manager: Donna Brown

Production Editor: Rebecca Conolly

Layout and Graphics: Kim Monteforte, Heidy Lawrance Associates

Special Art: Shelley Lea, Elizabeth Puhl (cartographer), Brent Savage, Rashell Smith

Proofreader: Pamela Erlichman

Indexer: Belle Wong

General and Administrative

IDG Books Worldwide, Inc.: John Kilcullen, CEO; William Barry, President

CDG Books Canada, Inc.: Ron Besse, Chairman; Tom Best, President; Robert Harris, Vice President and Publisher

IDG Books Technology Publishing Group: Richard Swadley, Senior Vice President and Publisher; Walter Bruce III, Vice President and Associate Publisher; Mary Bednarek, Branded Product Development Director; Mary Corder, Editorial Director

IDG Books Consumer Publishing Group: Roland Elgey, Senior Vice President and Publisher; Kathleen A. Welton, Vice President and Publisher; Kevin Thornton, Acquisitions Manager; Kristin A. Cocks, Editorial Director

IDG Books Internet Publishing Group: Brenda McLaughlin, Senior Vice President and Publisher; Diane Graves Steele, Vice President and Associate Publisher; Sofia Marchant, Online Marketing Manager

IDG Books Production for Dummies Press: Michael R. Britton, Vice President of Production; Debbie Stailey, Associate Director of Production; Cindy L. Phipps, Manager of Project Coordination, Production Proofreading, and Indexing; Tony Augsburger, Manager of Prepress, Reprints, and Systems; Laura Carpenter, Production Control Manager; Shelley Lea, Supervisor of Graphics and Design; Debbie J. Gates, Production Systems Specialist; Robert Springer, Supervisor of Proofreading; Kathie Schutte, Production Supervisor

Dummies Packaging and Book Design: Patty Page, Manager, Promotions Marketing

◆

The publisher would like to give special thanks to Patrick J. McGovern, without whom this book would not have been possible.

◆

Contents at a Glance

Cartoons at a Glance

Table of Contents

Introduction

C anadian history is a lot of fun. When CDG first approached me about
writing a ...*For Dummies* book, I jumped at the chance. Heck, I even
juggled a couple of other assignments in order to do it, and although this
turned out to be a much bigger undertaking than I ever imagined, it was well
worth it. Canadian history has always been one of my great passions, and it
was a thrill to finally take on the entire sweep of Canada's past, from top to
bottom, start to present.

It's a hell of a story. There are heroes and villains, tragedies and triumphs,
great battles and sudden betrayals, loyal refugees and long struggles for
social justice. Canadian history is a roller-coaster ride all right, but more
importantly, it tells us who we are, where we came from, and where we are
going. And when I say "we," I am not speaking in terms of racial background
or ethnic identity. I'm speaking of nationality. And a country: *Canada*.

Any place as eclectic and mixed-up as Canada will never be able to settle on a
single unified, homogenous national history that will please everyone, but
make no mistake: There *is* a history that we need to know. The interpretations
may vary — radically, at times — but there are still core events and important
leaders from our past that every Canadian should be familiar with.

> *We do not simply exist in a contemporary world. We have a past, if only
> we would try to grapple with it. . . . History matters, and we forget this truth
> at our peril.*
>
> — Canadian historian J.L. Granatstein

About This Book

Canadian History for Dummies is a crash course in cultural literacy. It covers
the essential dates, events, leaders, and historic themes from our past — and
present. It also includes more than 200 Web sites on related topics, so that
you can expand and explore further the areas that interest you. It's like having
access to an entire on-line library of Canadian history. Even better, it's free.
And trust me, there are some amazing sites out there in Cyberspace. I once
spent an entire afternoon going through the final days of Henry Hudson's
doomed expedition, and another day exploring the heartbreak of Canada's
disastrous World War II raid on Dieppe.

This book contains all the essentials of Canadian history, but I hope it will only be the start, a launching pad for further explorations of Canada's past. My goal is to whet your appetite and supply some interesting leads — but be warned: History is addictive. Start pursuing Canadian Web sites and haunting the Canadiana section of your local bookstore, and you may never resurface again. I speak from personal experience.

We all have those moments in life when we stop and look around and ask ourselves, "How on earth did I ever end up *here*?" And the answer lies, as always, in the contingencies of the past and the choices we made along the way. This book tries to answer that question on a national level: *"How on earth did we ever end up here?"*

> *History is the record of an encounter between character and circumstance. . . . And the encounter between character and circumstance is essentially a story.*
>
>   — historian Donald Creighton

History is about the impact of the decisions we make and the ripple effects that follow. It's a study of people and events, action and reaction, crisis and consequence. History can inspire us. It can anger us. It can teach us important lessons. It can be used as an alibi — or a weapon. But above all it is a story. In this case, the story of a country.

The "story" in history *is* important, and I have tried my best to give this book a narrative flow. I have also tried to introduce some lesser-known figures from Canada's past.

- ✔ People like Lizzie Cyr, the prostitute whose now-forgotten trial first set in motion a chain of events that led to the women's rights crusade of the Famous Five and the Persons Case that followed.

- ✔ Or the swashbuckling Sieur d'Iberville whose exploits are worthy of a Hollywood blockbuster.

- ✔ Or the Canadian diplomat, John Humphrey, who drafted the United Nations Universal Declaration of Human Rights. The UN Declaration set both the standards and the ideals of today's global village. It has had a huge impact on world events. Yet, few Canadians have ever heard of John Humphrey or are aware of what he achieved.

When I was living in the Loyalist town of St. Andrews, New Brunswick, I used to drive by a small island almost every day. I never gave it much thought until one day, just in passing, I noticed a historic marker up from the shore. When I pulled over, I discovered that right there — right there in front of me — was the legendary St. Croix Island (once known, for grim descriptive reasons, as "Bone Island"). It was on that tiny tuft of land that a band of French colonists first suffered through a horrific winter 400 years before. It was there, on that small island, that Acadia was born: the first permanent European presence on mainland Canada. And here I was, driving by it, week after week, blissfully unaware. I was sleepwalking past epic adventures. I was surrounded by ghosts, and I never even knew. I think that is how a lot of Canadians view their past: It barely registers with us and is only ever caught in passing — if at all.

> *Strangers in their own land . . .*
>
> — author Robertson Davies on the relationship many
> Canadians have with their country and its history

How This Book Is Organized

It's very simple. I took a straightforward chronological approach, with each part representing another step in Canadian development. You can jump around if you like, though I do recommend reading the chapters in any given part in the order they appear.

Part I: When Worlds Collide

This part deals with Canada's First Nations and their initial contact with Europeans, beginning with the Vikings and ending with the first tentative colonies in Newfoundland, the Maritimes, and along the St. Lawrence. The Native societies of Canada prior to first contact were incredibly complex and varied: ranging from the military and political alliances of the Iroquois to the northern trade empire of the Ojibwa; from the small-band subsistence hunters of the northern forests to the austere lifestyle of the plains; from the intricate arts and social caste system of the Pacifc Coast to the survival techniques and adaptive genius of the Arctic Inuit. This wasn't an empty continent that the European explorers first stumbled upon. Far from it.

Part II: The Rise of New France

Here I talk about the formative years of 1608 to 1701. It begins with Samuel de Champlain and the founding of French fur-trading colonies in the Maritimes and along the St. Lawrence. We look at the rise of an elaborate French culture in Canada, a sort of "Paris-in-exile," as well as its ongoing frontier war with the Iroquois Confederacy. Jesuit missionaries travelled deep into Native territory spreading both germs and the gospel among the Huron and other nations. A new breed of trader was born — the voyageurs and woodsmen of New France — even as England outflanked France to the north, in the Hudson Bay. A fierce rivalry between the two European countries erupted, and battles raged from Arctic seas to the outposts of Newfoundland.

Part III: The Fall of New France

I cover the fateful years 1701 to 1766, which deals with the conquest of New France by Britain, something that has been described as "the Big Bang" of Canadian history. During the Seven Years' War, Britain and France battled it out for final control of the continent. The Acadian colonists of the Maritime region were forced into exile, and the French fortress of Louisbourg, perched on the windswept coast of Cape Breton, was captured — and systematically destroyed. On the Plains of Abraham, outside the walled city of Québec, two armies faced off against each other: one British, one French. In a fierce 15-minute battle, the fate of Canada was decided.

Part IV: Canada: The Failed Republic?

Here you'll read about the tumultuous years of 1766 to 1838. When the American colonies broke free of Great Britain, the northern ones stayed loyal. In this, the American Revolution ultimately created, not one, but *two* new countries. In 1812, the Americans tried to finish the job and conquer Canada, and in 1837 rebellions within Upper and Lower Canada again tried to break the colonies free. Both attempts failed, and Canada remained independent of the United States. Meanwhile, in the vast interior of the continent, explorers were pushing their way overland — all the way to the Pacific.

Part V: The Roads to Confederation

This part looks at the energetic years of 1838 to 1891. This was an era of nation-building that marked the birth of modern Canada, as three colonies joined together to form a new Confederation. Under the terms of the 1867 British North America (BNA) Act, Canada's essential character was set. And soon after, the Canadians purchased the vast North-West and invited B.C. into the fold. On the plains, the Métis (of mixed Native and European background) led an armed rebellion against the government — and the last spike of the CPR was driven home, joining Canada "from sea to sea."

Part VI: The End of "English" Canada

The years between 1891 and 1929 were ones of optimism and disillusionment. It was an era that marked the high-point of English-Canadian imperial pride — and its decline. The events discussed in this part include the opening of the Canadian West, the Klondike Gold Rush, World War I, and the fight for women's rights. Canada's multicultural character (neither French, English, nor Native) first began to take shape during this time, as waves of newcomers arrived in search of prosperity. The First World War, which brought old-school European imperialism to a crashing halt, also marked Canada's "political independence." In was an age — not of nation-building — but rather consolidation, a time when Canada moved from colony to country.

Part VII: Dark Days

The dark years of 1929 to 1959 were a time marked by three disastrous events: the Great Depression of the 1930s, the slaughter of World War II, and the tense Armageddon-game of the Cold War. During the Thirties, the economy collapsed, the Prairies turned into a dustbowl, and labour unrest and socialist movements rose. Then suddenly, as an ally in the war against Nazi Germany, Canada found itself plunged into unexpected prosperity. This in turn led to the consumer society of the 1950s and the baby boom that followed. And all the while, the threat of nuclear war between the Capitalist West and the Communist East hung over our heads. Canada was a "Middle Power," in more ways than one. As a Soviet ambassador noted, Canada was "the ham in the Soviet–American sandwich."

Part VIII: Noisy Evolution

This part covers 1960 to 2000. It begins with the Quiet Revolution in Québec, a cultural renaissance that gave birth to renewed nationalism — and violence. Martial law was declared and mass arrests were ordered. The violent wing of the separatist movement was crushed, but not the political arm, and in 1980 a referendum on "sovereignty-association" was held — and defeated. Canada's Constitution came home with a Charter of Rights and Freedoms, but without the approval of Québec's PQ government. Later attempts at "bringing Québec into the Constitution" failed and the country teetered at the edge of collapse in 1995. Since then, things have simmered at a low heat without boiling over, and we entered the 21st century with the same unresolved issues and recurring themes that we started with at the dawn of the last century.

Part IX: The Part of Tens

Here you'll find great Canadian quotations (a sort of summarized history of Canada as told through some of the more memorable quips) as well as the most notable French-Canadian, English-Canadian and Native leaders, and a list of important political firsts for women. The information in this part is dealt with in detail in previous chapters, but is gathered here for quick reference.

Icons Used In This Book

As I noted in an earlier book, the three big themes of Canadian history are keeping the Americans out, keeping the French in, and trying to get the Natives to somehow disappear.

In *Canadian History for Dummies*, I've gone through and flagged these themes — along with some others. One of the trademarks of . . . *For Dummies* books is the use of icons. These are great when it comes to marking technical advice or computer tips, but when it comes to something like history — which is essentially a narrative, I thought it would be helpful to use "thematic icons," to mark the recurring patterns of Canadian history.

As a combination of chronological and thematic styles, this represents a new approach to presenting history. These icons allow you to follow the ongoing themes of Canadian history as they are played out. (And let me just say, I wish there were thematic icons in the margins when I was struggling through *Moby-Dick* back in college.) You can even read this book along thematic lines if you like, tracing the various "recurring dramas" of Canadian history as you go.

This eagle feather (an important symbol for most First Nations) signals issues dealing with aboriginal rights, from early colonial conflicts to current land claims.

From the wars of conquest to the present-day separatist movement in Québec, this icon marks one of the central elements of our national history: the relationship between French and English Canada.

The presence of the United States has had a strong impact on Canadian development, from the War of 1812 to our current "branch-plant" economy. Confederation itself was brought about partly by the threat of an American military invasion. So when you see this icon, brace yourself.

One of the defining traits of Canada is that it has preferred evolution to revolution. Canada gained its independence gradually, and this icon — a maple leaf rising — marks key moments along the way.

This icon signals areas of disagreement, either among historians or the public at large. I try not to take sides, but . . .

Want to learn more? You'll find a wealth of information at the Web site addresses marked by this icon. (*Note*: because of formatting rules, any Web sites contained *within* sidebars aren't flagged with an icon. So keep your eyes peeled for those ones as well.)

A quick note about these icons: The symbols I chose only *represent* the themes. They aren't meant to be taken literally. The Union Jack/fleur-de-lis icon, for example, is used in this book to represent everything from Acadia versus New England to the LaFontaine/Baldwin political alliance of the 1840s to Québec versus Ottawa in the 1990s.

The stylized maple leaf dates only to 1965, but is used here to symbolize Canadian independence from the earliest years of New France onward. It marks the Battle of Vimy Ridge, for example, even though the soldiers at that time would have been flying the Red Ensign, not the maple leaf.

A Final Note

Please let me know of any errors or omissions, especially on-line sites I may have missed, or ones that have since become defunct. (We re-checked all the Internet addresses just before this book went to press, but the Web is constantly changing, so if some of the sites have vanished, I apologize.) You can send any comments, complaints, or corrections to me care of the publisher.

> *I want History to jump on Canada's spine with sharp skates.*
> — Montréal poet Leonard Cohen

Don't worry, I won't be jumping on any spines! But it will be a heck of a ride. I hope you enjoy it.

Part I
When Worlds Collide

Starting off on the wrong foot. Early contact between Europeans
and Canada's Native groups didn't always go smoothly . . .

In this part . . .

We look at Canada's First Nations, from the Iroquois of the Eastern Woods to the buffalo hunters of the Plains, from the artists and noblemen of the Pacific Coast to the Inuit hunters of the Far North. Then we look at the first Europeans to arrive on our shores: the Vikings, the "Three Big C's" (Cabot, Cartier, and Champlain), and the two G's (Gilbert and Guy). We also look at the fate of some of the early Arctic explorers. Hint: It wasn't pretty.

Chapter 1

First Nations

· ·

In This Chapter

▶ The Iroquois Confederacy terrorizes its neighbours

▶ The Plains Indians create a Hollywood legend

▶ The Pacific Coast Nations try to figure out what to do with all their wealth

▶ The Inuit of the Far North adapt to a harsh environment

· ·

> *Canada has fifty-five founding nations rather than just the two that have been officially recognized.*
>
> — historian Olive Dickason

he first Canadians — the very first — arrived in prehistoric times when low sea levels created a temporary land bridge (Beringia) between Asia and Alaska. Early hunters, following the woolly mammoth, migrated overland into North America. When exactly this happened, no one is quite sure. Estimates range wildly from 100,000 to 10,000 years ago, depending on which expert you consult. The most commonly accepted view is that the first humans arrived roughly 15,000 years ago, with the oldest confirmed cultural site in the Americas being 13,350 years old (though sites in Alaska and Yukon suggest human occupation as long as 20,000 to 25,000 years ago). Either way, it was a long, long, long time ago: long before the birth of Christ, long before the pyramids were built, long before Moses led his people out of Egypt and into the Promised Land.

So, to say, as some do, that "we are all immigrants to Canada, even the Indians" is a gross distortion to say the least. Surely, any group whose roots in Canada go back to before the days of the pharaohs has a legitimate claim at being considered our "original" inhabitants and "first" nations. Indeed, when you hear commentators insisting that Native Canadians are "immigrants, same as everybody else," I guarantee you they have a hidden agenda — usually one aimed at trying to undermine Native land claims and treaty rights.

By the time the Europeans showed up, a wide variety of aboriginal societies had long since evolved and spread across every region of North and South America. The diversity was remarkable. In Canada alone, there were more than

50 separate Native languages, many of which were as different as Chinese and English. Today, only three of these — Cree, Ojibwa, and the Inuktitut language of the Arctic — are in a strong enough position to survive. Entire nations have vanished; entire cultures have been lost.

Still, calling the European invasion of Canada "a collision" is a bit misleading. The process occurred as much by stealth as anything, and it took centuries to unfold, with European trade goods often preceding the arrival of the Europeans themselves by several generations.

Trade is good. It allows people to redistribute materials, generate wealth, and improve their quality of life. Complex and long-standing trade routes were already in place among the First Nations long before the Europeans arrived. It is a myth that the Natives, gullible and innocent of the ways of the outside world, traded away valuable furs for trinkets. Far from it. They were notoriously shrewd in their dealings with the Europeans. The metal goods the outsiders brought in — the iron, the weapons, the axes, and especially the cooking pans — revolutionized Native life.

As the various Native societies jostled for position, ambushing, attacking, and attempting to outplay both their neighbours and the newcomers, a great social disruption occurred. This was inevitable: Cultures along trade routes are always transformed, and there is no doubt that European trade goods were both desirable and useful. And remember, the Europeans were also jostling for position. The French, Dutch, and English along the east coast battled it out for access to Native trade.

Not all imports were beneficial. Alcohol wreaked havoc among Native communities, and still does to this day. Native middlemen waged bloody wars of territorial control, and well-intentioned Christian missionaries caused terrible divisions within Native societies.

> *When the white man came, we had the land and they had the Bibles. Now they have the land and we have the Bibles.*
> — Chief Dan George

Even more deadly were the infectious diseases that the whites brought with them. The Europeans were crawling with germs, many of which were unknown in the New World. As a result, the First Nations had never developed a resistance to many of the illnesses the Europeans unwittingly introduced. Smallpox, measles, influenza, lung infections, and even the common cold all took a deadly toll on Native societies. Entire populations collapsed. It was a demographic catastrophe.

Here's just one example: The Huron Confederacy in what is now northern Ontario had a population of 25,000 in the year 1600. But once Catholic missionaries and French traders made contact, a smallpox epidemic swept through the Huron community, killing thousands and leaving the population at scarcely 9,000 by 1640 — a shadow of its former greatness. Demoralized, with their population depleted and the missionaries sewing seeds of discord among them (the community was divided between those who had been converted and those who had not), the Huron could no longer maintain their once vast farmlands. Fields were abandoned. Villages sat empty. And the Huron, a once proud and powerful people, were overrun by their Iroquois enemies and destroyed. (See Chapter 3 for more on the Iroquois defeat of the Huron.)

Ethnohistorian Henry Dobyns estimates that the Native population of North America was more than 18 million prior to European contact — a number that fell a whopping 95 percent over the next 130 years. Ninety-five percent, mind you! That was far worse than the Black Death of the bubonic plague in Europe. (Other ethnohistorians support Dobyns's conclusions, though they put the population at around 10 million prior to first contact.)

Not everyone agrees, however. More conservative historians, such as Alfred Kroeber, insist that the North American Native population was no more than one million prior to contact, and that any population decline was "moderate" and only partly due to disease. One thing *is* known from first-hand accounts and eyewitness reports: Disease did sweep through Native communities, did cripple their economies, did destroy their societies, and did leave haunting "ghost camps" in their wakes. This awful human toll is not really reflected in any statistic.

Today, there are approximately one million Canadians of aboriginal descent. The government distinguishes between three broad categories: Indian, Inuit, and Métis (mixed ancestry), of which some 550,000 are legally recognized, or *status*. Theirs is a history interwoven through Canada's, and it is a point worth remembering: This wasn't an empty continent that the Europeans stumbled upon, and it wasn't an empty land that we claimed as our own.

For an overview of the effects and impact Europeans have had on Native culture, www.inac.gc.ca/pr/pub/fnc/nwcm_e.html offers a wealth of information. This is part of a larger First Nations site presented by Indian and Northern Affairs Canada. It is one of the best on-line sources going, and I recommend it highly. For an extensive look at Canada's First Nations, by region and culture group, go there at www.inac.gc.ca/pr/pub/fnc/index_e.html and explore!

For the Museum of Civilization's overview of Canadian Native Groups, with some maps, go to www.civilization.ca/membrs/fph/stones/groups/grmenu.htm.

Figure 1-1 shows the distribution of Native Groups in Canada at the time of first contact.

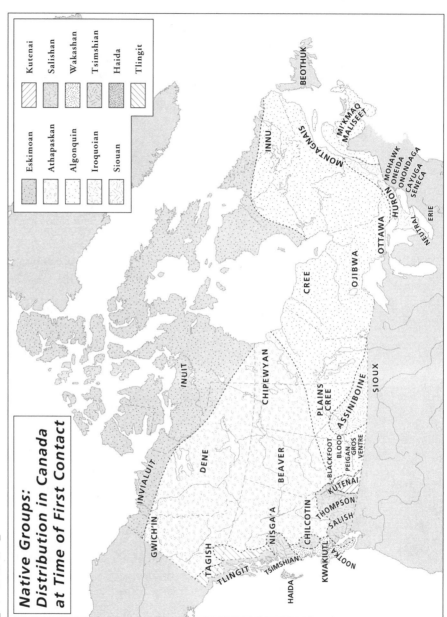

Figure 1-1:
Native Groups in Canada.

People of the Longhouse

Let's clear up one point of confusion right at the start: The term *Iroquoian* refers to the Native people who lived in the St. Lawrence–Great Lakes region. They shared a similar language and culture.

Among them were the Huron in the Georgian Bay area, the Neutrals in the Niagara region, and the Erie, who lived on the south side of Lake — well, you can probably figure that part out yourself.

The Iroquoian people were the northernmost farmers in North America, living in heavily fortified log-palisade towns and tending large farmland fields. Their communities contained as many as two thousand people, and they relied heavily on agriculture, especially maize, squash, and beans.

Their lifestyle centred around longhouse dwellings. These longhouses, some reaching almost 100 metres in length, contained the members of an entire extended family: as many as 50 people, living under one common roof. (How they did it, I'll never know. There were seven of us when I was growing up, sharing one bathroom and three bedrooms, and that was tough enough.)

The term *Iroquois*, however, usually refers to one specific group of Iroquoian people, namely, the Five Nations who inhabited key lands south of Lake Ontario in what is now New York State. From east to west, the Five Nations were Mohawk, Oneida, Onondaga, Cayuga, and Seneca. (They later became the Six Nations when the Tuscarora, a displaced Iroquoian nation from the south, joined them in 1722.)

Together, these Five Nations formed a powerful and important confederacy, one that played a crucial role in the early development of Canada (see Chapters 3 and 5).

The Great Law of Peace

[The Iroquois Confederacy] is in fact the oldest democracy on this continent. Its political system, which includes a voice for all and a balance of power between the sexes, existed when Europe still believed in the divine right of kings.

— author Ronald Wright

The founding of the Iroquois Confederacy (also known as the League of Five Nations) can be traced back fairly accurately to 1451 by a reference to a solar eclipse that occurred in the region — although other sources cite 1570. Either way, by the time the first Europeans arrived, the Confederacy was well established, giving the Iroquois both a united front and considerable political power.

Canada: An Iroquois nation?

Did the Great Law of Peace help to inspire the United States' own Constitution? This is a hotly contested issue that has been raging for more than 20 years. In 1988, the U.S. Senate formally acknowledged "the contributions of the Iroquois Confederacy of Nations to the development of the United States Constitution." But the matter is far from settled, and historians remain strongly divided over the idea.

Did the American Founding Fathers lift some of their ideas from the 117-article constitution of the Iroquois, one that had existed for hundreds of years prior to the American Revolution? Benjamin Franklin, for one, was impressed with what the "ignorant savages" of the Iroquois Confederacy had achieved — namely, the creation of a self-governing union that had "subsisted for ages, and appears indissoluble."

Certainly the Iroquois Confederacy, with its clear division between levels of government, provides a blueprint for the U.S. federal system (that is, states or provinces contained within a larger union). Canada, in turn, based its own version of the two-level federal system largely upon that of the U.S., making Canada — in spirit, anyway — "an Iroquois Nation." However, one aspect of the Iroquois constitution was *not* adopted: women's rights. Canada's Indian Act of 1876 took the vote away from Native women, something they had held for centuries under Iroquois law.

For more on the influence of the Iroquois Confederacy upon the Constitution of the United States, see "Forgotten Founders" at www.ratical.com/many_worlds/6Nations/FF.html and for a rebuttal, read "Tribal Lore" in the February 2000 issue of *LinguaFranca Magazine* (the article is no longer available on-line unfortunately).

The Confederacy was founded by the semi-mythical Dekanahwideh, a "heavenly messenger" born of virgin birth, who came from the north to bring peace and unity to the Five Nations in a time of great turmoil. The people were caught up in an endless cycle of blood feuds and revenge, and Dekanahwideh — together with his disciple Hiawatha — travelled from nation to nation, urging an end to the conflict. In its place, they proposed a Great Law of Peace that would bring the various nations "under one roof," like the families in a longhouse.

Slowly, and with great public debate, Dekanahwideh and Hiawatha managed to convince each of the five nations to join. The Mohawk were the first to accept, and thus were known as "the elder brothers" of the Confederacy. As a symbol of the new union, Dekanahwideh planted a great white pine, the Tree of Peace, beneath which he buried a war club. The roots of the great tree were depicted as spreading in all directions, and on top of the tree sat an eagle, ever vigilant.

Note: There is no connection between Hiawatha, co-founder of the Iroquois Confederacy, and the character with the same name who appears in the poem, *The Song of Hiawatha*, by Henry Wadsworth Longfellow. (It appears that Longfellow got the real Hiawatha mixed-up with the Native folk hero Nanabozho.)

The Great Law of Peace was, in effect, the working constitution of the Iroquois Confederacy. And because the Iroquois, like all First Nations, had no written alphabet, the entire law was passed on orally from one generation to the next for hundreds of years. No small feat, that. It was the equivalent of memorizing a 75,000-word book, longer than many of today's novels. (Imagine having to memorize and recite *Angela's Ashes* — again and again.)

As a memory aid, elders used a system of woven bands of shells, called wampum belts, to help guide their recitations. The centrally located Onondaga were designated the "wampum keepers," making them, in today's terms, the keepers of the public archives.

Romans of the New World

The Iroquois Nations have been dubbed "the Romans of the New World." They imposed their will upon a vast expanse of territory, they waged a series of apocalyptic wars against their neighbours, and they fought the French to a standstill. Feared in battle and ruthless in victory, the Five Nations eventually overran and destroyed all of their Iroquoian neighbours: the Huron, the Neutral, the Petun, the Mahican, and the Erie. Crippled by smallpox epidemics and demoralized by the constant attacks, one by one they fell under the might of the Iroquois Confederacy.

A confusion of names

The Mohawk aren't the only Native group to get their name confused or misapplied. The Huron referred to themselves as the Wendat. (Huron came from French slang meaning "ruffian" or "scruffy.") And, of course, the term "Indian" itself is a misnomer, mistakenly applied by Columbus in 1492 when he thought he had landed in the Indies.

Because this book is meant as a beginner's guide, I have used the more common or familiar versions of Native names. These are the ones you are more likely to encounter (in the same way that you will encounter "Germany" more often than Deutschland, or "Japan" more often than Nippon).

Here are some other examples:

Region	Common name	Actual name
Maritimes	Maliseet	Welustuk
Northern Woods	Ojibwa Chipewyan	Anishinabe Dene
Plains	Blackfoot Sioux	Siksika Dakota/Lakota
Pacific Coast	Nootka	Mowachaht

History as living artifact: False faces and corn husk masks

Two distinctive types of mask, one woven from husks and the other carved directly into a living tree and then "freed," were central to Iroquoian healing rituals. The wooden False Face masks were often wildly and even comically distorted, with bent noses and protruding lips. Along with the more abstract husk masks, they represented good spirits with magical curative powers. At various times of the year, members of the False Face Society would visit homes, dancing, chanting and tending to the ill — and in return they would receive offerings of tobacco and corn meal.

These masks have a deep religious significance even now, and they still play a key role in the ceremonies of today's Iroquois traditionalists, who are often upset at seeing False Faces displayed in public museums. Less reverential Iroquois entrepreneurs carve "false faces" for sale as souvenirs. To be authentic, these masks must be cut from living wood and blessed with a ceremonial burning of tobacco. When I asked a Mohawk carver recently whether the tourist-bought False Face masks have been properly sanctified in this manner, he just smiled . . .

Whenever Iroquoian warriors (Five Nations, Huron, and Neutral alike) captured prisoners in battle, they tortured them in a gruesome, prolonged, public spectacle that could last for days, after which the captors performed ritualized cannibalism, eating the heart of the captive if he had been particularly brave.

Of the Iroquois, none had as fierce or as feared a reputation as the Mohawk. Indeed, Mohawk is not their original name. They called themselves Ganiengehaka, "People of the Flint Country." But to their long-suffering neighbours, they were *mowak* — "eaters of men." The name, rendered by Europeans as "Mohawk," has stuck ever since, so much so that it is even used by today's Mohawk when referring to themselves.

Clan mothers and Faithkeepers

Like the Vikings, the Iroquois, although fearsome in battle, had a quiet home life. Their society was remarkably stable and well integrated. Iroquoian cultures were *matrilineal*. That is, both the larger clans and the extended families of the longhouse traced their descent along their mothers' side. Women wielded real power: Women owned the land (or, more accurately, acted as "caretakers"), and men protected it. The chiefs may have been men, but the women held the balance of power. (The Clan Mothers chose the members of the Grand Council of Chiefs and if any leader failed to follow the dictates of the Great Law, he could be removed by the Clan Mothers.)

The Iroquois, in essence, lived in a representative democracy, with votes given to the delegates of each Nation, and a unanimous decision needed to go to war (although the Nations often went to war separately as well). The main town of the Onondaga, the largest and most central of the Nations, acted as the capital of the Confederacy, a hub community where diplomacy and long-term strategy were hammered out.

Along with the Council of Chiefs and the Clan Mothers, Iroquois society also had a system of Faithkeepers and shamans responsible for attending to the spiritual and health-related needs of the community. The distinction between medicine and magic was never clearly drawn, and the same healer who had an encyclopedic knowledge of herbs would also exorcise evil spirits from ill bodies.

People of the North Woods

The forests of the Canadian Shield cut an immense swath across Canada, from what is now northern Québec, across Ontario, all the way to the Northwest Territories. In the north woods, the soil is thin and the land is rugged. Unlike their southern Iroquoian neighbours, the people of Canada's north woods lived a nomadic life based around small kinship bands. They were neither farmers nor politically united. Indeed, decentralization was the key to their survival. They lived in domed, bark-covered structures known as wigwams, which only held one or two families.

Two broad language groups are found in this vast area:

- ✔ In the northwest, the *Athapaskan* (including the Kutchin, Dogrib, Beaver, and Chipewyan — all of whom are also referred to as Dene).
- ✔ In the southeast, the *Algonquian* (including the Cree, Ojibwa, Ottawa, and on the Atlantic coast, the Maliseet and Mi'kmaq).

On the coast

Although the Algonquian language group was located mainly in the northern woodlands, it did stretch all the way to the Atlantic. The Mi'kmaq (also spelled *Micmac*) were the dominant Native group in what is now the Maritimes. They lived in semi-nomadic communities along the coast from Gaspé to Nova Scotia, and later migrated to Newfoundland as well. The Mi'kmaq were among the very first Native groups to encounter the Europeans, and as such, were the first to experience the upheaval and displacement that inevitably followed.

Incredible but true . . .

A later 1756 bounty has never been repealed. As of August 2000, it was still on the books. Meaning that, in Nova Scotia, if you handed in a Mi'kmaq scalp today you were entitled to 25 pounds, payable "by the Officer commanding at any of His Majesty's Forts in this Province."

The Mi'kmaq, along with the Maliseet in the Bay of Fundy region, befriended the early French settlers and allied themselves against the British. The British, in response, waged a brutal but unsuccessful war of extermination against them. (See Chapter 6 for more on this period.) Governor Cornwallis, the founder of Halifax, put a bounty on Mi'kmaq scalps and even brought in Mohawk mercenaries to help "eradicate" them. This is one of the reasons the present-day Mi'kmaq were less than enthusiastic when the City of Halifax decided to celebrate its Founding Father a few years ago.

The canoe as Canadian icon

The Natives of the north woods, and the Ojibwa in particular, were renowned for their elegant yet practical river-going craft. The birchbark canoe — light, easily repaired, and able to carry heavy loads — made extensive trade possible. It was the canoe that opened up the interior of Canada. Like the snowshoe and the toboggan, the birchbark canoe is a wonder of adaptive technology. And Canada, explored and exploited largely by river, was a nation born of the canoe. From the image of the early fur traders in their great flotillas to former prime minister Pierre Trudeau, paddling with the current in buckskin and beads, the image of the canoe, and the communion with nature that it suggests, has been adopted — or appropriated, depending on your point of view — by Canadians as a whole.

> *Canada is a canoe route.*
> — aphorism attributed to historian Arthur Lower

For more on the culture and craft of the canoe, including background on Native origins, visit www.civilization.ca/membrs/canhist/canoe/can00eng.html and also www.nativetech.org/brchbark/canoe.htm.

The wild man of the forest

For the Iroquois, cannibalism was a war ritual. But for the subsistence-level small-band societies of the northern woods, where starvation was a constant and real danger, cannibalism was looked upon with horror as the final

---

History as living artifact: The dreamcatcher

Central to the Ojibwa way of life was the Midewiwin religion, in which it was believed that the Earth was a living, interconnected whole. Every plant and animal contained a life force, and this in turn was connected to the concept of *Manitou*, usually translated as "Great Spirit" or, more accurately, as simply "Mystery." It refers to the unseen realities of life, beyond human understanding, but always present and very real. (The province of Manitoba is named in reference to this.)

Dreams were a contact point between the everyday world and the Manitou, and one of the best known Ojibwa artifacts — and one that has been adopted by other First Nations as well — is the dreamcatcher. Who knows, you may even have one hanging above your bed. They have become very popular lately, though not everyone who buys one understands its underlying significance.

Dreamcatchers invite good dreams in and "ensnare" bad ones. They also protect against illness and evil spirits. A baby's first protective talisman was a dreamcatcher, an intricate and finely woven web adorned with feathers, either owl (for wisdom) or eagle (for courage). In most dreamcatchers, a hole in the centre is left open to allow the good dreams to pass through, while blocking the bad ones. (In other Native cultures, it is just the opposite: The hole allows bad ideas and dreams to pass through and "catches" the good ones.)

---

breakdown of order. The most dreaded figure in Cree and Ojibwa mythology was the Windigo, an evil spirit who took possession of people's souls and led them into wild, anti-social behaviour — especially cannibalism. For some commentators, the Windigo has also come to represent a darker, underlying fear that has haunted non-Native Canadians for years: the image of a person who, "having spent too long in the wilderness, becomes a part of it." Northrop Frye saw this as a symptom of a larger "garrison mentality," a sense of living under siege, surrounded by the forces of nature. A very Canadian neurosis.

ON THE WEB

For more on the fascinating area of Native art and technology (with an emphasis on the Eastern Woodlands) go to: www.nativetech.org/.

A northern empire

The Ojibwa (also: Ojibwe and Ojibway) were the primary middlemen in the aboriginal fur trade, and they controlled the widest Native territory north of Mexico. The Ojibwa were, in their own way, "the Romans of the north woods." Part of a coalition known as the Council of the Three Fires, the Ojibwa moved south after the Fall of the Huron Confederacy, and later pushed west as well, displacing the Sioux — no small feat, considering what worthy opponents the Sioux were. In the words of historian J.M. MacDonald, the Ojibwa controlled "one of the largest Indian territories in history — an empire that stretched from southern Ontario and Wisconsin to Saskatchewan and western Montana." The Ojibwa are also sometimes referred to as "Chippewa," which gets really confusing because it sounds so similar to Chipewyan, which is an Athapaskan Native group with no connection to the Ojibwa.

For more on the Ojibwa, visit www.turtle-island.com/historytext.html.

People of the Plains

Quick! Close your eyes and — *wait*, don't close your eyes. Instead, just picture in your mind an "Indian." Odds are, you conjured up an image of someone from the plains, probably Sioux, dressed in buckskin, wearing a feathered headdress, perhaps riding a horse and firing a rifle at buffalo or — even better — at the U.S. Cavalry. The Plains Indians are, after all, the stuff of Hollywood mythmaking. These are the *Dances with Wolves* Indians, the ones who have come to represent the image of Native North Americans as a whole. Which makes it all the more ironic that the short-lived heyday of the Plains Indians was made possible almost solely because of two items introduced by the Europeans: the horse and the repeating rifle.

Of these, the horse was by far the more important. First acquired from Spaniards far to the south, they were traded north, arriving in the Canadian West in the mid-1700s. The horse changed everything. It gave the Indians greater freedom, greater speed, and better mobility. It also allowed them to expand the range of the hunt — and the range of their wars. With the horse, the People of the Plains attained a brief and brilliant ascendancy, one that lasted just a little over 100 years, but that would burn itself forever into the popular imagination. (The Spanish actually *re-introduced* the horse to the New World. Horses had existed in North America in pre-historic times, but had long-since been hunted into extinction.)

On the high plains, the most powerful presence was that of the Blackfoot Confederacy. The Confederacy waged war with and against the Plains Cree and Assiniboine to the north and east, and the Sioux and Crow to the south.

It was an austere, militant culture, one described by historian Arthur Ray as "extremely macho." If the Iroquois were the Romans of the New World, the Plains Indians were the Spartans.

The buffalo hunt

The People of the Plains were hunters. Their homes — tipis of raised poles and hides — could be taken down and put up quickly, and the mainstay of both their diet and their way of life was the buffalo. Great herds roamed the plains, often covering the horizon, and the buffalo (or, more correctly, *bison*) provided meat, robes, glue, sinew, and bowstrings. The hides were used for tipis, blankets, moccasins, and portable "bull boats" used in crossing streams. The dried dung was used for fuel. The ribs were used as sled runners, the hollowed horns as drinking goblets, the bladders as water bags and the tails as flyswatters. It was once estimated that the Plains Indians had over 300 different uses for buffalo. The buffalo were, in a way, "walking supermarkets."

Now, there were several ways to kill them. You could build a long fenced-in area that was wide on one end and narrowed toward the other, a "buffalo pound," and then corral the animals into it. Or you could ride alongside them and shoot them full of arrows, a difficult and dangerous undertaking. Or you could simply run them off a cliff.

At one cliff site in southwestern Alberta the bones lie more than ten metres deep. Named "Head-Smashed-In Buffalo Jump" (not in reference to the buffalo but rather to an unfortunate — and not very bright — young Native lad who one day decided to watch the hunt from directly *below* the cliffs), this site had been used for more than 5,000 years. In 1981, UNESCO (United Nations Educational, Scientific, and Cultural Organization) declared Head-Smashed-In Buffalo Jump a World Heritage Site.

Waste not, want not . . .

The buffalo hunt required discipline, skill, and patience, but the payoff was well worth it. The average buffalo weighs over 900 kilograms, and a good kill could bring in as many as 250 animals, producing — almost literally — a mountain of meat.

Even with drying, pounding, and skinning, a good deal of the meat ended up rotting under the hot prairie sun. (This was before refrigeration, remember.) As well, the Plains Indians believed they had to kill an entire herd, otherwise the survivors might escape and warn their fellow buffalo. So the notion that Native Canadians were holistic environmentalists in tune with nature is a wee bit exaggerated. They were hunters, they weren't park rangers.

However, the Native buffalo hunt pales in comparison to the wholesale slaughter undertaken by whites. In 1800, there were an estimated 60 million buffalo roaming North America from Mexico to Northern Alberta. By 1889, only 800 were left. This wasn't a hunt, this was carnage, what one commentator called "an orgy of marksmanship." Whites shot hundreds of buffalo a day,

History as living artifact: Medicine wheels

Although it's easy to miss, history is everywhere on the prairies — if you know where to look. The Plains Indians left thousands of stone markings across the plains. Dubbed "medicine wheels" by puzzled whites, these circle patterns, made of sun-bleached stones, radiate a stark, symmetrical beauty. Some, constructed by the Blackfoot, commemorate important battles. Others mark territory and serve as a warning to encroaching outsiders. Some are of a spiritual nature, in reference to Sun Dance ceremonies; others were made to honour the memory of great warriors who died in battle. Simply put, medicine wheels are geography made sacred.

Of North America's 150 known medicine wheels, 125 are in southern Alberta and Saskatchewan. Many of them date back thousands of years and are older than Stonehenge, older than the pyramids. And almost every known medicine wheel has been vandalized at some point, by New Age tourists, crass souvenir seekers, or picnickers who rearrange the stones to spell out their initials.

skinning the humps and leaving the rest to rot where they lay. There was also a darker intent behind the slaughter: The near-extinction of the buffalo, achieved with tacit government approval, crippled Native independence on the Plains. The real target was always the First Nations, not the buffalo. It was a ruthless strategy. And it worked.

For more on the many varied uses of the buffalo, check out `www.nativetech.org/essays/buffalo.html`. For Head-Smashed-In Buffalo Jump, with background on Blackfoot history, go to `www.head-smashed-in.com`.

The medicine bundle

Among the Blackfoot and the Plains Cree, the most sacred belongings were one's "medicine bundle," a small pouch containing bones, sacred stones, amulets, and magical objects. These bundles were sanctified by medicine men and renewed constantly, but the contents remained protected and secret.

In 1987, when a museum in Alberta wanted to put a medicine bundle on display, there was an outcry from the Plains Indians. After long debate and much discussion among the elders, it was finally decided that the Blackfoot Nation would provide the museum with a *replica* of a medicine bag — clearly labelled as such — that would contain a few key errors in its design and, more importantly, would be empty inside. Not all aspects of Native culture are meant for public consumption. More recently, in 2000, the Glenbow

Museum in Calgary, which has acted as a caretaker of many Native icons and rituals, announced that it would be returning the medicine bundles and other sacred objects in its collection to the First Nations from which they came.

The Sun Dance

Fewer coming-of-age rituals were tougher than the Sun Dance. Forget bar mitzvahs. These young men had a real ordeal to pass through. The Sun Dance (more accurately, the "Thirsting Dance") took place in mid-summer, usually after a buffalo hunt, and it involved feasting, chanting, conjuring, and rhythmic, hypnotic dancing that could last for days at a time. The most striking aspect was the rite of passage performed by the young men. In a display of physical endurance, they would insert skewers through their chest muscles and then attach themselves by a cord to a central pole. Under the punishing sun, in slow circles, the boys would turn and turn, leaning back against the skewers until they eventually ripped themselves free.

It should be noted that this ceremony was (a) only part of the larger Sun Dance, and (b) completely voluntary. No one was required to undergo the ordeal, but those who did bore their scars with great pride for the rest of their lives. (And come to think of it, something like this would certainly make bar mitzvahs more entertaining. *"Today I am a man . . . Ouch!"*) In the 1890s, the federal government decided to crush the Sun Dance. What had once been the central ceremony and most important ritual in Plains culture was driven underground and made illegal. It was like outlawing Thanksgiving.

People of the Pacific Northwest

From the austere landscape of the plains, I take you now to the Pacific Northwest. What a contrast! Here, amid the lush rainforests and wet green fjords and islands of the west coast, some of the most rich and complex Native societies evolved. Far from the subsistence lifestyles of the plains and the arctic, the people of the coast enjoyed abundant food and a relatively mild climate. They had lots of leisure time and a great deal of excess wealth. So much wealth, in fact, that it was a challenge at times just to dispose of it.

The Pacific Northwest was the most densely populated area of Canada. It has been estimated that almost *half* of Canada's total Native population was living in British Columbia at the time of first contact. At least 16 separate languages were spoken here, making it one of the most linguistically diverse areas anywhere on earth. And two of the languages (Haida and Tlingit) are isolates: unique and unrelated to any others. Imagine having Chinese spoken on one island, Portuguese on the next, and Swahili on the coast and you have an idea just how remarkable this region was — and is.

History as living artifact: The totem pole

Totem poles frightened and fascinated early European visitors, who assumed the poles represented pagan gods (or even demons) that were meant to be worshipped and appeased. In fact, most totem poles display the symbols and stories of a specific clan. They often acted like a family's coat-of-arms. They were also public displays of wealth, and the number and size of poles a house could raise was a matter of social esteem. Elaborate poles, some as tall as 20 metres and weighing up to four tonnes, were sunk into the ground and raised by ropes to great public acclaim and joyous celebration. There was a certain phallic pride involved as well. (One Nass River chief forced a rival to shorten his totem pole, not once but twice, a move meant to both humiliate and emasculate.) Some were even erected as "ridicule poles" designed to mock and shame debtors.

Totem poles originated among the Nisga'a of the Tsimishian and were later refined by the Kwakiutl, who added the outspread wings of the thunderbird. Mortuary poles containing boxes with the bodies of deceased chiefs were also raised. And among the Haida, portals to the house were often through entrance poles, all carved in the softwood cedar that was so indispensable to the culture of the coastal nations. (Indeed, they were as much a "people of the cedar" as they were a "people of the salmon.") Although most of the old stands of totem poles are now crumbling into ruin and neglect, or have been uprooted and moved indoors, the art of the totem has not died, and new poles continue to be carved by West Coast craftsmen. For an online study of totem poles visit www.moa.ubc.ca/ Virtual/Other/ prelude2/start.html.

Among the many First Nation groupings of the Pacific Northwest are the Haida of Queen Charlotte Islands; the Tlingit of the Alaska Panhandle region; the Tsimishian of the Nass and Skeena Rivers; the Kwakiutl along the middle coast; the Bella Coola enclave further inland; the Coast Salish of the Vancouver region; and the Nootka on the west coast of Vancouver Island.

Note: These are only the major cultural and linguistic groupings; they can be further divided into separate nations. It's a long list.

Of noblemen and slaves

Unlike almost all other Native groups, the concept of private ownership was both central and explicit among the coastal societies. When white traders began arriving in the late 1700s they were annoyed to discover that every square foot of land belonged to *someone,* and that fishing and hunting rights were clearly delineated. The taking of firewood, or even fresh water, required payment of some kind. No New Age socialist brotherhood here.

The Coastal chiefs were often vain and acquisitive, with their material wealth the key to their status. The people of the Pacific Northwest lived in a grand style, in wide plank houses 150 metres long supported by massive, decorated cedar beams. The size and splendor of the houses were duly noted and compared, and each house had its own history and even its own name. These were often unabashedly proud: *House Which Thunder Rolls Across, House That Other Chiefs Peer at from a Distance*, or — my personal favourite — *House People Are Ashamed to Look at as It Is So Overpoweringly Great.* (And, hey, if I ever buy a house, that's what I want on the mail box.)

Elaborate social structures evolved. Unlike the communal lifestyles of other Native groups, the coastal societies had a *caste system*, that is, one made up of several distinct and formal social classes. At the top were the nobles, from which the chiefs were drawn. Below them were the commoners. And below them were the slaves, usually taken as captives from neighbouring nations. (In some villages, the slaves made up a third of the population.) As well, among the Nootka of Vancouver Island, the whale hunters were elevated to almost mystical status as a separate class to themselves. They lived apart prior to the hunt and engaged in ritualized bathing and cleansing before boarding the long boats and heading out to sea.

But, most importantly, the coastal societies were able to support a whole sub-class of professional artists who apprenticed under masters and who studied their craft for years. The art of the Pacific Northwest is unparalleled: the fluid, stylized designs; the sublime shades of emotion in the masks; the whale fluke representing the whale, the beak representing the raven; the intricate interwoven patterns. It is one of the richest artistic traditions in the world. On the Pacific Coast, art and life were completely intertwined.

The culture and philosophy of the potlatch

The raising of a totem pole, the ascension of a new chief, or a marriage between nobles: Such events as these were marked by celebrations we call *potlatch*, a word derived in a roundabout way from the Nootka verb "to give." And boy, when they said "give," they weren't kidding. Artwork, food, slaves, cedar chests, land titles (that is, the right to fish or hunt on the host's land for a specified period of time), blankets, and sheets of decorative copper: Guests at a potlatch often returned so laden down with gifts that extra canoes had to be provided just to carry it all.

You see, the people of the Pacific Northwest had a very refined concept of wealth. They recognized something the Europeans did not: True wealth lies not in the amount one is able to hoard, but rather in the amount one is capable of *giving away.* Lavish gift-giving increases one's status. It was a case of "conspicuous generosity," as opposed to conspicuous consumption, a battle of vanity and pride. At some of these more ruthless ceremonies, riches were actually destroyed. Canoes were sunk, blankets were casually thrown into the fire, copper tossed away, and slaves killed on a whim and for the slightest offense: all as evidence of the host's great wealth. (Potlatches must have been an especially nerve-wracking time for slaves. "Why I am so rich, I can. . . well, let me see . . . Bob! Get over here!")

Potlatches served an important economic function as well. They were both a way of redistributing wealth and a subtle form of banking. After all, a potlatch had to be returned, and a village that gave one now would receive one later, often with "interest" since the responding potlatch would have to be, as a matter of honour, larger and richer than the first. This complicated web of "favours given" and "favours received" also helped promote social continuity.

The impact of white society on the potlatch

The potlatch was a synthesis of coastal life: celebratory, abundant, status-conscious, and artistic. However, with the introduction of European trade goods, the nature of the potlatch changed forever. Sewing machines, jewellery, and clocks were added to the list of gifts. Wealth became less evenly distrib-uted, and tribes with trade connections gave away gifts that others could never repay. Social debt meant social shame. Tensions rose. Among the Kwakiutl it took a distinctly nasty turn when chiefs set out to ruin rivals by inviting them to a potlatch and then piling an outrageous amount of gifts on them. The rival was forced to up the ante and the escalating war of gift-giving continued until one or the other was broken by it and reduced to poverty, with a dark cloud of unrepaid favours hanging over his name.

Missionaries complained that the potlatch was an obstacle to the proper "Christianization" of the coastal people. And in 1884, the Government of Canada, appalled at the "debauchery" and the "blatant disregard" for material wealth that the potlatch represented, outlawed the ceremony entirely and drove it underground. Giving gifts had become a crime. (The law would remain in effect right up until 1951.)

For an interesting but academic look at the potlatch, its history, and the social impact of the government ban go to www.anu.edu.au/~e950866/potlatch.

Caught in between: People of the Plateau

The semi-arid, high plateau of the British Columbia interior is a land of raging rivers, rolling hills, sagebrush deserts, sharp valleys, and sudden steep mountain ranges. In fact, calling it a plateau is a bit misleading.

Some of the First Nations in this region, such as the Kutenai (also spelled *Kootenay*) had originally been Plains Indians, but had been pushed back, into the mountains by relentless Blackfoot attacks. At least, that's the version of events the Blackfoot like to tell. The Kutenai insist a smallpox epidemic wiped out their plains cousins and left them stranded in the highlands. The Kutenai, a language isolate, were certainly more plains than mountain. They were a warrior society with no clans, no caste system, and no complex social hierarchy — and year after year they would return to the grasslands to take part in the buffalo hunt.

The Interior Salish, meanwhile, had entered the plateau the other way, moving inland from the Pacific Coast. In a sense, the Interior Salish are "river cousins," to the coastal nations. They adapted well to life in a harsher climate. They travelled in small, semi-nomadic bands and dwelled in pit houses, dug partly into the ground and often entered from the top. The Interior Salish hunted deer and fished the salmon-rich waters of the Thompson, Columbia, and Fraser Rivers.

They are also responsible for the modern legend of the Ogopogo, a monster seen regularly splashing about in the waters of Lake Okanagan. To the People of the Interior, it is *N'ha-a-itk*, a mythical figure represented in pre-contact petroglyphs. Far from the tourist-friendly version of Ogopogo that you see promoted on postcards and T-shirts today, N'ha-a-itk was a fearsome creature who would occasionally surface to pull men and animals under water in its jaws. The Native people in the area used to offer small, writhing animals as a sacrifice to the monster, but that doesn't look as good on postcards. *Suggested tourist motto*: "Take a dip in Lake Okanagan! You'll probably escape with your life!" (The modern Sasquatch, dubbed "Big Foot" in the U.S., can also be traced back to Native mythology, in this case a wild, hairy creature of Coast Salish lore. Which is to say, the legends of the First Nations have entered the public imagination.)

Just for fun, here is an Ogopogo Web site: www.sunnyokanagan.com/ ogopogo.

People of the Far North

The Inuit of Canada's Arctic inhabit one of the harshest and most unforgiving environments on earth. The winters are long and dark, the winds fierce, the summers short, and the resources scarce. It is the outer limit of the habitable world. (The Arctic was, in fact, the very last region on earth to be inhabited by humans.)

Crossing over from Siberia some 4,000 to 5,000 years ago, today's Inuit are part of a larger, transpolar culture. Although there are eight separate Inuit tribal groups in Canada, they all speak dialects of a common language: Inuktitut. (The Inuktitut language crosses several national boundaries, stretching from eastern Siberia, across Alaska and northern Canada, all the way to Greenland, creating a remarkable international linguistic community.)

Inuit contact with the outside world was fleeting until well into the twentieth century. Before that, the only whites they encountered were rough Yankee whalers, desperate English explorers lost in a sea of ice and, long before that, the occasional surly Viking. Not that first contact was any less traumatic for the Inuit. The Sadlermiut Inuit living on the northwestern shores of Hudson Bay (their culture seems to have been archaic and possibly unique among the Inuit) were completely wiped out by disease after the first whalers came through. The last Sadlermiut died in 1903, and the mystery of their origins remains.

The current population of Canada's Inuit is around 40,000 and many of them still hunt regularly, though most travel by snowmobile now, not dogsled. (Which may be faster, true. But if you get stranded and run out of food, you can't eat your skidoo.)

A further confusion of terms

The term *Eskimo* was originally derived from an Algonquian word, *eskipot*, meaning "eaters of raw meat," which was considered an insult. Today, the word *Eskimo* has largely been replaced with Inuit, meaning simply "people." Even so, the term *Inuit* only really refers to the people in the eastern Canadian Arctic. In the western area around the Mackenzie Delta, they prefer the term *Inuvialuit*. But to avoid confusion, and with apologies to the Inuvialuit, I'll be using Inuit as a general term throughout. (In northern Alaska, meanwhile, they prefer *Inupiat . . .*)

History as living artifact: The inuksuk

The Arctic above the treeline is beautiful but barren. The open tundra stretches out from horizon to horizon without distinguishing landmarks, and hunters travelling across this open landscape, often for great distances, need some kind of markers along the way. As guideposts, the Inuit erected stone cairns, called *inuksuk*, "that which stands in for a man" (also spelled "inukshuk"). Carefully stacked inuksuk can withstand the worst winds and the heaviest snowfalls. In the Arctic, there are lichen-covered inuksuk that have stood for hundreds of years — and more.

Inuksuk come in all sorts of shapes and sizes and serve a number of purposes. Gate-shaped cairns, built in a line across the landscape, serve as aids for navigation: You look through and line up the next one in the distance. Smaller ones, adorned with flapping scarecrow-like sprigs of arctic heather, help to herd caribou toward accessible hunting grounds. Some inuksuk point the way to food caches.

Others serve as warnings for dangerous terrain. Some indicate kayak-launching sites, and others were built as memorials to a person's memory. Each has its own distinct style and name, and its own distinct purpose — my favourite being the one called *inuksuk quviasuktuq*, "inuksuk built for the sheer joy of it." In 1999, when the Inuit territory of Nunavut was called into being, the legislature chose the inuksuk as its emblem.

Northern hunters

The Inuit were hunters, first and foremost: caribou, musk-oxen, whales, waterfowl, seals, and even polar bears, which are one of the few animals in North America that (a) have no natural enemies, and (b) aren't the least bit afraid of us. (Polar bears have even been known to stalk and attempt to prey on humans, and the Inuit have to be careful lest the hunters become the hunted. Inuit trackers often circle back to look for paw prints to make sure that no polar bears are following them.)

Moving seasonally from one camp to another, the Inuit would gather in groups of up to 100 in the winter. Summer hunting groups, travelling light, were usually less than a dozen. It was a small-scale but highly sociable society, where the emphasis was on sharing resources (up to and including spouses).

Central to the Inuit way of life was the caribou. Like the buffalo to the Plains Indians, the caribou was a "walking supermarket": It provided meat for food, fat for candles, hides for kayaks and summer tents, skins for bedding, bones for tools, and sinew for sewing. Even diapers were usually made from caribou skins.

Further examples of Inuit ingenuity

Here are more important contributions made by the Inuit:

- **Igloo:** The traditional winter dwelling of the Inuit, the snowhouse igloo is a structural marvel. Sliced blocks of fine-grained, compact snow are built up from the inside, in a narrowing, inward-leaning spiral. A final, all-important "keystone" block is nudged into place and a small hole cut for ventilation. In little more than an hour, a single hunter can create a self-standing dome of surprising strength. After watching an igloo being constructed, the English explorer John Franklin, amazed at the purity of the material and the elegance of its design, compared it to a Grecian temple. "Both," he noted, "are triumphs of art."

- **Parka:** Where would Canadians be without their parkas, eh? The original Inuit parka, made of caribou hide and often trimmed with fur, effectively sealed the wearer inside. Parkas were waterproof, wind-resistant, and durable. In one of the coldest climates on earth, the Inuit discovered a way to use their own body warmth to full adavantage. The Inuit parka has been compared to the spacesuits NASA developed. (I like that: spacesuits in a Grecian temple.)

- **Kayak:** If the birchbark canoe is the glory of the Ojibwa, then the glory of the Inuit is certainly the kayak. Made from skins stretched over a frame and ranging up to seven metres in length, the kayak are ideal for fast, sea-going journeys. Once seated inside his kayak, the Inuit hunter attaches his parka around the opening, sealing himself in and making the kayak both watertight and virtually unsinkable. If the kayak tips over, the hunter is able to flip it back up and resurface.

- **Umiak:** Although the sleeker, sexier kayak gets more attention, equally important was the broader-based, flat-bottomed umiak boat. These work-a-day vessels were used to transport families and supplies along coastal waters during the summer hunting season. Umiaks could carry more than 20 people at a time.

Go to www.tapirisat.ca/html/inuit_s.html for more on Canada's Inuit. For information on the Inuktitut language (with links to history and culture as well), go to www.arctic-travel.com/chapters/languagepage.html. For more on the inuksuk emblem of Nunavut go to www.arctic.ca/LUS/ Nunavut_info.html. For the National Library of Canada's "North: Landscape of the Imagination" site (with informative links) visit www.nlc-bnc.ca/ north/norint-e.htm.

Chapter 2

First Contact

• •

In This Chapter

▶ The Vikings come and go

▶ John Cabot puts his trust in cod, and Jacques Cartier thinks he's discovered diamonds

▶ Henry Hudson is swallowed up in the heart of a cold continent

▶ England launches its Empire — in Newfoundland

• •

"In 1492, Columbus sailed the ocean blue . . ." Christopher Columbus, an Italian mariner in the employ of Spain, wanted to reach the Indies, but he added a new twist. Instead of travelling overland or sailing around the southern tip of Africa, he decided to go *west* across the Atlantic Ocean, reasoning that since the world was round, he would eventually circle around and reach the Orient "from the back door."

His logic was sound, but there was just one snag. Two vast continents stood in the way. Columbus had, quite by accident, stumbled upon an unknown land, a New World. And nothing would ever be the same again.

> *A land may be said to be discovered the first time a European, preferably an Englishman, sets foot on it.*
>
> — Arctic explorer Vilhjalmur Stefansson

Most Native Canadians object to the use of the words "discovery" and "New World" when talking about the early contact between Europe and North America. "How can you say you discovered a country when there were people there greeting you from the shore?" But personally, I don't see what the problem is. The word "discover" doesn't carry the meaning of "uninhabited." I can speak about "discovering" an interesting shop in my neighbourhood. I can "discover" a new restaurant or a shortcut to work. Which, in a sense, is what the Europeans did.

They "discovered" a new continent: one that was populated by a variety of cultures and societies previously unknown to them. In that sense, it *was* a new world that the Europeans stumbled upon. And it *was* a discovery. And that is how I will be using those words throughout this section. Not in the sense of "uninhabited," but rather "previously unknown."

The Vikings

You think your ol' man was tough? Eric the Red was a murderer, an outlaw, an exiled wanderer, and a fearless explorer. It was Eric who led the first Viking expedition to Greenland in 982 A.D., setting up a colony on what was — at that time — the very edge of the world. And it was Eric's son Leif who would go beyond.

The Norsemen were Scandinavians (mainly Norwegian) who fought, explored, and traded over a wide range, from Russia to ancient Iraq. (The term "Viking," although often used as a general term for the Norse, really only refers to raiders in longships.) The Norse had already island-hopped their way to Greenland when a supply ship was blown off course and got lost in a heavy fog. When the weather cleared, the crew caught a glimpse of a distant, unknown shore, but they turned back without landing. Intrigued by this tale, Leif Ericsson, son of Eric, set sail in or around the year 1000 in search of these "unknown lands."

Leif and his men sailed west and soon landed on Baffin Island, which they named *Helluland* (Land of Flat Stones), though "Hell of a Land" might have been more accurate: It was a barren, rocky, windswept place. Turning southward, they came to the forested coasts of Labrador, which Leif named *Markland* (Land of Woods).

They continued south and, after two days at sea, again sighted land. It was a warm and pleasant locale, and Leif and his men set up camp to explore it. They found thick forests and wide natural pastures. Wheat grew wild, the streams teemed with salmon, and grapes lay heavy on the vine. Overjoyed, Leif named the area *Vinland* (Land of Wine) and returned with a shipload of lumber — as good as gold in treeless Greenland. With that single voyage, he made his fortune.

Leif himself never returned to Vinland, but his brother Thorvald did, with supplies and 30 men. They wintered at temporary camps and scouted areas for a possible permanent colony. Then they ran into the locals. The Norse called them *skraelings* ("barbarians"), but they were most likely ancestors of today's Labrador Natives, the Innu, or perhaps they were Beothuk or possibly Inuit; no one knows for sure. It was Thorvald who first encountered them. It happened during his explorations along the Labrador coast, when his men came upon nine Natives, asleep under skin-covered boats. The Norsemen attacked, killing all but one (who managed to escape). The Natives then returned in full force, and a high-pitched battle ensued. Thorvald was hit in the belly with an arrow and died soon after. It was the first recorded contact between Europeans and Natives, and it didn't bode well for the future.

Around 1012, a major expedition was launched: three ships with 160 settlers and assorted livestock (cows, ewes, a bull, a ram, and possibly pigs and goats as well). The settlers went ashore, probably in Newfoundland, and that autumn a baby boy was born. Named Snorri, he was the first European child to be born in the New World. The Norse settlers traded with the Native groups in the area, but the relationship was strained and it soon erupted into violence. Native hunters attacked the Norse camp, killing two men and scattering the rest. They were turned back only by Leif's warrior-like sister Freydis, who snatched up the sword of a fallen Norseman and, baring her breasts in defiance, faced the attackers head on. The Natives withdrew and the battle ended. (The Norse retaliated by ambushing a Native scouting party soon after.)

Bad weather and the constant threat of *skraeling* attacks took their toll, as did the physical and psychological isolation. The Vikings eventually abandoned their Vinland colonies, though they did continue to make occasional visits to North America for hundreds of years. As noted, the Norse/Native contacts were not always hostile. There are records of renewed trade between the two, and Norse materials have been found in several northern Inuit communities.

The tales of Vinland the Good were handed down in Icelandic sagas, and in 1914, Newfoundland historian William A. Munn published a detailed pamphlet, based on clues in the sagas, in which he argued that a Viking settlement must have been built near L'Anse aux Meadows on the northern tip of the island. Munn had practically pinpointed the spot, but it wasn't until the 1960s that a team of Norwegian archaeologists followed his advice. Some 50 years after Munn had first urged an excavation, the remains of a Norse settlement were unearthed.

The site contained homes, workshops, a bathhouse, a kiln, and a blacksmith's forge, marking the first time that iron was smelted in the New World. Archaeologists also uncovered fragments of wool spinning and knitting tools, which is especially important because it gives clear evidence that the Vikings had brought their wives with them and had intended to stay. But what the site *didn't* contain was just as significant: There were no large or extensive garbage piles, suggesting that the community itself was short-lived, lasting perhaps only a few years.

It is a remarkable site, nonetheless, and in 1978, L'Anse aux Meadows was declared a United Nations World Heritage Site, joining a list that includes the Great Pyramids of Egypt, the Taj Mahal, and the Grand Canyon — not to mention, of course, Head-Smashed-In Buffalo Jump, which I introduce you to in Chapter 1.

Is L'Anse aux Meadows Vinland? Is this the site that Leif the Lucky discovered? Or were these the remains of another ill-fated colony? Perhaps one led by Lief's brother or sister? Historians disagree even now, and much of the debate turns on the word *vin* itself. If the name does refer to wild grapes, Vinland must have been farther south, possibly in New England, but this doesn't seem to match the time frame and navigational clues recorded in the sagas. It is just as probable that Vinland *was* in northern Newfoundland. The word *vin* can also be translated as "pastures," and Vinland, in turn, as "Land of Grasses." Or perhaps the "wine-berries" Leif referred to were gooseberries, mountain cranberries, or plump red currants, which grow in that part of Newfoundland. Still others suggest that Leif might simply have been lying. He may have intentionally exaggerated the lush conditions of Vinland in order to attract settlers. Overall, though, the general consensus among archaeologists seems to be that L'Anse aux Meadows wasn't Vinland, but rather "a gateway to Vinland."

What does matter is this: The Vikings were here 500 years before Columbus. Even today, evidence continues to appear. Eight-hundred-year-old Norse spinning yarn was discovered on Baffin Island in 1984, and Norse artifacts — woven cloth, iron fragments, ship rivets, a carpenter's plane, and even chain mail — have been discovered as far north as Ellesmere Island, well above the Arctic Circle and much farther north than Iceland itself. In 2000, Newfoundlanders celebrated the 1,000 anniversary of the arrival of the Vikings, an event that included a replica Norse ship built and captained by a descendant of Leif Ericsson.

Still, it is important not to overstate the significance of the early Viking expeditions to the New World. The Vikings are really just a footnote in Canadian history. A fascinating footnote, to be sure, but still just a footnote. The voyages of Christopher Columbus, on the other hand, had a huge impact. Columbus changed the course of human history forever. The Vikings did not. They came, they saw, they went home.

> *We have found a good land — but are not likely to profit from it.*
> — Thorvald the unlucky, as he lay dying

The Parks Canada site at L'Anse aux Meadows can be found at parkscanada. pch.gc.ca/parks/newfoundland/anse_meadows/anse_meadows_e.htm. For a quick overview of the Vikings in Newfoundland, visit www.wordplay. com/tourism/viking.html. You'll find all kinds of great links on Viking exploration, far and wide, at www.win.tue.nl/~engels/discovery/viking. html. For the full story on Leif the Lucky, go to home.rmci.net/khwmd. For more on the Viking Landing at L'Anse aux Meadows go to collections.ic. gc.ca/vikings. And for more on the "Voyages to Vinland," visit www.aldstar. com/forum/origins/leif.

The Diffusionists Are Coming!

You thought Columbus discovered the Americas? You thought the Vikings were the first outsiders to skirt our shores? Guess again.

Irish monks. Ancient Hindu travellers. Greek explorers. English noblemen. Phoenician traders. Chinese sailors. Hebrew prophets. Polynesian seafarers. Even the Lost Tribes of Israel. All have been championed at one time or another as pre-Columbus, pre-Viking visitors to the New World. The theories abound. And not all of them are as crazy as they sound.

We now know that Irish monks almost certainly reached Iceland well before the Vikings. Did they continue west and reach North America as well? Why not? Some sources cite a ninth-century Latin text titled *Navigatio Santi Brendani Abatis* (*Voyage of St. Brendan the Abbot*) as evidence that the Irish did indeed discover America. In the text, St. Brendan describes sailing in his little ox-hide boat with a band of monks to distant lands, and he mentions ice floes that are strikingly similar to the icebergs off Newfoundland. But St. Brendan also writes about talking whales and an island where the birds sang in Latin. The evidence is circumstantial at best. Certainly the Irish *could* have reached North America prior to the Vikings. But did they? Remember, the fact that something could have happened doesn't mean it did.

Historians and archaeologists are sharply divided on these issues. On the one hand is the more conservative "standard" approach, that North American cultures evolved independently of the rest of the world, with only limited contact by the Vikings prior to Columbus. Opposed to this view are the "diffusionists," who insist that contact was ongoing throughout history. The diffusionists believe that societies develop less through independent evolution and more through widespread migration, intermittent contact, and the cross-borrowing of culture traits. Sounds sensible enough, except that it often leads them into outlandish conclusions as they attempt to explain the many cultural parallels that exist between the various far-flung regions of the world.

But again, not all diffusionist theories are as crackpot as they may seem. Certainly, the standard explanation that the first humans arrived by crossing a temporary landbridge between Asia and Alaska has been challenged lately by geological evidence that suggests the landbridge was actually impassable until several centuries *after* the first humans had already appeared. A rival view has developed, suggesting that the migrants arrived by boat, following the coastline north, along Siberia and then over. Others have suggested a second, separate migration across the Pacific, made by island-hopping Polynesians who settled in South America. Some have even suggested that ancient mariners arrived from what is now Spain, along the eastern coast of the icecaps.

Chinese sailors in British Columbia. Ancient Irish monks living amongst the Mi'kmaq. African hieroglyphics in Ontario. Shang Dynasty Chinese in Guatemala. Druids in Vermont. In the absence of real evidence, the imagination soars.

For more on the voyages of St. Brendan and the possible Irish discovery of North America, go to www.castletown.com/brendan.htm.

The Three Big C's

Cabot, Cartier, and Champlain: These are the three most important explorers in early Canadian history.

- ✔ **John Cabot** rediscovered North America after the Vikings. He claimed the region for England.

- ✔ **Jacques Cartier** discovered and explored the St. Lawrence River, and *he* claimed the region for France. (You can see where this is leading, can't you?)

- ✔ **Samuel de Champlain**, the "Father of New France," marked the shift from exploration to permanent settlement.

John Cabot and the cod

The next time you want to impress and annoy your friends with your ready wit and erudite sophistication, just say, in an offhand sort of way, "We were thinking that next year we might take a drive through Nova Scotia, maybe along the scenic Giovanni Caboto Trail." When they blink at this say, "Oh, you may know him as John Cabot." And make sure you smile in a condescending sort of way. You'll be a big hit at parties with this one, trust me. (Cabot was also known as Johan Cabot Montecalunyal, so if you really want to sound like a know-it-all . . .)

John Cabot was a contemporary of Christopher Columbus, and like Columbus, he was born in the Italian seaport of Genoa and raised in Venice. There is the distinct possibility that the two explorers knew each other in their youth. Certainly, John Cabot had — independently of Columbus — come to the same conclusion: that the world was round and that by sailing *west,* across the Atlantic, you would eventually circle around and reach Asia from the other side. It was a simple but brilliant idea.

Cabot was in Spain when the news broke that Columbus had "reached the Indies" by just such a route. Cabot tried to get backing for a similar expedition, but failed, so he went to England instead, to look for financial support from among the wealthy spice merchants of Bristol. Why England? Two reasons. First off, Spain had already claimed the middle latitudes. But just as importantly, Cabot reasoned that, if the world was indeed a globe, then the distances would become narrower the further north you went. England would thus be closer to Asia than was Spain. Cabot's logic was correct. There was just one problem: An entire continent blocked the way. (Not that there was any way Cabot could have known this at that time.)

The English king, Henry VII, still kicking himself for having passed on the chance to sponsor Columbus's original expedition, was told of Cabot's plans and he quickly gave his royal approval. No money, just approval. "Thanks a lot yer Highness." (And even then, Henry expected a kickback of one-fifth of any riches Cabot might bring back with him.) Cabot was only able to outfit a single ship, the *Matthew,* with a small crew of 18 men.

> *To seeke out, discover, and finde, whatsoever iles, countreyes, regions or provinces of the heathen and infidelles . . . whiche before this time have beene unknowen to all Christians.*
> — from the directives given to John Cabot by Henry VII

In May 1497, just five years after Columbus's first voyage, Cabot sailed from Bristol. His destination? The distant isles of the Orient! *Huzzah! Huzzah!* He got as far as Newfoundland . . .

Or maybe Cape Breton. No one is sure exactly where he landed (hence the name of Nova Scotia's scenic drive: the John Cabot Trail), but Cabot made quick work of it anyway. He erected a large cross and laid claim to the "New Founde Land" in the name of the King of England. He never did find a route to China, but he did find something just as valuable: fish. Lots and lots of fish. The seas off the Grand Banks were swarming with cod, so much so that Cabot claimed "they sometimes stayed his shippes." Why, the men onboard the *Matthew* did not need to sink lines to catch them, they had only to lower baskets and bring them up.

Was Cabot really the first? There is some indication that the Grand Banks were well known to Bristol fishermen *before* John Cabot set sail and that he merely "broke a trade secret." Either way, with Cabot the word was out. There was no longer any doubt that a new continent had been discovered, and Cabot is sometimes referred to as "the intellectual discoverer of America."

The strange disappearance of John Cabot

No gold, but lots of fish. Henry VII awarded Cabot for his discoveries with an annual pension of £20 and granted him permission for another voyage. And so, in 1498, John Cabot set out on a second expedition, again in search of a passage to the Orient. This time, however, he had a crew of 300 men and a fleet of five ships. It was all hoopla and excitement heading out, but alas, there are no records of Cabot ever returning. Because of this, most historians have assumed that Cabot must have perished en route. Or maybe not. There *are* records that Cabot (referred to as Antonio Gaboto) joined his son Sebastian on a 1501 journey to Greenland. So it looks as though he did make it to Newfoundland and back alive. But he never did reach China.

For background information on John Cabot and the importance of his discoveries, go to www.heritage.nf.ca/exploration/cabot.html. For more detail on Cabot (with lots of links at the end): www.win.tue.nl/~engels/discovery/cabot.html.

From Cabot to Cartier

After John Cabot's discovery, there were soon hundreds of ships prowling the waters off the Grand Banks. They came from England, Spain, France, and Portugal. But it was a transitory population, and no one seemed interested in setting up long-term permanent settlements. The Basques (from the southern area of Spain and France) maintained a whaling station on Newfoundland for more than 50 years, but only a few crumbling gravestones and a scattering of place names survive.

See Figure 2-1 for a map showing the location of early European settlements in Canada.

Note in minor C: Corte-Real the slaver

Along with the Major C's (Columbus, Cabot, Cartier, Champlain) another explorer is worth noting, if only because he set the tone for so much that would follow between the First Nations and the upstart Europeans. Gaspar Corte-Real, a Portuguese nobleman, skirted the shores of Newfoundland as early as 1500. The following year, he returned with his brother Miguel and a fleet of three ships, and captured and took as slaves more than 50 Native citizens. He sent his prisoners back to Portugal and then steered his own ship towards the Canadian mainland. He vanished without a trace. (I like to think that he was captured and beaten to death by relatives of the Natives he had kidnapped and enslaved.) When Gaspar failed to return, his brother Miguel set off with three ships to find him. He never came back either. So a *third* brother got ready to search for Miguel (who was searching for Gaspar). But the king refused to let him go, which was just as well. By that point, they were running out of Corte-Reals.

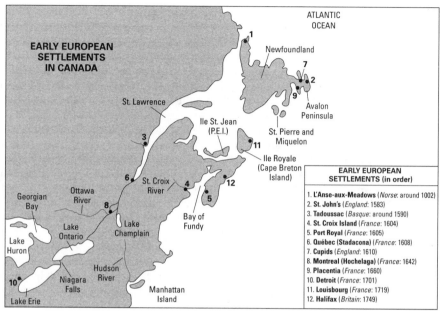

EARLY EUROPEAN SETTLEMENTS IN CANADA

ATLANTIC OCEAN

Newfoundland

St. Lawrence

Ile St. Jean (P.E.I.)

St. Pierre and Miquelon

Avalon Peninsula

Ile Royale (Cape Breton Island)

Georgian Bay

Ottawa River

St. Croix River

Lake Ontario

Lake Champlain

Bay of Fundy

Lake Huron

Hudson River

Niagara Falls

Lake Erie

Manhattan Island

EARLY EUROPEAN SETTLEMENTS (in order)
1. **L'Anse-aux-Meadows** (*Norse:* around 1002)
2. **St. John's** (*England:* 1583)
3. **Tadoussac** (*Basque:* around 1590)
4. **St. Croix Island** (*France:* 1604)
5. **Port Royal** (*France:* 1605)
6. **Québec (Stadacona)** (*France:* 1608)
7. **Cupids** (*England:* 1610)
8. **Montreal (Hochelaga)** (*France:* 1642)
9. **Placentia** (*France:* 1660)
10. **Detroit** (*France:* 1701)
11. **Louisbourg** (*France:* 1719)
12. **Halifax** (*Britain:* 1749)

Figure 2-1: European settlements map.

The Portuguese tried to set up a colony on Cape Breton Island around 1520, but failed miserably. And it wasn't until 1524 that France finally got around to sending an "official" expedition to the area. (French fishermen had been hauling in the cod for years, but the French courts had more or less ignored the Americas.) The King of France authorized an Italian explorer, Giovanni da Verrazano, to look for a short northern route to the Orient, and although Verrazano didn't find any such passage, he did establish a French claim on the eastern seaboard of North America. Sadly, Verrazano himself was later captured and eaten by cannibals in the Caribbean. It was a tough life, being an explorer.

Cartier's first voyage: Laying claim

On April 20, 1534, Jacques Cartier sailed out of the French seaport of St. Malo with two ships and a crew of 61 men. His mission? "To discover certain isles and countries where it is said there must be great quantities of gold and other riches." Unlike Cabot, Cartier knew exactly where he was going. He had probably accompanied Verrazano on an earlier failed quest for a passage to the Orient, and he certainly had been to the cod-rich fisheries of Newfoundland at some point.

Cartier made one important discovery right at the start: By sailing through the narrow northern strait, he proved that Newfoundland was in fact an island. He also had a flair for description. Earlier, when he landed on the rugged coast of Labrador, he dubbed the region "the Land God Gave Cain." Then, sailing west, he discovered an isle he dubbed "the fairest land 'tis possible to see." It would later be known as Prince Edward Island, and Cartier's ringing endorsement is still proudly recalled in tourist brochures even today.

Cartier next sailed up the coast of what is now New Brunswick, where he was met enthusiastically by a band of Mi'kmaq, who were well-versed in trade and eager to acquire European goods. Cartier followed the coastline north to the Gaspé peninsula, where he made contact with a group of Iroquoian people who were on a seasonal fishing expedition. In the presence of their chief, Donnacona, the French explorer erected a large wooden cross emblazoned with the words *Vive Le Roi de France* and claimed the land in the name of King François I.

Donnacona was understandably upset at this. In spite of the language barrier, the chief knew full well that Cartier was up to no good and he angrily denounced the explorer's actions. This early confrontation between European imperial claims and Native ancestral rights is an important moment in Canadian history, and it too set the tone for much of what would follow. Cartier knew that this land belonged to someone else.

> *Pointing to the cross [Donnacona] made us a long harangue . . . and then he pointed to the land all around about, as if he wished to say that all this region belonged to him, and that we ought not to have set up our cross without his permission.*
>
> — Jacques Cartier

In an attempt to soothe the irate chief, Cartier told him that the cross was merely a navigational marker, a landmark, and not a claim of ownership. Cartier plied Donnacona with gifts, hoping to win him over, and then, as a show of good faith, he kidnapped Donnacona's two sons and headed back to France. By European standards, it had been a successful journey all round.

Cartier's second voyage: Down the St. Lawrence

The two young men that Cartier kidnapped, Dom Agaya and Taignoagny, were taken back to France and given language lessons so that they could act as interpreters on later voyages. History tells us very little of the terrifying culture shock they must have experienced — something akin to being whisked away to another planet onboard a UFO — but they did lead Cartier back to their home village the following year.

In 1535, spurred on by rumours of a magical kingdom the Natives called "Saguenay," Cartier left St. Malo with three ships and a crew of 110 men. (There is some suggestion that the chief's sons invented elaborate tales of gold and wealthy kingdoms in order to convince him to take them home.)

Guided by his two captives, Jacques Cartier sailed into the mouth of the St. Lawrence River. And there, at the site of present-day Québec City, he came upon the village of Stadacona. Chief Donnacona was there to meet them, and was overjoyed at seeing his sons again, but he treated Cartier coldly — and understandably so. Later, when Cartier expressed an interest in sailing further upriver, Donnacona became angry. The Stadacona controlled trade along the St. Lawrence, and Cartier had no right bypassing them.

Cartier went anyway, and soon arrived at an even larger village: Hochelaga (at present-day Montréal). The village was impressive. It had 50 longhouses, open fields, and palisade walls. More than a thousand people came out to greet Cartier, and he was led on a royal procession through the village. (Villagers later brought their sick and lame to Cartier, asking him to heal them.) Cartier climbed a forested hill, which he named "Mont Royal," and planted yet another cross in the name of France. From the top of Mont Royal (which would later become pronounced "Montréal"), he could see the treacherous Lachine Rapids, and he knew then that this was not the passage he was searching for. Disheartened, he turned back.

Canada: Just a village at heart

Where does the name Canada come from? Several fanciful explanations have been put forth. Some have claimed the name was derived from early Portuguese explorers who scribbled *acada nada* ("nothing here") on their maps. Oddly enough, it has the same meaning in a southern German dialect, where *keine dah* (pronounced *"kana dah"*) means "nothing there." I even read one tongue-in-cheek rendering that suggested the name Canada came from the lament of early colonists who had been put on a strict beer ration and were heard to cry, "Oh! Can a day!"

The truth is almost as strange. Canada is a country named — by mistake. When guiding Cartier down the St. Lawrence on his return voyage, Donnacona's sons, Dom Agaya and Taignoagny, used the word *kanata*, meaning "our village."

(Although, I have also seen *kanata* translated as everything from "a collection of houses" to "village dwellers" to "yonder be our wigwams." Seriously. There is another version as well, which has the term derived from the Native word, *kanatats*, meaning "strangers.") Anyway, Cartier misunderstood what they were saying and assumed that the word — which he rendered as "Canada" — referred to the region as a whole. The St. Lawrence was originally called the "River of Canada," and this in turn was later expanded to include the area that is now the heartland of Quebec and Ontario. Today, it is the name of a vast nation stretching from the Atlantic to the Pacific to the Arctic. At 9,970,610 km squared, Canada must surely be the biggest "village" on earth.

Cartier and his men spent a harrowing winter back at Stadacona. Scurvy, a crippling disease caused by a simple vitamin C deficiency, ravaged his crew, killing 25 men. Concerned, the Indians provided Cartier with a cure of boiled cedar, and in exchange, Cartier introduced several new infectious diseases into their community.

Cartier then upped the ante, taking Chief Donnacona prisoner along with four others. As Cartier prepared to sail back to France, the Stadacona tried to barter for their chief's life, offering Cartier five other prisoners "as gifts" instead. So, with a shrug, Cartier took them as well, sailing for home in the spring of 1536 with a total of ten Native prisoners in tow. He was a very talented kidnapper, our Jacques.

Cartier's third voyage: Fake as a Canadian diamond

The great chief Donnacona, "Lord of Canada," never made it home again. He died in France, far from his family, a token "savage" in a strange land. (French historians insisted that Donnacona died "a good Christian, speaking French.") Only one of Cartier's captives survived, and she remained in France. When Cartier finally returned to the Stadacona in 1541, more than five years after kidnapping their chief, he found that their mood had soured considerably. Hmmm, I wonder why.

Cartier attempted to establish a French colony along the St. Lawrence, but he failed. The Indians had turned against him, the climate was harsh, and the mythical Kingdom of Saguenay was nowhere to be found. Thirty-five colonists were reportedly killed in conflicts with the Stadacona Iroquois, and Cartier had had enough. He left for France with a handful of gold and some "Canadian diamonds" he had managed to excavate. A second attempt at establishing a colony had already been launched, under the leadership of Sieur de Roberval, a French nobleman. But by the time Roberval set sail from France, Cartier was already hightailing it for home. The two expeditions met in St. John's harbour, going in opposite directions. Like Cartier, Roberval failed as well.

Alas, Cartier's "gold" was iron pyrites — "fool's gold" — and the "diamonds" mere quartz. Cartier's third voyage had been a complete fiasco, and all it did was introduce a new expression into the French language: *Faux comme un diamant du Canada*. "As fake as a Canadian diamond."

The mythical Kingdom of Saguenay had proven to be a mirage, the Canadian equivalent of El Dorado, and French interest in the New World waned. Still, Jacques Cartier had achieved a lot, even if he hadn't uncovered any great wealth: He had discovered and charted one of the world's great rivers, the St. Lawrence, and he had given France a claim on the mainland.

For more on Jacques Cartier and his voyages, go to the Virtual Museum of New France at `www.mvnf.civilisations.ca/explor/explcd_e.html`. For a biography of Cartier, with helpful links, try `www.win.tue.nl/~engels/discovery/cartier.html`.

Champlain to the rescue

Samuel de Champlain succeeded — *barely* — where Cartier and others had failed. Against all odds, Champlain managed to establish, and maintain, a permanent French colony on the mainland of North America. This marked an important shift in Canadian history, from exploration to settlement. The fur trade and missionary zeal fuelled the early inland French colonies, and Champlain — a champion of both — is known appropriately as "the Father of New France."

St. Croix Island

In 1604, not a single European settlement existed north of Mexico. A scattering of temporary fishing stations had been built on Newfoundland and along the shores of the St. Lawrence, but nothing permanent had taken root. The adventurous French trader, Pierre de Monts, decided to change that once and for all.

With a young Champlain tagging along as a sort of unofficial navigator/mapmaker, de Monts set sail from France with an eclectic band of noblemen, craftsmen, and Swiss mercenaries. De Monts arrived in the Bay of Fundy and, following the shore, eventually entered a river he named "St. Croix" for its cross-like formation. There, on a small island in the middle of the river, de Monts built a settlement that included a grand residence for himself and rough barracks for the men, as well as a communal kitchen, a blacksmith stand, and even a small chapel.

Most of the buildings were behind protective walls, with cannons at either end for defense. The Maliseet Indians in the area had been watching the French colonists intently, and de Monts was fearful of an attack. He shouldn't have worried. It appears that the Maliseet were more concerned for the French settlers' survival — if not their sanity. Didn't they know the river could get blocked with ice during winter? Apparently not. The island, de Monts noted, was roughly on line with the south of France. How cold could it possibly get?

That year, snow began falling on October 6. By early December, there were ice floes in the river. It would turn out to be one of the bitterest winters in a hundred years, and de Monts and his men suffered terribly. Stricken with scurvy, their gums bled and turned black, their teeth became loose and fell out, their arms and legs became swollen, and a terrible pain convulsed their stomach and bowels.

Trapped on the island for weeks on end, terrified of an impending (and imaginary) Indian attack, and weakened by disease, they began to die one by one. The bodies piled up, and by spring, when supply ships from France finally arrived, 36 of the original 80 colonists were dead. It had been an ordeal, a Trial by Ice, but from this tentative start France had gained a foothold on the continent. It was a bittersweet victory at best.

Port Royal

De Monts's attempt at establishing a beachhead on St. Croix Island was a near disaster, but rather than give up he moved his settlement across the Bay of Fundy to a cove he dubbed "Port Royal," on the inner shore of what is now Nova Scotia (near present-day Annapolis Royal). From this, the colony of Acadia would eventually grow. Port Royal was the first *successful* European presence on the mainland of Canada.

At Port Royal, de Monts built a single, interconnected *habitation*, with palisades, a central courtyard, and cannons for protection. He also planted a garden, something often hailed in history books as "a first," even though several First Nations had been farming extensively inland for hundreds of years before de Monts began tending his little patch of vegetables.

More noteworthy was the "Order of Good Cheer" (*L'Ordre de Bon Temps*), a social club founded by Champlain as a way of maintaining morale among the scurvy-ridden, stir-crazy Port Royal colonists over the winter. Members of the order took turns arranging entertainment and festive meals for the others. They are also credited with staging the first theatrical production in Canadian history, the 1606 play *Le Théâtre de Neptune,* based on the Roman myths of the sea god set in a New World context. The play was written by colonist Marc Lescarbot, a poet, playwright, and wandering academic who travelled extensively in the region and left behind vivid descriptions of life in early Canada. (So, next time someone suggests a night at the theatre, you can casually wonder aloud, "I wonder if anything by Lescarbot is playing.")

The habitation at Port Royal has been rebuilt, with an on-line "walking tour" at parkscanada.pch.gc.ca/parks/nova_scotia/port_royal/Port_royal_ e.htm. (This site also includes a history of Port Royal and more on the Order of Good Cheer.) Another "virtual tour" of Port Royal, with history and background, can be found at www.wvda.com/heritage/portroyal.html.

Québec City

De Monts left Port Royal in 1607, in a bit of a huff after the French Crown cancelled his trade monopoly. But although he himself never returned to the New World, de Monts still remained active in pursuing trade and encouraging settlement. Egged on by Champlain, he decided to fund a second colony, this one inland on the St. Lawrence, the great river that led into the heart of the continent.

Go Habs! Go!

Ever wonder why a hockey team dubbed the Montréal Canadians is nicknamed "the Habs" (as in "the Habs and the Hab nots")? It refers to the early French settlers, called *habitants*. And that, in turn, refers to Champlain's 1608 habitation at Québec, making it a sports nickname that goes back four hundred years. (The term "champs," however, has nothing to do with Champlain, but you may want to try convincing some of your more gullible friends. Mike, if you're reading this, now you know.)

In 1608, Samuel de Champlain sailed up the St. Lawrence with a small band of colonists. Where the river narrows, a great natural rock formation rises up. It was "the Gibraltar of North America," the future site of Québec City, and it was here, at the base of these cliffs, that Champlain built *his* habitation: a cluster of connected buildings modelled on Port Royal.

Samuel de Champlain had a tough assignment. A wild-eyed, lawless community of Basque traders had already set up camp on the St. Lawrence at Tadoussac, and they openly scoffed at Champlain's claims to authority.

That first winter, scurvy again took a deadly toll. Twenty of Champlain's twenty-eight men died, a terrible death rate. But those eight survivors proved it could be done, and a new colony was born.

Now, if you've been paying attention, you're saying to yourself, "Hey, wait a minute. Hadn't Cartier already visited that area? Wasn't that where the village of Stadacona used to be?" And you'd be right. This was indeed the same location where, 70 years earlier, Jacques Cartier had kidnapped Chief Donnacona and mined the quartz and mica he mistook for diamonds. However, by the time Champlain arrived, the Stadacona had vanished. So had the Hochelaga further upriver at the site of Montréal. Intertribal warfare had turned the entire St. Lawrence region into a no-man's land, and in some ways Champlain was fortunate to be entering a war zone. It made it easier for him to stake a claim. No one is exactly sure what happened to the St. Lawrence Iroquois during the 70 years between Cartier's visit and Champlain's, but disease appears to have played a major role in their disappearance. Prior to Cartier's 1535 voyage, an "epidemic and plague" had broken out in St. Malo, and there is the strong possibility that Cartier and his men brought the epidemic over with them.

The Quest for a Northwest Passage

Canada began as an obstacle, blocking the way to the treasures of the East, to be explored only in the hope of finding passage through it.

— scholar and theorist Northrop Frye

It was driving the Europeans crazy. At every turn, Columbus's would-be short-cut to the Orient was blocked by vast and vaguely defined lands. Verrazano and others, sailing north, had demonstrated that the coast was continuous from Florida all the way to the Bay of Fundy, and Cartier had dashed any hope that the St. Lawrence River might be the Passage to the Indies. Because England was the northernmost of the newly emerging imperial powers, it was only natural that she would turn her gaze to the cold and mysterious Arctic Ocean. (But it's important to note that at this stage the English were minor players in the New World land grab, a game dominated at that time by Spain and Portugal.)

Elizabeth I, the "Virgin Queen," was determined to have a trade route of her own, far from the Spaniards and across the shortest possible distance from England. The first great champion of a Northwest Passage was an explorer named Humphrey Gilbert, who published a *Discourse to prove a passage by the northwest to Cathay and the East Indies,* in 1576. In it, Gilbert argued that if ships could somehow manage to thread their way through the treacherous waters of the High Arctic, they would eventually reach Cathay and Cipango (that is, China and Japan). And so began the quest for a Northwest Passage, one that would last for more than three hundred years and cost hundreds of lives and millions of pounds, and achieve very little. The men who went in search of a Northwest Passage took an enormous risk. They were sailing off the map, into darkness.

Fool's gold: The voyages of Martin Frobisher

The first explorer to take up Gilbert's challenge was Martin Frobisher, a big, blustering larger-than-life professional adventurer. Popular historian Pierre Berton describes Frobisher as "a onetime pirate and slaver, choleric and passionate, heavy of frame, florid of feature, violent of temper and 'full of strange oaths.'"

In 1576, Martin Frobisher sailed into the Arctic on board his tiny ship, the *Gabriel.* At the southern tip of Baffin Island, he entered the bay that now bears his name. What he had hoped was a passage to China turned out to be a fjord-like dead-end, and Frobisher grew impatient. These were unknown lands and dangerous waters. He made tentative contact with the Inuit in the area, and even took one on board to act as pilot. But when five of Frobisher's men returned the Inuit pilot to shore, they were captured and never seen again. Frobisher was livid, and in response he took an Inuit hunter hostage. He had hoped to barter the hunter for his own men but the tactic failed, and Frobisher was forced to raise anchor and return without the missing sailors. The Inuit captive, meanwhile, was taken back to England where he died soon after from a common cold.

Frobisher's journey wasn't a total failure. As a gift for Queen Elizabeth, he brought back the horn of a strange "sea unicorn" (that is, a narwhal tusk) as well as a small sample of rock he thought might contain coal. Mere coal? Perish the thought. A shifty metal assayer quickly pronounced that the rock contained not coal, but gold! The news broke and a gold-rush fever gripped the merchants and investors of London. Shares for the next journey were sold at inflated prices, and the following year Frobisher sailed back to Baffin Island with three ships in tow. The focus had now shifted from finding a passage to discovering gold. After taking possession of the land in the name of Queen Elizabeth I, he began mining "the black ore."

Relations with the Inuit grew worse and worse, and the hostility soon escalated into open conflict. In a barrage of arrows from the Inuit, Frobisher himself was hit in the buttocks, but survived. Throughout the summer, Frobisher continued to search for the crewmen who had been taken prisoner on the previous expedition. Sadly, although Frobisher came across traces of them (clothing and personal items) in hastily abandoned Inuit camps, the men themselves were never seen again. First contact was going from bad to worse. Frobisher kidnapped three Inuit — a man, a woman, and a small child — and took them back to England, where they were toured about and feted in a grand style before dying, one by one, of disease.

Frobisher came back with almost 160 tons of ore in the hold, and Elizabeth was overjoyed. She named the new region *Meta Icognita* (Latin for "the Unknown Limits") and all but danced with glee. Before the final reports on the ore were in, Frobisher headed off again, on a third voyage, with an entire fleet of ships and some 400 men. His goal in 1578 was to mine the land and set up a northern English colony. After several harrowing mishaps on the ice floes, the fleet finally landed on Baffin Island and immediately began chewing up the land-scape. The notion of an Arctic colony quickly abandoned, Frobisher returned loaded down with more than 1,200 tons of rock. He was convinced it was worth a fortune.

But there was no gold in the ore. Or at least very little. Turns out, the earlier evaluations had been (suspiciously) incorrect, and Frobisher's shiploads of rock were worthless. Much of it was dumped overboard, the rest was used in construction to repair manor walls. It was a scandal that ruined several of Frobisher's backers, and to this day, the culprit behind the fraud has never been determined. Frobisher himself appears to have been innocent. He remained in Elizabeth's good books and was later knighted for his role in defending England from an invasion force from Spain (the famous Spanish Armada).

With the dream of Arctic wealth gone, the North was once again perceived as being not a destination but an obstacle: something to be conquered, something to be travelled through, a riddle to be solved. The search for a Northwest Passage resumed, most notably with the voyages of John Davis in 1585, 1586, and 1587. Davis rediscovered Greenland, which had been abandoned and more or less forgotten since the Norse settlements, and crossed the strait that now bears his name to reach Baffin Island. He probed the fjords and coastline of the island, searching in vain for a passage to China. The riddle remained unsolved.

Land of Desolation . . .

— name given to the Arctic by John Davis

For more on the Frobisher expedition, with an emphasis on the Inuit perspective, go to www.civilization.ca/membrs/canhist/frobisher/frint01e.html. A history of the Arctic, including the voyages and perceptions of early Europeans, can be found at arcticcircle.uconn.edu/HistoryCulture/index.html.

The lonely fate of Henry Hudson

Poor Henry. Put yourself in his shoes. You are one of the great navigators of your day. You have just discovered a vast inland sea, leading into the very heart of an uncharted northern continent. You have sailed farther into the interior than anyone has before. But in doing so, you have pushed your motley crew of sailors to the breaking point, you have failed to find the coveted "passage to the Orient," and you are about to pay for it with your life in one of the loneliest deaths in the history of Canadian exploration.

In 1610, Henry Hudson set sail in search of the Northwest Passage with a crew of 22, onboard his ship *Discovery*.

Discovery was a popular name among explorers: Captains James Cook and George Vancouver both sailed ships of that name up the Pacific Coast, and the tradition continued into the space age when NASA launched the space shuttle *Discovery,* named in honour of both Hudson's and Cook's ships.

Hudson became the first person to navigate the treacherous 450-mile strait that separates northern Québec from Baffin Island, a bottleneck of churning arctic currents and unpredictable ice floes. When he made it through and entered the bay that now bears his name, Hudson was convinced he had "won the passage" to the Orient, and he set a course due south, for sunnier climes. But at the bottom of James Bay, he ran into a dead end.

As summer slipped away, he sailed back and forth, trying desperately to find a way through. It was no use. Winter was setting in and Hudson was forced to beach his ship and hunker down. Within ten days, the bay had frozen them in. They were stuck. Hudson hadn't come prepared to winter in North America, and his provisions were running dangerously low. Trapped in the ice, submerged in a bleak sub-arctic winter, the crew was put on starvation rations and was soon reduced to eating moss to survive. (Back in London, meanwhile, a new play by William Shakespeare was opening. The title? *A Winter's Tale*.)

Henry Hudson was a bold navigator but a terrible leader. In today's terms, he lacked "people skills." At turns petty, cruel, and apologetic, Henry Hudson could never make up his mind whether he wanted to be loved or feared. And in the end, he was neither. The following spring, when it became clear that Hudson had no intention of returning to England but was instead determined to push on in search of the fabled passage, the crew rebelled in mutiny. They bound Hudson's arms and set him adrift without food or water in a small boat with his young son Jack and a handful of supporters (some loyal, some ill, and some just plain unpopular).

The ragtag mutineers considered becoming pirates and plundering the shore off Newfoundland, but in the end, they decided to make a run for home. On a small island near the tip of northern Québec, the crew stopped to kill seabirds for food and were ambushed by a band of Inuit hunters, who dis-emboweled two of the men with spears and riddled two more with arrows. (The image of the jolly, happy-faced Eskimo is a modern invention.) By the time the mutineers came limping back to Europe, the main ringleaders of the uprising were dead.

Not that it mattered. The English courts were less concerned about the mutiny than they were intrigued by the possibility of a Northwest Passage. The Indies seemed to be within reach, and Henry Hudson was all but forgotten in the excitement. It is shameful how little concern Hudson's backers showed for him. They even sent one of the mutineers back to the Arctic in Hudson's own ship, to continue the search for the passage and — oh, yes, maybe look for Henry if he found the time. (He didn't.) Not a single mutineer was ever convicted for the crimes they committed.

The drama of the mutiny has long overshadowed Henry Hudson's very real accomplishments. He had discovered the second great sea route into the Canadian interior: the Hudson Bay. The first route, along the St. Lawrence and Great Lakes, was discovered and controlled by the French. The Hudson Bay would belong to England.

For an informative and gripping biography of Henry Hudson, with a blow-by-blow account of the mutiny, go to: www.georgian.net/rally/hudson.

The mystery of Henry Hudson

What of Henry Hudson and his small band set adrift in James Bay? Were they adopted by local Natives ? Or killed outright? Did they even make it to shore? There are legends among the Inuit of a boat found adrift, filled with dead white men and a single, shivering boy (Henry's son?). The Inuit tied the boy up like a dog and, presumably, he died soon after. Other theories suggest that Hudson and the others were taken captive and then sold into slavery to the Indians in northern Ontario, where a rock was reportedly found with the haunting inscription *"H.H. 1612 captive"* on it. Unfortunately, the rock itself can't be located and only a photograph of it remains.

A more recent theory suggests that Hudson and the others somehow managed to navigate their way out of the Bay and across the Arctic Circle to the Norwegian island of Spitzbergen, where a grave marked "Hudson" was discovered in 1823. Fascinating, but unlikely. A more plausible ending is that they took shelter on nearby Danby Island, where a row of wooden stakes was discovered twenty years later. Were these the remnants of a makeshift shelter built by the outcasts? No one knows for sure, and the fate of Henry Hudson remains shrouded in mist and mystery. One historian has even challenged the notion that Henry was trying to find the passage at all, arguing that a mariner as worthy as Hudson knew full well he was in a deep bay and not on an open sea, and that he was in fact looking for gold.

Rule Britannia! An Empire Founded by Fog?

The sign beside St. John's City Hall says it all: "Canada begins right here." Newfoundland is Mile Zero, the outer edge of the country, England's first overseas colony, and the place where the sun first rose on the British Empire. An empire, oddly enough, that was founded by fog.

Note: It's "England" up until 1707, and "Britain" after 1707, when England and Scotland were joined under one crown.

Although John Cabot had given England an apparent "dibs" on Newfoundland, the Grand Banks were in fact an international free-for-all. It was "fish fever" (like gold fever, but smellier). In Catholic Europe, you see, Fridays and fast days were still strictly "meat-free," and for 153 days a year, fish was served in its stead. Cod was "the beef of the sea," and great shipping fleets crowded in along the coast of Newfoundland every year, with as many as 10,000 fishermen plying the waters of the Grand Banks, making them the richest fishing grounds in the world.

The fisheries of Newfoundland are inexhaustible and are of more value to the Empire than all the silver mines of Peru.
— English essayist Sir Francis Bacon, in 1608

Cod required great quantities of salt to preserve it for the journey home. When the fish were hauled in they were immediately packed in salt barrels, a process called "wet" or "green" fishing. The salt that came from mines was too coarse and uneven, so the fishing fleets used "solar salt," taken from the sea and sun-dried, usually in the sunnier Mediterranean regions of Europe. England, however, with its damp climate and northern foggy weather, could barely scrape together enough to salt an egg. France and Spain, on the other hand, had tons of the stuff. "*Mon Dieu*, what are we going to do with all this salt?" they would often say, just loud enough for England to hear. And then they would laugh.

Blame it on the fog, but the English were forced to improvise. They developed a new process, called "dry" fishing, whereby the catch was first taken ashore and dried on racks before being lightly dusted with just enough salt for the return voyage. "Salt cod" as it was known, gave English fishing crews a sudden competitive edge. It also brought them onshore, and that was a crucial turning point. It wasn't long before English and Irish fishermen began building makeshift towns and summer settlements along the coves and crannies of Newfoundland's coast. Now, if you consider these shoremen as true "inhabitants" (most historians don't, but I do), then Canada's permanent European presence began, not in New France or Acadia, but in Newfoundland. And all because of that damn foggy English weather.

By 1992, the once "inexhaustible" cod stocks of Newfoundland had collapsed. For a full history of the northern cod fisheries, from Cabot to the present, visit www.stemnet.nf.ca/cod/home1.htm. (You can also reach this site by going through the Government of Canada's digital collections at the following address: collections.ic.gc.ca/cod/index.htm.)

The two Gs

England wanted to control the coast of Newfoundland, and from it the Grand Banks. Or rather, they wanted to control the southeast *Avalon peninsula*, which juts out into the shipping lanes and waters of the Grand Banks. (A lot of what is referred to as "early Newfoundland history" is really a history of this peninsula, which was as important to the cod fisheries as the St. Lawrence would later be for the fur trade.)

Two men played a crucial role in England's move to take control of Avalon: our old friend Humphrey Gilbert (early advocate of a Northwest Passage), and John Guy.

"Lend me your ears!"

An earlier attempt at launching an English colony on Newfoundland had already failed when Humphrey Gilbert sailed into St. John's Harbour in the summer of 1583. Gilbert was actually on his way to establish a colony somewhere else, but he stopped in at Newfoundland and claimed it as well for good measure.

Some 36 different ships — from Spain, Portugal, France, and England — were in harbour at the time, but that didn't deter Gilbert. Waving a royal charter, he announced that he was taking possession of Newfoundland's southeastern shores in the name of Elizabeth I, Queen of England. He then began confiscating (i.e., stealing) supplies from the various ships and demanding, ahem, "tax" payments. Now, this might have *looked* like outright piracy, but because Gilbert had first *claimed* the island it didn't count. (That Gilbert, he was a clever one all right.) He also proclaimed that the Church of England was now the official religion and that anyone making "dishonourable remarks" about Queen Elizabeth would have their ears cut off.

With the site of John Cabot's original landfall still a source of controversy, most historians consider Gilbert's proclamation of August 5, 1583, as the true beginning of the British Empire, and Newfoundland its first colony. Gilbert, alas, came to a less than heroic end. On his way back to England, Gilbert's flagship, the heroically named *Squirrel,* ran into a storm and went down with all hands. Men on an accompanying ship heard Gilbert's famous last words ringing out: "We are as near to heaven by sea as by land!" What that means exactly, I couldn't tell you.

Pirate-fodder

In spite of Gilbert's brash proclamation, it wasn't until 1610 that the first "official" attempt was made at establishing a permanent English colony in Newfoundland. A company of merchant adventurers in London and Bristol had been given title to the region, and they appointed a man by the name of John Guy to be the colony's first governor. With 39 hardworking colonists, Guy landed at Cuper's Cove (later dubbed Cupids). The men cleared the land, planted grain, imported livestock, and built homes. Two years later, 16 women joined them, and Guy was proud to report that the colony was "very honest peaceful and hopefull and very lykelye to be profytable." It was the first successful year-round English colony in Newfoundland history.

But things soon soured. The seasonal fishermen didn't want them there. The weather was harsh, farming was all but impossible, and — just to keep things interesting — pirates were roaming the coast. One in particular, the "Pirate Admiral" Peter Easton, caused all sorts of grief, plundering settlers and fishermen alike from his fortress in Harbour Grace, not far from Guy's colony. Looting and stealing, stealing and looting, Easton ranged as far south as the Caribbean and as far west as the Azores. At one point, an entire French squadron sailed in to do battle with Easton and his "pirate fleet." They were destroyed.

Now, there is an important distinction to be made between "pirates" and "privateers." Pirates were outlaws, pure and simple. But privateers plundered the seas *legally* onboard privately held warships. Like pirates, they raided and looted and killed — but they did so with prior approval, on assignment to "vex" their sovereign's enemies. Some of Britain's greatest naval heroes, such as Martin Frobisher, began their careers as privateers. Peter Easton was originally a privateer as well, but when he lost his official commission he turned to piracy. (A small step, granted.)

Easton actually treated the Cupids colonists fairly well — at one point he even provided them with protection for their harvests — and he is even considered something of a folk hero, the "Robin Hood of Newfoundland," so to speak. But legends aside, Peter Easton was still a pirate, and pirates were the bane of John Guy's existence. Guy pleaded for help from England but all attempts at bringing Easton to justice failed. (During one raid, Easton even managed to capture the very sheriff sent from England to arrest him.) Frustrated by the lack of success and harried by pirates, John Guy finally left Newfoundland for good in 1615, never to return. The settlers began drifting away, livestock died, and by 1631 the colony had collapsed.

However, the site itself continued to be used as a fishery and seal-hunting base for years, and many of the original settlers and their children stayed on and were eventually joined by others. In this sense, then, John Guy has a legitimate claim as "the Father of Newfoundland," Newfoundland's answer to Samuel de Champlain.

For more on the Two G's (Gilbert and Guy) and other sponsored settlements in Newfoundland, go to www.heritage.nf.ca/exploration/sponsored. html. (This is part of the larger Newfoundland and Labrador Heritage site, which contains a wealth of information — but it is tricky to navigate. So be careful, it's easy to miss subheadings.) For more on the Avalon Colony specifically, go to www.heritage.nf.ca/avalon. Scenic tours of the Avalon Peninsula, where so much of Newfoundland's early history was played out, can be found at www.wordplay.com/tourism/scenictours/avalon/ avalonregion.html. For the "Canadian Privateers' Homepage" (yes, Canadian privateers have their own homepage!) visit www.chebucto.ns.ca/~jacktar/ privateering.html.

The Beothuk

The Beothuk of Newfoundland were the original "Red Indians," a term coined in reference to the custom they had of painting their bodies with red ochre. The Beothuk hunted seals off the shore and caught salmon in the rivers that emptied into the sea. Caribou herds, long since extinct, once migrated down the interior of Newfoundland every autumn, and the Beothuk moved inland to intercept them, building elaborate fenced pounds to corral them in.

Slow death

The Beothuk were wary of whites, and the first settlers who came to their shores gave them reason to be. The Irish and English fishermen who moved into the coves, seasonally at first and later year-round, cut off the Beothuk's access to both the sea and the shore. These settlers — *these trespassers* — ignorant of the salmon's life cycle, began stringing nets across the rivers, disrupting the migration upstream, and squeezing out the Beothuk's food supply.

In retaliation, the Beothuk began cutting nets and pilfering supplies from the settlers. The settlers, in turn, began shooting the Beothuk on sight. Later, when furriers started moving inland, stealing Beothuk deerskins and raiding their villages, hostilities escalated. The killings lasted for more than two hundred years, from 1613 to 1823, and ended only because by that point there were very few Beothuk left to shoot. If it was war, it was a very lopsided one. The Beothuk never organized "hunts," never launched indiscriminate massacres, and never killed a single woman or child. The white settlers did all of the above. For more than 50 years, it was perfectly legal to kill Beothuk. And even after a proclamation was issued in 1769 making it a crime, the killings continued anyway. An entire people were starved, hounded, and hunted into oblivion and not a single white settler was ever brought to any kind of real justice.

Mi'kmaq Indians had recently arrived on the island and were also clashing with the Beothuk. At first the Beothuk kept them in check, but with the introduction of firearms, that changed. The Beothuk had a genuine abhorrence of guns. The Mi'kmaq did not. They traded with the whites and were in turn armed by the whites. Tradition has it that the Mi'kmaq were offered bounties for each Beothuk killed, but this has been disputed.

When the government finally did try to intervene, they only made matters worse. Once it became clear that the Beothuk were on the verge of extinction, well-meaning officials decided that they should capture a Beothuk, teach him or her the benevolence of white civilization, and then use them as a "peace messenger." Unfortunately, to do this, the government offered a bounty on live Beothuk, which only encouraged the hunters rather than discouraged them. One little Beothuk boy, just four years old, had his mother shot out from beneath him as she fled with him on her back. The little boy was then taken in for the reward money. In another encounter, a Beothuk woman named Demasduwit was taken prisoner by bounty hunters, who killed her husband in front of her and then dragged her away, leaving her newborn baby behind. Demasduwit was taken out to be "civilized," in order to act as a future ambassador of sorts, but she died before she could be re-introduced to her society. A corpse was sent back instead.

In 1823, three Beothuk women — a mother and two daughters — surrendered to white settlers. They were starving and were, perhaps, the last of their people. The mother and one of the daughters soon died, leaving only Shawnandithit, who comes down to us as the Last of the Beothuk. She left behind a small collection of sketches and notes, painfully remembered and related to William Cormack, a man who set up the Beothuk Institute to "preserve and study" the Beothuk — should any still exist aside from Shawnandithit. (In 1822, Cormack had walked across the island in search of Beothuk to "preserve," but the interior was eerily empty, and he succeeded only in being the first white man to traverse Newfoundland.)

Dying from tuberculosis, Shawnandithit struggled to relate the story of her people and their passing. It was a tale that always ended with her capture, and here, Cormack writes, "ends all positive knowledge of her tribe, which she never narrates without tears." The Beothuk were gone forever. An entire people destroyed.

But was it genocide?

Local Newfoundland historians get quite upset when the extinction of the Beothuk people is referred to as "genocide." They insist that such charges are a slander on the early settlers, one that portrays them as vindictive, callous, and uncaring. To which I reply, "If the shoe fits . . ."

Anthropologist Ingeborg Marshall, a leading expert in the field and author of the definitive work *A History and Ethnography of the Beothuk*, makes it quite clear: The deciding factor in the destruction of the Beothuk was the ruthlessness and brutality of the early English settlers, who showed a "total disregard for the humanity of the native population." Calling it genocide makes some people queasy, because the word conjures up Nazi death camps and official government pogroms. Fine. Let us define our terms then:

The 1948 United Nations Genocide Convention states that "genocide, whether committed in time of peace or in time of war, is a crime punishable under international law." Article Two of the convention reads:

Genocide means any of the following acts committed with intent to destroy, in whole or in part, a national, ethnic, racial or religious group:

(a) Killing members of the group;

(b) Causing serious bodily or mental harm to members of the group;

(c) Deliberately inflicting on the group conditions of life calculated to bring about its physical destruction in whole or in part;

(d) Imposing measures intended to prevent births within the group;

(e) Forcibly transferring children of the group to another group.

By current war tribunal standards, the settlers in Newfoundland who took part in the ongoing harassment and violence against the Beothuk would have been indicted.

The Beothuk Indians were eliminated. Cut off from the coasts and pushed back into the interior, they were starved out, hunted down, and persecuted. And even worse than the sporadic violence and slow strangulation they faced was the relentless disregard with which they were treated. The Beothuk — and here I borrowed a phrase from Irving Abella, writing about the plight of Jewish refugees some 200 years later — were treated with "an indifference that bordered on contempt." If it wasn't genocide, what was it?

A wealth of information on the Beothuk can be found at the Newfoundland and Labrador Heritage site mentioned earlier: www.heritage.nf.ca/aboriginal/beothuk.html. (The authors at this site insist it wasn't genocide but rather "a complex mix of factors" that killed off the Beothuk. You can read the evidence and decide for yourself.) For an alternate site on the Beothuk (part of a larger First Nations history) visit www.dickshovel.com/beo.html.

Part II
The Rise of
New France
(1608–1701)

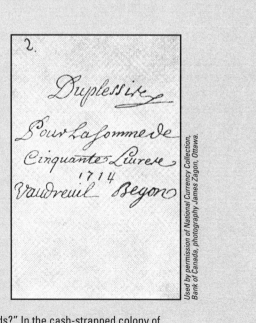

"Buddy, can you spare a 2 of diamonds?" In the cash-strapped colony of New France, playing cards were sometimes used in lieu of money.

In this part . . .

*W*e take a look at the struggle to establish a French fur-trading colony along the St. Lawrence. The French fight it out with the Iroquois and send Jesuit missionaries deep into the interior to build a mission among the Huron. But the English outflank them to the north, establishing posts along the Hudson Bay, and all sorts of hijinks ensue. Pirate attacks, Iroquois invasion forces, civil war, mail-order brides, and a frontier commando attack: stick around, it's a hell of a story.

Chapter 3

The Early Years

●●

In This Chapter

▶ The Kirke brothers take Québec

▶ The Jesuits establish missions deep in the interior

▶ The Iroquois Confederacy destroys Huronia

▶ Acadia is wracked by a civil war

●●

*B*y the time Champlain arrived on the scene, the St. Lawrence River was already bustling with activity. More than 500 ships from half a dozen European nations were fishing its waters, but in spite of all the hubbub, it was still a seasonal, transitory population: None of the makeshift communities along the river were occupied year-round. Samuel Champlain changed that. Even more importantly, he turned his gaze inland. . . .

The St. Lawrence had first been explored as a passage to either the Orient or to the elusive (and nonexistent) Kingdom of Saguenay. When that failed, the river became a fishing and whaling lane. Now, under Champlain, it became something more: a fur-trading artery and a "highway" into the heart of the continent. It was a fundamental shift in perspective, from coast to interior.

So crucial was the St. Lawrence to early Canadian development that historian Donald Creighton puts it at the very centre of the drama: The struggle and expansion was, in essence, the story of "the commercial empire of the St. Lawrence." The St. Lawrence would be Canada's central transportation system and the focus of economic expansion. Control the St. Lawrence and you controlled the interior. Control the interior and you controlled Canada.

Life and Times of Samuel Champlain

In some ways, Champlain is just as important for what he *didn't* do: He never gave up, he never gave in, and even when things were at their worst, he kept coming back for more. If there is ever a medal for sheer perseverance, it'll have Champlain's name on it. A tireless promoter of the struggling young colony, he literally criss-crossed the ocean, petitioning the courts and cajoling merchants and investors back in France, as he laid the foundation of what would one day be Québec. Champlain was also a master cartographer: He explored the waterways of the St. Lawrence and the Great Lakes, probing farther than anyone had before, and his maps were strikingly accurate.

Champlain built his *habitation* upriver at Québec (from the Algonquian *kebek*, "where the river narrows") because he wanted to avoid the rowdy Basque whalers at Tadoussac. His authority didn't include Tadoussac, which was just as well. The Basques gave him a rough welcome as it was. One traitorous French colonist, a locksmith by the name of Jean Duval, even hatched a scheme to assassinate Champlain and invite the Basques to come in and take over. Champlain, however, caught wind of the conspiracy and quickly put a stop to it. He had Duval hanged and then skewered the man's head on a spike, putting it on prominent display as a warning to others.

Iroquois versus Canadien: The lines are drawn

The Basques were the least of Champlain's problems. He faced a far more serious threat from the Iroquois, which was largely his own fault. In 1609, the Montagnais Indians asked Champlain to join them and others on an expedition against the Iroquois to the south. Champlain, not wanting to insult or provoke his fur-trading allies, agreed to go. It was a decision that would have far-reaching impact for generations of Canadiens.

It was also the first time European weapons had been turned against the Iroquois and it was a lesson they would never forget. Champlain, wearing an armoured chestplate and firing a matchlock musket, killed several Iroquois outright and helped scatter the rest. Over the next six years, Champlain would take part in several raids against the Iroquois, and in doing so would make lifelong enemies of them, and of the Mohawk in particular.

The Huron in the Georgian Bay area of the Great Lakes, meanwhile, wanted to trade directly with the French and they sent an invitation for Champlain to join them for trade negotiations. The Montagnais tried their best to block this but in 1615, Champlain made the trek to Huronia. That summer, he joined in another raid against the Iroquois. He was wounded by an arrow and spent the winter in Huronia recuperating, but overall the trip was a resounding success. The following spring, Champlain returned to Québec with a fleet of canoes filled with furs.

The alliance between New France and Huronia had been sealed in blood and profit. They had a common enemy (the Iroquois) and a common goal (increased trade). The Huron could now funnel furs from the northwest directly to the French without having to deal with other middlemen along the way who inevitably jacked up the prices. (Mind you, the disgruntled Montagnais, although now cut out of the loop, still had control over the waterways, and they continued charging tolls on canoes passing through. From mighty middlemen to mere toll collectors — no wonder they later turned on the French and betrayed them to the English.)

In choosing sides and arranging an alliance with the Huron, Champlain had plunged New France into an ongoing war against the Iroquois Confederacy, though "war" is probably not an accurate description. It was more of an ongoing feud, handed down from generation to generation on both sides. I suppose Champlain had little choice in the matter. After all, the best furs came from the north, and the powerful Huron Confederacy controlled that trade. It made sense to side with them, right?

Still, you have to wonder. It's true that the French needed the Huron more than the Huron needed them, but overall the trade was *mutually* beneficial. If Champlain had remained neutral, the Huron would have still brought in furs. Their canoes would have been riddled with Mohawk arrows when they arrived, of course, but New France may have been able to play one confederacy off the other. If Champlain had trod more carefully, he may have avoided being drawn into the conflict. It certainly would have spared the Canadiens almost one hundred years of hardship and heartbreak.

After the 1615 alliance with the Huron, New France would exist under a state of almost constant siege, as the battles with the Iroquois ebbed and flowed, flared up and died down, through numerous campaigns, truces, and sudden vicious attacks on both sides. It was a tumultuous existence, and Champlain must be held at least partly responsible for this.

A historian friend of mine scolds me for such musings. "It's easy to say the feud could have been avoided in the comfort of hindsight," he notes. "But history happens in the present tense. It turns on specific decisions in specific contexts. How could Champlain have said no to the request from the Huron to accompany them on those fateful raids? He couldn't have." As well, other historians have argued that the basic alliances were already in place when Champlain showed up and that French traders had already thrown their lot in with the Huron. Personally, I'm not so sure Champlain's options were that limited.

Coureurs de bois and voyageurs

To encourage trade and to suss out the neighbourhood, Champlain began sending out men to live among their Native allies, to learn their language and customs, and to become familiar with the lay of land. Champlain, ever the map-maker, wanted to chart the geography of the fur trade, and the adventurers he sent out, later dubbed *coureurs de bois*, "runners of the woods," played an important role in this. They also helped bridge the culture gap between Native and Canadien societies.

The coureurs de bois were the forerunners of the French *voyageurs*, or "travellers," who would paddle deep into the continent each year in flotillas of canoes to collect furs. The "original coureur de bois" was Étienne Brûlé, who spent twenty years among the Huron and whose life reads like an adventure novel. When Champlain arrived in Huronia, Brûlé had already spent five years there and was on hand to greet him. Brûlé acted as an interpreter, cartographer, diplomat, and spy. He even died in a suitably dramatic fashion, in an incident shrouded by mystery, apparently assassinated by the Huron when he attempted to negotiate a trade deal that would have bypassed them.

The first habitant

In the early years, New France was little more than a trading post perched on the edge of a vast frontier. Until settlers took up the plow and made a commitment to stay, the colony would never take root. And so, in 1617, Samuel Champlain asked Louis Hébert, a former Acadian colonist, to settle in New France. Not that Champlain had to twist his arm. Hébert was working as a pharmacist/herbalist back in Paris at the time, and he missed the freedom and adventure of the New World. So off he went, dragging his wife Marie and three children with him. Known as "the original habitants," Louis and Marie cleared the land and planted crops, making them both the first farmers and the first true settlers of New France. The slow transformation of New France had begun, from fur trading outpost to a colony of farming communities.

Between Brûlé and Hébert you have the two ends of the spectrum. The traveller vs. the settler. The forest vs. the farm. The coureur de bois vs. the habitant. In many ways, the history of Canada has been the slow triumph of Louis Hébert. And though we like to picture ourselves as a nation of hearty coureurs de bois, it was the habitants who built this country. As Canadians we are much closer in spirit to Louis Hébert than to Étienne Brûlé.

Canada is a land pinned between the memories of habitant and voyageur
— from *Why I Hate Canadians*

Baltimore's mansion

Many a dream has died on Newfoundland's rocky shores, and more than one starry-eyed romantic has tried — and failed — to set up their own private version of a New Jerusalem on this cold and wind-swept isle. Of such attempts, the most notable was the colony founded at Ferryland by the divinely inspired George Calvert (a.k.a. Lord Baltimore). In 1621, Calvert sent over a dozen colonists to the peninsula he named "Avalon" (in reference to the legendary spot where Christianity was first introduced to England). It was a name intended to inspire heroic acts of greatness among the colonists. Then Calvert spent a winter on the Rock and changed his mind.

I have sent [my family] home after much sufferance in this wofull country, where with one intolerable wynter were we almost undone. It is not to be expressed with my pen what wee have endured.

From "Avalon!" to "wofull country," Newfoundland never was a place for sissies. The Ferryland colony struggled on, but the Baltimore family more or less abandoned it, turning their gaze south to Maryland and the city that would one day bear their title. The French, meanwhile, began a colony of their own at Placentia Bay around 1660, just across the Avalon Peninsula from the English. A few years later, they added a fortress, and this set the stage for a whole slew of attacks, counterattacks, and other such tomfoolery.

For a brief bio on Brûle, the "original coureur de bois," visit www3.ns.sympatico.ca/educate/brule.htm, and for a bit more on Hébert, the "original habitant," visit www.acpo.on.ca/claude/hebert-a.htm.

Company of One Hundred

New France may have begun as a fur-trading colony, but it had a clear spiritual directive as well. From the start, Champlain considered it an outpost of salvation among "the savages." Concerned that open trade with the French would debase the Indians without properly "civilizing" them, he urged the Récollet friars near his hometown in France to come to the New World and begin missionary work.

Champlain's motives were an odd mix — bartering both in pelts and in souls — but he never let these contradictions faze him. Converting the Natives, he declared, would "cement their commercial ties with the French as well as save them from eternal hell-fire in the next world." With the arrival of Récollet missionaries in 1615, Native culture faced a different sort of assault. It was no longer a matter of mere trade. Their very culture and belief systems were now on the bargaining block.

The Récollets were followed by the Jesuits ten years later, who gave the drive to convert the Indians renewed vigour. The Jesuits were fearless, driven, some would say obsessive, men. They ranged the world from Japan to South America, preaching the Good Word. There was no jungle thick enough, no portage long enough to stop them. The Jesuit Campaign signalled the beginning of the end for that great northern Confederacy. (For more on the role of the Récollets and Jesuits, see the section called Black Robes later in this chapter.)

Tensions were rife in the colony of New France as well. The fur traders were mainly French Protestants (that is, *Huguenots,* who were, at that time, in open revolt back in France). And these traders, along with the coureurs de bois, didn't want missionaries running loose disrupting Native societies and interfering with business. The trader versus the missionary: It was a conflict of world views that would occur time and time again. The Jesuits quickly went over the traders' heads and made an appeal directly to Cardinal Richelieu back in France. Now, who do you think won? Whose arguments do you think went over better with *Cardinal* Richelieu? Those of a band of profiteering Protestant traders or those of a highly respected Catholic order? It's a no brainer, folks. In 1627, the earlier trade monopolies were cancelled and in their place the Company of One Hundred Associates was established, with Richelieu himself at the helm.

The Company of One Hundred Associates (*Compagnie des Cent-Associés*) was less concerned with profits than with proselytizing among the Natives and with bringing out more "pious" settlers. To finance these efforts, they came up with a clever plan. It was the same way college students pay for pizza: everyone would kick in a set amount, the money would be pooled, and any profits/pizza would be shared equally. But, as anyone who has ever watched a bunch of students standing around scratching their heads and adding up their quarters only to keep coming up short knows, schemes like this often fail. And so it was with Richelieu's attempt at co-operative "spiritual" capitalism. It floundered for years before being put out of its misery by Louis XIV.

Pop quiz for the slow-witted: How many people originally invested in the Company of One Hundred Associates?

For an overview of New France, including information on Champlain and the Company of One Hundred, visit `www.crosswinds.net/~gapellet/history.htm`. The Virtual Museum of New France also has an excellent section on Champlain at `www.vmnf.civilization.ca/explor/explcd_e.html`.

The Kirke brothers take Québec

There is a key distinction between *pirates* and *privateers*. Both plundered the seas and robbed ships of their bounty, but pirates were "independent operators." Privateers, in contrast, were working under a charter from their king or queen. That is, they were *licensed* pirates.

As you can imagine, the distinction was a fine one, and at times it was hard to tell one from the other. The unfortunate Captain Kidd, for one, began as a legitimate privateer, but when he overstepped the bounds of his charter he was tried and executed — unfairly — as a pirate. Legend has it that Kidd's fabled treasure, with which he tried to barter for his life, lies buried at the Oak Island "money pit" in Nova Scotia.

The Kirke brothers were privateers — though in the minds of many Québec historians they were little more than pirates. There were five of them, and they earned lasting notoriety when they captured Québec in 1628.

Led by the oldest brother, David, the Kirkes made a *de rigueur* stop to torch and terrorize the poor Acadians and then sailed boldly up the St. Lawrence. They quickly captured the Basque whaling station at Tadoussac and set up a river blockade. Having cut off Québec from the outside world, they sent word to Champlain demanding his surrender. Champlain refused, but luck was on the Kirkes' side. The hapless Company of One Hundred Associates (you remember them) had just outfitted their first big expedition. Amid much publicity and hoopla, they had loaded up around twenty transport ships with supplies and colonists and sent them on their way. When the ships passed the Gaspé peninsula, they ran smack into the Kirkes, who "rounded them up like sheep."

The Kirke brothers captured 18 ships and took 600 people prisoner. In the stores was food, livestock, even — ironically — cannons sent from France to provide the settlers with protection from just this sort of thing. It was magnificent plunder. The Kirkes made a fortune and Québec, still dependent on French supplies, faced starvation and ruin. The brothers departed as winter set in, leaving the settlers in dire straits. It was a cruel strategy, but it worked. By the time the Kirkes returned the following summer, Champlain was forced to surrender and was taken back to England as a prisoner. It was a complete and decisive conquest — but Champlain would be back.

New France and Acadia remained in English hands for the next four years as the Kirkes pulled in huge profits from the fur trade. This might very well have ended the French presence in Canada forever, except for one small quirk of fate. Over in England, Good King Charles was running dangerously short of money. Indeed, he was so strapped for cash that in 1632 he agreed to give back the French colonies in exchange for a large lump-sum payment, in a deal brokered by our old pal Cardinal Richelieu. And the dream of New France was again resurrected.

The death of Champlain

Samuel Champlain returned to Québec in 1633 to find that the Kirkes had stripped the colony right down to the window frames. It was a sad homecoming for the Father of New France, and Champlain himself had only two years of life left in him. He remained active almost to the end, and even founded a post at Trois-Rivières in 1634, but his dream of a great inland colony along the St. Lawrence had yet to be fulfilled. He died on Christmas Day 1635, an exhausted man. At the time of his death, fewer than 200 people were living in New France. All that work and so little to show for it.

Still, Champlain *had* persevered. He had struggled against insurmountable odds and he had done his absolute best. Without Champlain, the entire enterprise would have collapsed. Without him there would have been no New France, no Québec, and no French-Canadian presence in Canada today. For that reason alone he deserves to be honoured.

And what of the Kirkes? Well, David was given title to the Avalon Peninsula and became the first governor of Newfoundland. He moved to Ferryland, chased off the stragglers from Lord Baltimore's old colony, and spent the rest of his days fighting lawsuits from the Calvert family (whose lands he had usurped) and taxing the locals to the brink of oblivion. He eventually ended up in jail. Like I said, there is a fine line between pirate and privateer. And an even finer one between pirate and landlord.

The Newfoundland and Labrador Heritage site (www.heritage.nf.ca/ exploration/sponsored.html) has more on both Kirke's tour-of-duty as governor and the ill-fated Baltimore colony at Ferryland. For a fascinating look at Newfoundland's French colony, Placentia, visit collections.ic.gc.ca/ placentia/.

Black Robes

The Récollets were the first missionaries to arrive in Canada. They made the journey to Huronia, but their strategy was ill conceived and they met with little success. They wanted to make the Natives "first become human" (that is, European) by forcing them to relocate on farms, adopt European dress, and learn to speak French. Champlain supported this approach, but it failed utterly.

The Jesuits, who arrived in 1625, took a completely different tack: They were determined to meet the First Nations on their own terms. Rather than expect the Natives to come to them, the Jesuits went to the Natives. They lived among them, learned their languages and customs, and converted them one soul at a time. It was a far more effective approach.

Impact of the Jesuits

The Jesuits were messengers of a specific god. *Their* god. Native spirituality had to be undermined, and because of this, the Jesuits had a vested interest in everything they did. I certainly admire the bravery, selflessness, and sincerity of the Jesuits. But there is no disguising the deep social rifts they created.

The Huron tolerated the presence of the Jesuits because the Huron wanted to continue their military trading alliance with the French, but blatant incentives to become baptized were soon introduced: Christian Huron were given preferential treatment and better rates of barter, and guns were later sold only to "Christianized Indians." Huron who had been baptized were told they had to make a complete break with traditional rituals and customs, including burial rites — a crucial part of Huron culture.

Huron society broke into two camps: those who converted and those who refused. When a smallpox epidemic, introduced unwittingly by the Jesuits, swept through, killing more than half the population, suspicious Huron turned their anger at the black-robed priests. (Even worse, the disease killed a high number of the elderly, which was devastating to the continuity of traditional skills and culture.) The Jesuits were feared and resented as sorcerers. People were baptized on their deathbeds, often against their family's wishes, and when the Jesuits declared that only *Christian* Huron would go to Heaven, many hurried to be baptized so that they would not be separated after death from family members who had already been converted.

So great were the social divisions, that some of the non-Christian Huron even considered forming an alliance with their old enemies the Iroquois as a way to combat the Jesuits and stop the erosion of traditional Native values.

Ste. Marie Among the Hurons

Leading the mission to Huronia was Jean de Brébeuf, a devout and hardworking priest. An exceptional linguist, Brébeuf oversaw the first Huron dictionary and grammar book. He also wrote in great detail about Huron society and has been described, accurately I think, as "Canada's first serious ethnographer." Brébeuf, always sensitive to Huron customs, wrote up a list of instructions for new priests. Among Brébeuf's instructions and one that I think can be applied as a general motto in life:

Do not paddle unless you intend always to paddle.

That is, either commit entirely or don't bother.

The founding of Montréal

Montréal began in 1642 as a would-be spiritual utopia, founded by a group of religious visionaries in Paris who wanted to build a New Jerusalem in the wilderness. They chose a devout and energetic young soldier, Paul de Chomedey de Maisonneuve, to lead an expedition — a crusade in essence — to establish a new colony upriver from Québec on the island discovered by Jacques Cartier.

When he got to Québec, Maisonneuve was warned that his mission was suicidal. The Iroquois were waging war against the habitants along the St. Lawrence, settlers had fled, crops were rotting in the fields, and the very existence of New France was now in question.

But Maisonneuve scoffed at this warning, declaring (in his best heroic voice, no doubt): "I have come here not to deliberate but to act! It is my duty to found a colony at Montréal! I would go if every tree were an Iroquois!"

So off he went with his brave band of forty. They named their community Ville-Marie, and among those first settlers was Jeanne Mance, a nurse and administrator who was as much a co-founder of Montréal as was Maisonneuve. Dubbed the "Angel of the Colony" by the people she cared for, Mance built the community's first hospital, Hôtel-Dieu, where she treated colonists and Natives alike. Under her guidance, the small colony grew to 500 within 20 years.

Brébeuf was later replaced as superior by Jérôme Lalemant, and in 1639, under Lalemant's directives, the Jesuits began construction of a fortified mission named Ste. Marie Among the Hurons in the heart of Huron territory (near present-day Midland, Ontario). As both a sanctuary and a base of operations for the Jesuits working in the area, Ste. Marie Among the Hurons was designed to be self-sufficient and self-contained. A bastion of faith, a spiritual fortress, deep in the savage wilderness!

Or at least, that is how romantic historians have portrayed it over the years. Considering that the Huron lived in well-established villages with elaborate and extensive housing and broad-based agriculture, the Jesuit bastion was less "a pocket of civilization" than it was an embassy. Ste. Marie Among the Hurons was expanded over the years to include a hospital, a church, and separate dwellings for converted Huron. It was soon a hive of activity with as many as 43 lay brothers and priests operating out of it.

Apocalypse then: The fall of Huronia

In 1648, the Iroquois unleashed a full-scale attack on the Huron. Weakened by smallpox, divided by Christianity, and facing Iroquois fur blockades, the Huron could barely muster a defence against the onslaught. The Iroquois overran and destroyed one village after another in an apocalyptic campaign designed to wipe out the Huron Confederacy once and for all. Several Jesuits were killed during the assault, among them Jean de Brébeuf. (His bones lie buried at the Martyrs' Shrine in Midland, Ontario.)

On May 15, 1649, the Jesuits withdrew from Ste. Marie Among the Hurons and burnt the mission to the ground so that it would not fall into Iroquois hands. The Jesuits then fell back to a small island in Lake Huron and tried to start anew. They were joined by thousands of Huron refugees seeking sanctuary, and after a horrific winter of famine and disease, the Jesuits were forced to abandon the island as well. They retreated to Québec with a band of six hundred Huron followers. A small community of Huron live in the Québec City suburb of Lorette even today.

The rest of the once mighty Huron Confederacy was scattered to the four winds. The Huron became Canada's Lost Tribe. Some fled north. Some went south and wandered for years before settling in the United States. Others were captured and absorbed into the Iroquois Confederacy. And still the Iroquois juggernaut continued: the Petun, the Neutral, the Erie — one by one, they fell. Would New France be next?

You can find a history of the Huron and the fall of Huronia at www.dickshovel. com/hur.html. Ste. Marie Among the Hurons has been rebuilt near the original site at Midland, Ontario. Their Web site isn't extensive, but it's worth a quick look (www.saintemarieamongthehurons.on.ca/english/index.html).

The Canadian martyrs

At times you have to wonder if the Jesuits who came to Canada didn't have some sort of death wish. After all, dying for one's faith was an act of martyrdom and was often the first step on the road to sainthood. The Iroquois killed no fewer than eight Jesuits, five during the fall of Huronia alone. The Jesuits, devout and unarmed, were often brutally tortured first, and the descriptions of their ordeal are agonizing to read: They were tied to stakes and skinned alive, they had their fingernails pulled out, they were forced to endure "mock" baptisms of boiling water, they were — but that is quite enough. Suffice it to say their suffering was enough to make Stephen King queasy. The Catholic Church has canonized all eight Canadian martyrs as saints.

> *By martyrdom, a disciple is transformed into an image of his Master,*
> *who freely accepted death on behalf of the world's salvation.*
> — Second Vatican Council

One martyr, Isaac Jogues, was actually tortured *twice*. Captured in an ambush by the Iroquois in 1642, he later managed to escape — but only after having endured relentless torment and humiliation at the hands of his captors. Ever the optimist (when the Iroquois cut off his left thumb, he later expressed gratitude that they hadn't taken his right thumb as well so that he could still "write to his brethren") Jogues went back to the Iroquois voluntarily in 1646, as an "ambassador of peace." They killed him.

Visit `www.jesuits.ca/martyrs-shrine/biograph.htm` to find biographies and portraits of all eight Canadian martyrs. (Of course the martyrs have their own Web site. *Everybody* has their own Web site.) Another, similar site worth a glance is `www.martyrs.org/History.htm#picture`.

Meanwhile, Back in Acadia . . .

Port Royal, the main habitation in Acadia, was abandoned in 1607 when the settlement's leader, Pierre Du Gua de Monts, a wealthy French merchant, lost his trade monopoly to the area. De Monts turned his attention to the St. Lawrence and helped launch the colony at what is now Québec City, but not everyone was convinced Acadia was a lost cause. In 1610, one of de Monts's associates, Jean de Poutrincourt, sailed back to Port Royal to start anew. He had been a member of the original expedition and had in fact acted as de Monts's governor, and he understood full well the difficulties he would face in trying to re-establish a colony in Acadia. Still, when he arrived, Poutrincourt was both surprised and touched to discover that the Mi'kmaq had maintained the Port Royal habitation and garden in good repair during their absence. Perhaps it was an omen of better things to come?

Membertou: The unsung Father of Acadia?

Sure, de Monts and Poutrincourt and the others get all the kudos, but the people most responsible for the success of the early Acadian settlements were the Mi'kmaq. They gave their support and help to the French, and — more importantly — they didn't launch the type of attacks against the Acadians that the Iroquois did against the settlers of New France.

Credit goes to the Mi'kmaq chief Membertou for setting the tone of co-operation and friendship right from the start. Membertou was a real character, though we should probably speak of him in the plural. He claimed he was over 100 years old and had been on hand to greet Cartier when he explored the Maritimes more than seventy years before. But it is much more likely that the name "Membertou," being highly honoured, was handed down from one generation of chiefs to the next, a practice found in other First Nations as well.

A prophet, a medicine man, and a chief of great standing, Membertou was proud to the point of vanity (he expected to be greeted at Port Royal by a salvo of gunshots saluting his arrival). Unusual for his culture, he was also monogamous. That is, he only took one wife at a time. (Other chiefs kept as many as seven wives, a practice that horrified the oh-so-celibate Jesuit priests.) Generous towards and protective of the fledging French colony, Membertou eventually converted to Catholicism and on his deathbed urged his people to maintain their alliance and friendship with the Acadians.

Argall attacks!

Unfortunately for the eternally optimistic Poutrincourt, things in Port Royal soon went sour. Bickering and infighting among the colonists, stirred up by a pair of troublemaking priests, led to a schism, and a breakaway colony was set up across the bay. In spite of these internal problems, the Acadian colony began to grow and even started to branch out along the coast.

But trouble was a-brewin' down south. The English, you see, had established a colony of their own at Jamestown, Virginia, and in 1613 they launched an attack against Acadia. Led by the notorious privateer Samuel Argall, they fell upon the breakaway Jesuit colony, killing one priest, wounding several settlers, and razing the buildings. They then stopped at St. Croix Island (now deserted) and tried to eradicate any evidence of French occupation there. The goal was to drive the French from the Bay of Fundy entirely and physically erase all traces of their prior claim to the area. Argall eventually sacked Port Royal, torching the buildings and burning the fields. He then carried his prisoners back to Virginia. *Mission accomplished!*

Poutrincourt had been away at the time, and when he returned he found "the fort in ruins and the inhabitants starving." The long, slow process of rebuilding Acadia began anew, but without Poutrincourt. He gave up and went back to France. The lesson was clear: Acadia, exposed to English attacks along the coast, would always be in a precarious, vulnerable position.

The first Nova Scotian

There was already a New France and a New England, so why not a New Scotland? In 1621, James VI of Scotland granted all of Acadia to a nobleman and poet by the name of William Alexander, who promptly renamed it "New Scotland" *(Nova Scotia)*. The king created a new order of knights, "the Baronets of Nova Scotia," and issued both a flag and a coat of arms for the territory. Sure, it was a little presumptuous of James to go around granting French colonies to his buddies, but Sir William, "the first Nova Scotian," was persuasive.

In 1629, a band of settlers led by Alexander's eldest son arrived at Port Royal and built a settlement they dubbed Charlesfort. With Acadia no longer under direct French control, the Scots were able to set up camp unopposed. They farmed the land, they struggled through harsh winters, and they maintained friendly relations with the Mi'kmaq. But in 1632, Acadia was handed back to France and the short-lived Scottish community was forced to disband.

For a history of the Scots in Nova Scotia, including William Alexander, visit www.chebucto. ns.ca/Heritage/FSCNS/ScotsHome.html.

For more on the early years of Acadia, visit www.geocities.com/~timhebert/origin.htm (part of a larger Acadian site) or ourworld.compuserve.com/homepages/lwjones/acadhist.htm (part of an Acadian genealogy site). The Museum of Nova Scotia also has information on the Acadians and Mi'kmaq (www.ednet.ns.ca/educ/museum/arch/infos/info.htm). For an extensive history of Port Royal, visit users.andara.com/~grose/portroy.html.

The Acadian Civil War

It has all the hallmarks of a really splendid melodrama: the arch villain, the loyal wife, the heroic last stand, and the final betrayal. The Acadian Civil War, basically a feud between competing French fur traders, was more than simply an exciting sideshow of history. It had a far-reaching impact.

The story begins in 1636, when Charles d'Aulnay inherits the rank of "Governor of Acadia" from his cousin. D'Aulnay (usually referred to as "the dastardly d'Aulnay") built his fort near the site of the original Port Royal. There was just one snag: Acadia already had a governor. His name was Charles La Tour and he had *his* base across the Bay of Fundy at the mouth of the Saint John River (at what is now the city of Saint John, New Brunswick). A case of competing monopolies, the two trade zones were vague and overlapping. It was a recipe for disaster.

D'Aulnay, a high-born aristocrat and former naval officer, looked down on La Tour, a commoner backed by merchants, a man of suspect loyalties, the son of a shameless social-climbing debtor. Charles d'Aulnay was determined to drive La Tour from the Bay of Fundy and he began petitioning the French court to that effect. When that failed, he went on the offensive.

"The lioness of Acadia"

La Tour is the more sympathetic character. He had made his life in Acadia. He had married a Mi'kmaq woman, he spoke the language, and he doted on his three daughters. More than one historian has noted that, while other French colonists (including Champlain) referred to the Mi'kmaq as *savages*, meaning "uncivilized" in the original French, La Tour did not. He was always careful to refer to them instead as *people of the country*.

In 1639, the now-widowed La Tour arranged a second marriage to a woman back in France, one Françoise Marie Jacquelin. She is commonly known as "Madame La Tour," but women didn't take their husbands' surnames at that time, so we will refer to her as Jacquelin. Destined to go down in history as "the lioness of Acadia," Jacquelin joined her husband at Fort La Tour in 1640, just as things were heating up between the two Acadian communities.

Within weeks of her arrival, tensions had boiled over. D'Aulnay launched an ambush on La Tour's ships in which several died, including one of Jacquelin's loyal guards, who died in her arms. It was Jacquelin's "baptism of blood" and she never forgot it.

The La Tour/d'Aulnay civil war would rage for the next five years, and although La Tour counterattacked and held his own, he was losing the propaganda battle back in France. D'Aulnay had friends in high places and La Tour, in desperation, turned to the English for help. It was in the spring of 1645, while La Tour was in Boston trying to drum up support and supplies, that d'Aulnay launched his biggest assault.

Tipped off that La Tour was away, d'Aulnay decided to make his move. He sailed across the bay to Fort La Tour and sent word to Jacquelin, demanding immediate and unconditional surrender. But instead of a white flag, she ran up a red banner. It was a flag of war, a flag of defiance, and it demonstrated that Jacquelin had no intention of surrendering. The battle raged on and off for three days. Grapeshot and cannon fire rained down, but when d'Aulnay's forces attempted to swarm the fort, they were met by fierce resistance and hand-to-hand combat, led by Jacquelin herself.

D'Aulnay fell back and asked for a truce. If Jacquelin would surrender the fort, he gave his word that her men would not be harmed in any way. Jacquelin, out of ammunition and with her fortress in near ruins, agreed to d'Aulnay's terms. But — and here is where the "dastardly" part comes in — once he was in control of Fort La Tour, d'Aulnay quickly went back on his promise. In one of the most underhanded betrayals in Canadian history, d'Aulnay forced Jacquelin to watch, with a noose around her neck, as he hanged her loyal supporters one by one. He then threw her into a prison cell where she died a few weeks later under suspicious circumstances. ("Died of a broken heart," they said, though some suspected poison.) Victory was complete. D'Aulnay was now the undisputed Lord of Acadia.

The return of Charles La Tour

The story doesn't end there. In 1650, a canoe d'Aulnay was travelling in capsized, and he died of cold and exhaustion after dragging himself to shore. (Another version has him drowning, pulled down by the weight of his armour while a Mi'kmaq servant he had recently beaten looked on impassively.) With his old nemesis out of the picture, Charles La Tour returned to Acadia, and — in a surprising manoeuvre — he managed to talk d'Aulnay's widow into marrying him and thus avoided an ongoing conflict with d'Aulnay's estates. The feud was over and the two sides, united by marriage, set about the difficult task of rebuilding the devastated Acadian fur trade.

When the struggle between La Tour and d'Aulnay began, Acadia ranked with, if not above, Québec in French colonial schemes. At its end, she was left exhausted, easy prey for expanding New England. She became a political pawn. . . .

— historian M. A. MacDonald

Visit `chardonnay.niagara.com/~merrwill/default.html` for more on women in Canadian history, including Madame La Tour and other heroines. You can also find biographies of all of the main figures in early Acadian history at `www.blupete.com/Hist/BiosNS/1600-00/List.htm`.

Chapter 4

Life in New France

• •

In This Chapter

▶ Louis XIV makes New France a royal province

▶ The Great Intendant Jean Talon arrives on the scene

▶ "Daughters of the King" sail in

▶ An odd form of Canadian feudalism takes root

• •

After the fall of Huronia, the coureurs de bois (French-Canadian woodsmen) were forced to take over as middlemen in the fur trade. This drew the traders of New France deeper into the Northwest. It also further antagonized the Iroquois. And let's face it, the Iroquois were an easy group to antagonize. A short-lived truce between New France and the Confederacy collapsed in 1658 and the attacks began anew.

> *The history of New France prior to 1665 was overwhelmingly shaped by the Indians. Throughout that period, they outnumbered the Europeans and were militarily superior to them.*
> — historian Bruce G. Trigger

Of Myth and Men: The Battle of Long Sault

In 1660, the French settlers decided to take the battle to the Iroquois. Led by a soldier-turned-saviour by the name of Adam Dollard, a small band of 17 Frenchmen were joined by a larger group of Huron, along with a handful of Algonquin, intent on ambushing Iroquois trade canoes. They ran instead into a full invasion force, 300 strong, on its way to Montréal. What followed was a dramatic Alamo-style siege, as Dollard and the others took refuge in an abandoned stockade at Long Sault. For seven days, the battle raged.

The most dramatic moment occurred when Dollard hoisted a barrel of lit gunpowder above his head and prepared to throw it at the Iroquois. Unfortunately, that snapshot of history, with Dollard in full heroic pose, fails to tell what happened next. The gunpowder keg got snagged on a branch and fell back into the fort, where it exploded, causing irreparable damage. As their Huron allies abandoned them, only nine French defenders remained. The end was nigh. The Iroquois overran their position, killing several survivors outright and carrying off others to be ritualistically tortured.

The noble Adam Dollard died in battle, but he succeeded in stopping a full-scale invasion of Montréal. Nineteenth-century historians in Québec later elevated the Siege of Long Sault to mythic stature, and hailed Dollard as both a saviour and a sacrifice. (They gave the story clear religious overtones, portraying Dollard as a secular martyr and unofficial saint.) Even today, people in Québec celebrate not Victoria Day but *Fête de Dollard*, every May, in honour of "the saviour of Montréal."

This romantic version of Dollard and the Siege of Long Sault has been challenged. For one thing, it is highly unlikely that Dollard himself, a relative newcomer to New France, would have been "leading" the Huron. Nor is it certain that the Iroquois were in fact intent on conquering Montréal (though the evidence does seem to suggest they were). Historian Daniel Francis has even argued that, "far from saving New France, the Dollard incident probably served to provoke the Iroquois into redoubling their attacks the next season."

> *Depending on which school of interpretation one believes, Dollard was either a brave and selfless martyr in the righteous missionary cause, or a klutzy bandit who escalated hostilities with the Iroquois.*
> — columnist Peter Black

Peter Black is a Quebec-based radio producer and one of my favourite online columnists. You can find his piece on Adam Dollard (part of the larger "Log Cabin Chronicles" site) at www.tomifobia.com/dollard.html. The about.com French-Canadian culture site has some more info on Dollard as well.

A Royal Province

In 1660, the year that Dollard made his celebrated "last stand at Long Sault," the entire population of New France was only around 3,000 people. This was a far cry from the English colonies on the eastern seaboard, which were bursting with 100,000 colonists or more.

Fortunately, the *true* Saviour of New France was at hand. Forget Dollard — the real person responsible for rescuing the struggling colony was the Sun King himself, Louis XIV. On the advice of his astute and able advisor Jean-Baptiste Colbert, Louis cancelled the Company of One Hundred Associates and elevated New France to the position of "royal province," under the direct authority of the King Himself. (The Company of One Hundred had actually "sublet" its monopoly to a third party by this point, so cancelling it was more an act of euthanasia than anything.) Rule by royal decree: It was a drastic measure, but it worked. Within ten years the colony had more than doubled in size. Louis XIV had indeed "saved" New France.

> *The King regards his Canadien subjects, from the highest to the lowest, as his own children.*
> — the ever-paternal Louis XIV

Mercantilism and triangular trade

Mercantilism is one of those Big Ideas of history (like Marxism or progress or bell-bottom pants) that have an immense impact regardless of whether or not they are actually true. Many Big Ideas are not. Mercantilism, for one, is based on the notion that trade is a zero-sum game. That is, wealth is finite. The pie can only be cut so many ways and more for you means less for me.

Mercantilism was the working assumption of imperialism. In practical terms, it meant that the major trade nations were convinced they had to sell more goods than they purchased in order to thrive. Colonies were meant to be exploited. Indeed, it was almost the definition of a colony: *that which exists to be exploited by the mother country.* Ideally, colonies should not cost more to administer than the value of the goods they supplied. In other words, they should be cash cows.

Under mercantilism, the object of trade was not to increase the standard of living or improve infrastructure. No. The point was to amass as much wealth as possible, especially gold, and usually at the expense of other nations. It was a highly interventionist system, and a far cry from free trade. As a firm believer in mercantilist theory, Jean-Baptiste Colbert, Louis XIV's chief advisor, developed a system of self-supporting "triangular trade" back and forth between France and its colonies in Canada and the Caribbean. The system worked like this:

- The Canadian colonies would ship furs, fish, timber, and minerals.
- The Caribbean colonies would supply rum, molasses, and sugar.
- And France, in turn, would supply textiles and manufactured goods.

Colbert's system of "triangular trade" put New France in a key, cornerstone position. No longer a colonial backwater, it was — in theory at least — now considered a vital player in the grand imperial scheme. And a new position was created to manage these affairs: that of colonial administrator, or *intendant*.

The Great Intendant

"So he was, like, the first Minister of Beer and Babes?"
"Yes," I say with a weary sigh. "Something like that."

My friend Mike has been listening to me go on and on about Jean Talon and his many accomplishments. It's easy to get caught up in the sheer drama of history, and while researching this book, I would often regale (inflict?) my family and friends with tales from the past. Mike, however, had selective hearing. "Beer, you say?"

Jean Talon, the first intendant of New France, was a remarkable man. In just two terms, and six years over all, he turned everything upside down. He represents a new kind of hero. Neither an explorer, nor a soldier, nor a martyr: He was, if such a thing is possible, a *virile bureaucrat*.

Jean Talon arrived in 1665 and immediately set about transforming New France from a struggling fur-trading colony into a robust royal province, one with an integrated infrastructure and all the luxuries of home. Unlike most bureaucrats, who have a problem for every solution, Jean Talon had a thousand solutions for every conceivable problem. He built the colony's first shipyard. He imported livestock, he established new communities, he brought in looms and encouraged colonists to weave, he even created Canada's first family allowance, and he introduced the novel idea that landowners should actually *reside* on the property that belonged to them.

True, many of his major projects fizzled and died after he left, but give the man his due. He was a catalyst to impressive growth. Jean Talon encouraged numerous shops, inns, and factories to set up, and he even built the colony's first commercial brewery in 1668, making him (unofficially) the Father of Canadian Beer. Alas, it was an idea slightly ahead of its time. The habitants preferred wine and brandy and Talon's brewery eventually closed down. No matter, he was already on to the next project at full gallop. Determined, energetic, imaginative: By the time he left for good in 1672, he had helped launch a remarkable transformation. Even more importantly, he had arranged for hundreds of young women to immigrate to New France.

Jean Talon and the spiral staircases

Ever wonder why the buildings in Montréal are so narrow? Ever wonder why the staircases have to twist and turn to stay inside property lines? You can thank Jean Talon for that. It actually made a lot of sense. Rather than large cookie-cut squares of lands, Talon divided lots into narrow strips, usually bordering a shoreline, with the houses huddled together and the fields stretching back into the hills. (This system had started to evolve before Talon arrived, but he entrenched it as *the* way of allotting land in New France.)

This system of narrow "ribbon" farms, with the houses lined up at the end, kept settlers near each other for protection. It also allowed the maximum number of people access to water. By 1700, the St. Lawrence shoreline from Québec City to Montréal was virtually one extended, unbroken line of farmhouses. The island of Montréal was laid out in a similar fashion, and as succeeding generations divided their property among offspring, the lots became narrower still. Today, from an airplane, Québec's distinct history is laid out for all to see in the province's unique, thin strips of farmland.

The empire strikes back

Unlike the Iroquois Confederacy, which was a working democracy, Louis XIV ruled by divine right. It was an approach he summed up famously with the phrase, *"L'état, c'est moi"* ("I am the state"). He wasn't going to take any guff from a band of New World nations. With the fall of Huronia, the Iroquois had become the region's dominant military force and had pushed the French colony to the brink of dissolution. Something had to be done.

The year 1665 was a turning point in the history of New France. Not only did it see the arrival of the Great Intendant, Jean Talon, it also saw the arrival from France of some 1,100 soldiers of the elite Carignan-Salières Regiment. Their mission? To end the Iroquois threat once and for all. The French soldiers marched on the Iroquois homeland, torched a couple of villages and set up a highly visible garrison duty at Montréal and Trois-Rivières. And although they only spent three years in New France, and never fought a major engagement with the Iroquois, the impact of the Carignan-Salières Regiment was immense nonetheless.

The presence of the regiment alone acted as a strong deterrent, and in 1667 the Iroquois agreed to a cease-fire. It was a peace that would last for twenty years, during which the colony of New France would flourish. Cathedrals and grand homes were built. Land was cleared, farms were built, and high society soirees, elegant as anything back in Paris, were held in banquet halls and manorial residences. And though the Carignan-Salières Regiment itself was recalled once the peace treaty with the Iroquois had been established, some 400 soldiers and officers stayed behind and were granted vast tracts of land by Jean Talon. Many married "good local girls." Some married "daughters of the king."

Filles du roi

Jean Talon was not happy. Not at all. He had commissioned the colony's first census and the results weren't very promising. The ratio of eligible men to women was hopelessly lopsided. There were far too many bachelors and not enough young women of marriageable age. In a population of 3,200, there were around 720 unmarried males and only 45 single females. True, this was great for the women, who could pick and choose, but it was terrible for the society as a whole. Population growth had stalled.

Fortunately, Jean Talon was a man of action, a man of bold plans and quick decisions. If there were too few women, the solution was simple: bring in more. Between 1663 and 1673, under Talon's urging, Louis XIV sponsored nearly 800 young female settlers. They were called *filles du roi* ("daughters of the king") and their transportation and settlement costs were covered by the Crown. Almost all were married soon after their arrival, some within days, and they began clearing the land and raising families. The *filles du roi* helped spark a population explosion that saved New France just as surely as had Louis XIV and his soldiers. Of the more than six million Québécois in Canada today, most can trace their roots back to these adventurous women.

In the genes?

So who were these women, these Mothers of New France? Who were the *filles du roi*? Many were orphans; most were of "modest birth." A few (secretly) were widows escaping poverty, but the majority were simply young women looking for a better life in the New World. In this, they brought a spirit of adventure and risk-taking with them. (If, as some geneticists now suggest, there is indeed a "risk-taking" gene, then surely Québec has a higher than usual share.)

Some *filles du roi* were beggars from the ghettos in Paris, but more than a few were educated women from upper-class families. The *filles du roi* from more noble backgrounds usually married the officers of the Carignan-Salières Regiment, and from this came the lively mix of today's Québécois: soldiers, beggars, orphans, and aristocrats. And royal mail-order brides.

Reluctant husbands

But what about the men? The women chose their own husbands, but not all of the men were eager to get married and settle down. In fact, some of them were downright hostile to the idea. They enjoyed the rugged freedom of a frontier bachelor lifestyle, and they often refused to take a wife. This, Jean Talon would not tolerate. In a letter to Colbert, he outlines the harsh measures he took to force the men to choose a bride:

I have ordered that [bachelors] be deprived of the right to trade and hunt, and that the honours and privileges of church and community be withheld, other than by decree, if within fifteen days of the arrival of vessels from France they are still not married.

Want to know the funny part? Jean Talon never married.

For more on the *filles du roi,* check out the Virtual Museum of New France (www.mvnf.muse.digital.ca/popul/filles/s-fil-en.htm).

Feudalism: Canadien style

To a certain extent, New France had become a "little Paris." It was a pocket of French culture transplanted into the St. Lawrence valley. If this made for elegant balls and airs of refinement among the upper echelons, it also meant that certain anachronistic elements were preserved and kept alive in Canada long after their demise elsewhere. One such example was the distinct form of feudalism that took root in New France in the 1620s and that would last for more than two hundred years, ending only in 1854, long after the French Revolution had wiped out the hereditary rights of the landed gentry back in France.

The seigneurial system

Based on European concepts of feudalism and landownership, the *seigneurial system* in New France was first devised by Cardinal Richelieu but extended and strengthened under Jean Talon. In it, the Crown "granted" land titles to certain deserving individuals and institutions. These were usually soldiers, noblemen, or religious organizations, but — especially in Canada — they could also be wealthy or well-connected commoners.

Estates belonged to a *seigneur,* or "lord," on the condition that he develop it. This usually involved building and maintaining a manor, a mill, and even a fortress. To achieve this, the seigneur brought in labourers who lived on his land and worked it. Although these tenants, known as *habitants* in Canada, (though the formal term was *censitaire*) did not fully own the lands they worked, they could pass it on to their children, making them owners in effect if not fact. The habitants paid a lease and had certain obligations to the lords of the estate, such as giving him a portion of their harvest. But in Canada the relationship between the lords and the tenants never did descend to the nastier depths it did in Europe if only because, in Canada, landowners were required to live on their estates (though many did not). Seigneurs often worked alongside their tenants, and this also helped to blunt social barriers.

Was the seigneurial system bad for New France? Did it hold the colony back? Or did it encourage growth? A system of feudalism, even as mild as this one, hardly seems appropriate amid the rough-hewn egalitarianism of the frontier, no? In the Anglo-American colonies, where individual initiative was better rewarded, expansion occurred at a staggering rate. In contrast, New France seemed more class-conscious. Growth was more methodical and less pell-mell, and historians are still split on whether the seigneurial system was beneficial or detrimental to the development of New France.

One thing is for sure: By 1700 a new nationality was taking shape, one that saw itself as neither French nor European, but *Canadien.* And the habitants that tilled the land were adamant about one thing: They were *not* mere peasants. They had far more freedom than their European counterparts. They ate better, had a healthier lifestyle and bigger families, and were not nearly as deferential to authority. Officials from France were already complaining that the habitants of Canada were "too proud."

Church and State

For 30 years the Jesuits had effectively run New France. As a royal province, power was wrestled away from the Church and focused on the governor and his intendant instead. Still, the colony retained a strong theological element, and one that would colour and enrich Québec society right up until the 1960s. (Or hinder and harm it, depending upon your bias.)

The bishop and the widow

Two of the most influential religious leaders in the early years of New France were Marie de l'Incarnation and Bishop Laval.

Marie was a widow from Tours, France, who began to hear voices and experience mystic visions. Abandoning her young son, she entered the secluded world of the Ursulines (a religious order for women) and later sailed for Canada, arriving in Québec in 1639. She established a convent and worked hard, educating young women and translating religious texts into Native languages. Marie wrote vividly about life in New France, both spiritual and secular, and found time to compile Algonquian and Iroquoian dictionaries. She managed to be both devout *and* level-headed.

So too did François de Laval. The Jesuit bishop arrived in Québec in 1659 and quickly asserted his authority (though he wasn't named Bishop of Québec until much later). An austere and determined man, Laval fought long and hard against the ongoing liquor trade with the First Nations. He built numerous churches and in 1663, he founded Canada's first college, the theological Séminaire de Québec (forerunner of today's Laval University). The headstrong holy man often clashed with rulers of New France. As one early, browbeaten governor complained, Bishop Laval "listens to no one."

Mère d'Youville and the Grey Nuns

They called her "the tipsy sister" because of her family's alleged involvement in brandy trafficking. In 1737, Marie-Marguerite d'Youville, a widow who raised two children on her own before devoting herself to charitable work, founded a religious society that would later be known as the Grey Nuns (though the order itself was not formally recognized until 1755). With her fellow sisters, Mère d'Youville established a hospice for orphans, abandoned children, "fallen women," the destitute, and the elderly. The Grey Nuns were an active organization that invested in everything from orchards to bakeries, and which ran a hospital during the final British assault on New France. After Mère d'Youville died in 1771, word spread of her miraculous powers, her healing touch and her deep spirituality. The first Canadian-born candidate for sainthood, Mère d'Youville was canonized by Rome in 1994.

The Virtual Museum of New France (www.mvnf.muse.digital.ca/somm-en.htm) is one of the best history sites going. Well-designed, informative, and easy to use. Recommended! Be sure to have a look.

Slavery in New France

Slaves were brought and sold in Canada for more than 200 years, under both French and British rule. In New France, they were imported as early as 1680, and the clergy were among the biggest slaveholders. Black and Native slaves were owned by Catholic convents and hospitals run by the nuns, as well as by merchants and the upper class. And if there is any doubt that the Canadiens could be just as cruel as the English and Americans, consider the following passage taken from the *Code Noire* of New France, outlining the "proper" treatment of slaves:

If a Black tries to escape, we cut off his ears and we brand a fleur-de-lis on his shoulder with a hot iron; if he tries to escape a second time, we cut the hamstrings on the back of his legs. If he is so bold as to try again, it's death.

Chapter 5

The Fur Wars

All hail the mighty beaver! Canada's largest rodent and furriest national icon!

It might have been a passage to China that first brought Europeans to Canada. And it might have been the codfish and whales that brought them back. But it was the beaver that gave them a reason to stay. Beaver-felt hats were all the rage in Europe: The underpelts were warm and water-resistant and could be made into exceptionally fine felt. The Europeans had long since trapped their own beavers pretty well to extinction, so the hat-makers turned their eyes on Canada.

Aside from the obvious financial bonanza it created, the fur trade had an immense impact on the development of Canada in two important ways:

✔ Furs with thicker underpelts naturally came from colder climes, and this in turn drew traders and explorers into the north and the west. The interior of Canada was opened up largely in the quest for furs.

✔ Unlike the fisheries, the fur trade was heavily dependent on Native suppliers. It brought the First Nations and the early colonists into a tight market relationship, one that initially favoured Natives but which would later turn against them.

Other animals were trapped as well — marten, otter, mink, fox, and wolf — but it was the beaver that was central to the entire economy. Indeed, beaver pelts were used as a standard of currency, with the value of any given trade item estimated by the number of prime pelts it was worth. It's no exaggeration when historians state that the real founder of New France (and Canada) was the all-mighty beaver: a buck-toothed, web-toed water rat, but still a proud national icon.

The French originally had a free rein in the northern fur trade, but in 1670 that would change forever when the English entered the scene in a big, big way. The struggle between the two countries would reach new rollicking heights.

Heritage Canada has more information on Canadian emblems, including the Mighty Beaver (www.pch.gc.ca/ceremonial-symb/english/emb_other_beaver.html). Another fun site on Canadian emblems can be found at home.ican.net/~marlatt/craig/symbols.html.

A Northern Shortcut

If you look at a map of Canada — go ahead, I'll wait — you may notice something interesting: The St. Lawrence River is not the only water route into the interior. Instead of paddling upriver on birchbark canoes, making gruelling portages and fighting white-water rapids, why not take a shortcut around the northern tip of Québec and into the Hudson Bay? That way, you could send in huge ocean-going vessels and simply load up on furs. Even better, you could deal directly with the Cree trappers of the north and cut out the middlemen entirely. Brilliant, no?

Voyage of the Nonsuch

Two couriers de bois, Pierre-Esprit Radisson and Médard Chouart des Groseilliers, proposed just such a scheme. It was cunning. It was bold. It was brash. And it was of absolutely no interest to the French court. Nor did the merchants of Montréal have any intention of being bypassed in such a flagrant way. So, with a shrug and a sigh, Radisson and Groseilliers went over to the English. (The two countries were technically at peace at that time, but it was still considered something of a betrayal.)

In 1668, an English consortium agreed to fund an expedition to the "great inland sea." Two ships set out, the *Eaglet* with Radisson on board, and the *Nonsuch* with Groseilliers. The *Eaglet* was forced to turn back, but the *Nonsuch* made it through. The traders built a small makeshift post at the bottom of James Bay, and word soon got out. In the spring, some 300 Cree suppliers arrived and Radisson did a brisk trade, returning to London in 1669 with a cargo of beaver pelts in the hold. The expedition was a resounding success. Radisson and Groseilliers had been right on the money.

Or had they? Canadian history books have long given credit to these two audacious French-Canadian woodsmen for discovering and promoting this northern trade route. But were they really taking the initiative, or were they simply reacting to leads given to them by the northern Indians? In *Canada's First Nations*, historian Olive Dickason argues persuasively that the role played by Radisson and Groseilliers has been greatly inflated. With the collapse of the Huron Confederacy and the turmoil along the waterways, Dickason insists that it was the Cree trappers who first proposed the Hudson Bay route. Radisson and Groseilliers simply reacted.

For a brief bio of Radisson and Groseilliers have a look at the site `www.lafete.org/v_ger/ex/rgE.htm`.

Here before Christ

The voyage of the *Nonsuch* changed the course of North American history forever. Within days of Groseilliers' triumphant return to London, investors were lined up and a Royal Charter was issued for a "Company of Adventurers" who were given exclusive trading rights over the lands that drained into the Hudson Bay. It was a vast area, most of it uncharted, and the company was made "true and absolute Lordes and Proprietors." This great basin, dubbed Rupert's Land (after Prince Rupert, the company's first governor), covered almost 40 percent of Canada's present territory. This territory was later expanded over the Rockies, all the way to the Pacific, and north to the Arctic.

> *At the peak of its expansion [the Hudson's Bay Company] controlled nearly three million square miles of territory — nearly a twelfth of the earth's land surface and an area ten times that of the Holy Roman Empire at its height.*
> — popular historian Peter C. Newman, *Empire of the Bay*

Founded in 1670, and still with us today (though no longer trading in furs), the Hudson's Bay Company is probably the oldest commercial enterprise in existence — anywhere. It was said the initials HBC actually meant "Here Before Christ," and in a sense that was true. The Company of Adventurers *did* precede missionaries into much of the northwoods.

I grew up in the former fur trading community of Fort Vermilion, Alberta, and I can assure you the HBC was a central, almost suffocating presence. They were northern lords in every sense of the word. We used to joke that their motto was, "The Hudson's Bay Company: we screwed your grandfather, we screwed your father, and we're going to screw you."

Whose bay is it? (Or should that be "who's"?)

Have you noticed something odd about the name of the company and that of the actual bay? The punctuation is different. The company is called *Hudson's Bay*, but the body of water itself is *Hudson Bay*. What's the deal with that?

Well, it turns out that the possessive form actually came first. It used to be standard practice when naming a location after its discoverer. (For example, it was originally *Vancouver's Island*.) But about a hundred years ago, and on the not unreasonable grounds that these features did not actually belong to the explorers they were named after, the Canadian Cartography Society decided to drop the use of possessives. The Company did not. It retained its apostrophe, and has been proudly confusing students ever since.

For an entertaining, full history of the Hudson's Bay Company, check out www.hbc.com/hbchistory/. For the Hudson's Bay Company informative archives, visit www.gov.mb.ca/chc/archives/hbca/index.html.

Company of the North

The competition was heating up. The Hudson Bay shortcut allowed the English to outflank the French in the north and deal directly with the Cree. At first, French traders responded by making the arduous overland canoe trek north to James Bay to intercept Native canoes en route to doing business with the English. But by 1682, the HBC was operating no fewer than five separate trading posts along the Hudson and James Bays. Flotillas of Cree canoes arrived in the spring, weighted down with furs, and a great deal of trade was now being diverted from the French. It is, however, important to note that this increased competition was good for the First Nations. They didn't have to travel as far and they could bargain harder and obtain better prices for their furs.

With a resolve borne of desperation, the Montréal merchants went on the offensive. In 1682, they banded together to form the Company of the North (*Compagnie du Nord*) and in 1686 they decided to strike at the very heart of the English operation.

North America's first commando raid

Under the leadership of the brilliant tactician Pierre de Troyes, a strike force of fast-running voyagers and trained military officers left Montréal heading upriver towards the HBC forts on James Bay.

De Troyes wanted to hit the English from behind before their supply ships arrived in the spring, which meant leaving before the snows had completely melted. It was a punishing, 12-week trek up along the Ottawa River and then down through uncharted lands, over countless portages and across rugged dangerous terrain. By the time they reached James Bay the men were exhausted and malnourished. Just getting there had been an achievement. They would now have to fight as well. De Troyes immediately began plans to capture three of the HBC's forts.

Described as North America's "first commando raid," De Troyes' strike force caught the English completely by surprise. In one case, they were literally in their nightshirts and without sentries posted. The voyageurs, travelling in birchbark canoes, hadn't been able to carry any heavy artillery with them, so De Troyes used captured English weapons — and even one of their own ships — against them. The French scaled palisade walls, they knocked down six-inch gates with battering rams, they battled with muskets and sabres, and, in the end, they captured all three forts.

By the time the last of the James Bay forts fell, De Troyes and his men were in ragged repair, half-starved and desperate, but the English never knew this. In a truce meeting with their governor, De Troyes neatly bluffed his way to victory. When the English governor toasted the French king with a glass of wine during peace talks, De Troyes took a sip and said, with a sniff, that he had much better wine back at his camp and invited the Englishman to join him there for a drink. The governor declined, which is just as well; De Troyes had no wine (and indeed, very little food or ammunition either).

It should also be noted that the De Troyes expedition had another objective as well: to arrest any coureurs de bois they discovered along the way who were working for the English. At the top of their "most wanted" list? Our old friend Pierre Radisson, who was now wanted by the French on charges of treason. Radisson was a man of, how shall I say, "fluid" loyalties. Having delivered Hudson Bay to the English, he was granted a pardon by France, only to go back to the English again when he found himself being taxed out of profits. Radisson had gone from France to England to France, and then back again to England. In spite of this, he is still considered a hero in Québec today.

You take the river, I'll take the bay

The De Troyes expedition was a brilliant success. Although outnumbered and outgunned, the small band of voyageurs and officers managed to capture three heavily fortified trading posts, effectively giving France control of the lower Hudson and James Bays. It also marked the beginning of a long tug-of-war for control of the northern fur trade, as forts changed hands back and forth. The nature of the coming French/English showdown was becoming clear: The English would focus on the Hudson Bay, Newfoundland, and the mid-Atlantic seacoast; France would hold the St. Lawrence River, the Great Lakes, and Acadia. (No one bothered to consult the First Nations about any of this.)

A Tale of Two Travellers

The Hudson's Bay Company charter required them to explore and open up the interior, but they didn't take the directive very seriously in the early years. Instead, they focused on trade, clinging to the coast and keeping expenses to a minimum. New France was much more active in this regard.

"The boy Kelsey"

The few expeditions that the HBC did sponsor were concerned first and foremost with increasing profit. So it was when the Company sent young Henry Kelsey west in 1690. His goal was not to map and record, but to make contact with First Nations farther inland for the sole purpose of expanding HBC trade. Kelsey spent two years in the interior. Travelling with Cree companions, he became the first European to reach the Canadian plains, and he peered in awe and amazement at the vast herds of buffalo that stretched across the horizon. Kelsey kept an odd, eccentric journal written partly in rhyming couplets. He saw great sights and vast panoramas, and made contact with mighty nations — but the Company made almost no use of his discoveries. They didn't bother following up on them, and Kelsey's journey was all but forgotten.

> His skin to gett I have used all y ways I can
> He is mans food & he makes food of man
> — Kelsey's memorable description of the grizzly bear

For a brief bio on Kelsey, with links, visit www.win.tue.nl/~engels/discovery/kelsey.html.

La Salle

The HBC's lacklustre response to Kelsey's trip contrasts sharply with the enthusiasm shown by France for the voyages of La Salle, made at around the same time. In 1682, René-Robert, Cavelier de La Salle undertook an ambitious journey: He followed the Great Lakes inland and then turned south, down the Mississippi, all the way to the Gulf of Mexico. In doing so, he cut a swath through the interior of the continent and became one of France's most celebrated explorers.

At the muggy Mississippi delta, La Salle raised the Royal Arms of France and claimed all lands that drained into the Mississippi and its tributaries in the name of Louis XIV. And why not? The English had claimed the Hudson Bay basin; France would have the Mississippi. La Salle named this vast region "Louisiana," after his king.

La Salle was a man of grand schemes. On an earlier voyage, he had departed from his seigneurial farm on the south side of Montréal on a canoe headed for China. He was convinced he would discover the elusive and mythical "Western Sea" (the French equivalent of the Northwest Passage) that would lead to the spice kingdoms of the Orient. Nor was La Salle's optimism unusual. In 1634, an explorer by the name of Nicollet had set out on a similar journey, and had even donned a flowing silk robe for his anticipated meeting with "the Emperor of China." Nicollet discovered Lake Superior, but no sea passage to the Indies. La Salle failed as well, and when he returned, suitably chastened, his neighbours cruelly nicknamed his farm "La Chine" (China) and the name stuck ever since.

The always-fascinating Virtual Museum of New France (`www.vmnf.civilization.ca/explor/explcd_e.html`) has more on La Salle, as well as Nicollet and other French explorers.

Return of the Iroquois

The French were a little *too* successful when it came to their western expansion. The Iroquois Confederacy had set up fur-trading colonies of their own on the north shore of Lake Ontario and had begun trading with the Ojibwa. The French were trespassing on territory that the Iroquois now claimed. Armed by their English allies in New York, the Iroquois began ambushing Native fur canoes that were destined for New France. Even worse (in the eyes of New France anyway), the Iroquois, by setting themselves up as the new middlemen between the Ojibwa to the north and the English to the south, were gaining a heightened power in the area.

The Lachine massacre

In 1684, the French launched a raid deep into Confederacy territory. It turned into a humiliating fiasco, but the French were undeterred. In 1687, when a delegation of forty Onondaga envoys arrived to negotiate a ceasefire, they were seized and sent back to France as slaves. The French followed this up with a massive invasion, several thousand strong, into the very heart of the Seneca homeland, burning villages, destroying fields, and desecrating graves. In retaliation, the Iroquois launched an attack of their own.

In August 1689, the Iroquois fell on the small community of Lachine, killing two dozen settlers and carrying off almost 60 more for ritualistic torture and execution. It was a terrifying massacre, true. But history books, especially those espousing the heroic age of New France, rarely put it in the context of a larger war that had been launched as much by the French as by the Iroquois. The attack on Lachine is usually presented as an unmotivated act of sheer sadism. In fact, the victims had been caught between hammer and anvil, in a vicious game of power politics.

"For God and King!"

The Lachine massacre marked the start of more than ten years of terror for the citizens of New France, as the Iroquois attacks increased. No one felt safe. In 1692, the 14-year-old heroine Madeleine de Verchères defended her family farm from the Iroquois while her father was away on business. Having donned armour and fired a cannon to warn other habitants along the valley, Madeleine rallied her brothers and tenants with a ringing battle cry that sounds as though it were scripted: "Let us fight to the death! For our homeland and our religion! For God and King!"

Alas, much like Adam Dollard's defence of Montréal, the legend of the plucky young Madeleine de Verchères has also come under scrutiny. Most of the facts were related by Madeleine herself, and it turns out that many of her claims were, well, a wee bit embellished. For one thing, the number of Iroquois she first eluded to grew over the years from a single warrior to 45 "blood-thirsty braves." That's the problem with history, it turns into myth so easily. Still, Madeleine's bravery was real enough, and she did succeed in saving her father's estate and in warning others.

Phips and Frontenac

*Arrogant and vain, stubborn and impatient, imperious and careless as
to how he obtained and spent money, he was nonetheless a man of
immense energy, courage and insight.*
> — historian Arthur Lower's assessment of Count Frontenac

The confrontation between the governor of New France, Louis de Buade,
Comte de Frontenac, and the upstart New England adventurer William Phips
is one of the classic moments in early Canadian history, one that has all the
elements and drama of a staged scene.

Frontenac had first been appointed governor of New France in 1672, but had
been recalled ten years later amid acrimony and constant quarrelling with the
other colonial administrators. Frontenac was a highbred man of extravagant
tastes and "colossal vanity." (He insisted that others address him not as
"Governor Frontenac," but as "High and Mighty Lord.") Frontenac left New
France in 1682 and we might never have heard from him again, had it not
been for two things: the Lachine massacre of 1689 and Frontenac's own
high-flying lifestyle.

The Frontenac massacres

Frontenac enjoyed luxury. He was forever living beyond his means and was
already heavily in debt when news reached France of the Iroquois attack on
Lachine. Frontenac, now an old man, was being pursued by creditors and
yearning for one last grasp at glory. He successfully petitioned the king to be
allowed to return to New France and "deal with" the Iroquois problem.

Easier said than done. Once Frontenac was back in New France he found that
the Iroquois were not at all interested in his peace overtures. If anything,
their attacks grew. Frontenac realized that the root of the problem lay in the
English settlers to the south who were both arming and encouraging the
Iroquois campaign against New France. And so, in the winter of 1689, Comte
de Frontenac sent Canadien and Native warriors on a brutal guerrilla assault
against the English. They fell upon the Schenectady settlement, massacring
men, women, and children, killing 60. Two parallel forces wreaked similar
havoc as dozens more were killed, some after they had surrendered. But
Frontenac's plan backfired, and rather than cow the English settlers, the
attacks only strengthened their resolve.

A monumental clash of egos

In 1690, the New Englanders sent a strike force under William Phips to mete out some "justice" of their own. They captured Port Royal and pillaged the innocent Acadians, destroying homes, looting farms, and even desecrating church altars. Flushed with success, Phips immediately began making plans for an attack on Québec. (You'll notice a pattern here: first Acadia, then Québec. It was one that would be repeated by the English again and again.)

The force under Phips's command was immense: more than 30 ships and 2,300 armed men. Québec braced itself for the onslaught. In some ways, the confrontation between Frontenac and Phips was a study in contrasts. Frontenac was of noble French stock. Phips came from humbler origins. Born in a cabin on the edge of a lawless frontier, Phips was an uneducated treasure hunter who had made it rich with the discovery of sunken Spanish gold, which he parlayed into royal favour and a knighthood from the English King. But on another level, Phips and Frontenac were very similar. Both were men of mighty egos: thin-skinned, proud, and determined not to bend.

Having arrived late in the season, Phips set up a blockade across the St. Lawrence and sent a messenger to Frontenac issuing an ultimatum, the gist of which was: *You have one hour to surrender.* Frontenac straightened himself, looked the messenger in the eye and said, in words that echo through history even now:

> *I have no reply to make to your general other than from the mouths of my cannon and muskets! He must learn it is not in this fashion that one summons a man such as I. Let him do the best he can on his side, as I will do on mine.*

In some ways, Frontenac's defiance helped ease the humiliation of the earlier conquest, when Champlain had surrendered to the Kirkes. But it also under-lined the increasingly self-sufficient nature of New France. The colony, no longer completely dependent on France for aid and supplies, could not be beaten by a simple blockade. In this sense then, with Frontenac's rebuttal, we hear the first early stirrings of Canadian independence.

In the end, however, it was less Frontenac's bravado that beat the English than it was that greatest of all Canadian foes: the weather. Winter set in early and Phips, frustrated and running out of time, launched a poorly planned attack on Québec City, which failed brilliantly. Just three weeks after his triumphant arrival, Phips was forced to slink back to Boston, his men hungry and cold and suffering from smallpox.

Acadia: Caught in the middle

Have you been keeping track of the number of times that Acadia was captured and sacked?

✔ Samuel Argall in 1613

✔ The Kirke brothers in 1628

✔ William Phips in 1690

And that's not all! Port Royal was sacked in 1654 as well, and Acadia remained under nominal English control until 1670. (Even the Dutch had a go at conquering Acadia at one point.) I tell you, it's a headache just trying to keep it straight. Between the First Conquest in 1613 to the Final Conquest in 1710, the region changed hands no fewer than *11* times. It was a misfortune of geography more than anything. Pinned between the continental designs of England and France, Acadia found itself caught in a permanent crossfire.

Phips usually disappears from Canadian history books at this point, a sort of stumblebum clown who was outplayed by the proud French nobleman. But in fact, he became governor of Massachusetts and — to his eternal credit — helped stamp out the Salem witchcraft hysteria that was tearing New England apart. (Women were being put to death in a religious frenzy of accusations and unfair trials.) Governor Phips put an end to this nonsense. Satan, as it turned out, was an easier opponent than old Frontenac.

And as for Frontenac? He continued to harass and attack the English, and is, of course, still a hero in Québec, where the separatists in that province not long ago announced that, should Québec ever become a sovereign nation, they would name their currency the *frontenac*. Sigh.

For the Heritage Project's "Frontenac minute," go to (and explore!) www. heritageproject.ca/media/minutes/expanded/fronte.htm. For more on the dramatic 1690 face-off between Phips and Frontenac visit canadahistory. com/quebec.htm (part of a larger Canadian History Site).

Iberville the Swashbuckler

You remember the five Kirke brothers? The ones who captured Québec and sent Champlain packing? Well, the Le Moyne brothers were New France's answer to the Kirkes. There were 12 of them, no less, from a seigneurial farm near Montréal, and their exploits put the Kirkes to shame.

Pierre (#3 son) was the most famous and feared of the Le Moyne brothers, and is known in history books by his title, Sieur d'Iberville. Iberville and two other brothers had taken part in De Troyes' audacious "commando raid" against the English in the Hudson Bay. (It was Iberville and one of his brothers who scaled the walls of the first fort, leading the others into the fray.) And Iberville himself would lead four more military expeditions against the English in Hudson Bay between 1688 and 1697.

Rampage in Avalon

Between his fourth and fifth expedition to Hudson Bay, Iberville was sent south to attack an English fort in what is now Maine. The English there had been harassing Natives on their way to trade furs in Acadia. In retaliation, Iberville sacked the fort, took the English prisoner, destroyed the walls, and burnt the buildings. After that he turned his hungry gaze toward Newfoundland.

The French, remember, had established a base a few years earlier at Placentia on the west side of Avalon Peninsula. The English were on the east, with their cannons facing outward toward the sea. In between was a scattering of small English villages. No one had ever attempted an overland attack in Newfoundland before, but Iberville had a secret weapon, something the Newfoundland fishing colonists had never before seen: *snowshoes*.

Iberville led a band of Canadiens and Indians across the peninsula like "an Angel of Wrath." It was less a military expedition than it was a rampage: Iberville and his men destroyed 36 settlements, killed 200 settlers, took 700 more prisoner, destroyed 90 vessels, and pillaged a fortune in dried cod. The dead were scalped and the scalps sent back to Governor Frontenac as war trophies. St. John's lay in ruins. Ferryland was a smouldering waste. Every single English settlement on the Avalon Peninsula was taken — with one exception: the colony at Carbonear, where the hot-tempered merchant William Pynne earned the distinction of being the only settler to turn back Iberville's forces. No small feat that. Over the years the French would attack the vulnerable and often unprotected Newfoundland fishing coves again and again. But the tough little community of Carbonear was never taken.

Hampshire and the Pélican

In 1697, Iberville sailed into Hudson Bay onboard his flagship the *Pélican*. He came to take the York Factory fort from the English, but on the way had become separated from his fleet in a heavy fog and he arrived in the Bay alone. No matter. His other ships would catch up, and sure enough, three masts soon appeared on the horizon.

As they slipped into view, Iberville's chest tightened. They weren't French. They were English. And they were armed. Iberville was up against a powerful Royal Navy frigate, the *Hampshire*, and two armed merchantmen ships of the Hudson's Bay Company. Together, they had 124 guns to Iberville's 44, and they were headed straight for him. Iberville's Day of Reckoning was at hand. The Scourge of the Bay was about to be destroyed.

Outgunned three to one and cornered against the shore, the only option was surrender. But this Iberville could not do. Instead, he set sail for the English ships in a wild headlong attack. He came crashing alongside the *Hampshire* with his guns blazing. The *Pélican* was hit by a broadside that toppled tackles and rigging, but she fired back, point blank, and scored a direct, devastating hit. Iberville then steered his ship *between* the other two English vessels. He blasted them from both decks, and broke free from the trap.

Having "run the gauntlet," Iberville might have hightailed it out of there. Instead, he reeled his ship about and came back. The captain of the *Hampshire* couldn't believe Iberville's tenacity. It was like trying to fight off an especially determined terrier. For nearly four hours, Iberville battled the three English ships, taking hard hits but delivering worse. By the end, the *Pélican* was little more than floating wreckage, but Iberville refused to back down. He fired on the *Hampshire* with deadly aim, puncturing the hull at the waterline. The English ship hit a shoal and went down with all hands.

Iberville now turned to face the armed merchantmen, but they had had enough. One quickly surrendered and the other made a run for it. The *Pélican*, leaking badly, was unable to pursue. Iberville had destroyed one ship, captured another, and sent the third one fleeing. His crew bailed out as the *Pélican* herself went down, but Iberville was not yet through. When his own fleet finally did show up, they went on to capture the York Factory fortress as well. It would remain in French hands for the next sixteen years.

Iberville never returned to Hudson Bay. Instead, he focused his attention on the south, where he helped launch French colonies in Louisiana and what is now Alabama. The French had expanded and entrenched their sphere of power from the Hudson Bay all the way to the Mississippi Delta. And Iberville, the Canadien, remains one of France's greatest "empire builders."

For more on Pierre Le Moyne d'Iberville and his larger-than-life exploits, check out the Virtual Museum of New France www.mvnf.muse.digital.ca/Explor/iber_e1.html. For more on Iberville's rampage in Newfoundland see www.infonet.st-johns.nf.ca/providers/green/de'iberville.html.

Peace at Last?

NATIVE RIGHTS

By 1700, the tide had begun to turn against the Iroquois. With their population diminished, their ranks depleted, and their territory overextended, they began to reconsider their campaign against New France. The Algonquian and their French allies had pushed the Iroquois back, into their original territory south of Lake Ontario, and in 1701 the Iroquois and the Canadiens signed a peace treaty. The Iroquois agreed to maintain neutrality in any future Anglo-French conflicts, and New France relented and allowed the Iroquois to trade in the interior. In this sense, 1701 marks the end of an era. (Indeed, a splinter group of Iroquois would later align themselves with the French and move to the Montréal area of Kahnawake and Oka.)

> *The Iroquois had not been defeated. In fact, they had fought the French to a standstill, and they would endure as an independent power in their own land until well after the passing of New France.*
> — historian Christopher Moore

In 1701, it seemed as though peace was finally at hand. The Iroquois Wars were over. Farming had replaced the fur trade as the main economic activity, and a remote post had been built in the interior, on the western shore of Lake Erie, by a French nobleman named Cadillac. The settlement was dubbed "city of the straits," or *D'étroit* for short. Perhaps New France would survive after all.

Part III
The Fall of New France
(1701–1766)

General James Wolfe, Conqueror of Canada, got little respect from his own officers. In this caricature, the uptight general is seen inspecting the latrines.

In this part . . .

We look at the final struggle between Britain and France. The colony of Acadia is captured first and kept under British rule for 40 years. As the struggle for the continent heats up, the Acadians are forced into exile. On the Plains of Abraham, outside the walled city of Québec, the British invader James Wolfe faces off against the French defender, Louis-Joseph de Montcalm. The fate of Canada is about to be decided . . .

Chapter 6

Acadia

· ·

In This Chapter

▶ Acadia is conquered — again

▶ The French build a fortress at Louisbourg

▶ The English counter by founding Halifax

▶ Governor Lawrence orders the mass deportation of Acadians

· ·

*N*o sooner had New France signed a peace treaty with the Iroquois than they were plunged into conflict against the English. Queen Anne's War, as it was known, began in 1702 and would rage for 11 years. The French launched attacks against New England, and the New Englanders responded in kind. As usual, Acadia found itself caught in the middle. Although the Acadians were generally peaceful and law-abiding, they were also an easy target and as such they faced the brunt of English retaliations.

Acadia, at the Maritime gateway to the St. Lawrence, was a strategic location. It acted as both a sentry post and a buffer zone, protecting Québec and the inland settlements of New France from English aggression. France was always more concerned with denying Acadia to the English than with developing the area in its own right. And Acadia, the most-conquered colony in North American history, was about to be conquered yet again — this time for good.

The Final Conquest of Acadia

When war was declared, one of the first to take advantage of it was the "avenging Puritan," Colonel Benjamin Church, who launched a brutal attack against Acadia in 1704 and again in 1705. Not that Church needed much of an excuse: He had been leading raids against the Acadians since 1696. (In total, he would plunder and pillage Acadia on at least five separate occasions.) Church, a self-described "fierce messenger," was a grim man: obese, sadistic, and stubborn. He killed prisoners, breached dikes, flooded fields, stole altar pieces, and burnt farmhouses to the ground. He even killed family pets, as he recounts in a cold matter-of-fact style:

What's in a name?

Québec means "where the river narrows." Nova Scotia means "New Scotland." Canada means "village." And Newfoundland means, well, "Newfoundland." But what of Acadia? The origins are obscure, though the name does seem to have been derived from the Greek myth of Arcadia, a "pastoral paradise." Others have noted the similarity between Acadie, as it is properly known in French, and the Mi'kmaq suffix *e'katie*, meaning, "land of." This suffix appears in several Maritime place names, such as Shubenacadie, Tracadie, and even Passamaquoddy (rendered "Pesmacadie" on older maps). It is also possible that Acadia is a combination of the two: Greek mythology reinforced by already existing Native names. Old World and New, blended into one. This is the version I prefer. It's more poetic somehow.

> *When the Acadians returned [from hiding] they were troubled to see their cattle, sheep, hogs, and dogs lying dead about their houses, chopped and hacked to death with hatchets.*
> — the ironically named Church, recounting his oh-so-heroic exploits

The capture of Port Royal

The Acadian governor, Daniel de Subercase, pleaded for help from France, but none came. Alone and unloved, the Acadians still managed to turn back two full-scale invasions before the colony finally fell in October 1710.

English commander Francis Nicholson led the assault: a massive combined colonial and British force of 3,500 men and a fleet of 45 ships. Resistance was futile. Inside Port Royal, the French governor could barely muster 300 ill-equipped soldiers, "dressed in rags." France had sent no reinforcements and the crops had failed that year, leaving the defenders short of food. As the English cannons rained down, Subercase was forced to surrender.

> *Rarely in the history of human conflict had so little been achieved by so many against so few.*
> — historians Horwood and Butts' take on the 1710 conquest

Acadia had been taken before. Indeed, the flags of competing countries had gone up and down over Port Royal so many times that the Acadian settlers often had trouble knowing under whose rule they now belonged. So, when Acadia fell once again in 1710, the inhabitants weren't too concerned. No one knew then that this time it would be forever. Heck, the terms of surrender didn't even include all of Acadia; they referred only to Port Royal and the immediate vicinity. So calling it a capture is slightly misleading. As we will see, Acadia would be lost more by treaty than by battle.

Even then, the fight was far from over. French, Acadian, and Native allies counterattacked, ambushing an English force and killing more than 30 soldiers at a spot that has since become known as Bloody Creek.

Nor were the Acadians under British military rule passive or deferential to their new overlords. Their independent nature was already asserting itself, and within weeks, the British Governor was complaining that his Acadian subjects refused to pay their taxes and were being "highly unco-operative."

The Iroquois come to Nova Scotia

Francis Nicholson changed the name of Port Royal to "Annapolis Royal" in a reference to Queen Anne. (Nicholson was one of the Queen's darlings. She referred to him as "our trusty and well beloved colonel.") He sent the captured French troops home and left the garrison in the hands of Samuel Vetch, his second in command. Trouble began almost immediately. The Acadians, as noted, went out of their way to avoid paying taxes and they sent excuse after excuse, each one lamer than the next, for why they had been unable to cough up the required tithe. Their horses were sick. The ice was too thin for them to make the journey in winter, and the crops needed tending in spring. English attacks had left them in poverty. How could they pay? Vetch seethed and stewed. Annapolis Royal, bombarded by successive English raiders, was now barely inhabitable and his men began deserting.

A far more serious threat came from the Acadians' Native allies, who continued to harass and ambush the British. To counter this, Vetch brought in a band of 100 Iroquois mercenaries to fight fire with fire, guerrilla attack with guerrilla attack. The Iroquois spent only a year in Acadia, they operated as a separate unit, and they never fought a direct battle with the Mi'kmaq. But their very presence was a deterrent. The Iroquois were feared. Their reputation had preceded them and during their tour of duty, Mi'kmaq attacks sharply abated. (Iroquois mercenaries would be brought in to fight the Mi'kmaq again under Governor Cornwallis. It was a very effective ploy.)

1713: The Treaty of Utrecht

"New France" referred to all of France's North American colonies, primarily:

- ✔ **Canada:** the St. Lawrence heartland
- ✔ **Acadia:** the Maritime region

But, as we will see, place names were notoriously vague back then, both in common usage and on maps.

The war ended with huge concessions on the part of France. Louis XIV paid for his losses in Europe by giving up land in North America, and in the Treaty of Utrecht, France relinquished its claim to both the Hudson Bay and Newfoundland (except for fishing rights off the north shore). France also surrendered "all of Acadia comprised in its ancient limits."

Ah, but there's the catch. Where exactly were Acadia's "ancient limits"? As noted, maps were notoriously vague back then. France insisted that only the peninsula of Nova Scotia had been ceded. They kept possession of both *Ile Royale* (Cape Breton) and *Ile St. Jean* (P.E.I.). They also claimed the area that is now the coast of New Brunswick, something that Britain hotly disputed. Far from having "conquered Acadia," the British in Nova Scotia were now hemmed in by the French on three sides, with the major Acadian communities in the area now controlled by Britain.

In spite of this mess, the Treaty of Utrecht ushered in 30 years of peace, during which both New France and Acadia flourished.

For biographies on the main players in Acadian/Nova Scotia history (1700–1763), visit www.blupete.com/Hist/BiosNS/1700-63/List.htm. Another informative site on early Acadia is at ourworld.compuserve.com/homepages/lwjones/acadhist.htm.

Louisbourg

France had not given up. Far from it. Almost immediately, plans were drawn to strengthen French claims to the area. And the very summer that the Treaty of Utrecht was signed, 160 dispossessed French settlers from the former Newfoundland colony of Placentia set sail for Cape Breton, where they founded the settlement of Louisbourg. Other communities were also established, but Louisbourg was made the military and administrative capital for the island and in 1719 construction began on an enormous fortress. It would be one of the greatest ever built in the New World.

Still, it is important not to confuse the two: the community and the fortress. Louisbourg was a "garrison town," true, and the fortress was central to life. But France had grander designs than simply a military outpost guarding the entrance to the St. Lawrence. Although the windy, exposed lands of Cape Breton might not seem like the ideal location for a colony, France had its reasons. Louisbourg was on a large, ice-free harbour that faced open sea and was within range of the Grand Banks fisheries. Louisbourg was also on the trade routes between France's Caribbean colonies and Québec. Ships could complete a circuit, with Louisbourg as a port of call for both warships and trading vessels. (The old "triangular trade" scheme from Chapter 4.)

The goals of the Louisbourg settlement were as follows:

- ✔ To exploit the still-lucrative cod fisheries.
- ✔ To provide a home for Acadians and other displaced colonists.
- ✔ To protect Québec and the entrance of the St. Lawrence.
- ✔ To act as a "lynch pin" in France's intercolonial trade system.

White elephant?

The fortress at Louisbourg was a massive undertaking, and one that would take 26 years (!) to complete and would cost a fortune in royal funds.

> *Are the streets being paved with gold over there? I fully expect to awake one morning in my Palace at Versailles and see the walls of the Louisbourg fortress rising above the horizon.*
> — Louis XV, complaining about the high cost of defense

Was the fortress at Louisbourg really the white elephant it is made out to be? Not everyone agrees. It has been pointed out that Louisbourg, although an immense undertaking for North America, was a fairly minor one by European standards. The cost of a year's work at Louisbourg was less than the cost of outfitting a single large warship. In return, France got a naval port, a commercial and trading centre, a military presence, a fisheries base, and a cornerstone of its intercolonial "triangular trade." A bargain.

No, it wasn't the cost that made Louisbourg a white elephant; it was the very concept itself. It was more a dinosaur than an elephant. The heavy, defensive walls were already out of date, made obsolete by modern cannons. Louisbourg was a symbol of a previous era. What were needed were low-lying defensive ditches and protective earthworks, not a high and haughty mighty fortress. The location was a poor choice as well. There was no dominant height of land available to build the fortress upon, and the surrounding hills were danger-ously close. (As the French would learn the hard way, the hills were ideal spots for setting up siege cannons.)

A thriving community (in spite of everything)

Louisbourg may have been a lousy fortress, but it was a rousing commercial success. It was the town and the harbour that gave Louisbourg its vitality, not its lumbering, poorly conceived fortress. The foundation of the economy was cod, but Louisbourg itself quickly evolved into a wide-ranging trade centre. Ships from the West Indies, Europe, and even New England plied her waters, as many as 200 vessels a year, making it one of the busiest sea ports in North America. The warehouses, taverns, and inns of Louisbourg were humming with commerce and activity.

You'll find an informative look at Louisbourg, past and present, at `collections.ic.gc.ca/louisbourg`.

Acadia: The Golden Years

In British-controlled Acadia, life went on. In fact, the Golden Age of Acadia (1713–1743) took place under British rule. During the benign neglect of French rule, the Acadians had been forced to trade illegally with their New England neighbours (whom the Acadians had dubbed *nos amis l'ennemi*, "our friends the enemy"). Now that Acadia was held by the British, the attacks ceased, the smuggling more or less ended, and trade with the English colonies was not only legal, it was actively encouraged.

Life was good, the birth rate was high, and Acadia was at peace. For more than 30 years, the colony prospered. The Acadians had an integrated, mixed economy, and they enjoyed a religious freedom not allowed to Catholics in Britain, nor Protestants in France. There was just one problem . . .

Although they didn't act like it, the Acadians were still a conquered people. And, according to the conventions of the day, conquered people were either (a) deported or (b) defanged. The first possibility seemed more likely, and in the early years the Acadians expected to be expelled at any time. (In 1714 they sowed two years' worth of crops and didn't bother planting more, so sure were they that they wouldn't be around the following fall to harvest it.)

The French King wanted them to move to Louisbourg, and a few Acadians were sent to scout the location, but the report they sent back was discouraging. The Acadians were farmers not fishermen, and the thin, infertile soil and poor grazing lands of Cape Breton weren't suited to their lifestyle.

There were other French-held territories to which the Acadians could have relocated, but the British blocked all attempts at a mass migration. They forbade the Acadians from building or importing boats (if they were going to leave, they would have to leave walking) and from selling their property or livestock (if they were going to leave, they would leave empty-handed). Why did the British want the Acadians to stay put? Simple. If the Acadians — who now numbered in the thousands — were to move to Louisbourg, it would have created the largest and most powerful French colony on the continent.

So, since the Acadians weren't going to be deported, at least not anytime soon, they would have to be "defanged" instead. No problem. The Acadians were neither militant nor heavily armed. All that the British needed was to get them to swear an oath of loyalty. Easier said than done.

The neutral French

As early as 1714, British governors were complaining about the Acadians' "argumentative" nature. (The French governors had made similar complaints, noting with a disapproving sniff that the Acadians were, in effect, "semi-republicans.") The issue of the oath was a case in point. As a matter of both pride and principle, the Acadians refused to swear an unconditional oath, and they held out for almost 40 years.

True, the Acadians had been forced to swear oaths to England on at least two occasions before (once in 1690 after Phips conquered Port Royal and again in 1710 following the final siege as one of the terms of surrender), but after the Treaty of Utrecht, the British wanted to take it even further. They wanted the Acadians to make a solemn vow, "before God," that they would take up arms alongside the British in times of war. This, the Acadians could not do.

"Taking up arms against Britain's enemies" would, of course, mean taking up arms against France. Even worse, and much more dangerous, it would mean taking up arms against their old allies the Mi'kmaq. The Mi'kmaq were, ironically, far more loyal to France than were the Acadians, and when word got out that the Acadians were considering "switching sides" the Mi'kmaq made it clear — in not so subtle terms — that they would consider such an act to be a personal betrayal. That is, if the Acadians had taken the full oath, they would have risked making mortal enemies of the Mi'kmaq. It was a very real threat, and it hung over the Acadians' heads like an axe about to fall.

Fortunately, the Acadians were master negotiators and they knew they held the trump card: They could simply leave. When an early British governor threatened to deport them if they refused to sign an unconditional oath, the Acadian delegates said, "Fine, see you later," and the governor, fearful that they would move to Cape Breton and strengthen the Louisbourg colony with their numbers and expertise, quickly relented. Eventually, the Acadians agreed to a *conditional* oath, which included the following provisions:

- The Acadians would never be required to take up arms against France or the Mi'kmaq.
- They would be free to leave British territory at any time.
- The authority of the Catholic priests would be respected.

The British governor pulled a fast one, however. The above concessions were offered only verbally. The official English-language version of the oath made no mention of them, and stated, simply: "I do sincerely promise and swear that I will be faithful and bear true allegiance to His Majesty King George the Second, so help me God."

Even this was considered too lenient. The British Lords declared it null and void but they were never able to get better terms, and a second oath more or less repeated these terms. From 1730 on, the Acadians were known as "the neutral French" and they lived in peace under British rule.

The stubborn neutrality of the Acadians annoyed both the British (who considered them unreliable subjects) and the French (who considered them near-traitors), but the Acadians kept their word. When the English finally did attack Louisbourg in 1745, the Acadians didn't take sides or get involved. They never led the uprising that France urged or Britain feared, but in the end they couldn't avoid being pulled into the conflict. Their refusal to take an unconditional oath would come back to haunt them.

A landscape transformed: The Acadian dikes

Talk about determined. The Acadians turned back the very tides themselves. No small feat when you consider that the Bay of Fundy has the highest tides in the world, rising and falling as much as 15 metres in some areas. During its retreat, the tides of Fundy expose vast swaths of sediment-rich land, and the Acadians developed an ingenious system of drainage and dikes to transform these saltwater marshes into lush meadows. The construction and constant maintenance of the Acadian dikes (unique in the history of North America) required an ongoing collaborative effort on the part of the settlers, something that fostered a sense of both community and solidarity. Having transformed the landscape, the landscape transformed them.

This is also one of the reasons that the Acadians hadn't come into conflict with their Mi'kmaq neighbours. They didn't encroach on Native hunting grounds. Rather than clear the forests, the Acadians farmed instead on reclaimed lowlands. (Remnants of these original dikes can still be seen in the Hopewell region and in the rich Tantramar meadows.)

Visit www.lafete.org/v_ger/ex/vendE.htm for a brief bio of La Vérendrye.

The Vérendryes go west

Pierre La Vérendrye was the first Canadian explorer to be born in Canada, and though he failed in his goal of discovering an overland route to the elusive Western Sea (the French equivalent of the quest for a Northwest Passage), his accomplishments were impressive nonetheless. Along with his four sons and a nephew, La Vérendrye pushed west with a flotilla of canoes, breaking free of the Great Lakes and the Canadian Shield. In the 1730s and '40s, the La Vérendryes built a string of French trading posts along the waterways of the interior, effectively undercutting the HBC in its own backyard.

Among the posts they founded was Fort Rouge in 1738 at the fork of the Red and Assiniboine Rivers, making them the unofficial founders of Winnipeg. They discovered the Saskatchewan River, whose twin branches were the key to the interior, and two of the sons even glimpsed the distant foothills of the Rockies. They had given France a vast claim on the interior, but La Vérendrye himself was treated with near contempt by the French courts for his failure to find gold or a passage to the Orient. His 15-year search for a route to the Western Sea had bankrupted the family and cost him the life of his oldest son, Jean-Baptiste, who was killed and scalped in a Sioux ambush.

Cold War in Acadia

The peace couldn't last forever. In 1744, France and Britain were once again at war and Acadia was once again on the front lines. France launched a raid against Annapolis Royal (formerly Port Royal) in an attempt to recapture Acadia, but it failed when support ships did not show up. That winter, the ill-kept soldiers back at Louisbourg boiled over in mutiny. The uprising was quickly put down, and more than a dozen soldiers were charged and eight were hanged, but it didn't bode well for the future.

The Louisbourg fortress was *finally* completed in 1745 — just in time for its first attack. Aided by British warships, a ragtag band of New England volunteers captured the low hills behind Louisbourg and all but surrounded the fortress. After 46 days, Louisbourg fell. It was a humiliating defeat for France and a valuable lesson for Britain. New France was a colossus with feet of clay, ready to be toppled. The war ended in 1748 and Louisbourg was returned to France, but the peace treaty was little more than a temporary ceasefire, and both sides immediately began making preparations for war. It was less a "peace" than it was an armed truce, a cold war, a sabre-rattling staring match along the Acadian frontier. There is a famous Chinese curse: "May you live in interesting times." Well, things were about to get very interesting for both the Acadians and the Canadiens.

For a detailed account of the 1745 capture of Louisbourg, visit www.
thehistorynet.com/AmericanHistory/articles/0895_text.htm.

Warden of the North: The founding of Halifax

There were "howls of protest" from the New England colonies when Britain
handed back Louisbourg to the French, but that wasn't the end of the story.
Even before the war had ended, Lord Halifax of the British Trade Board had
presented a plan for a fortified town to be built on the east coast of Nova
Scotia, deep in the natural harbour that the Mi'kmaq called *Chebucto*. Why
shouldn't Britain have a Louisbourg of its own?

So, led by Colonel Edward Cornwallis, some 2,500 rough-and-ready colonists
set sail from Britain. Many of the settlers were cockney paupers from the
worst slums of London, true, but the operation was well planned and well
executed nonetheless. Cornwallis arrived in Chebucto on June 21, 1749,
ahead of the colonists, and when the others arrived, they drew building lots
and laid-out a gridwork plan for a fortified town. Halifax was born. (Actually,
Halifax was his title, not his name. Just be glad they didn't choose the
alternative, "Dunkville," after Lord Halifax's real name: George Dunk.) The
settlement of Halifax was Britain's answer to Louisbourg. The capital of Nova
Scotia was moved there from Annapolis Royal, and Cornwallis took over
duties as governor.

> [Most] are poor idle worthless vagabonds that embraced the opportunity
> to get provisions for one year without labour, or sailors that only wanted
> a passage to New England. . . . Many of the settlers are without shoes,
> stockings or shirts . . .
>
> — Cornwallis's evaluation of the founders of Halifax

Pop quiz: What do you call someone from Halifax? Why, a Haligonian, of course.
(Hey, it could be worse. They could be called "Dunkers.")

The Mi'kmaq resistance

The Acadians may have remained neutral, but not the Mi'kmaq. And not the
"warrior priest," Abbé Jean-Louis Le Lourte. With their ancestral homeland
divided between two competing European powers, the Mi'kmaq — allied with
France — waged an ongoing frontier battle against the British for years. Many
Mi'kmaq had converted to Catholicism, and the French fur trade and lowland
farming rarely interfered with their nomadic lifestyle. They had no love of the
English, and using massacres and psychological terror, the Mi'kmaq kept
them huddled behind garrison walls for years.

The Masterless Men

It wasn't just Acadian priests and Mi'kmaq warriors who were giving the British a hard time. In Newfoundland, in 1750, a young sailor by the name of Peter Kerrivan deserted the British Navy along with two cohorts. They fled into the hills near Ferryland, where they were later joined by Irish apprentices who wanted to escape their cruel fishing lords. It was a harsh time, when working boys were practically owned by their masters, and the Kerrivan Gang became outlaws from British "justice." The sailors, together with the Irish youngsters, were known as the Society of Masterless Men. They robbed and plundered, and lived off the land, hunting caribou in the interior and trading on the sly with colonists and fishermen.

This brazen independence could not be tolerated by the British Navy, which sent in several military expeditions against the Masterless Men to capture and kill them. But Kerrigan and the others eluded the British forces, drawing them into dead-end bogs and false-cut trails. Four young Irish boys were eventually captured and hanged by the British Navy, but the Masterless Men themselves were never broken. Even now, they live on as folk heroes in Newfoundland lore.

Egging the Mi'kmaq on was Abbé Le Loutre, one of the most fascinating characters in early Canadian history. Denounced by Cornwallis as "a good-for-nothing scoundrel," Le Loutre was a man of the cloth, a missionary who lived among the Mi'kmaq and adopted their customs and culture. He was also an expert rabble-rouser, a "Moses of the Mi'kmaq" who encouraged vicious attacks against English settlers and threatened disobedient Acadians with the same. Le Loutre built churches and preached the gospel even as he paid the Mi'kmaq for English scalps. The British in turn put a bounty on Le Loutre's head, but so renowned had the priest become that when they did capture him he was imprisoned rather than executed. He was later returned to France, where he received a hero's welcome.

The cold war heats up

Cold wars have a way of escalating, and so it was in Acadia. Like a great game of chess, France and Britain countered each other, fort for fort, outpost for outpost. Thousands of Protestant settlers — English and German — were brought in to counter the Acadian presence. The fishing community of Lunenburg, for one, was settled in 1753 almost entirely by "foreign Protestants," namely, German and Swiss colonists from allied regions in Europe, making Lunenburg an unofficial New Germany.

Britain held only peninsular Nova Scotia; the area that is now New Brunswick was disputed territory. With only a narrow strip of land (the Isthmus of Chignecto) separating them, the French and British built opposing forts right across from each other:

- ✔ Fort Beauséjour on the French side.
- ✔ Fort Lawrence on the British side.

Fort Lawrence had been named after its founder, Charles Lawrence, who would later become Governor of "Acadia or Nova Scotia" (as it was still known). In 1755, Lawrence sent a young officer by the name of Robert Monckton to capture Fort Beauséjour. Although France and Britain were technically at peace over in Europe, in North America it was a different story. Under Monckton's command, British troops and New England volunteers captured the French fort as the majority of Acadians outside it once again stood aside, refusing to launch a general uprising. If they thought this would endear them to their British lords, they were sadly mistaken. The balance of power had shifted dramatically in Britain's favour. With the threat to their western flank removed, the British could now turn their full attention on their decidedly "un-loyal" Acadian subjects.

The historic community of Lunenburg has been named a UNESCO World Heritage Site. To find out more, visit `parkscanada.pch.gc.ca/unesco/OLD/Old_e.htm` and `www.ovpm.org/ovpm/sites/alunen.html#DKN`.

The Expulsion of the Acadians

Charles Lawrence was a military man. A man of duty. A man of action. For him, the world was divided into allies and enemies, for or against. The Acadians fit neither category. With the fall of Fort Beauséjour, the cold war had heated up. An attack on Louisbourg was imminent, and after that, Québec itself. But first the Acadians under his rule would have to be dealt with. They must either take an unconditional oath or they must leave. Cornwallis had made a similar threat, but he had backed down at the last moment. Lawrence, however, was not bluffing. And so it was that he conceived and carried out what he called "the final resolution."

Lawrence and his council summoned a delegation of Acadians and demanded that they take the oath. When they refused, they were thrown into jail. The delegates argued that they were being held illegally. For 40 years they had remained neutral. For 40 years they had never taken up arms against Britain. What more did Lawrence want from them? When a second delegation arrived, demanding the release of the prisoners, they were imprisoned as well. The moment of reckoning was at hand.

At Grand Pré

The Minas Basin was the "breadbasket" of Acadia and Grand Pré was its most developed and prosperous community. It was here at Grand Pré, on September 5, 1755, that Acadian farmers gathered at the church to hear a royal proclamation being read. It was a bombshell: The Acadians had been declared "non-citizens." Their land and livestock were to be confiscated, and their farms destroyed. A mad clamour broke out, but the British soldiers were already in position and they began rounding up unarmed settlers. More than 2,000 Acadians were taken prisoner at Grand Pré alone. They were herded into transport ships at gunpoint as the British troops fanned out, laying waste to generations of hard work and toil. The soldiers burnt farms, homes, mills, and barns — some 700 buildings in the first wave alone. The Great Expulsion had begun.

For a detailed history of the Acadians, with an emphasis on the genealogy and the deportations, visit www.genweb.net/acadian-cajun/origin.htm. Parks Canada has a Grand Pré site at parkscanada.pch.gc.ca/parks/ nova_scotia/grand_pre/grand_pre_e.htm.

The voyages

I would have you not wait for the Wives and Children coming in but Ship Off the Men without them.
— from Governor Lawrence's instructions

The expulsion of the Acadians was a displacement unprecedented in North American history, and it happened with remarkable speed. "In a matter of months," writes historian Christopher Moore, "Acadia ceased to exist." In the confusion and chaos, families were torn apart: parents were separated from children, husbands from wives. Villages and homes were destroyed so that any Acadians who managed to escape would have no place to seek shelter or warmth after the British troops had departed.

The transport ships were grossly overcrowded even by the standards of the day. The Acadians were packed onboard to the point of suffocation. Squalid, dismal, dangerous: they were not so much ships as they were floating prisons. When the first boatload arrived in New York, the Acadian refugees were described as "poor, naked and destitute."

The Acadians were scattered throughout England's North American colonies, as thousands more fled to the French-held territories of *Ile Royale* (Cape Breton) and *Ile St. Jean* (P.E.I.), but the escape was only temporary. When Louisbourg was captured in 1758, the deportations began anew. The Acadians were hunted down methodically, and among the officers leading the persecution was Robert Monckton, who left scorched earth in his path. (Which makes it all the more ironic that one of the strongholds of Acadian education and culture today is the city named — and misspelled — after him: Moncton, New Brunswick.)

Those who resisted were locked up. Hundreds were sent to England where they spent seven years in internment camps. Those "repatriated" to France found themselves in a foreign country. After more than 100 years in the New World, the Acadians found France an alien environment. Within years of arriving in France, most had departed, many of them for Louisiana, which had become an "Acadia-in-exile." Their descendants would become known as *Cajuns*.

Others pushed north, into the Madawaska region of what is now northwestern New Brunswick, where they evolved into a rough-hewn, independent lumbering culture known as *les Brayons*.

The deportations lasted from 1755 to 1762, during which the Acadian region was almost completely depopulated. Some 10,000 people were forcibly evicted and sent as refugees to distant lands. Of those, more than 3,000 died, either in shipwrecks or from smallpox, typhoid, and yellow fever brought on by their ragged condition and unsanitary holding pens.

For an "Acadian Odyssey": collections.ic.gc.ca/acadian/intro.

"A criminal soul"

Were the deportations necessary? Was Lawrence justified in his actions? Some say he was. Refugees, after all, are a hard fact of war. Conflict displaces people, and at that time deportations were a common enough occurrence (though never of the scale or scope of the Acadian exile). A century before, when the French had captured the island of St. Kitts in the West Indies, they promptly deported 2,500 English colonists — and were so proud of their actions that they even issued a commemorative medal marking the event. Under Frontenac, the French, intent on capturing Albany and New York, had made plans to round up and exile the settlers. Louis XIV had expelled Protestant Huguenots from France, and when the French led their rampage across the Avalon Peninsula of Newfoundland in the 1690s, they too had deported the English settlers they captured.

On the basis of these and other examples, some historians have defended Lawrence's decision as regrettable but justified. Personally, I'm not so sure. Aside from the usual "two wrongs don't make a right" argument, a few key points are worth remembering:

✔ The deportations happened during peacetime. True, the frontier was effectively at war by 1755, but no official declaration had been issued.

✔ The English had originally gone out of their way to *stop* the Acadians from leaving. The Acadians were there because of British policy, not in spite of it.

✔ The British had accepted an earlier conditional oath.

✔ The Acadians had lived and worked the land for 40 years under British rule, during which they had never led a general uprising against the British nor had they taken up arms for France.

The deportations were carried out at a local level. Governor Lawrence and his Council notified Britain only after the decision had been made, and though Britain gave its approval once the policy was underway, the ultimate responsibility lies firmly with Lawrence. French-Canadian historians have long since dismissed him as a cruel and cold man, a "criminal soul" in the words of one. Lawrence even made John Robert Colombo's list of the Most Despised Canadians of All Time, coming in at #2. (To find out who #1 was, read on.) Lawrence himself never gave the deportations much thought and he certainly never regretted it. He died, unexpectedly, after a grand ball in Halifax in 1760, while the deportation orders were still in effect.

The Return of the Acadians

In 1764, after New France had been conquered, the ban on Acadians was lifted and the deportation orders cancelled. Like the Huron, the Acadians had become a Lost Tribe. Unlike the Huron, however, the Acadians were able to regroup and return. They had survived lootings, shipwrecks, mutinies, starvation, forced labour, mass arrests, and imprisonment. Slowly, they began to make their way home.

Some 3,000 Acadians returned to Nova Scotia, only to discover that the lands they had cleared and farmed for generations had been given away to New England squatters (dubbed "Planters"). With the best estates taken, the Acadians had to start again from scratch. This time, they took the oath.

The biggest single demographic change that resulted from the deportations was that the centre of Acadian culture shifted north, into New Brunswick. The lifestyle changed too, as farmers became fishermen (or, in the case of the Brayons, lumberjacks). The Acadians suffered through years of hardship and poverty following their return, but through it all they knew that they had done nothing wrong. They were a people who had stood on principle and had suffered greatly for it. That they have survived without being overcome by anger and bitterness is even more remarkable.

Evangeline

When the American poet Henry Wadsworth Longfellow heard accounts of the heartache and loss caused by the expulsion of the Acadians, he composed a long, sad narrative poem about it, entitled *Evangeline: A Tale of Acadie*. First published in 1874, nearly 100 years after the events described, the poem tells the story of two young lovers, Evangeline and Gabriel, who are separated at Grand Pré and spend the rest of their lives trying to find one another. They meet only at the very end, when Evangeline, now a kindly, grey-haired nun, comes upon Gabriel, bent and stricken with pestilence. They get one final kiss just as Gabriel dies.

The dominating theme of Longfellow's vision is that of terrestrial Paradise Lost, and one lost without proven original sin.
— historian Naomi Griffiths

Translated into French, Longfellow's epic poem had an enormous impact upon the Acadian sense of identity. *Evangeline* gave a voice and focus to their community, and it soon replaced the oral traditions of the older Acadians as their main source of information and inspiration. Today, a statute of the fictional Evangeline stands outside a chapel at Grand Pré, Nova Scotia, not far from where the first deportations began.

They have maintained their historic neutrality even today. Throughout the rise and fall of tensions between French and English Canada, the Acadians have, for the most part, steadfastly refused to be drawn into the conflict.

You'll find a historical perspective on Evangeline and Acadia at www.ac.wwu.edu/~jay/pages/evangel.html.

Chapter 7

The Conquest

- -

In This Chapter

▶ A frontier clash in the Ohio Valley sparks a world war

▶ The British capture Louisbourg — and then systematically destroy it

▶ The French are defeated on the Plains of Abraham

▶ France eventually surrenders, abandoning the Canadiens to British rule

- -

Franco-Ontarian writer Lyse Champagne calls it "the Big Bang of Canadian history," and she's right. The Conquest of New France by Britain in 1760 changed Canada forever. As a nation, we are dealing with the fall-out still.

Was it a disaster? A misfortune? A triumph? An unavoidable outcome? The end of New France has been interpreted in wildly different ways over the years. The Catholic clergy once saw the Conquest as "a blessing in disguise," one that protected Canadiens from the later violence and atheistic republican values of the French Revolution. In the 1960s, the Conquest became politicized as an ongoing symbol of Anglo oppression. Others have scoffed at this, insisting that the Conquest was an imperial conflict that neither destroyed nor crippled French Canada in the long run. (The very real power wielded by Québec today does seem to bear that out.) Historian Fernand Ouellet would have nothing to do with the peculiar cult of victimhood that developed in Québec, and author Gilles Lalande called Québec's constant preoccupation with the Conquest "a perpetual alibi."

However, it isn't only Québec nationalists who have been obsessed with the Conquest. English Canadians have long gloried in it, just as surely as French Canadians have lamented it. "Didn't we beat them on the Plains of Abraham?" It is a common enough bleat, and a sentiment that lies just below the surface of a lot of grassroots Anglo rhetoric in Canada today. But as we will see, this is one of the Great Delusions of Canadian history. *We* didn't beat them, because *we* didn't exist. English Canada hadn't been invented yet. Any Canadians on the Plains of Abraham spoke French. And however one chooses to interpret it, it was still conquest. "And conquest," writes historian Susan Mann Trofimenkoff, "is like rape."

People are often very surprised that Quebeckers say they are still affected by an event that took place over two hundred years ago, while other peoples have already overcome more recent, more devastating defeats. They forget the fundamental difference between defeat and conquest. A conquest is a permanent defeat, an institutionalized defeat.

— Québec commentator Christian Dufour

Pop quiz: How long did the Seven Years' War last in Canada? *Answer*: Nine years. It's a trick question, of course. The war began in North America in 1754, two years before it spread to Europe.

The Shooting Starts

A volley fired by a young Virginian in the backwoods of America set the world on fire.

— essayist Horace Walpole

The trouble began in the Ohio Valley, west of the Appalachian Mountains. Like the Mississippi, the Ohio River was a strategic highway into the interior. The American colonists were determined to move in, and the French were just as determined to block them. In 1753, the Governor of New France sent in a military expedition to cut a trail and build an outpost, dubbed Fort Duquesne. When the Governor of Virginia caught wind of this, he dispatched a young officer by the name of George Washington to deliver a letter "ordering" the French to leave. The French all but laughed in his face. ("I fart in your general direction," as Monty Python might put it.)

Washington left and came back the following year with 150 armed men. He ambushed a Canadien patrol, killing ten including the commander. These would be the first deaths in what was to become a world war. Following the attack, Washington and his men — "assassins" in the eyes of the Canadiens — beat a hasty retreat to a temporary shelter they dubbed Fort Necessity. The French surrounded it and opened fire, and Washington was forced to surrender. He slunk away, defeated. All of this occurred during peacetime.

Council at Alexandria

The humiliation could not go unanswered, and in April 1755, the governors from several British American colonies gathered at Alexandria, Virginia, to plot their revenge. They decided on a four-prong assault against the French: at Niagara, Lake Champlain, Acadia, and — of course — Fort Duquesne itself.

General Braddock, a blustering and fearless man, led a strike force of 2,500 redcoats and militiamen into the Ohio Valley. As the advance guard marched along in parade-ground formation, a small band of Canadien, French, and Native allies were lying in wait. It was less an ambush than it was a turkey shoot: The British were gunned down by invisible enemies lurking in the forests. Braddock died cursing and waving his sword ineffectively. The British lost 977 men, the French 23, and the attack on Niagara was quickly cancelled. Of the four campaigns planned, only one succeeded; Fort Beauséjour on the Acadian frontier was captured, clearing the way for the deportations that followed. (Check out Chapter 6 for more about the Acadian frontier.) Other than that, 1755 was a disastrous year for the British.

France's Native allies

These Indians claim to be and in effect are independent of all nations, and their lands incontestably belong to them.
> — Intendant Bigot following a conference with Native delegates

When war began, New France was badly outnumbered. The entire population of Canada was less than 60,000 at that time, compared to 1.2 million inhabitants in the Thirteen Colonies, a difference of 20 to 1. But these numbers don't give an accurate picture. For one, the British American colonies were not a united front; they often bickered and fought amongst themselves. For another, the British Americans had almost no support from the First Nations. (Although some Iroquois did fight alongside the British, for the most part they didn't play a major role.) The French, in contrast, had very close ties with several of the Algonquian nations, especially the Abenaki, the Maliseet, and the Mi'kmaq. They also made alliances with the Ojibwa, the Ottawa, the Potawatomi, the Miami, and the Illinois. Almost all the First Nations in the northeast sided with the French — including a breakaway group of Mohawk in the Montréal region.

Early French victories

The Canadian-born Governor of New France, Pierre de Vaudreuil, was an avid supporter of what the French called *la petite guerre*, "small warfare," which employed the quick-running techniques of Native warriors, striking hard and fast and then melting back into the woods. As later historians have noted, for Vaudreuil offense was the only defense. In this, the governor clashed with his newly appointed military commander, General Louis-Joseph de Montcalm, who took a more cautious and conventional approach.

Confused by all these wars? Here's why

By this point, you may have gotten the impression that the early years of Canadian history were just one extended slugfest between Britain and France. And you'd be right. For more than 150 years the two sides fought it out, often during times of "official" peace. And if that's not confusing enough:

- The North American phase of a war had a different name than it did in Europe. (For example, in the U.S. the Seven Years' War is known as "the French and Indian War.")

- The dates were often different as well. (For example, as noted, the Seven Years' War actually lasted nine years in North America.)

The important thing to know is this: The Seven Years' War was the final conflict between Britain and France for the control of North America. The conflict began on the frontier and then spread to Europe, where it eventually drew in a complex web of alliances (Britain, Prussia, and Hanover on one side; France, Austria, Sweden, Saxony, Russia, and Spain on the other). Winston Churchill called it the first "true" World War because it was fought on four continents and ranged as far as India. In North America, however, it was strictly a British/French grudge match.

Here is a summary of the many various conflicts that led up to the Seven Years' War and the Conquest of Canada, along with some of the highlights.

1613: Samuel Argall attacks Acadia in an attempt to drive the French from the east coast.

1629–33: The Kirke Brothers capture Québec, taking Champlain prisoner.

1654–70: Acadia is under English control.

1686: De Troyes leads "North America's first commando raid" against HBC posts in James Bay. Although England and France are technically at peace over in Europe, in Canada the "fur wars" will rage for years.

1688–97: *War of the League of Augsburg* (in North America, *King William's War*, 1689–97) William Phips captures Acadia and then sails on to Québec, but Governor Frontenac stands tall and the attack fails.

Iberville captures HBC forts with wild abandon and leads a rampage across the Avalon Peninsula of Newfoundland.

1702–13: *War of the Spanish Succession* (in North America, *Queen Anne's War*)

Acadia is captured and Port Royal is re-named Annapolis Royal.

With the Treaty of Utrecht, France cedes claims to the Hudson Bay, Acadia, and Newfoundland (other than fishing rights off the north shore). After the war, the French found Louisbourg.

1713–43: Thirty years of peace, considered a "Golden Age" for both Acadia and Canada.

1740–48: *War of Austrian Succession* (in North America, *King George's War*, 1744–48)

Louisbourg is taken in 1745, but is later returned to France by treaty. The British immediately begin building Halifax.

1756–63: *Seven Years' War* (to the Americans it's known as the *French and Indian War*, 1754–63)

The Acadians are expelled, and the British again capture Louisbourg.

Québec is taken, and in the Treaty of Paris, France cedes all its territories in North America, except for a pair of small islands off of Newfoundland. It is the end of New France and more than 150 years of conflict between Britain and France for control of North America.

In spite of their differences, both men more than proved their worth in the early stages of the conflict. When war was officially declared in 1756, the first years saw one French victory after another. Canadien and Native raiders struck deep, burning farms on the outskirts of Boston and coming within 50 miles of Philadelphia — at that time the largest English-speaking city in the world, after London. Widespread panic ensued.

> **1756:** Vaudreuil leads a force against Fort Oswego on the east shore of Lake Ontario. Montcalm takes over and captures the fort. In doing so, he wrestles control of the Great Lakes away from the British.

> **1757:** Montcalm captures Fort William Henry in upper New York, a stunning victory marred only by the Indian massacre that follows. Even as the French try to stop them, warriors fall upon unarmed prisoners, killing at least 50 and carrying off 100 more to be tortured. The massacre outrages Britain — and horrifies Montcalm.

> **1758:** At the French outpost of Fort Carillon, Montcalm turns back a massive attack by the British and prevents a full-scale invasion of Canada. (Québec's current provincial flag is said to be derived from the war banner Montcalm flew during the defense of Fort Carillon.)

Visit `www.canadianheritage.org/galleries/warsbattlesrebellions` `0100.htm` for a look at the Canadian Heritage picture collection of battles from 1600–1758.

The Fall of Louisbourg

Montcalm's heroic defense of Fort Carillon in 1758 would be the last major victory France would have for two years. With the British Navy blockading the supply lines to Canada, one French stronghold after another was either captured or abandoned. Forced to pull out of Fort Duquesne, the French blew it up first — thus ending their dream of controlling the Ohio Valley. The British occupied the site and built Fort Pitt, named after their newly appointed prime minister, William Pitt. (It would later become Pittsburgh.) But the most important battle would occur in the east, at Louisbourg.

The attack on Louisbourg was launched in June 1758, when a fleet of ships carrying 12,000 British troops under the command of General Jeffrey Amherst set sail from Halifax. Behind the walls of Louisbourg were scarcely 4,000 men, soldiers and local militia combined. Sealed into the harbour and cut off from French support, the French garrison's only hope lay in holding off the invaders until winter set in. The British, in contrast, wanted to take Louisbourg as quickly as possible so that they could continue on to Québec.

Playing card money

Imagine going in to work one day to pick up your paycheque and having your boss flash you a nervous smile as he fans out a deck and says, "Pick a card, any card." Well, that's more or less what happened in New France when the governor ran out of money to pay the wages of soldiers stationed at Québec. Facing a near mutiny, the governor's intendant began issuing playing cards instead of currency. He cut each card into four, penned in an amount on the back, and attached his personal seal. The cards were used like regular currency and then exchanged for real money once the supply ships from France arrived. At one point, more than two million livres of cardboard notes were in circulation (the livre being the standard of currency in New France). This, in turn, caused runaway inflation in the colony. The Crown solved the problem by redeeming the notes — but at only *half* their face value. Playing cards and other similar cardboard notes were used in lieu of money from 1685 right up until 1759, making them the first true "currency" ever issued in Canada — though the beaver pelt, long a standard of barter, could also be considered currency. Either way, between playing cards and beaver pelts, you have the proud origins of Canada's current economic system.

On the very first day of the attack, a reckless young officer by the name of James Wolfe charged headlong into enemy fire, wading ashore as shells exploded around him. Wolfe and his men captured a key French position and cleared a beachhead for the British. After that, it was only a matter of time before the great fortress fell — and even then, it took almost two months for the French to finally surrender. (Part of the blame lay with Amherst's painfully slow approach to laying siege.) Although Louisbourg was indeed taken, the attack on Québec had to be postponed until the following year.

To find out more about Louisbourg, visit the Parks Canada site: `parkscanada.pch.gc.ca/parks/nova_scotia/fortress_louisbourg/Fortress_louisbourg_e.htm`.

The Bank of Canada's Currency Museum (`collections.ic.ca/bank`) is a fascinating place. Go there for more info, including a facsimile of the playing card money of New France.

1759: The Battle for Québec

In 1759, the odds were stacked against New France. The British outnumbered them

- ✔ three to one in ships
- ✔ four to one in regular troops
- ✔ ten to one in money

The French were outgunned, outmanned, and outplayed. It was a lopsided fight, true, but then again, France didn't need to *beat* the British, all they had to do was wear them down. If they could drag out the conflict long enough, the war would become so expensive an undertaking that the British taxpayer would demand a ceasefire. If they could hang on for just one more year . . .

> *The Conquest of Canada was by no means foreordained or inevitable.*
> — historian W. J. Eccles

Key players

The final battle for Québec was dominated by a handful of strong but flawed figures — it was a battle of personalities as much as one of geography. Here then are some of the key players involved in the Conquest of Canada. Many of them, you have already met.

Pitt: "Saviour of the British Empire"

By 1757, the French were clearly winning the war. Defeat after humiliating defeat piled up on the British, and they might well have called the campaign off entirely had it not been for one man: William Pitt, wild, temperamental, and possibly insane, who came steamrolling into power with the declaration that "Nobody else can save this country." As prime minister, Pitt threw all his energy into the war effort, making an enormous commitment on behalf of Britain in terms of money, men, and ships. For Pitt, a student of military history, the primary theatre of war was not Europe but North America. He was determined to bring the French "to their knees" and capture Canada once and for all. It became both a crusade and an obsession.

Amherst: "The methodical commander-in-chief"

Amherst was a cautious leader — overly cautious, some might say. Having taken Louisbourg after a long, drawn-out siege, he was made commander-in-chief for North American operations. While James Wolfe led a strike force against Québec City, Amherst advanced — slowly, methodically — up Lake Champlain, capturing French forts one at a time. This was supposed to be part of a pincher move (Wolfe from the east, Amherst from the south, and a third column from the west along Lake Ontario) but Amherst's advance was so slow and plodding that his arrival outside the gates of Montréal was delayed until 1760, long after the matter had been settled by Wolfe.

Wolfe: "The reckless Hamlet"

Jeffrey Amherst and James Wolfe were opposites in almost every way imaginable. Where Amherst was cautious, Wolfe was reckless to the point of mental instability. (More than one historian has suggested that Wolfe may have had a death wish. I'm inclined to agree.) As Gordon Donaldson so aptly put it, it wasn't death that Wolfe was afraid of — but failure. Wolfe had made a name for himself with his daring charge at Louisbourg. Just the sort of man Pitt was looking for. When a fretful advisor ran to George II to warn him that James Wolfe was "a madman," the King replied, "Mad, is he? Then I hope he will bite some of my other generals." Thin, sickly, indecisive, rash, morose, moody: General Wolfe was a cold and aloof figure to his men. "He neither drinks, curses, gambles nor runs after women," one captain complained. James Wolfe was just 32 years old. The assault on Québec would be his first independent command. It would also be his last.

Montcalm: "The reluctant general"

Wolfe would face off against General Montcalm, the victor at Carillon and Oswego. Poor Montcalm. He didn't want to be over in the colonies, fighting alongside Indians. He was deeply homesick for his chalet back in France and his heart was never really in it. Montcalm, a wounded war hero, was a capable but unimaginative commander. Even when he did win a battle, he didn't follow up on it, preferring instead to withdraw and wait for the British to make their next move. This wasn't necessarily a bad strategy, but it drove Governor Vaudreuil up the wall. Vaudreuil often criticized Montcalm for refusing to take the initiative, and there was some truth to the accusations: Montcalm did tend to *react* to events, rather than control them. Ironically, it was only when he abandoned this approach and acted impulsively that he lost everything: the battle, the colony, and his life.

> *I think I would give up all my honours to be back with you, but the King must be obeyed. The moment I see you again will be the best in my life.*
> — Montcalm in his last letter to his wife, written in 1759, shortly before he died in battle

Vaudreuil: "The Canadien governor"

Pierre de Vaudreuil was the first native-born Canadien to be made governor of New France. As such, he was fighting to defend not a mere colony but rather, his homeland. If Montcalm was too pessimistic, Vaudreuil was far too optimistic. He was a man of grand schemes and bold pronouncements and as often as not, all he did was get in Montcalm's way. The two men argued constantly. Vaudreuil was a Canadien. Montcalm was French. Vaudreuil wanted to take the battle to the British. Montcalm wanted to play it safe. Vaudreuil favoured Native war techniques. Montcalm preferred a defensive campaign based on set European formations. The result? A governor and a general who were working at cross-purposes. It was a clash of both personalities and world views that would prove fatal for New France.

Bigot: "The corrupt intendant"

François Bigot was a repulsive little man. Corrupt, decadent, and oily in his social flattery, Bigot squeezed money out of the colony even as it faced extinction. While the habitants starved, Bigot held feasts and grand balls — fiddling while Rome burned, so to speak. And yet, somehow, he managed to keep New France's coffers full and its troops fed and equipped.

Earlier historians heaped a great deal of scorn on Bigot (most of it deserved) and some even held him personally responsible for the Fall of New France. In Chapter 6, I introduce you to Charles Lawrence, Governor of Acadia and #2 on John Robert Colombo's list of Most Despised Canadians. Well, now you know who holds the #1 spot. Recently, however, Bigot has been re-evaluated. He is now portrayed as either:

(a) a product of his time — most of the public officials back then were corrupt, it was almost expected of them;

(b) a scapegoat — he faced criminal charges back in France after the colony fell; or

(c) a miracle worker who kept the colony supplied even as he lined his own pockets.

Which interpretation is correct? All of the above. He *was* repulsive. He *was* effective. And he *was* later turned into a scapegoat.

Lévis: "The finest soldier on the field"

If Bigot was the buffoon, Lévis was the Knight in Shining Armour. An astute and brave officer, François-Gaston de Lévis was one of the few people capable of getting along with both Vaudreuil *and* Montcalm. When Montcalm blundered his way to defeat and Vaudreuil panicked and fled Québec City, Lévis marched right back and attempted to retake it. And the following spring, in a full-scale rematch, Lévis came within a whisker of defeating the British and taking back the walled city. *The bottom line*: If Lévis had been in charge, the British most certainly would *not* have captured Québec — at least, not that year. History is full of such tantalizing "might-have-been's."

The British armada arrives

The habitants watched in fear and awe as it passed: one-quarter of the British Navy, more than 140 ships, stretching along the St. Lawrence for 50 miles. Wolfe had been put in charge of an invasion fleet of 13,500 men, including a strike force of almost 9,000 soldiers from the best units in Britain.

> *It was the best trained and equipped army North America had seen, supported by the biggest and best fleet.*
>
> — popular historian Gordon Donaldson

Admiral Charles Saunders steered his fleet of great ships through the tricky waters of the St. Lawrence and dropped anchor east of Québec City. Here then was the problem: How to take Québec? Known as "the Gibraltar of the New World," it was perched atop towering protective cliffs, and Montcalm refused to come out and play. The one key tactical mistake the French made was in not defending the south shore of the St. Lawrence across from the city. Vaudreuil's engineers had assured Montcalm that British cannon didn't have the range, but in this they were sadly mistaken.

The British captured the heights across from Québec City and pointed their guns at the city. On June 12, when the first cannonball was fired, it splashed harmlessly into the St. Lawrence as the Canadiens jeered. The next one, however, flew right over the Lower Town and crashed into the Upper. The Great Bombardment had begun. Iron and fire rained down, and Québec burned. The cannons pounded the city night and day, killing civilians by the score and destroying hundreds of homes. The prolonged destruction served no military purpose other than to terrorize and punish the city's inhabitants. As Francois Bigot so succinctly put it: "*M. Wolfe est cruel.*"

Visit `parcscanada.risq.qc.ca/fortifications_e` for more on Québec City's fortifications, unique in North America.

Summer of terror

> *[If] we find that Québec is not likely to fall into our hands . . . I propose to set the Town on fire with Shells, to destroy the Harvest, Houses & cattle, both above & below, to send off as many Canadians as possible to Europe, & to leave famine and desolation behind me.*
>
> — General James Wolfe in a letter to Amherst

Wolfe continued to pound the city as his frustration and anger mounted. With Lévis back in Montreal preparing for an assault that never came, Montcalm was forced to play a game of cat-and-mouse with Wolfe. When Wolfe moved, Montcalm countered. When Wolfe attacked, Montcalm responded. The British general was becoming more and more erratic: He sent his men into crossfires, he worried himself sick, and he contradicted his own orders. One of his officers began ridiculing him behind his back, drawing mocking caricatures of the general and collecting evidence for the court martial he was sure would follow Wolfe's botched expedition.

Boiling with impotent rage, James Wolfe now turned his full wrath against the Canadiens. With instructions "to burn and lay waste the country," Wolfe turned his American Rangers loose against the habitants living along the St. Lawrence. The buck-skinned Rangers were the British American equivalent of the *coureurs de bois* — but meaner. They burned homes, took scalps, and slaughtered livestock. On the south shore alone, the British destroyed more than 1,000 homes and left the harvests in ruins. It was an act of sheer spite.

As summer slipped away and autumn came with a chill in the air, Wolfe knew he was running out of time. He decided to make one last attempt before leaving. Earlier, he had spotted a break in the cliffs west of the city, at a cove called l'Anse-au-Foulon. If Wolfe could somehow land his men undetected and then scale the cliffs, he might be able to put his army on the plains behind the city and draw Montcalm out into the open . . . and so it was, on a moonless night in mid-September, that a flotilla of 30 flat-bottomed boats slipped silently downriver with the tide.

The paths of glory

Before his departure from England, Wolfe's sweetheart, Katherine Lowther, gave him a small, leather-bound copy of Thomas Gray's poem, *Elegy Written in a Country Churchyard*, which contained the following passage:

> The boast of heraldry, the pomp of power
> And all that beauty, all that wealth e'er gave
> Awaits alike the inevitable hour —
> The paths of glory lead but to the grave.

Legend has it that Wolfe recited this to his officers shortly before the final battle, his voice lingering on that last fateful line. He then said softly, "Gentlemen, I would rather have written those lines than take Québec." Later historians have since debunked this version of events as romantic nonsense, but the fact remains that Wolfe *had* underlined the above passage. And certainly, as events would show, that final line was indeed prophetic. *The paths of glory lead but to the grave.* Wolfe's copy of Gray's *Elegy*, with the fateful passage underlined by the General himself, is now held by the University of Toronto.

On the Plains of Abraham

As the boats glided down the St. Lawrence, a French sentry spotted them and called out from the shore, but the British managed to bluff their way past and, just before dawn, they landed at the cove. An advance guard climbed the narrow trail and overpowered the French post at the top as the rest of the troops followed, pulling themselves up along handholds of roots and vines, up onto the Plains of Abraham. It was September 13, 1759.

Although the name has a nice Biblical ring to it, suggesting sacrifice and redemption, the plains were actually named after a settler who had farmed in the area. It was here that the future of Canada would be decided. By daybreak, Wolfe had positioned more than 4,500 troops on the Plains of Abraham. The surprise was complete. General Montcalm had been convinced that the final attack, if it came, would be on the other side of the city at the Beauport shore. When an aide suggested the British might try to climb the cliffs, Montcalm had snorted with derision. "We do not need to imagine that the enemy has wings," he wrote in his journal, "so that in one night they can cross the river, disembark, and climb the obstructed cliffs." But now, they had done just that. As he hurried to assemble his troops, Montcalm looked out at the redcoats that were lining up behind the city, and complained, "They have no right to be there."

Wolfe had managed to drag up only two light cannons. Montcalm decided that time was of the essence and that the British had to be attacked immediately, before they could dig in and strengthen their position. For the first time since the British arrived, Montcalm acted impulsively. He had 3,000 reinforcements somewhere behind the British lines — a message had been sent and they were on their way — but he didn't wait for them to arrive. Instead, Montcalm gathered the troops he had on hand and threw open the city gates . . .

The battle lasted only 15 minutes. The British had formed a "thin red line," two men deep, and the French advanced in a ragged charge, the regulars and the Canadiens stumbling over each other. Native snipers were picking off British soldiers from nearby woods, but Wolfe stood his ground. Then, when the French were only 30 paces away, the order was given. The redcoats raised their muskets and fired, one platoon after the next in rolling thunder across the Plains. Smoke filled the battlefield. The British re-loaded and advanced, emerging from the smoke like ghosts. They fired a second volley, and that was all it took. The French broke and ran.

Montcalm, atop his magnificent black horse, was hit in the stomach and thighs. He reeled in the saddle but refused to fall. Instead, he slowly rode back behind the walls of Québec, where he later died. His last words were ones of gratitude that he would not live to see the English inside the city.

Wolfe fell on the battlefield, hit twice — in the wrist and stomach — before a sharpshooter finally split open his chest. As he lay dying, a great cheer went up. "Look, sir!" one of his men cried. "They run!" "Who run?" Wolfe asked anxiously. "The enemy, sir. They give way everywhere."

And so ended the Battle of the Plains of Abraham. The two sides had been roughly equal and had suffered roughly the same number of losses: 650 on each side. It is worth noting that the battle, in itself, hadn't resolved anything. The British had won a field. That was it. If anything, they were in a dangerously exposed position. Québec fell not because the British won, but because the French lost their nerve. Vaudreuil panicked and fled with his troops along a side road. Five days later, the city's bewildered commander (who had been left behind without any clear instructions) surrendered the city. The Canadiens hadn't been conquered by the British; they had been abandoned by France.

Endgame

The Chevalier de Lévis was furious. When he met Vaudreuil and the rest of the French army on the road to Montréal, he all but denounced them as cowards. Lévis immediately marched his troops back to Québec, but by the time he arrived, the city had already been taken and a tough little Scotsman by the name of James Murray was now in charge. As the snow began to fall, Lévis withdrew to Montréal. He would be back.

The British garrison suffered miserably. Wolfe's bombardment had reduced the city almost to rubble, more than a third of the dwellings were ruined, and firewood was scarce. Sentries froze to death, soldiers starved, and sickness and despair swept through the camp. More than 1,000 men died that winter, far more than had fallen in battle on the Plains of Abraham itself.

Counterattack

As the first snows began to melt in April, and before the ice had left the river, Lévis made his way back to Québec intent on a rematch. Incredibly, James Murray made the same mistake as Montcalm: He rushed into battle outside the walls. Lévis led him into a trap and pounced. The Battle of Ste-Foy (sometimes known as "the Second Battle of the Plains of Abraham") was an impressive victory for the French. The British were forced to flee back into the city, abandoning valuable artillery in the field. Lévis set up camp and waited for help to arrive from France. It had all come down to this: a race across the Atlantic. Lévis could have retaken Québec City with just a few reinforcements, but none came. Unknown to Lévis, the British had defeated the French Navy in Europe and no help was coming. The ships that did arrive were British, and Lévis, bitterly disappointed, marched his men back to Montréal. (In fact, a few French supply ships did try to get through, but by then it was too late.)

Amherst arrives — finally

The British advanced on Montréal from three sides: east from Québec City, west from the Great Lakes, and south along the Lake Champlain river system. As the noose tightened, Lévis could barely muster 2,000 men against the British force of 17,000. When Amherst arrived, he sent a message to the governor: "I have come to take Canada, and I will take nothing less." Lévis wanted to fall back to a small island and fight it out to the death, but Vaudreuil vetoed this heoric — but suicidal — approach. Would they at least be able to march out of Montréal with their heads held high and their regimental flags flying? No. Amherst, in a somewhat petty move, refused to allow them their military honours even in defeat. So Lévis and his men burnt their banners so that none would fall into English hands as war trophies, and then laid down their arms. It was September 8, 1760. New France had fallen.

And what of the First Nations that had fought alongside the French and the Canadiens for nine long years? A separate peace had been concluded with some of them before New France had surrendered, and at Montréal, Article 40 of the Terms of Capitulation included a partial protection for Native Canadians: "Indian Allies [of the French King] shall be maintained in the lands they inhabit; if they choose to remain there."

For more on the Conquest of Canada, see canadahistory.com/conquest. htm (part of a larger, integrated Canadian History site). For the "Discriminating General's" Seven Years' War Web site, go to www.militaryheritage.com/ 7yrswar.htm.

The Battle of Signal Hill

Here's a quirky historical fact for you: The last battle for Canada was fought not in Québec but in Newfoundland.

No doubt, readers in Newfoundland will be rolling their eyes and muttering darkly at this. "Quirky historical fact? *Hardly!*" In Newfoundland, the Battle of Signal Hill is a well-known and often told tale. But outside the province it isn't. So here goes:

The important thing to remember is that the Conquest of New France did *not* end the Seven Years' War. Far from it. The war continued to rage elsewhere, from the West Indies to India. At Louisbourg, in 1760, the British began systematically demolishing the French fortifications, rendering the site useless and ending any possibility of a future threat should it be handed back to France at a later date. The French, meanwhile, needed *something* to bring to the bargaining table once the shooting stopped. (When it came time to negotiate a treaty it was important to have territory worth swapping for, and the French had very little to offer.) So, in the spring of 1762, France launched an attack on Newfoundland, intent on capturing St. John's and holding it as a bargaining tool.

With a force of 800 men, including some 160 or so Irish mercenaries, the French landed and quickly captured Fort William in St. John's Harbour. They then set about ransacking settlements in the area, sinking hundreds of fishing boats and causing all sorts of unnecessary damage. The French looted and ravaged and had a grand old time. Then the British arrived.

Led by Colonel William Amherst (Jeffrey's brother), 1,500 British soldiers poured in — and Amherst had mercenaries of his own, Swiss and Germans, as well as Scottish regulars from Cape Breton. Amherst's men first attacked the French outpost on Signal Hill, overlooking the harbour. Signal Hill was every bit as imposing a natural defense as Quebec. The cliffs rose up straight from the sea, and the heights could be approached only from one angle. In spite of this, the British managed to overrun the French position without much of a fight. They then turned the French guns around and pointed them down on Fort William. One day of shooting was all it took. The French surrendered on September 18, 1762, exactly three years to the day after Québec City itself had surrendered.

Signal Hill would be the last battle of the Seven Years' War to be fought in North America, and with it went any hope France had of retaining a "bargaining chip." When the French were beaten at Signal Hill, Canada was lost to them forever . . .

Go to `www.infonet.st-johns.nf.ca/providers/green/jingo69.html` for more on Newfoundland's early military history.

Chapter 8

Aftermath

In This Chapter

▶ Canada is put under British military rule

▶ The Treaty of Paris ends the French empire in North America

▶ The First Nations boil over in a rebellion against the British

▶ A Royal Proclamation "clarifies" the situation

Quelques arpents de neige ("a few acres of snow")
— the off-hand dismissal of Canada by French man of letters Voltaire

As Voltaire's breezy comment suggests, France was not overly traumatized by the loss of New France. The Canadiens, however, had reason to be concerned. In Acadia, the British had rounded up settlers and deported them by the thousands. An entire way of life had been destroyed. Would the British do the same thing in Canada now that they were in control?

No. Following the Conquest, French-Canadian society was *not* shattered. Nor were the Canadiens deported. As historian Fernand Ouellet has pointed out, after the Conquest life went on more or less as it always had. The average Canadien lived the same, worked the same, and held the same beliefs. In this sense, the Conquest was more of a disaster to the ruling elite of New France than it was to the average habitant. (If nothing else, the vindictive British raids against their farms had finally ended.)

Rather than force the Canadiens to leave, the British actively encouraged them to stay. Why were there no deportations? Two reasons: For one, the French military presence had been wiped out in North America and therefore the Canadiens were no longer perceived as a threat. But it also came down to personality, and specifically the character of the man named military governor: James Murray. (You remember him. He was the one who suffered through that first terrible winter in the ruins of Québec City and was then soundly defeated by Lévis the following spring, as described in Chapter 7.) James Murray was a hard man and James Murray was a military man. But he was in no way a cruel man.

Canada under British Military Rule

When the French surrendered at Montréal in 1760, the Terms of Capitulation were not particularly severe. True, French laws, customs, and institutions were not protected, but neither were they banned. The Canadiens were allowed to retain possession of their lands and property, and — just as important — they were allowed to continue practising their religion. James Murray had no intention of impoverishing the habitants, either financially or spiritually. Great Britain was a Protestant stronghold, and the Anglican Church was made the "established" (i.e., government-supported) denomination of Canada, but the Catholic Church itself was not banned, nor was it actively persecuted.

True, the Church had been put in a precarious position — it had lost a great deal of money and property during the war, and many of its clergy had fled to France — but it was still intact and was, indeed, one of the few social institutions remaining for the Canadiens. Of church, state, and military, only the first was still standing. The French governors were gone and so were the military elite. In this vacuum, the Catholic Church would play an increasingly important role in French-Canadian society (a role that would last right up until the 1960s). Later historians have criticized the Church for "stunting" Québec's development as a mature society, and there is some truth to this, especially in the area of education. But give the Church its due. Without it, French-Canadian society might never have survived at all.

1763: The Treaty of Paris

On February 10, 1763, France signed away an empire. Under the terms of the Treaty of Paris, the French ceded control of the following:

- ✔ Canada (that is, the St. Lawrence heartland)
- ✔ the rest of Acadia (including Cape Breton and P.E.I.)
- ✔ any claim to the Ohio Valley and the Great Lakes
- ✔ and French Louisiana

All that was left of France's once vast empire in North America were two small islands off the coast of Newfoundland — St. Pierre and Miquelon — which are territories of France to this day. Oddly enough, Britain wasn't completely sure it wanted to keep Canada. As the Seven Years' War drew to a close, there was heavy pressure on Pitt to give back the Canadian colonies and keep the Caribbean sugar-rich island of Guadeloupe instead.

Some are for keeping Canada, some Guadeloupe. Who will tell me what I shall be hanged for not keeping?
— William Pitt on the opposing pressures he faced

In the end, Britain chose Canada, but by then Pitt had been ousted from the prime minister's office and — even more importantly — a new king, George III, was on the throne.

The Pontiac Rebellion

For the British, it must have felt like they were trying to put out a grassfire. No sooner had they quashed one blaze than another flared up. With the Treaty of Paris signed, Britain now held claim to the vast interior of the North American continent. They barely had time to catch their breath, however, when a new challenge to their authority reared up. It came from France's former Native allies.

The great alliance

The British had signed peace treaties with *some* of the First Nations in the St. Lawrence area prior to the Conquest, but not with those of the interior. As the British began moving in and taking over French posts throughout the region, resentment among the Natives grew. Ironically, the first signs of dissent began with the Seneca of the Iroquois Confederacy who had fought alongside the British and now found themselves shunted aside as English settlers moved in, many of them taking up residence on Seneca lands.

A Native medicine man, known as "the Delaware Prophet," began urging a return to their traditional Native roots. He wanted the First Nations to reject the ways of the whites and the brandy trade that had caused such havoc. The time had come to drive the "red-coated dogs" from the region. The Prophet's message was picked up by the Ottawa war chief Pontiac and soon became both a rallying cry and a crusade. With Pontiac at the helm, a widespread alliance took shape that included Ojibwa, Ottawa, Potawatomi, and Seneca.

You have conquered the French. You have not conquered us. We are not your slaves. These lakes, these woods and mountains were left us by our ancestors. They are our inheritance, and we will not part with them.
— the Ojibwa chief Minweweh, allied with Pontiac,
in an address to the British

The frontier exploded in violence. More than 2,000 settlers were massacred and 400 soldiers killed. With the single exception of Detroit, every fort west of Niagara was captured. The rebellion lasted for two years and shook the British authorities to the core. When Pontiac finally entered peace talks, he made it clear that the British would be considered only tenants on Native lands, not owners. They could occupy trading posts, but that was all. The British, of course, had no intention of keeping their word, but they agreed anyway and the Native alliance soon fell apart, as the Nations once again began bickering amongst themselves. Chief Pontiac, disillusioned and reviled, was later killed by an assassin from a rival Nation.

Biological warfare

It was at the height of the Pontiac Rebellion that General Amherst earned lasting notoriety as an early proponent of "biological warfare." Amherst hated the Indians, hated them with a passion. Like many classically trained European military men (French and British alike), Amherst felt that the Native and Canadien techniques of forest warfare were cowardly and cruel. One should face one's enemies in the open, like proper soldiers. Far from being considered heroic, the guerrilla warfare of *la petite guerre* (see Chapter 7 for a description of this type of warfare) was deemed "barbaric." This from the people who had systematically destroyed hundreds of farms and bombarded civilian targets with heavy artillery, remember.

Amherst suggested a ruthless strategy of his own for dealing with the Native rebels. Why not secretly circulate smallpox-infested blankets among the Indians? In such a manner one might yet destroy what Amherst called, "this execrable race." No one knows whether or not Amherst ever carried out these orders. The evidence suggests that he was recalled to Britain before he could put his experiment into action. But another officer, stationed at Fort Pitt, did present unruly Native leaders with a "gift" of blankets and handkerchiefs taken from a smallpox hospital, which triggered an epidemic.

For more on the British attempts at biological warfare, visit www.nativeweb. org/pages/legal/amherst/lord_jeff.html. And you'll find more on Pontiac at detnews.com/history/pontiac/pontiac.htm.

The Royal Proclamation

It was a little too late, but the Royal Proclamation of 1763 did address many of the grievances that the First Nations of the interior had expressed. Of course, by that point the Pontiac Rebellion was already boiling over.

The Proclamation (which didn't actually take effect until August 1764) established the boundaries and organization of Britain's colonies in North America. Among its key points were the following:

- ✔ The St. Lawrence region of New France became the newly created "Province of Québec," with Murray carrying on as Governor.

- ✔ The "Province of Nova Scotia" was expanded to include the remaining territories of what had once been French Acadia (in today's terms: Cape Breton, P.E.I., and New Brunswick). Nova Scotia now covered the entire Maritime region.

- ✔ But the most striking feature of the Proclamation was its approach to Native lands. To encourage a more "orderly" expansion, settlement was prohibited west of the Appalachian Mountains, and anyone wishing to trade in the interior would have to get a license first. The interior, off-limits to settlers, was reserved as "Indian territory" and would be administered through a Superintendent of Indian Affairs, located in London, whose job it was to arrange land treaties with the First Nations prior to development. This policy was designed to stabilize the still volatile Native interior and maintain the fur trade with a minimum of disruption.

The American colonies were outraged. Wasn't that one of the main reasons they had gone to war with France in the first place — to open up the Ohio Valley and the interior to stout-hearted settlers? Britain seemed to have done exactly what France had set out to do: block westward expansion. (In fact, the Proclamation was intended as a temporary measure, but that was no comfort to the expansionist-hungry land speculators — er, settlers.)

The Royal Proclamation of 1763 marked the first time that Britain gave legal recognition to prior aboriginal land rights. The key passage reads:

> *Any Lands whatever, which, not having been ceded to or purchased by Us . . . are reserved to the said Indians.*

You may be thinking, "Well, duh. If the land hasn't been formally given up, *of course* it still belongs to the original inhabitants." But the ramifications of this statement are enormous. According to the terms of 1763, any land not given up by treaty still belongs to the First Nations — *even now*. The Proclamation has become the legal cornerstone of many comprehensive Native land claims, although its validity has been challenged many times in court. Does the Proclamation include British Columbia as well, which hadn't even been discovered in 1763? What about squatters' rights? If whites have been living in an area for generations, don't they have legal claim as well? These are issues still being argued by lawyers and Native groups alike.

The bottom line: The Royal Proclamation of 1763 has had a long and often acrimonious effect on Canadian aboriginal law. And though it is not part of Canada's current Constitution, the Proclamation is referred to specifically in section 25 of the 1982 Charter of Rights and Freedoms. Which is to say, it's going to be a part of our legal landscape for a long time to come.

For more on Canadian aboriginal law, with links to the complete text of the Royal Proclamation of 1763 and other documents, go to `www.bloorstreet.com/200block/brintro.htm`.

Canada under Civil Rule

The Royal Proclamation of 1763 also sought to make Québec more attractive to English settlers by promising to introduce British law and to restrain the seigneurial system of land ownership (a semi-feudalistic system of "lords" and "worker-tenants" known as habitants — discussed in Chapter 4). Even then, very few farmer-colonists were enticed to settle in this cold, remote, northern French-speaking Catholic colony. But a handful of adventurous English-speaking merchants did set up shop in Montréal, which was still the main commercial centre of the fur trade.

The birth of English Canada?

Nothing annoys a Newfoundlander more than to hear someone speak of the years after 1760 as "the birth of English Canada." As Newfoundlanders are quick to point out, St. John's was a bustling trade centre long before Champlain ever arrived on the scene. So let me weasel out of it by saying that the years after the Conquest saw the birth of *mainland* English Canada. (Nova Scotia had a smattering of English-speaking settlements as well, mainly New England Planters who had moved in and taken over Acadian lands, as I mention in Chapter 6, but I won't get into that.)

Either way, the first "Canadians" — with an *a* not an *e* — were English-speaking merchants who came to Montréal in pursuit of fur-trade profits.

As you can imagine, tensions between the Canad*iens* and the Canad*ians* quickly surfaced. And though the English-speaking merchants were small in number, they were very vocal in their demands. Governor Murray, however, had grown to like and admire the habitants, whom he considered "perhaps the bravest and best race" on earth, and he sided with them against the increasingly shrill rhetoric of the merchants. (He described the merchant tradesmen as "the most cruel, ignorant, rapacious fanatics who ever existed.")

The Royal Proclamation had promised English law and assemblies, but Murray blithely ignored this. And although he was suspicious of the Catholic Church, he defended its role in the lives of the habitants and he worked closely with, and through, the clergy. (He even helped rig the selection of a bishop.)

Governor Murray delayed calling a meeting of the Assembly because he knew full well it would run roughshod over the wishes of the Canadiens, and he allowed French laws and customs to be followed in the courts, something that further antagonized the merchant class. They eventually took their complaints all the way to London, and Murray was recalled to face a parliamentary inquiry in 1766. He was cleared of all charges, but he never returned to Canada again.

Go to gbms01.uwgb.edu/~wisfrench/library/articles/trask/trask. htm for a survey of English attitudes toward the newly conquered Canadiens.

An ominous prediction

The American colonists were upset. They had been excluded from the interior and were increasingly annoyed by what they perceived to be the "greediness" of English merchants in Montréal. There were dark clouds on the horizon. Britain's American colonies were becoming more assertive, more aggressive — more independent. How long would they be content to remain mere colonies of the Motherland? Omens were everywhere:

- ✔ Even as the British were celebrating their Conquest of New France, James Murray had commented, "If we were wise, we would return Canada to France. New England needs something to rub up against."

- ✔ During peace negotiations, a pamphlet was circulated in Britain urging the government to *keep* the sugar islands and give back Canada. Unless there was a French threat, the pamphlet warned, the American colonies would begin demanding outright independence.

- ✔ After the Conquest, the French first minister, Duc de Choiseul, shrugged and said that, without a French enemy to unite them, the American colonies would soon start squabbling with Britain itself. The loss of the American colonies would be a far greater catastrophe for Britain than France's loss of Canada. And he was right.

Part IV
Canada: The Failed Republic?
(1766–1838)

The best thing about winning an election is that you get to make fun of the losers. In this caricature, the defeated radical reformers of Upper Canada are being mocked. Soon after, however, the colony boiled over in armed rebellion — and the laughing stopped.

In this part . . .

We look at three attempts to turn Canada into an American-style republic: the invasion of 1775, the War of 1812, and the Rebellions of 1837. Each of these failed and by the end of this tumultuous period, Canada's destiny in North America was clearly separated from that of the United States. At the same time, fur traders were pushing deeper into the vast interior of the Northwest. They would eventually cross the continent and reach the Pacific Ocean . . .

Chapter 9

Canada and the American Revolution

• •

In This Chapter

▶ The American colonies rebel against British rule — and invade Canada

▶ Thousands of Loyalist refugees arrive

▶ New Brunswick and Upper Canada (Ontario) are created

▶ Captains Cook and Vancouver explore the Pacific Coast

• •

*I*f the Conquest was the Big Bang of French-Canadian history, the American Revolution was the Big Bang of English-Canadian history. America went. Canada stayed. And that has made all the difference.

> *Who is a Canadian? Well, the political answer is that he is an American who avoided Revolution . . .*
> — scholar and theorist Northrop Frye

With the help of their former enemy, France, the Thirteen Colonies of the eastern seaboard broke free from British rule and formed a new political union: the United States of America. But it is important to remember that the American Revolution ultimately created not one country, but *two*: the shiny new Republic of the United States on the one hand, and the scattered northern colonial leftovers on the other, which would eventually be pieced together to form the Dominion of Canada.

The Pot Boils Over

The war against France and her allies had pushed Great Britain to the brink of financial ruin. New France had been captured, but at a staggering cost; the British national debt had soared to £130 million. (To put that in context, the most Britain had ever collected in taxes in a single year until then had been £15.5 million.) So why not make the North American colonies chip in?

Shouldn't they help pay for their own defence? It sounded reasonable, except for one detail: the colonies did not enjoy full British citizenship and had no delegates in London. The cry *"No taxation without representation!"* rang out in the American colonies, as Britain was denounced as "a tyranny." It was against this atmosphere of impending violence that the British government decided to revamp its policies regarding the French Canadians.

The Québec Act

In 1766, Governor Murray (whose exploits are discussed in Chapters 7 and 8) was replaced by the aristocratic Guy Carleton. But if the English merchants in Montréal thought things were going to change in their favour, they were sorely disappointed. Carleton continued along the path set by Murray. He too was sympathetic and supportive of the old French elites and often openly antagonistic toward the small Anglo minority. Nor did Carleton hold out much hope that the French Canadians would ever become assimilated and properly "anglicized." Instead, he predicted that the French in Canada would exist "to the end of time."

Carleton spent four years back in London trying to convince the British authorities to restructure the governmental framework of Québec. With the American colonies about to erupt in rebellion, it was crucial that Britain made sure their French-Canadian subjects were appeased. Britain couldn't afford to fight rebellions on two fronts, and Carleton's arguments won out. He returned to Québec with almost all of his recommendations approved.

The Québec Act of 1774 revoked most of the Royal Proclamation of 1763. The Royal Proclamation (described in Chapter 8) had promised an elected assembly of Protestant landowners, but Murray had refused to enact it. (He knew full well that an assembly that excluded 95 percent of the population would be a disaster.) The Québec Act gave up any pretext of granting Québec an elected assembly. Instead, the colony would be administered directly by the governor and a handpicked council — but one that could include French Canadians.

The Anglo merchants were outraged at this, but Carleton was no fool. He appeased them by greatly expanding the territorial boundaries of the colony. The Ohio Valley and the Great Lakes were given back to Québec, and with it the heartland of the old French fur trade.

The following are other key sections of the Québec Act:

✔ French civil law was reinstated for matters of property.

✔ English law was retained for criminal matters.

✔ The seigneurial system of land holding (which I explain in Chapter 4) was confirmed.

✔ And the Roman Catholic Church was granted rights not allowed back in Protestant Britain, including the right to raise money through tithes.

It was a masterful compromise, or a muddled mix of French customs and English business ambitions, depending on your bias. Either way, it was very, very Canadian.

The Québec Act set off a storm of protest in the American colonies. As far as they were concerned, Carleton had pandered to the French Catholics to the north and had in fact reinstated New France in all but name. Once again the Americans had been blocked from expanding into the interior. (First by "Indian Territory," as I explain in Chapter 8, and now by the greatly inflated territory of Québec.) Once again, the anger and rhetoric rose.

"Join us!"

> *By His Excellency, George Washington, Commander in Chief of the Army of the United Colonies of North America. To the inhabitants of Canada: Friends and Brethren, the unnatural Contest between the English Colonies and Great-Britain has now risen to such a height that Arms alone must decide it . . . Come then, my Brethren, unite with us in an indissoluble Union, let us run together to the same Goal.*
> — from a proclamation issued in both French and English

In 1775, the American colonies held a Continental Congress to map out their strategy against Britain. They drew up a list of "Intolerable Acts" committed by the British, and prominent on the list was Carleton's Québec Act. The Americans had invited the Canadians to send a pair of delegates to the Continental Congress, but no one took them up on their offer. Why?

Why did Canadians, both French and English, resist the lure of the American Revolution? Why didn't they swarm onto the streets as well, shouting "Liberty!" and "Down with King George!"? Well, it wasn't so much that they were loyal to Britain as they were wary of the Americans. Historians don't all agree, but the general consensus on the "un-revolutionary stance" of the Canadians is this:

✔ **English Canadians**, many of them recent arrivals from the American colonies, were delighted to have access to all that land added by the Quebec Act, so they decided to play it safe and remain more or less neutral.

> ✔ *French Canadians*, meanwhile, had been urged by their clergy and seigneurs to resist the Americans' call. And anyway, why change one foreign ruler for another? At least their British overlords were fairly benign. What would become of French-Canadian culture under the Americans? Remember, George Washington and his rebels had denounced both the Catholic Church and French law in their call to battle. The Americans were much less tolerant than were the British, and their call to French Canadians to join them in their fight against British oppression was, for the most part, ignored.

So, although the Americans confidently expected Canadians to join them in their struggle, they were sadly mistaken. (It is one of the enduring delusions of Americans that everyone — especially Canadians — secretly wishes they could become Americans. We see this pattern again and again: from the 1775 invasion to the War of 1812, to the present.)

However, it is also worth noting that Governor Carleton was just as deluded about French-Canadian sentiments. He fully expected that the habitants, grateful for the concessions of the Québec Act, would rally round the British flag and take up arms against the Americans. Carleton had assumed that his sympathetic approach to French customs and traditions had won over *les Canadiens*. And he too was sadly mistaken.

1775: The Invasion of Canada

Canada must be demolished!
— from a speech given by an American rebel leader

George Washington — wealthy slave-owner, champion of liberty, and future first president of the United States of America — decided that the time to act was now. The Continental Congress approved a full-scale invasion of Canada. The Americans firmly believed that Canadians, both French and English, were yearning to be "liberated" from British rule. The Americans also wanted to prevent Britain from using Canada as a base for strikes against the American colonies — and they knew a good land grab when they saw one. From the start, from the very moment of its inception, the United States was an expansionist country.

The capture of Montréal

In September 1775, the Americans launched a two-pronged attack:

- ✔ One column of men, 1,500 strong under the command of Richard Montgomery, would strike at Montréal.

- ✔ A second column of 1,200 men, led by a former British officer-turned-rebel by the name of Benedict Arnold, would make the difficult journey up along the Kennebec River towards Québec City.

Here was the plan: Montgomery would first capture Montréal and then march on Québec, where he would meet up with Arnold's men. Together, they would capture both the city — and Canada.

After a long seige, Montgomery captured Fort St. Jean outside Montréal, and Governor Carleton was forced to flee, abandoning the city on November 11, just a day before Montgomery's men marched in. Carleton himself had to slip past the Americans in disguise. With a rebel army now in control of Montréal, he retreated to Québec City and hastily began preparations for the final showdown.

The siege of Québec City

On December 3, the Americans converged on Québec City. Arnold's troops were in disarray. The overland wilderness route had proven near fatal, and Arnold had lost half his men to desertions, disease, and death before the first shots were even fired. His troops were half-starved and exhausted.

The French Canadians, meanwhile, were staying ruthlessly and relentlessly neutral. They cheerfully sold supplies to both sides, American and British, but refused to fight for either. The Americans were baffled. Carleton was livid. For him, the French-Canadian neutrality was a clear betrayal. He had expected 18,000 loyal habitants to present themselves for service; only a few hundred ever did. The rest just shrugged and said, "You two want to fight it out, go ahead. Me, I've got fields and livestock to tend."

Only later did French-Canadian support turn against the Americans, and that was only after the rebels tried to pay for provisions with their useless paper money. (Yes, there was a time when the Almighty American Dollar was held in disdain.) If that wasn't bad enough, the American troops began looting habitant farms and terrorizing families.

The American invasion was running out of steam. Winter had set in and December 31 was fast approaching. Many of the troops were under contracts that expired at the end of the year, so, in the middle of a howling snowstorm, in the early hours of the final day of December, Montgomery and Arnold launched an attack on Québec's Lower Town. Montgomery was shot dead in the first skirmish, but on the other side of town, Arnold's troops managed to break through a street barricade. Arnold himself was hit in the leg and carried back by his men, but the assault pushed on. To their dismay, the Americans found themselves facing a *second* barricade as British troops fired on them from above and behind. The invaders were trapped. (First rule of military strategy: Take the high ground first.)

The battle turned into a brawling street fight amid the maze of warehouses and narrow alleyways of the Lower Town. (Second rule of military strategy: Try to avoid marching into unfamiliar streets in the middle of the night during a raging blizzard.) The Americans stumbled about blindly. More than 400 were taken prisoner and as many as 100 were killed. The bodies lay silent beneath the falling snow as the paper banners they had pinned to their caps, "Liberty or Death," fluttered on the wind. Some of the bodies were discovered only in the spring, after the snows had begun to melt. The British, in comparison, had lost just three men in the battle.

The attack on Québec had been an utter failure. Although American replacement troops arrived and camped out on the Plains of Abraham for several months, when British reinforcements arrived in the spring, the Americans fled — abandoning their camps so quickly that Carleton and his men found dinners still warm and uneaten. The Invasion of Canada was over. Governor Carleton received a knighthood for his defense of Québec City, though some grumbled that he had been too timid, that he had let the Americans get away and had failed to follow up on later victories. (Like Montcalm, Guy Carleton did take a somewhat reactive approach to defense.)

The Americans withdrew from Canada completely on July 2, 1776. Two days later, the Continental Congress issued a Declaration of Independence. They were no longer rebels. They were now the self-proclaimed government of a new republic. (Benedict Arnold, however, would cross back to the British side and be denounced as a turncoat by the Americans. Even today, the name "Benedict Arnold" is a synonym for "traitor" in the U.S.) After the Declaration of Independence, there would be no more talk of "reforming" the British Empire: only of breaking it apart. After the Declaration, there could be no compromise and no negotiations — this is something worth keeping in mind when Québec separatists talk about a "unilateral declaration of independence." When that happens, there will be no turning back.

Nova Scotia: The Fourteenth Colony?

Here is a question that historians have debated for years: Why isn't Nova Scotia part of the United States? If ever there was a colony ripe to follow the Americans, it was Nova Scotia. When the Revolution began, the colony had a population of around 19,000. Fully *half* of these were settlers from the American colonies, the so-called "Yankee" Nova Scotians. The American rebels certainly expected them to join the fight. So too did the British officials! They braced for an armed uprising from their "bitter bad Nova Scotian subjects." But none came.

Aside from two fervent but ineffective rebel campaigns, one in Maugerville (near present-day Fredericton) and the other in the Chignecto Isthmus (which was quickly put down), Nova Scotia stayed loyal. Or at least, noncommittal. Which, in this case, was just as important.

Make no mistake: Nova Scotian colonists were just as embittered about British neglect as were their American cousins down the coast. And as historian Ernest Clarke has clearly shown, the majority of Nova Scotians *were* sympathetic to the rebel cause. So why didn't they join the Revolution and become "the Fourteenth Colony"? Some possible reasons:

✔ "Nova Scotia" at that time was little more than a geographic description. There was no unified sense of political identity. Most of Nova Scotia's population was scattered in small coves along the coast, without a central political capital aside from Halifax, which was a British military base. (The garrison at Halifax was a strong deterrent to armed rebellion as well.)

✔ As American ships plundered Nova Scotian settlements in the name of liberty, many colonists who had been wavering went over to the British side. (It should be noted, however, that it was the wealthier residents who were upset. The average Nova Scotian fishermen had just as much reason to fear British "press gangs," who swooped in and forced men into naval service.) The anger and resentment aimed at American privateers has been exaggerated over the years, but it did play a crucial role in Nova Scotia's decision not to join the American cause.

✔ More important was the spiritual revival that had recently swept across the colony. Dubbed "the Great Awakening," it was lead by a charismatic prophet named Henry Alline, the Apostle of Nova Scotia, who preached neutrality in the so-called War of the Georges (i.e., George Washington and King George). The apocalyptic battle between Great Britain and her Protestant colonies was a sign that the end was nigh. A new age was about to dawn, and a spiritually awakened Nova Scotia was destined to become the New Jerusalem. Alline's crusade gave the scattered settlements a sense of destiny and spiritual identity at the very time when political alliances were tearing North America apart.

> ✔ Finally, credit is due to the colony's much-maligned governor, Francis Legge. Historians have described Legge as "a bully and a fool," but on the very eve of the Revolution, he managed to undermine the grievances of many Nova Scotians by cancelling an unpopular tax and suspending compulsory militia service (two bones of contention among Nova Scotian colonists). In doing so, he took the wind out of the rebels' sails.

A Tale of Two Islands

The bland indifference of the French Canadians infuriated Governor Carleton, who apparently expected devout loyalty from a people who had been conquered by the British just 15 years earlier. But, in a way, their lacklustre support for Britain had been just as crucial. Without a widespread French-Canadian uprising, the American invasion had faltered and failed. Nova Scotia too had stayed loyal, in spite of widespread "rebel sympathies." But what of the other two northern colonies: Newfoundland and P.E.I.? Why didn't they join the American cause?

P.E.I.: "Land of the absentee landlord"

Prince Edward Island was a colony founded by absentee landlords. In 1767, the island had been divided into townships and then parcelled out to British investors in a lottery: The lots were numbered and, almost literally, "drawn from a hat." The newly awarded landowners were required to settle on their estates within ten years and pay a small annual rent to the government. But many didn't and development in P.E.I. lagged for years.

In 1769, P.E.I. (then known as "St. John's Island") was separated from Nova Scotia to create a new colony. Smaller than Cape Breton, and smaller than the Avalon Peninsula, P.E.I. was an anomaly right from the start: a feudalistic little isle with its own distinct form of colonization, unique in Canadian history. It was, in a way, the English-Canadian answer to the seigneurial system, and it set the stage for the bitter class war that followed, one that set tenants against proprietors. It would shape much of the Island's early history. (P.E.I.'s first governor, Walter Patterson, made a fortune selling and reselling land — and was later hounded out of office for it.)

The Land Question, as it was known, bedevilled the Island for more than 100 years, and only began to be resolved in 1873, after it had joined Confederation as Canada's smallest, but scrappiest, province. Still, for all the internal dissent and land-ownership issues, the Islanders themselves knew full well that they had staked a claim on Paradise Itself: the island that the Mi'kmaq called *Abegweit*, often translated as "cradled on the waves."

There are only two types of people in the world: those from the Island, and those who wish they were from the Island.

— common P.E.I. expression

During the Revolution, a pair of American privateers attempted to liberate Charlottetown, the colonial capital, by looting homes and kidnapping several officials, but for the most part, the American Revolution was little more than a sideshow as far as the Islanders were concerned. They had more important things to deal with: crops, absentee landlords, local corruption. This is still a common enough point of view on the Island. I once worked for a transportation and shipping company in P.E.I. and I remember trying to discuss the latest Québec proposals emanating from Ottawa. I was cut short by my boss, who asked, pointedly, "And what does that have to do with the price of potatoes?"

Newfoundland: "The neglected outpost"

The tale of P.E.I.'s colonial development stands in stark contrast to that of Newfoundland, where Britain had banned permanent settlements since 1698. (Only seasonal workers and merchants were "officially" allowed to reside in Newfoundland.) The British plan was to exploit the island solely as a fishing station, and it is a point worth remembering — and one that says a lot about the stubborn character of Newfoundlanders: The island was settled *in spite* of British imperial policy, not because of it. As late as 1789, the British government had declared that "Newfoundland is in no respect a British colony and is never so considered in our laws." And this was when there were already some 15,000 people settled on the island.

No other colonial group, not even the Acadians, was left so completely to fend for itself as were the Newfoundlanders . . .

— historian S. F. Wise

With no legal protection or title to their land, the Newfoundland settlers, especially in the remote outports, were easy prey for the merchants and shipowners who set up shop in St. John's. The "fishocracy," as they were known, kept Newfoundland fishermen in crippling debt, year after year, even as the cod fisheries themselves made investors rich back in Britain. And yet, in the face of terrible neglect and openly hostile British policies, Newfoundland — oddly enough — continued to attract far more people than did the "garden colony" of P.E.I., where settlement was being actively encouraged. Neglected, remote, and closer in spirit to London than Boston — is it any wonder that the political upheaval in the American colonies to the south had little impact among the Irish-Anglo colonists of Newfoundland?

The Loyalists

The American Revolution was, above all, a civil war, one that tore communities and families apart. And as the rebels gained control, they expressed their anger at those colonists who had remained loyal to Great Britain. A favourite punishment was to strip Loyalists, cover them with hot tar and feathers, and run them out of town. The Loyalists ("Tories" in American history books) were from every walk of life. Many were farmers. A few were aristocrats. All were caught between opposing forces: new world republicanism versus old world monarchy. Mob rule versus plodding British traditions. Freedom versus tyranny. Tyranny versus freedom.

In 1778, Louis XVI of France signed a "mutual defence pact" with the Americans, and what had been an internal colonial conflict now became a world war. For France it was Round Two, and the French involvement would help tip the scales once and for all. When the British army was trapped at Yorktown, Virginia, in 1781, they faced a land and sea force that was more than half French. American historians have since performed an amazing feat of magic, causing the French soldiers at Yorktown to all but vanish in a puff of smoke. But Yorktown wasn't an American victory; it was a *Franco-American* victory. In some ways, the American Revolution was simply the final chapter of the Seven Years' War.

The great exodus

> *They sacrificed everything save honour*
> > — inscription on a Nova Scotian monument to the Loyalists

After the Battle of Yorktown, the rebel forces continued to gain strength. By 1783, the British army, along with thousands of Loyalist supporters, had fallen back to New York City, their last remaining stronghold in the Thirteen Colonies. Guy Carleton, now the commander of British forces in America, managed to keep George Washington's army at bay long enough to organize a mass evacuation. Ships crowded along the docks as refugees pushed on, carrying what belongings they had managed to escape with. It was a scene of panic and sadness, Exodus and Lamentations rolled into one.

Nearly 100,000 Loyalists fled the United States during the final days of the Revolution. Of those, some 50,000 went north into what is now Canada, most of them to Nova Scotia (or "Nova Scarcity" as they wryly dubbed it), which at that time included what is now New Brunswick.

They arrived as ragged broken exiles: defeated, dismayed, but determined to start anew. In this, they embody a certain indefatigable heroic spirit. Like the Acadians before them, the Loyalists were convinced that they had been entirely in the right. It was small comfort. "Nothing but wilderness before our eyes," wrote one exhausted Loyalist refugee on the shores of the Saint John River. "The women and children did not refrain from tears."

> *I climbed to the top [of the hill] and watched the sails disappearing in the distance, and such a feeling of loneliness came over me that, although I had not shed a single tear through all the war, I sat down on the damp moss with my baby in my lap and cried.*
> — a Loyalist woman describes her feelings after arriving in Saint John (her grandson would be Leonard Tilley, a future premier of New Brunswick and a key Father of Confederation)

The town of Shelburne, Nova Scotia, founded by Loyalists, became an instant boomtown with the influx of refugees — at one point it was the largest community in British North America. But the promise soon paled, and within three years most of the settlers had moved on and Shelburne was all but deserted, a ghost town on a cold and unforgiving shore.

In an earlier book, I described the Loyalists as "the original boat people." I took a lot of flak for that, especially from the descendants of the United Empire Loyalists who wrote in demanding that I be, well, tarred and feathered. An image of the "genteel departure" of Loyalists has taken root in Canada, but nothing could be further from the truth. It was desperate and heart-wrenching, and the Loyalists were — by definition — political refugees.

When they arrived in Québec, Governor Frederick Haldimand wanted them to keep on moving. The Loyalists were notoriously anti-French, and the governor didn't want them settling among the habitants. Instead, Haldimand sent an expedition to survey the north shore of Lake Ontario as a possible area for settlement. (Among the communities created was Kingston.) Other Loyalists moved into the sparsely populated southwest region, into what is now the Eastern Townships of Québec. Since land was granted to anyone willing to swear allegiance to George III, a veritable flood of supposedly "loyal" Americans swept in. It was soon difficult to tell the difference between genuine Loyalists and mere land speculators.

Still, the impact of the Loyalists on Canadian society cannot be underestimated. They changed the dynamics and the tone of British North America forever. They were the first significant influx of English-speaking immigrants to arrive, and their influence was far greater than that of the small number of English merchants who had preceded them. Indeed, the Loyalists established English-Canadian traditions and attitudes that have lasted right up until the present, and which are so imbedded in Canadian society that they often go unnoticed. It is a conservative outlook that prefers evolution to revolution, and one that is deeply suspicious of radical solutions. In the deepest, purest sense, these values are "anti-American."

With the French Canadians, the Loyalists form indisputably the most basic historical ingredient of Canadian nationhood.

— historian Kenneth McNaught

For Loyalist songs from the time of the American Revolution and all sorts of links, including historic propaganda, both Loyalist and anti-Loyalist, visit users.erols.com/candidus/music.htm. You'll find the United Empire Loyalists' Association of Canada site at people.becon.org/~uela/uela1.htm. For a wealth of Loyalist and genealogy links, go to www.islandnet.com/~jveinot/cghl/loyalist.html.

The Black Loyalists

At the height of the American Revolution, Great Britain issued a proclamation promising freedom and sanctuary to any slaves who deserted their American masters — something that enraged the "liberty-loving" Americans. When George Washington closed in on New York, one of his demands was that slaves and "other property" be returned to their owners. But Guy Carleton refused. Blacks who had been granted freedom would not be returned to slavery. And so, the great exodus of Loyalists included approximately 3,000 free Blacks — as well as hundreds of slaves. Indeed, many Loyalists brought their slaves with them when they came to Canada.

Sadly, as the Black Loyalists soon discovered, they had won their freedom and little else. They received only begrudging support from the authorities and open hostility from the other settlers. Marginalized, attacked, harassed, and given the worst land available, many gave up entirely.

In 1792, some 1,200 Black Loyalists left Nova Scotia for the free state of Sierra Leone in West Africa — where further hardships waited. Today, Canadians take a certain misplaced pride in the history of the Black Loyalists, but it is important to remember that the Blacks who came north were not welcomed with open arms. Far from it. They were shunted aside and treated badly. The remaining Black community in Nova Scotia, with roots going back to the American Revolution, is struggling even today.

New Brunswick: The Loyalist province

The influx of Loyalists into Nova Scotia was so great that two new colonies had to be created just to handle it:

✔ **New Brunswick**, which was carved out of greater Nova Scotia in 1784.

✔ **Cape Breton Island**, which was made a separate colony in 1784 as well (returned to Nova Scotia in 1820).

What's in a name?

If you have a keen eye and a copy editor's attention to detail, you may have noticed something odd about the spelling of the two Loyalist towns mentioned in this chapter: St. Andrews and Saint John. The first is abbreviated, but the second is spelled out. Why *Saint* John and not *St.* John? They did this to avoid confusion with St. John's,

Newfoundland. Add to that Frederick Town and the city misspelled after Robert Monckton, and all three of New Brunswick's largest centres — *Saint John, Fredericton,* and *Moncton* — have had some weird quirk of spelling applied to them. Perhaps the Loyalists were in such a rush they forgot to pack a dictionary.

More than 14,500 Loyalist refugees had flooded into New Brunswick, swamping the sparse population of 3,000 that had settled in the region before the Revolution. Together with the Acadians, who had been pushed further north and along the eastern coast, the Loyalists would create in New Brunswick an odd "colony of defeated dreams."

They settled mainly along the Bay of Fundy, in coastal communities such as St. Andrews and Saint John, or else inland along the Saint John River. Among the arrivals were some 700 slaves and perhaps 300 free Blacks. Some of New Brunswick's forgotten Black pioneers may very well lie buried in unmarked graves near the second tee of the St. Andrews golf course.

Colonel Thomas Carleton, younger brother of Guy Carleton, was named the colony's first lieutenant-governor — a position he would hold for the next 30 years ("lieutenant" because his brother Guy remained governor over *all* of British North America). A capital was established at Frederick Town, later rendered Fredericton, deep inland, away from the coast and the threat of an American invasion. (To this day, the blue-collar city of Saint John resents the fact that lazy, languid Fredericton was made the capital. And the Saint John/ Fredericton rivalry must surely rank as one of the longest-running municipal feuds in Canadian history.)

The Treaty of Paris (not to be confused with the Treaty of Paris)

The American Revolution ended with the Treaty of Paris. But wait a minute, didn't we read about this already, back in Part III? Actually, there have been several Treaties of Paris. The only two you need to worry about are these:

✔ **The Treaty of Paris (1763):** Ends the Seven Years' War. New France is ceded to Britain. *Winner:* Great Britain. *Loser:* France

> ✓ **The Treaty of Paris (1783):** Ends the American Revolution. Americans win their independence. *Winner:* U.S.A. *Loser:* Great Britain.

When peace talks began, the British negotiator wondered aloud whether Great Britain should simply hand over Canada to the United States as a "peace offering." (You'll see this pattern again and again: Britain pandering to American expansionism by offering them a piece of Canada. With friends like that . . .) As it was, the entire Ohio Valley — an area to which Canada had a clear and prior claim — was happily ceded to the Americans. The border was now drawn at the Great Lakes.

During negotiations, Britain betrayed its First Nations allies shamelessly, handing over Iroquois and other Native lands — which weren't theirs to give. The Americans, in turn, promised to compensate Loyalists who had been forced to leave. (They didn't. It was a hollow promise.)

The Revolution and the Iroquois Confederacy

The Iroquois Confederacy was torn apart by the American Revolution.

> ✓ The Mohawk and most of the Seneca joined the British side.

> ✓ The Oneida and the Tuscarora supported the Americans.

> ✓ The Onondaga and the Cayuga remained neutral at first, but when American raiders invaded their territory, burning villages and destroying crops, they went over to the British side as well.

The Mohawk communities in the Montréal area (Oka, Kahnawake, and Akwesasne) wavered, but for the most part supported Britain.

Two important Mohawk leaders emerged during the Revolution: the clan mother Molly Brant and her brother, Joseph. Women played a key role in Iroquois society, and Molly Brant was instrumental in keeping the Mohawk united. Under her leadership, the Americans were blocked at the Niagara peninsula. Which is to say, if it wasn't for Molly Brant, southern Ontario might very well be part of the United States today.

Joseph Brant (also known by his Mohawk name, *Thayendanegea*), was equally effective as a war chief. It was Joseph who first rallied the Mohawk and the Seneca to the British cause, and it was Joseph who led a brilliant — and terrifying — campaign against the American interlopers who were so intent on expanding into Native territories. Although commissioned as a British officer, he continued to fight as a war chief.

He was the most notable Indian of his day, a leader in peace and war and a champion of his people.
— popular historians Philomena Hauck and Kathleen M. Snow
on the legacy of Joseph Brant

The Iroquois were not defeated in war; they were defeated in peace. Following the British capitulation, more than 2,000 Iroquois Loyalists were forced to move north into what is now Ontario. Brant led one group, mainly Mohawk, Cayuga, and Onondaga, that settled along the Grand River valley. (He chose that area because it was across the border from their former allies, the Seneca, who had decided to remain in what is now New York State.) At the Six Nations Reserve, Joseph Brant built a school, a church, and a sawmill. The community later grew into the city of Brantford.

A second group of Iroquois followed another war chief, John Deserontyon, to the Bay of Quinte on Lake Ontario. Molly Brant ended her days in Kingston. The great Iroquois Confederacy had been shattered by the American Revolution. The Great Tree of Peace had been uprooted. (For more on the Iroquois Confederacy, see Parts I and II.)

For more on Joseph Brant: www.indians.org/welker/brant.htm.

Upper Canada Is Created

In the wake of the American Revolution, Guy Carleton returned to Canada as governor. He now had a fancy title, Lord Dorchester, and a simmering resentment about the "un-loyal" French Canadians, towards whom he still nursed a grudge. Indeed, French-Canadian historians often talk about the governor in the plural, as though speaking of two different people: the "good" Guy Carleton who was in charge from 1766 to 1778, and the "bad" Lord Dorchester, from 1785 to 1795.

It's true that Carleton was indecisive during his second term as governor. And it's true that he did manage to alienate both the French Canadians and the newly established English elites, but this wasn't really his fault. He was simply the first in a long line of leaders to be caught in that permanent Canadian paradox: how to reconcile the competing goals of French and English Canada.

Note: Different dates are sometimes given for Carleton's first term as governor. Although he took over in 1766, he wasn't officially promoted to governor until 1768.

The Constitutional Act of 1791

During his absence, Lord Dorchester (the governor formerly known as Carleton) had urged the union of the remaining colonies of British North America, but it was an idea ahead of its time and nothing came of it. Instead, the Loyalist immigrants petitioned to have the large, sprawling colony of Québec (which stretched from the St. Lawrence to the Great Lakes) cut in two. This was accomplished with the Constitutional Act of 1791, which divided the colony along the Ottawa River:

✔ *Upper Canada* in the west (which would one day become the province of Ontario), would be English.

✔ *Lower Canada* in the east (which would one day become the province of Québec), would be French.

Simple, no? To think that so many of our current and ongoing national woes can be traced back to that early decision to separate Canada along cultural and linguistic lines. It is also worth noting that the terms "upper" and "lower" did not designate status. They simply referred to the upper and lower reaches of the St. Lawrence, which flows east from the Great Lakes. (When I first moved to the Maritimes, I was surprised to learn that the term "Upper Canadian" was still used, usually with a slightly negative nuance, to refer to people from southern Ontario.)

Why had the American colonies boiled over in the first place? The rebels said it was because of a lack of freedom. The British government disagreed. They felt the problem had been *too much* freedom. And so, Great Britain sought to limit the "mob rule" of democracy and rampant republicanism in its remaining colonies. To achieve this, the Constitutional Act strengthened both the power and the prestige of the governor. Major decisions would now be made directly by the governor and an un-elected council, appointed from among established families and modelled roughly on the British House of Lords. There was an elected assembly, true, but it did not have any final authority.

The colonial hierarchy of Canada was thus established:

1. Governor/Lieutenant-Governor (representing British authority);

2. Council (appointed by the governor to help him run the colony);

3. Assembly (elected; representing male landowners).

It was a strange mix of imperial and republican world views, a hodgepodge of contradictory and self-cancelling impulses, with an *appointed* council overseeing an *elected* assembly. Historian Jean-Pierre Wallot called it "a hope-inspiring but largely unworkable colonial parliamentary system, at the same time democratic and aristocratic."

RELATIONS

Keeping track?

Are you managing to keep straight the many, varied acts and proclamations that have been issued since the Conquest of 1760? Here is a quick review:

1763: **Royal Proclamation** — creates the Province of Québec — limits French laws and customs — promises an elected assembly that excludes Catholics (the governor, James Murray, refused to implement this) — limits Québec's territory to the St. Lawrence valley — acknowledges prior Native land rights.

1774: **Québec Act** *(pre-Revolution)* — revokes most of the Royal Proclamation and eases restrictions on French laws and customs — allows the seigneurial system to continue — recognizes the rights of the Catholic Church — greatly extends the territory of Québec to include the Ohio Valley and the Great Lakes

1791: **Constitutional Act** *(post-Revolution)* — divides Québec into two colonies: English Upper Canada and French Lower Canada — stops short of true representative government — sets aside land as "clergy reserves" — limits the seigneurial system to Lower Canada.

If you count the military rule of 1760–63, Canadians had now lived under *four* different constitutions in just over 30 years.

If you'd like to read these documents first-hand, here are some sites to visit:

For the original text of the 1763 Royal Proclamation, www.solon.org/Constitutions/Canada/English/PreConfederation/rp_1763.html.

For the 1774 Québec Act, original text and commentary: www.nlc-bnc.ca/confed/lowercan/equebact.htm.

For the 1791 Constitutional Act, original text and commentary: www.nlc-bnc.ca/confed/lowercan/e1791act.htm.

When it came to land ownership and civil law, Upper and Lower Canada would operate under very different rules:

- ✔ ***Upper Canada:*** private ownership and sales of land were allowed (with a seventh of all land granted to the "Protestant Clergy" — not defined, but presumed to be the Anglican Church).

- ✔ ***Lower Canada:*** the semi-feudalistic seigneurial system was reaffirmed.

The "hyperactive" Father of Upper Canada

Upper Canada was Britain's first inland colony in North America. And if Samuel Champlain was the Father of New France, then John Graves Simcoe was certainly the Father of Upper Canada.

Simcoe, an acclaimed commander of a Loyalist corps during the Revolution, was a man of grand schemes and big dreams. As the colony's first lieutenant-governor ("lieutenant" because, like Thomas Carleton in New Brunswick, Simcoe was subordinate to Guy Carleton, who was still the overriding governor of all the British mainland colonies), Simcoe saw in Upper Canada a chance to "win back" the rebellious American colonies, to show them the errors of their ways. In the backwoods north of the Great Lakes, in what would one day be the heartland of Ontario, Simcoe set about building "a little England" in exile. Simcoe was determined that Upper Canada would one day become a shining beacon to the world, a living example of the superiority of British government.

Convinced that the Americans secretly dreamed of becoming Canadian (there's a twist for you!), Simcoe began offering lands to anyone prepared to renounce the Revolution and swear loyalty to Britain. *Free land, you say?* Once again, a rush of "late Loyalists" arrived. Alas, many of Simcoe's wilder schemes never panned out. (He seems to have been under the impression that you could call towns into existence simply by plotting them on a map.) Land speculators quickly began buying out individual grants and amassing huge tracts of real estate — among them a man by the name of Hamilton.

Even worse, rather than concentrate the land allotted as clergy reserves, it was decided to distribute them throughout the newly surveyed townships, as part of a "Chequered Plan." This would later prove to be an obstacle to full development because it blocked continuous settlement and often prevented farmers from clearing adjoining lands.

But in spite of this, Simcoe achieved a remarkable amount in a short time. In just four years (1792–96), he launched an extensive system of surveys and roads and established a working political and legal structure that was indeed a model of British institutions. He also founded a garrison at a boggy river delta on the shores of Lake Ontario that he dubbed York. The Natives called it "Toronto."

> *John Graves Simcoe: the Founding Father of the biggest, richest, least-loved and most-resented city in Canada!*
> — from *Bastards & Boneheads*

Simcoe and the slaves

Here is a provocative thought: We like to think that governments are, almost by nature, corrupt. Or at the very least, amoral. We like to believe that true morality comes from below, from the common people. Truth is, throughout history there have been times when it is the government that sets the moral standard and leads the way, often against intense public protest. Case in point: slavery in Canada.

Lieutenant-Governor John Graves Simcoe had a genuine and deep revulsion towards slavery, and the landowners and Loyalists refugees that had arrived in Upper Canada had brought along hundreds of slaves. (Iroquois Chief Joseph Brant, for one, owned many slaves, and he brought them with him when he came to Canada.) In spite of this, and in the face of strong public opposition, Simcoe forced through legislation banning slavery in Upper Canada.

Peter Martin, a representative of the Black community in Upper Canada, first made the request for a ban on slavery, and Simcoe quickly agreed. When the Slave Act of 1793 was passed, Upper Canada (that is, Ontario), became the first place in North America, and indeed, in all the British colonies, to formally abolish slavery.

Because of public opposition, the legislation did not set free existing slaves — but it did bar any future slave trade. The elected assembly was outraged nonetheless, and they introduced a bill of their own to have slavery reinstated. Simcoe refused. He hemmed and hawed, and delayed passage of the bill so long that it eventually died. The lesson? It was the ruling elites that ended slavery in Canada, and not the decent common folk.

Into the Interior

With France now out of the picture, you would think that the Hudson's Bay Company would have been in its glory. The fur trade of the Northwest was all theirs now, right? Ah, but trade abhors a vacuum, and no sooner had France been removed from the picture than there was an immediate rush to take over the old inland trade routes. Scottish and American merchants hired seasoned voyageurs and picked up where the French had left off.

Three elements came together to create a very serious headache for the Hudson's Bay Company:

- ✔ French-Canadian knowledge
- ✔ Native suppliers
- ✔ Scottish financing

Montréal was the gateway to the newly revitalized fur trade, and the city boomed. The HBC, accused of "sleeping beside a frozen sea," was jolted into action. For more than 100 years they had been content to sit on the coast of the great bay and let the Native trappers come to them. Now, they were forced to go inland. They did so reluctantly at first, sending small expeditions into the James Bay lowlands to scout the area. In 1769 they sent a young employee named Samuel Hearne on an epic overland journey, across the wind-swept, barren lands of the Arctic in search of a rumoured — and elusive — vein of rich copper.

Hearne's trek, the first to reach the Arctic Ocean by land, is one of the most remarkable stories of Canadian exploration, but it unlocked very little trade for the HBC. More significant was the founding of Cumberland House in 1774 (in what is now eastern Saskatchewan), the very first inland trading post in HBC history.

Instead of fast-running canoes, the HBC used larger, flat-bottomed boats designed by employees from the Orkney Islands of Scotland. Named "York boats" after the trading post where they were first tested, they could be sailed *or* rowed and could carry twice the load of the largest freight canoe. The York boats had a distinct "Viking" look about them, and for good reason: the Orkney Islanders are of mixed Nordic and Scots backgrounds. By using canoe relays and York boats, the HBC was able to expand its operation inland — especially along the North Saskatchewan River.

The HBC faced other challenges as well, the most notable being the fact that their employees worked for a salary. The Nor'westers (see below) were on commission, and as such, were far more motivated in their search for furs.

You can read Samuel Hearne's own account of his remarkable journey at `web.idirect.com/~hland/sh/title.html`.

The North West Company

The American Revolution had a subtle but profound effect on the development of Canada's Northwest as well. With war raging in the south, the Canadian fur trade was forced to shift further north. By 1778, Peter Pond, a Montréal trader originally from Connecticut, had pushed all the way into the woodlands of what is now northern Alberta and established a trading post near Lake Athabasca, on the waterways that flowed into the Arctic. This in turn opened up the deep north to the fur trade, an area so rich it was dubbed "the New Peru."

The following year, fur traders in Montréal organized a joint venture dedicated to expanding into the Arctic and as far as the Pacific. They called themselves the North West Company, and it signalled a new era in the fur trade: daring, dashing, and often violent. By 1800, the Nor'westers had established what historian S. F. Wise called "the first transcontinental economic system in Canadian history."

Jay's Treaty

After the American Revolution, tensions shifted to the frontier. According to the terms of the Treaty of Paris, Great Britain had promised to abandon its forts in the Ohio Valley. But on the pretext that the Americans hadn't lived up to their side of the bargain by not compensating Loyalists for their losses,

Britain refused to leave. The matter wasn't settled until 1794, when the Jay's Treaty was signed. In it, Britain finally agreed to evacuate its western forts. The treaty also guaranteed Natives the right to cross the border without having to pay duty. It is this treaty that the Mohawk invoke today in their clashes with the government. Canada Customs says they are smuggling. The Mohawk say they are exercising their ancestral and legal rights.

"Un homme du nord!"

With the Americans now to the south, Canadian fur traders were forced to confine their activities to the Northwest. Every spring, as the snows melted and the ice broke, flotillas of heavy freight canoes left Lachine, near Montréal, loaded with trade goods.

The voyageurs, paddling eighteen hours a day at times, fought their way upstream along the Ottawa River and then onto the sea-like expanse of Georgian Bay and Lake Huron, with their terrifying squalls and sudden storms. At the headwaters of Lake Superior lay Grand Portage, a gruelling 14-kilometre cross-country trek, which the voyageurs made while lugging heavy packs and canoes. At the other end, they rendezvoused with the even more rugged *hommes du nord*, "men of the north," traders who wintered inland.

A rough, rollicking frontier community had evolved at the rendezvous point of Grand Portage. The men of the north sneered at the Montréal voyageurs who had to run home before winter set in, and as the liquor flowed the taunts would start. The northmen liked to pound their chests and declare, *"Je suis un homme du nord!"* The hardworking Montréal men would then punch them in the face. It was all good fun, after which the two would go their separate ways. The voyageurs would return to Montréal in canoes filled with pelts. The northmen would head west in lighter, smaller canoes, back to their distant trading posts, weighed down with the next season's trade goods.

Go to `www.civilization.ca/membrs/canhist/canoe/can00eng.html` for portraits of the great canoes of the fur trade.

On the Pacific Coast

The Pacific Northwest was among the last major coastlines in the world to be explored by Europeans.

The first to arrive was Vitus Bering, a Danish sea captain working for the Russian Czar. Bering crossed the narrow strait that bears his name in 1741 and reached the islands off the coast of Alaska. Bering himself died on the journey, but the survivors made it back with seal and otter pelts in tow and within a few years the Russians were building trading posts in Alaska.

Now, it just so happens that the Spanish had claimed the entire Pacific Ocean for themselves. They were down in Mexico, but when they heard rumours that the Russians had crossed over, they decided to send an expedition of their own to the Pacific Northwest. By 1774, the Spanish had reached the islands now known as the Queen Charlottes, where they met and traded with the Haida who lived there. Over the next few years, the Spanish would eventually travel all the way to the cold windswept shores of Alaska. It was a far cry from Aztec gold and the silver mines of the south.

James Cook

First the Russians. Then the Spanish. And now the British.

Even as the American Revolution raged on the east coast, the British sent an expedition to the Pacific. In 1778, the renowned navigator James Cook began charting the western shores of Vancouver Island (which he thought was part of the mainland). Captain Cook had already discovered Hawaii, which he dubbed the Sandwich Islands, and had explored Australia and New Zealand. As a young man, he had helped navigate Wolfe's armada through the tricky waters of the St. Lawrence.

When Cook first encountered the Mowachaht people, he asked them the name of their land. Thinking he wanted directions around a smaller island, they replied *"Nutka, itchme"* (roughly: "Go around that way.") Cook, mistaking it for a place name, dubbed the region "Nootka." The name stuck and was eventually applied to the Mowachaht themselves.

So warm was the welcome he received that Cook nicknamed the inlet "Friendly Cove." Cook traded with the Nootka people for sea otter pelts and then, after probing further north along the Alaskan shore, sailed back to Hawaii — where he was killed in a dispute with the Polynesian islanders. But Cook's crew made it back to China, where they sold the sea otter furs for a small fortune. Word soon got out, and the great coastal fur trade was under way. Like the beaver in the Northwest, the sea otter, with its luxurious pelt, was a highly valuable commodity. And, like the beaver, the sea otter would become a victim of fashion — hunted to the brink of extinction. Unlike the beaver, however, the sea otter has never fully recovered from the onslaught.

You can find more on Cook's encounter with the Nootka at www.hallman. org/indian/cook.html. For more on the life and explorations of James Cook, with links to several informative sites, visit www.pacificcoast.net/ ~regent/cookbio.html.

The Nootka confrontation

In 1788, an English trader by the name of John Meares arrived in Friendly Cove and set up shop. The chief Maquinna was on hand to meet him and he agreed to let Meares build a warehouse/trading post on the shore — something that Meares later insisted was a writ of ownership.

When the Spanish heard about this, they threw a fit and immediately dispatched two ships of their own under the command of the hotheaded Captain Esteban Martínez to confront the British upstarts at Nootka Sound. (With the growing international tensions, it really couldn't be called "Friendly Cove" anymore). And no sooner had the Spanish arrived than in sailed an *American* ship. Martínez had had enough. Disregarding the Americans, who weren't considered much of a threat, Martínez seized one of Meares' vessels. He then began constructing a pair of island fortresses.

On June 24, 1789, Captain Martínez took "possession" of Nootka Sound and the entire Pacific Northwest in the name of the Spanish king. No one bothered to consult the people who were already living there, of course. (And anyway, it was a trade monopoly Spain wanted, not land.)

More British ships sailed blithely in, unaware of the Spanish presence, and one by one they were boarded and captured. The British had been planning to build a fort of their own, and had brought in a shipload of hired Chinese tradesmen. The Spanish captured them and immediately put them to work building their fortresses instead. It was an incredible moment in Canadian history: British prisoners, Spanish swashbucklers, Chinese workers, and baffled Natives, with American traders lurking in the background, all jostling for position on a remote cove on the far side of Vancouver Island.

Back in Europe, an all-out war now loomed between Britain and Spain. Frantic negotiations brought about a last minute compromise: the Nootka Convention of 1790, which was a restraining order of sorts. British ships would be allowed to trade along the Pacific Coast, but only if they kept a safe distance from Spanish bases. The Spanish, however, ignored this ruling and continued to exclude British traders entirely. Spanish troops commanded by Don Pedro Alberni were brought in, and the sabre-rattling continued.

Vancouver and Quadra

Spain now had a clear military presence in the Pacific Northwest, and by 1792 they were building another base on the coast. Renewed negotiations between Spain and Britain began at Nootka Sound:

✔ Spain was represented by the commander of the Spanish Pacific Fleet, Juan Francisco de la Bodega y Quadra.

✔ Great Britain was represented by Captain George Vancouver, who had sailed with Cook and was even now surveying the Pacific Coast.

The two men had a great respect and admiration for each other, but in spite of this negotiations did not go smoothly. Both sides claimed the same trade zones. Neither was willing to budge, and in the end the two men agreed to disagree. Vancouver would spend the next two years conducting a thorough and meticulous survey of the Pacific Coast, and he named the vast island "Quadra's and Vancouver's Island" in this spirit of co-operative disagreement. (Vancouver was the first to realize that it was in fact an island, something Cook had missed.) It would later be shortened to simply Vancouver's Island.

The showdown over Nootka was eventually settled back in Europe, when yet another Convention was drawn up and signed in Madrid in January 1794. It established Nootka as an "open port." Both Spain and Britain could trade there. They would compete alongside each other for Native furs, but neither side could interfere with the other, nor could they build a permanent base.

Spain, overextended in the New World, eventually withdrew from the Pacific Northwest entirely, leaving behind a wealth of Spanish place names and not much else. The British stayed on. Although they had recently lost their Atlantic seaboard colonies in the American Revolution, they had now staked a claim on the Pacific. And their next showdown would not be with Spain, but with the United States. During the ten years that followed the 1794 Convention, more than 50 American ships would arrive on the Pacific Coast to trade in furs, compared to just 9 vessels from Britain.

The age of the fast-running clipper ships was at hand. Sea otter pelts were loaded up and taken to China in these high-rigged vessels, where they were traded for silks, porcelain, and spices. A single trip could make a man his fortune, and soon the coasts were swarming with vessels of all nations — though the Americans, dubbed "Boston men," were clearly becoming the dominant presence. By 1825, the sea otter had been almost entirely wiped out.

The village of Gold River, B.C., has a Web site (www.island.net/~goldriv/index1.html) that includes some information on the history of the Spanish as well as the First Nations in Nootka Sound. For more on the explorations of the Northwest Coast, with biographic summaries of the main players from Bering to Quadra to Vancouver, go to mmbc.bc.ca/source/schoolnet/exploration/ee_nwc.html. At www.hallman.org/indian/.www.html you'll find a history of the Northwest Coast.

Chapter 10

The War of 1812

In This Chapter

▶ The North West Company pushes overland to the Pacific

▶ The U.S. declares war on Great Britain — and promptly invades Canada

▶ The Americans are pushed back and defeated

▶ Violence erupts in the Selkirk Colony of what is now Manitoba

*T*he War of 1812 was Canada's War of Independence. For the British, it was an annoying distraction at a time when it was fighting the French Emperor Napoleon. To the Americans, it was a war of conquest. To the Canadians, one of survival. Between 1812 and 1814, Canada won the right to *not* be American.

> *Perhaps the most striking thing about Canada is that it is not a part of the United States.*
>
> — historian J. Bartlet Brebner

The Lead-up to War

What goes around, comes around. Louis XVI, having aided and abetted the Americans in their republican revolution, now found himself swept away by a revolution of his own, which erupted in France in 1789.

Under the cry of *"liberty, equality, fraternity!"* French revolutionaries abolished the monarchy, arrested Louis XVI on charges of treason, and attempted to establish an American-style republic in Europe. (I have friends from Paris, and they hate it when I point out that the French Revolution was modelled largely upon the American one. They insist it was simply "a coincidence.") The democratic zeal didn't last very long, however. Louis and his wife Marie Antoinette had their heads lopped off by a guillotine. A ruthless little general named Napoleon seized power and launched France on a European war of conquest.

What is important to realize, from a Canadian perspective, is this:

- ✔ The French Revolution led to the Napoleonic Wars of 1793–1815.
- ✔ The War of 1812 was the North American phase of this conflict.

The Louisiana Purchase

Spain had been forced to return the vast Louisiana territory to France in 1801. Two years later, Napoleon, eager to raise capital and wanting to concentrate his resources on conquering Europe, agreed to sell the entire region — the very heart of a continent — to the Americans.

For $15 million, the United States acquired land stretching from the Gulf of Mexico to the Great Lakes basin. The U.S. had doubled in size and extended its western borders all the way to the Rockies. New Orleans, the Cajuns, and the entire Mississippi river system now belonged to the Americans. It is a lesson worth noting. When French-Canadian historians insist that the Conquest of New France was a disaster, they need to be reminded: It could have been worse. Much worse.

> *It is foolish to waste our time in expressing fruitless regrets and unattainable desires. . . . If the Treaty of Paris had saved us for France, what would have become of us? Assuming we would have escaped the bloody Reign of Terror [of the French Revolution], it is more than probable that Napoleon would have sold us to the Americans without even consulting us, as he did with Louisiana.*
> — editor and Québec nationalist Henri Bourassa in 1902

Governor Craig's "Reign of Terror"

In Lower Canada, the government had become divided along cultural and linguistic grounds: The governor and his ruling council were English, the elected assembly was primarily French (and as I point out in Chapter 9, the assembly did *not* have final authority). The council often overruled the assembly, and thus, the new French-Canadian elite — lawyers, doctors, artisans, surveyors, and wealthy farmers — found themselves blocked from having any real power. They formed the *parti canadien* to fight for a more responsive system of government. Specifically, they wanted the governor to be required to choose his council from among the majority members of the elected assembly. In 1806, the party launched a newspaper, *Le Canadien,* to further their cause. Although denounced as dangerous subversives, what they were asking for was, essentially, the same parliamentary rights enjoyed by citizens in Britain.

Governor James Craig responded with an iron fist. He branded the members of the *parti canadien* "demagogues" and "desperadoes," and he dissolved their assembly. Twice. During the elections of 1810, Craig seized the presses of *Le Canadien* and had the editors and distributors imprisoned, all without fair trial or warning. If Craig thought this would crush the growing demands of Canadian democracy, he was wrong. The *parti canadien* was re-elected, stronger than ever, and a weary and exhausted Craig asked to be recalled. With war now looming, it was just as well.

James Craig was replaced in 1811 by the bilingual and more conciliatory George Prevost. Prevost called off Craig's campaign, he appointed Canadians to the courts and the militia, and within months had calmed things down. In this, Prevost played a key role in ensuring French-Canadian loyalty in the war with the United States that followed.

Overland to the Pacific

The contest between Canada and the United States would cross the continent and be played out on the Pacific Coast as well, where both sides had staked a claim at the mouth of the Columbia River — a major trade route into the western interior. The Canadians arrived first, pushing their way overland.

They were led by three determined men.

Alexander Mackenzie: "From Canada, by land"

A dashing Scottish Nor'wester by the name of Alexander Mackenzie was the first person to cross North America above Mexico. He made it on his second try. The first time he tried to reach the Pacific, he took a wrong turn and ended up at the Arctic Ocean instead. (The river he travelled down now bears his name, though he himself called it the "River of Disappointment.")

Undaunted, Mackenzie went back to Britain and boned up on his navigational skills, and in 1793, he tried again. Relying heavily on voyageurs and Native guides, Mackenzie followed the Peace River into the Rockies and then portaged, hiked, and paddled his way through an endless sea of mountains and down to the Pacific itself. After spending a terrifying night under the threat of imminent attack by the warlike Bella Bella, Mackenzie beat a hasty retreat, but not before he dabbed his name and the date on a large boulder. It was the most famous graffiti in Canadian history:

Alexander Mackenzie, from Canada, by land, 22nd July 1793

Mackenzie later left the North West Company and joined a breakaway band of disgruntled traders who called themselves the "New North West Company" (better known as the XY Company, after the marks they used to identify their goods). The XY Company was formed in 1797 and began a cutthroat rivalry with the NWC. Mackenzie joined three years later, after which it became known, unofficially, as "Alexander Mackenzie & Co." (In 1804, the company was reconciled with the North West Company, and they again focused their competition against the Hudson's Bay Company.)

Simon Fraser: "Hell's Gate"

When the American president, Thomas Jefferson, read about Mackenzie's overland trek to the Pacific he knew he had to act fast to cut off those brash Canadian Nor'westers from taking over the entire west coast. So Jefferson dispatched a pair of explorers, Lewis and Clark, to travel to the mouth of the Columbia River and raise the U.S. flag. The North West Company, in turn, sent in an expedition under Simon Fraser to discover the headwaters of the Columbia and then follow it down to the sea. Unfortunately, Fraser followed the wrong river (the one that would later bear his name), and found himself up against the Hell's Gate rapids. Fraser and his band managed to claw their way through the canyon, but it was a harrowing experience — "We had to pass where no human being should venture," he later wrote — and it became clear that this river route was of no real commercial use.

David Thompson: "Just a little too late"

A short, stocky Welshman, David Thompson *twice* came across the mountain source of the Columbia River — one of the great trade quests of his day — only to take a wrong turn both times. In the summer of 1811, he finally made it. Thompson stumbled upon the upper Columbia again, and this time he followed it all the way down to the sea . . . only to find a U.S. flag fluttering in the breeze when he arrived. Members of the American Fur Company, under the powerful mogul John Jacob Astor, had sailed in and built a fort of their own. Some of the building's logs still had green branches attached. Thompson had arrived just a few weeks too late.

David Thompson was a master mapmaker. Described as "the greatest land geographer who ever lived," he charted the tortuous riverways of the B.C. interior and built a series of important trading posts, but died unknown and in poverty. (Thompson is also credited with the first recorded sighting of a UFO in Canadian history, when he described a "large blob" flying through the air while camped out near a frozen lake in Manitoba in 1792.)

The Discoverers Web (www.win.tue.nl/~engels/discovery/alpha.html) has links to bios on Mackenzie, Fraser, and Thompson. You'll find information on the Gwich'in people that Mackenzie encountered during his voyage to the Arctic Ocean at www.civilization.ca/membrs/archaeo/nogap/plgwich.htm.

"Free trade and sailors' rights!"

With Britain bogged down in Europe fighting Napoleon, the Americans saw their chance at capturing Canada — and they took it. Not that they didn't have genuine grievances:

- ✔ Britain had placed France under a naval blockade, preventing it from conducting trade with neutral nations. The United States, as the major "neutral trader," was hurt by this. Even worse, using the blockade as an excuse, Britain had captured nearly 400 American vessels, often within sight of the U.S. coast.

- ✔ Adding insult to injury, the British Navy had also asserted its right to board foreign ships and press any British citizens they found (sailors, deserters, or traders) into military service. The Americans considered this an affront to their autonomy and an insult to their flag, but the British didn't care. In 1807, they fired upon a U.S. vessel, the *Chesapeake*, killing several men, before boarding the ship and arresting four so-called deserters — two of whom were American citizens. Britain later apologized, and released the Americans, but the damage had been done.

Add to that the Americans' suspicions that Britain was aiding and encouraging Native attacks along their Western frontier, and you have all the justification you need. Under the battle cry, "Free trade and sailors' rights," the United States of America decided to strike at Canada.

A mere matter of marching

Strangely enough, American history books usually portray the United States as the underdog in 1812. Why? Because they were up against the might of the British Empire. But that isn't entirely accurate. Great Britain was tied up in Europe, and Canada lay poorly defended and exposed. The Americans knew this, and for all the glorious cries of sailors' rights and free trade, the War of 1812 was basically a land grab. Consider the real odds:

- ✔ Population of the United States: 7.5 million.
- ✔ Population of Upper Canada: less than 80,000.

Indeed, the entire population of the British North American colonies combined was less than half a million. How could the Americans possibly lose? Thomas Jefferson, now retired, advised President Madison that the conquest of Canada would be "a mere matter of marching." Henry Clay, Speaker of the U.S. House of Representatives, boasted that the Kentucky militia alone would be enough to deliver Canada. Again, wasn't it the dream of every Canadian to one day become a citizen of the United States?

We can take Canada without soldiers. We have only to send officers into the provinces and the people . . . will rally round our standard.
— William Eustis, U.S. Secretary of War

And so, on June 18, 1812, the United States of America declared war on Great Britain — and made immediate plans for the Conquest of Canada. Only the New England states had been opposed. (The New Englanders would continue to trade with their Maritime cousins throughout the conflict.)

The War in Upper Canada

Upper Canada certainly looked like easy pickings. The original Loyalist population had been swamped by an influx of American settlers whose true loyalty remained in doubt. Would the newcomers take up arms for the American cause? Or for Canada? These questions hung in the air like a dark cloud. Fortunately (for Canada), the U.S. forces were very poorly organized: Many militia groups refused to cross state lines, and rather than concentrate their attack, the Americans opted for a scattered, multi-pronged approach. Even worse, they were about to come up against two master tacticians.

Brock and Tecumseh: "Walking tall"

Most of the people have lost all confidence. I however speak loud and look big.
— General Isaac Brock, one of the saviours of Upper Canada

In Upper Canada, Isaac Brock, the man in charge of defending the colony from the American invaders, was a brilliant strategist and an inspiring leader. In the opening days of the war, he would make all the difference.

While some historians denounce the theory that "great men," make much difference to history, it is hard to see how Upper Canada would have resisted invasion without Isaac Brock.
— historian Desmond Morton

Brock was determined to take the battle to the enemy. He wanted to counter-attack relentlessly and keep the Americans off balance. In this, Canada's Native allies would play a crucial role.

Led by the great Shawnee chief Tecumseh and his shamanistic half-brother, Tenskwatawa, a great pan-Native alliance took shape. It brought together a dozen different Nations: Shawnee, Ottawa, Delaware, Miami, Wyandot, Chippewa, Fox, Potawatomi, Dakota, Kickapoo, Sauk, and Winnebago. All were united in a common goal:

✔ To stop American expansion into Native territory,

✔ and to secure a sovereign First Nations homeland in the interior, west of the Ohio River and stretching from the Great Lakes to Florida. It was territory that the United States of America now insisted it "owned."

The First Nations Alliance fought alongside the British for tactical, not loyalist reasons.

Isaac Brock held Tecumseh in high regard, calling him "a sagacious and gallant warrior." Tecumseh, in turn, admired Brock's fierce determination. (Legend has it that when they first met face-to-face, Tecumseh turned to his men and said, "This is a *man*!") Together — as friends, allies, and equals — the British general and the Shawnee chief would save Upper Canada.

"Join us!" (Part two)

On July 12, 1812, American General William Hull marched 2,500 men out of the fortified walls of Detroit and into Upper Canada. The invasion had begun. Hull, confident that the Canadians would flock over to the American side, issued a public proclamation that read, in part:

> *Inhabitants of Canada! The army under my command has invaded your country, and the standard of the United States now waves over the territory of Canada. To the peaceable, unoffending inhabitants, it brings neither danger nor difficulty. I come to protect, not to injure you. The United States offers you Peace, Liberty, and Security. Your choice lies between these and War, Slavery, and Destruction. Choose then, but choose wisely . . .*

The capture of Detroit

The Americans didn't know what hit them. At their post on Mackinac Island, at the northern tip of Lake Huron, they woke up to find themselves surrounded by a band of British regulars, French-Canadian voyageurs, and some 300 Native warriors. The fort surrendered without a shot being fired.

Meanwhile, in the south, Brock turned his attention on Detroit. Having issued his brave proclamation, General Hull was now huddled behind his garrison walls. The Americans were terrified of the Natives, and Brock and Tecumseh used this to full psychological advantage. The British general sent a fake communiqué along enemy lines advising his superiors that he needed "only" 5,000 more Native warriors for the final assault on Detroit. The message was duly captured and handed over to Hull, who almost choked in fear.

Tecumseh then marched his men along the edge of the woods, just out of range but in full view of the American garrison. The warriors slipped into the woods and then hurried around to join the end of the line. They then marched past again. Tecumseh sent the same men by three times and the Americans never caught on. Their estimates of Tecumseh's forces ranged as high as 3,000 warriors. In fact, Tecumseh had fewer than 600 men on hand.

The Shawnee chief urged Brock to attack Detroit immediately, while the Americans were still afraid, and Brock agreed. His officers were aghast. They reminded Brock that the Americans outnumbered them by almost 1,000 men and were well entrenched and well stocked with munitions. But Brock was adamant. The attack must go ahead. "We are committed to a war," he reminded his men, "in which the enemy will *always* be our superior in numbers and ammunition."

In fact, no attack was needed. General Hull was so undermined by fears of an Indian massacre that he caved in almost immediately. All it took were a few cannon shots and a threatening ultimatum from Brock. The Americans surrendered Detroit on August 16, 1812, and Tecumseh and Brock rode in, side by side, as the Stars and Stripes were lowered. Inside they found a wealth of weapons and supplies. General Hull, once a hero in the War of Independence, went home to face a court martial on charges of cowardice.

Fort Dearborn (now Chicago) had also fallen, and with the capture of Detroit and Mackinac, the Americans suffered the greatest loss of territory in their nation's history. The entire western frontier had been taken, and the brutal massacre of American prisoners by Native warriors following the fall of Fort Dearborn sent shock waves across the U.S. In Upper Canada, it was a different story. Spirits soared. Volunteers signed up for the militia. And the Iroquois (who had been neutral up until then) now joined the British side, led by the Mohawk leaders John Norton and John Brant, son of Joseph. (You'll find more on Joseph Brant in Chapter 9.)

Brock died a few months later, leading a foolhardy but heroic charge up the Queenston Heights on the Canadian side of the Niagara River. Tecumseh died the following year, at a bitterly fought battle at Moraviantown (near present-day Chatham). As the U.S. Cavalry fell upon them in waves, the British broke and ran. But Tecumseh stayed and fought to the death. The Americans then went among the bodies, taking scalps and mutilating corpses. When they found what they mistook to be Tecumseh's body, they skinned it for souvenir razor straps to take back to Kentucky.

The capture of York (Toronto)

By November 1812, the Americans had gained control of Lake Ontario. The following spring a fleet of American vessels landed at York, the village capital of Upper Canada, and more than 1,700 American soldiers poured ashore. British troops trying to stop them were slaughtered on the beaches and the rest of the garrison, under the command of Roger Sheaffe, fled — but not before setting the York munitions building on fire. (They didn't want their stock of gunpowder falling into American hands.) The deafening explosion rocked the town, sending a mushroom-shaped cloud skyward. Dozens of Americans died in the explosion, including their leader, General Zebulon Pike. In retaliation, the American troops spent the next few days looting and pillaging the town. They burned the assembly buildings to the ground and made off with the parliamentary mace as a war trophy.

Roger Sheaffe had been the true, unsung hero at Queenston Heights, taking over when Brock died and leading the British to a brilliant tactical victory. Now, he was the scapegoat of York. Never mind that the American force was overwhelming, and that Sheaffe had both denied them munitions and had lived to fight another day. The ruling elite of York, led by the dour and self-righteous minister Dr. John Strachan, denounced Sheaffe's "cowardice."

Laura Secord: "The Americans are coming!"

Don't be fooled: The real Laura Secord looked nothing like the frail Southern belle that adorns boxes of Laura Secord Chocolates. (Not only do the chocolates have no connection to the Secord family, but the company is now owned by Americans.) The real Laura Secord was a pioneer and a mother of five whose husband had been wounded and left for dead during the Battle of Queenston Heights. Laura had gone to the battlefield, found him, and taken him home. She was nursing her husband back to health when the Americans arrived and took command of the Secord homestead.

Laura overheard the officers discussing their plans for a surprise attack at Beaver Dams, and the following morning she set off on an epic 32-kilometre trek across the war zone to warn the British. When she finally climbed the Niagara Escarpment, her feet were bleeding and night had fallen. Mohawk sentries took her to see Lieutenant James FitzGibbon. Tipped off by Laura Secord, FitzGibbon set up an ambush at Beaver Dams (now Thorold, Ontario) on June 24, 1813. The Mohawk war cries frightened the Americans into surrender, and FitzGibbon and his men took almost 500 Americans prisoner, including the commander. "Not a shot was fired on our side by any but the Indians," wrote FitzGibbon, approvingly. "They beat the American attachment into a state of terror." At Stoney Creek, two weeks earlier, the American invasion had been stopped. At Beaver Dams it was turned back.

Visit the Heritage Minutes site (www.heritageproject.ca/media/minutes/expanded/lsecor.htm) for more on Laura Secord.

The War in Lower Canada

Although the war was fought mainly in Upper Canada, and particularly along the Niagara Peninsula, the Americans also invaded Lower Canada. In the autumn of 1813, the Americans launched a two-pronged attack against Montréal:

- ✔ The first would strike north from New York, along Lake Champlain and the Chateauguay River.

- ✔ The second would come in from the west, along the Great Lakes and the St. Lawrence.

Both attacks failed: the first in a Canadian woodland ambush, the second in an open-field, European-style engagement. And French Canada was saved.

The Battle of Chateauguay

Chateauguay is remembered as a true *Canadian* victory, the British having played no part in it. Led by the gallant Charles de Salaberry, a small band of French Canadians, along with English-Canadian and Mohawk allies, turned back an American invasion force 4,000 strong. Salaberry had positioned his men well, behind log barricades on a ravine overlooking the Chateauguay River. Hidden in the forests were men blowing horns and making a racket to create the impression of a much larger force lying in wait. The Americans were cut down as they tried, in vain, to break past. Convinced that this was just the advance guard of Canadians, they eventually broke and ran. Chateauguay was a key victory, and one that has since gained an almost mythical appeal: French, English, and Native Canadians, working together to push back an American invasion. Legend even has it they camouflaged themselves amid the forests with red maple leaves.

For the Parks Canada Battle of Chateauguay site, go to parcscanada.risq.qc.ca/chateauguay/en/index.html.

The Battle of Crysler's Farm

The second American strike force, approaching from the west along the St. Lawrence, fought a very different sort of battle — but lost just the same. As the rough Kentucky general, James Wilkinson, advanced towards Montréal, the redcoats were in hot pursuit. And at a boggy field near present-day Cornwall, the British and Canadians forces under Colonel Joseph Morrison finally caught up to the Americans and faced off against them in a classic "thin red line." (Actually, it was drab and drizzly that day and many of the redcoats were hidden under grey overcoats, but "the thin grey woollen line" doesn't have quite the same ring.) The Americans had run up against a wall. They flung themselves against the Canadians and the Brits, but failed to break through. The attack eventually crumbled, and the Americans retreated.

Along the Seacoast

In Newfoundland, the War of 1812 was a distant conflict. They had more immediate issues worth fighting for. A crusading surgeon named William Carson was spearheading a campaign to establish civil government. With its growing population and a bustling capital at St. John's, Newfoundland could no longer be considered "a transient outpost." Carson, along with the St. John's merchant Patrick Morris, would eventually win the battle, and in 1817, the British government finally recommended a year-round governor for Newfoundland and, later, full colonial status.

In the Maritime colonies, the war was closer than in Newfoundland, but the region still felt more secure than Upper or Lower Canada: The British Navy patrolled their shores and the garrison at Halifax deterred any notions of a full-scale Yankee invasion. If anything, the Maritime colonies experienced an economic boom during the war years. Shipbuilding, the fisheries, the timber trade: all flourished. The export of square-hewn timbers to Britain soon surpassed even the fur trade of Lower Canada, and times were good. Mind you, the East Coast did see its share of action during the War of 1812.

Shannon and the Chesapeake

You remember the *Chesapeake*? The ship the British once fired on and then boarded to round up deserters? Well, the *Chesapeake* was back. The U.S. ship was being refitted and re-armed in Boston harbour when the British frigate *Shannon* sailed into view. The captain of the *Shannon*, Philip Broke, sent a formal challenge to his American counterpart, James Lawrence:

> As the Chesapeake *appears now ready for sea, I request you will do me the favour to meet the* Shannon *with her and try the fortune of our respective flags. Choose your terms but let us meet.*

And on June 1, 1813, the *Chesapeake* sailed out of Boston to meet the *Shannon* in battle. It was an epic fight. The two ships came crashing in alongside each other, and Broke's men swarmed onto the American ship's deck. It was less a battle than it was a brawl, the men fighting with sabres and muskets alike. Lawrence was killed, and Broke was seriously wounded. But the Nova Scotian seaman William Wallis went on to capture the American ship and tow her back to Halifax as a trophy. When the victorious *Shannon* appeared, a great cheer went up from the docks.

Burn, Washington! Burn!

Why is the White House white? Because we burned it, that's why. Or at least, the British did. In August, 1814, and in direct retaliation for what the Americans had done in York, the British captured and burned Washington, D.C. The attack came as a complete surprise, and President Madison and most of his defending army ran away so fast that the battle became known, sarcastically, as "a race." The British spent the next two days ransacking the U.S. capital and torching public buildings. When the President's own residence was badly damaged and the walls scorched, the building was hastily rebuilt and the exterior painted over with whitewash. It became known as "the white house." After Washington, D.C., the British then sailed north and attacked the city of Baltimore. (It was during this attack, with "the bombs bursting in air," that a young American lawyer wrote the words to the song that would eventually become the U.S. national anthem.)

Unfortunately, in spite of its spectacular successes along the Atlantic coast, the British suffered a crushing defeat inland, on Lake Champlain. Governor George Prevost led a full-scale attack against Plattsburgh but lost his nerve when American ships blocked his advance. It was a complete fiasco, with Prevost beating an embarrassing retreat. As more than one historian has observed, if Prevost had used his superior firepower properly, much of what is now upper New York State would belong to Canada.

The Battle of New Orleans

You know that annoying American song about how they fired their guns and the British "started runnin'"? They're referring to the Battle of New Orleans, which occurred on January 8, 1815. (Of course, we could sing our own version based on the burning of Washington, D.C. "We fired our guns and the President started runnin' — and so did his Cabinet, the officers, and most of the army.") Yes, the Americans did indeed win the Battle at New Orleans, and in a very convincing manner, under the command of Andrew Jackson. But the battle itself occurred *after* the war had ended. A treaty had been signed at the Belgian city of Ghent on Christmas Eve, 1814, but word hadn't reached North America yet. In short, the Battle of New Orleans was a grand victory that meant very little — not that I want to rain on anyone's parade.

See Table 10-1 for a comprehensive timetable of the War of 1812.

Table 10-1		A Timetable of the War of 1812
1812	June 18	United States declares war on Great Britain
	July 12	General Hull invades Upper Canada
	July 17	Native warriors, British regulars, and French-Canadian voyageurs capture Mackinac
	August 16	Brock and Tecumseh capture Detroit
	October 13	Battle of Queenston Heights — Americans are ultimately pushed back, but Brock dies
1813	April 27	General Dearborn captures York (Toronto)
	June 1	H.M.S. *Shannon* defeats U.S.S. *Chesapeake*
	June 6	Battle of Stoney Creek — American advance is stopped cold
	June 22	Laura Secord's long walk
	June 24	Battle of Beaver Dams — Americans turned back
	July 31	Americans re-capture York
	October 5	Battle of Moraviantown — Tecumseh dies
	October 25	Battle of Chateauguay — American invasion force defeated by French and English Canadians
	November 11	Battle of Crysler's Farm — Americans defeated
1814	July 3	Americans capture Fort Erie
	July 5	The Battle of Chippewa sees Iroquois fighting Iroquois as Mohawk on the British side clash with Seneca warriors on the American side
	July 25	Battle of Lundy's Lane — a confusing and bloody conflict that ends in a stalemate (though both sides claim victory)
	August	British capture and burn Washington D.C.
	September 11	Americans defeat a much larger British force at Plattsburgh — Prevost makes an unseemly retreat
	September 12–15	British attack Baltimore
	December 24	Treaty of Ghent ends the War of 1812
1815	January 8	American victory at Battle of New Orleans

So Who Did Win?

Do you want to know the strangest thing about the War of 1812? The Americans think they won it. Really. Do you want to know what's even stranger? They're right. Not in a military sense, of course. On the battlefield, the Americans lost. They didn't even come close to obtaining their goal: the Conquest of Canada. But war is, above all, a *political* tool, and what counts in the end are the long-term results, not individual heroics.

In the treaty hammered out by Britain and the United States, the territories were returned to their original borders and the Americans were given a free rein in the West. Britain's First Nations allies had been completely shut out of the negotiations. So were the Canadians. (The Americans had refused to allow either at the table.) And so, in the end, the United States came away with its sovereignty reaffirmed.

> *The United States had lost a war and won a conference.*
> — popular historian Bruce Hutchison on the outcome of the War of 1812

Once again, Britain had betrayed its First Nations allies — utterly and shamelessly. The Americans were allowed to extend their borders deep into Indian Territory (an area previously reserved by the British as Native lands) and they now waged a war of extermination and displacement against the First Nations while Great Britain looked the other way. By 1817, Indians were being forcibly removed from the Ohio Valley.

The War of 1812 was the end of an era for the First Nations. No longer needed as allies or to provide a buffer zone, their usefulness to the British had come to an end. After 1812, the hope for a sovereign pan-Native homeland in the heart of the continent was lost forever. Native autonomy was no longer a consideration. Instead, Natives were to be settled, "civilized," and assimilated into white society as either farmers or as wards of the state. (The cost of this, by the way, was to be covered by the sale of Native lands.) Who won? Who lost? The final score stands like this:

- ✔ The Americans won
- ✔ The Canadians broke even
- ✔ The First Nations lost

In 1817, the Rush-Bagot Agreement limited the naval armaments that either side could place on the Great Lakes. It was the beginning of what would one day become the "longest undefended border in the world."

A second agreement in 1818 set the western border between the United States and Canada at the 49th parallel, from the Lake of the Woods straight across to the Rockies. At the mountains, it got trickier. Remember how the Nor'westers had built forts on the Columbia River? Well, both sides now claimed that area, a wide swath of land called the Oregon Territory. Britain and the United States agreed to joint occupation — for the time being. The modern boundaries of Canada were slowly taking shape. Just as important, a sense of English Canadian identify was forming.

> *In an odd way, the war did help to change Upper Canada from a loose aggregation of village states into something approaching a political entity. The war, or more properly the myth of the war, gave the rootless new settlers a sense of community.*
>
> — popular historian Pierre Berton

The Re-Living History War of 1812 site (`library.thinkquest.org/22916/exmain.html`) has lots of graphics and is recommended. For Galafilm's wide-ranging War of 1812 site, go to `galafilm.com/1812`. Other excellent War of 1812 sites, all highly recommended, include:

- `members.tripod.com/~war1812/index.html`
- `tor-pw1.attcanada.ca/~htfergus/AmericanWar.html`
- `www2.andrews.edu/~downm/`
- `www.militaryheritage.com/1812.htm`

Lord Selkirk and the Pemmican Wars

Not all of the battles during this period were with the United States. In the Northwest, a "new nationality" was taking shape: the Métis, who were a mix of French, Scots, and Native. A frontier people, largely French-speaking and Catholic, the Métis had developed a lifestyle based largely on that of the buffalo hunt. They also supplied provisions to the North West Company — especially the all-important *pemmican* (dried meat, usually buffalo or moose, mixed with berries and fat and pounded flat, it would keep for years). Pemmican fuelled the entire fur trade, feeding voyageurs and Métis traders alike.

The Hudson's Bay Company, meanwhile, had fallen under the control of Scottish investors led by Thomas Douglas, Earl of Selkirk. A sincere and idealistic man, Selkirk wanted to create a homeland for displaced Scots and Irish tenant farmers. He had already established similar colonies in P.E.I. and in Upper Canada, and in 1811, the HBC granted him a vast tract of land in the Red River valley. The following year, a small colony was established near the junction of the Red and Assiniboine Rivers (in what is now downtown Winnipeg). Intentionally or not, Selkirk placed his colonists smack dab in the middle of the NWC and Métis trade routes.

The Nor'westers were convinced that the colony was really a ploy for the HBC to establish a base for further penetration into the interior. Even worse, the Selkirk colonists were soon threatening to launch an embargo on pemmican supplies (arguing that the meat was being taken from land that they owned). The North West Company chased the colonists away and burnt their settlement to the ground. But Lord Selkirk, as dogged as he was naive, re-established the community with the help of an HBC armed force. Tragedy followed.

On June 19, 1816, at a cluster of trees known as Seven Oaks, a band of Métis suppliers led by Cuthbert Grant clashed with a small group of settlers. What followed was either a massacre or a battle, depending on whose side you take. Twenty-one settlers were killed, including their governor, Robert Semple.

Seven Oaks, still celebrated by the Métis as a defining moment in their nation's history, marked the beginning of a violent campaign between the HBC and the NWC, one that would be known as "the Pemmican Wars." After the bloodshed at Seven Oaks, Lord Selkirk sent in troops and seized a NWC fort, arresting several traders, including one of the company's leaders. And the small, beleaguered farming community at Red River, a remote outpost of British society, somehow managed to survive.

At www.cyberus.ca/~mfdunn/metis/links/Metis.html you'll find links to almost 200 different Métis sites (including a recipe for pemmican). For more on the Métis: www.sae.ca/mbc/people/history.html. For more on Cuthbert Grant: www.precourt.com/stfran/cuthbert/Default.htm.

Chapter 11

The Rebellions of 1837

In This Chapter

▶ The North West Company merges with the HBC

▶ Canada is ruled by cliques

▶ Rebellions erupt in Upper and Lower Canada

▶ American rebels launch border raids aimed at "liberating" Canada

*T*he War of 1812 stopped what might have been a natural progression: the eventual absorption of the northern colonies into the United States. After the war, bitter anti-American attitudes took root among the Canadian ruling class, and any attempt at broadening the democratic process was branded as "Yankee republicanism."

Among the French Canadians in Lower Canada, the struggle was not against Americanization, but *anglicization*. Irish and English immigrants were arriving, and the French Canadians were afraid of being slowly assimilated, of losing their culture, their religion, and their language.

British North America now consisted of the following colonies:

✔ **Upper Canada** (Ontario),

✔ **Lower Canada** (Québec),

✔ **New Brunswick**,

✔ **Nova Scotia** (with Cape Breton returned to it in 1820), and

✔ **Prince Edward Island**

The senior administrator, or *governor*, was based in Lower Canada. The other colonies were run, fairly independently, by *lieutenant-governors*. Historians, however, often use the term "governor" to refer to both. For example, Thomas Carleton (in Chapter 9) is often referred to as "the first Governor of New Brunswick," even though he was, technically, a lieutenant-governor.

Newfoundland, meanwhile, was in a class of its own, ruled by a separate governor, but lacking even the basics of representative government.

NWC + HBC = Monopoly

The Pemmican Wars that began in 1816 (see Chapter 10) devastated the fur trade. What had once been a commercial rivalry was now, in the words of Peter C. Newman, "a guerrilla war, fought along a four-thousand-mile front," as the Hudson's Bay Company and the North West Company battled it out. The struggle for supremacy had exhausted both companies and undermined the NWC's position among the First Nations. With the death in 1820 of Lord Selkirk, the HBC-backed founder of the colony at Red River, and the diminishing profits involved in running two parallel competing trade networks, a ceasefire was called. And in 1821, the Nor'wester William McGillivray, once a stubborn foe of the HBC, helped negotiate a union between the two. The North West Company, with its line of forts and hinterland expertise, was absorbed into the Hudson's Bay Company, and the golden age of the Montréal-based fur trade was over.

As historian Alan Wilson notes, after 1821, the HBC "ruled unchallenged from the Arctic to the Pacific." The great fur brigades that had left Lachine every spring passed into history. But by then, the city of Montréal had developed a broad enough merchant base that it was able to absorb the loss of fur trade without much disruption. (By 1830, the population of Montréal had passed 40,000, compared with just 2,800 in York, the capital of Upper Canada.)

After the merger of the two fur-trade companies, there was a sharp drop in the liquor trade to the Indians (the NWC in particular had used whisky to win over suppliers). But the merger also allowed the HBC to flex its newly monopolized muscle. The First Nations were now at a clear disadvantage, and the terms of trade were greatly reduced. The economic clout of the Native fur suppliers had been lost. It was an end of an era for them as well.

Selkirk's original Red River colony, meanwhile, struggled on, against all odds and through Biblical plagues of grasshoppers, droughts, floods, and prairie fires, to become the first permanent colony on the Canadian prairies. With the frontier at peace and the Americans repulsed, the next challenge to Canadian colonial stability would come not from outside, but from within.

Lead-up to Rebellion

The 1830s saw two separate rebellions erupt in British North America:

- ✔ in Lower Canada, led by the aristocratic Louis-Joseph Papineau, and
- ✔ in Upper Canada, led by the newspaperman William Lyon Mackenzie.

Reign of the "Little Emperor"

The decades after the merger were the glory years for the Hudson's Bay Company. And the man who dominated that era was a stocky, red-haired Scot named George Simpson, nicknamed "the Little Emperor." Following the overtrapping and excessive competition of the NWC days, Simpson closed down unnecessary posts, laid off extra traders, worked to halt the liquor trade with the Indians, and introduced conservation measures to protect the beaver population.

Simpson was a tough and resourceful man, and for nearly 40 years he effectively ruled the HBC's northern frontier. Under his direction, the company reached the Pacific Coast, building posts on the Columbia River and Vancouver Island. A tireless traveller, Simpson spent years criss-crossing HBC territory in a narrow-beam "express canoe," arriving at far-flung posts with his crew of Iroquois voyageurs, flags flying and piped in by a Scottish bagpiper in full regalia. Of his many epic and adventurous journeys, he once remarked, "It is strange that all my ailments vanish as soon as I seat myself in a canoe."

The causes behind the rebellions were similar — a colonial administration that was woefully out of touch with its subjects — but there were some very important underlying differences as well. In Upper Canada, the rebellions were more clearly an ideological and political crusade. In Lower Canada, they had the added complexity of race and language.

Political faultlines

As I explain in Chapter 9, the Constitutional Act of 1791 created all sorts of conflict. The root of the problem was in having an *elected* assembly under the control of an *appointed* council. The two were always at each other's throats, and in Lower Canada (Québec), the situation was aggravated by the fact that the elected members were mainly French Canadians, while the governor's handpicked council was made up largely of Anglo merchants. However, even with the cards stacked against them, the French-Canadian Members of the Assembly soon became masters of British parliamentary technique. Among other things, they were able to insist on establishing French as a working language of government.

Still, for the most part, the elected assemblies in both colonies could wield their power only in a negative manner. That is, they could block the government, but they could not lead it. New laws and government spending had to be approved by both the council *and* the assembly, so, although the assembly could not impose its will on the government, it could paralyze it. It was a system that encouraged political blackmail and heavy-handed power plays. The two sides were at constant loggerheads.

Government by clique

British immigrants poured in — more than 125,000 arrived in the 1820s alone. Most were either (a) lower-income immigrants trying to escape economic hardships and start anew, or (b) upper-middle-class Brits hoping to become "big fish in a small pond." Which is to say, Canada was settled largely along social extremes. (The U.S., in contrast, was more middle-class in its roots — and its outlook.) The poorer immigrants, especially those from Ireland, arrived as "human ballast" in lumberships that would have otherwise been empty on their return voyage. The vessels were dubbed "coffin ships."

For a first-hand look at the undercurrents of class conflict in early Canada, I recommend *Roughing It in the Bush*, by Susanna Moodie, a journal-like account of an English gentlewoman's experiences in Upper Canada. In it, Moodie often expresses her dismay at the rough-hewn egalitarianism of frontier life — something that horrified a well-bred lady such as herself. A system of oligarchy ("rule by a small group") soon became entrenched in all the British North American colonies, but it was especially marked in Upper and Lower Canada, where influential coalitions of wealthy landowners, merchants, and government officers had taken root:

- ✔ **The Chateau Clique** in Lower Canada (named in reference to the inordinate amount of time the members spend hanging out at the governor's residence, Chateau St. Louis).

- ✔ **The Family Compact** in Upper Canada (a stodgy mix of conservatives, Loyalist families, and self-proclaimed "defenders of 1812").

It is a sad fact that history favours crisis and conflict. The upheavals of Upper and Lower Canada dominate this age — and justly so. As we will see, the rebellions led by Papineau and Mackenzie set in motion a chain of events that would transform the empire and change the future of British North America forever. However, it is also worth noting that while this brouhaha was going on in the Canadas, the most successful and stable colony at that time was Nova Scotia.

Halifax, with a population of 15,000 and a bustling international seaport, was the very picture of civility when compared to Upper Canada. (One traveller noted that Halifax had "more refinements, more elegance and fashion," than any town in America.) Nova Scotia had a ruling elite as well, one more commercial in nature, led by aristocratic families such as the Uniackes. Indeed, all of the colonies faced the same problem: a distant and unresponsive government in London and an arrogant and often corrupt ruling class at home. But it was in the Canadas that the breaking point was reached.

Canals, practical and otherwise

The 1820s were a "golden age" of canal-building. Most of the canals were intended as practical transportation projects: The Lachine Canal bypassed the rapids along the St. Lawrence, and the Welland Canal bypassed Niagara Falls. But the Rideau Canal, linking Kingston and the Ottawa River, was built for military reasons. The St. Lawrence formed the border with the U.S. along that stretch and the British decided to create a second water route further inland, away from the American threat. The building of the Rideau Canal was an epic misadventure, an engineering ordeal that cut through 200 kilometres of swampland forests and took more than 6 years and 500 lives to build. The project went over its original budget by 700 percent, and in the end, it achieved very little, other than ruining the career of the man in charge of the project: Colonel John By. The lumber town at the mouth of the canal was named Bytown in his honour — but was later changed to "Ottawa," after the river that flowed past it.

You can find out more about the history of the Rideau Canal at the Parks Canada site (parkscanada.pch.gc.ca/parks/ontario/rideau_canal/rideau_canal_e.htm).

The Rebellion in Lower Canada

In Lower Canada, the seigneurial system had failed to protect even the elites of French-Canadian society. By 1830, more than half of the traditional seigneurial estates were now in the hands of English-speaking lords who had purchased and traded their way into positions of power. Along with the wealthy merchant families of Montréal (such as the Molsons and the McGills), they dominated the ruling Chateau Clique.

Opposed to them stood a young, professional French-Canadian elite — the yuppies of their day — who had gained control of the elected assembly under the radical *parti patriote,* but were barred from any real power on the basis of their religion and language.

In 1834, denouncing the governor's appointed council as an agent of "evil and discontent," the *parti patriote* drew up a long list of grievances, entitled *The 92 Resolutions.* Among their demands: They wanted the elected assembly to have control over public revenues, and they wanted the government to be "responsible" to voters by requiring the governor to choose his council from among elected members.

Papineau the patriote

The leader of the *parti patriote*, and the key architect of *The 92 Resolutions,* was an aristocratic reformer by the name of Louis-Joseph Papineau. Labelled "a divided soul" by one historian, Papineau was an odd mix of contradictions: an aristocrat and land-owning seigneurial lord who was fighting both for radical reforms and to preserve traditional French-Canadian values.

> *Louis-Joseph Papineau is one of the most puzzling men in Canadian history. . . . In theory he was a conservative; in practice he was a revolutionary. He believed in a republic, but he wanted it to be ruled by country gentlemen like himself.*
> — man of letters and gentle anarchist George Woodcock

Lower Canada's economy was suffering. The crops had failed. Immigrants were flooding in. And — because it never rains but it pours — cholera epidemics had swept through the cities, leaving hundreds dead. Rumours grew that the disease had been introduced intentionally by the English, to wipe out the French-Canadian population. A militant youth wing appeared, calling themselves *fils de la liberté* ("Sons of Liberty"), and they began brawling it out with the equally militant English-speaking Doric Club.

It was in this heightened atmosphere of hysteria that Britain finally sent its response to *The 92 Resolutions* — and the answer was: *No.* The Assembly of Lower Canada had waited three years only to have the door slammed in their face. Great Britain had rejected every major proposal the French Canadians had made — and the result was war. "The British ministry has set the seal of degradation and slavery upon us!" screamed a leading *patriote* newspaper. The time had come. There could be no turning back.

Papineau, a charismatic and forceful orator, spoke at angry public gatherings, whipping the crowds into a frenzy. Several prominent English Canadians also threw their support in with the *patriotes,* among them Dr. Wolfred Nelson, a veteran of 1812. Nelson called for a revolutionary assembly to be held in the town of St-Denis in the Richelieu Valley, long a hotbed of anti-government dissent. Papineau, now hailed as the George Washington of French Canada, was starting to have serious second thoughts. At the conference, he tried to calm the angry calls for open rebellion. Much had been won through parliamentary protest, he reminded them. And much more could still be won. But the crowds would have none of it. Dr. Nelson leapt to his feet and in his awkward, imperfect French yelled, "I disagree! The time has come to melt our spoons into bullets!"

The Battle of St-Denis

With the Richelieu Valley in turmoil, the governor sent British troops and Canadian volunteers in to arrest the *patriote* leaders and disperse the rabble. Led by Dr. Nelson, the *patriotes* blockaded the road and waited for the troops to arrive. It was a telling mix of men behind the barricades: habitants, lawyers, doctors, and notaries. Papineau, however, was nowhere to be seen. He had fled the site of the coming showdown and spent the next ten days hovering around the periphery before finally escaping to the United States. (Papineau had crawled through a gutter even as the British troops intent on arresting him pounded on the front door of his sister's manor.)

On a bitterly cold day in late November, British troops walked into a crossfire. A fierce gun battle followed, and the British were forced to flee, leaving six dead soldiers and a cannon behind. The Battle of St-Denis was the *patriotes'* first victory. It would also be their last. Just two days later, a second British force attacked nearby St-Charles, killing 60 *patriotes* and arresting dozens more. The rebellion had come too soon. It had been ill prepared and poorly co-ordinated, and the *patriotes* were now on the run.

The Battle of St-Eustache

Having subdued the rebel forces in the Richelieu Valley, the government now turned its attention to the area around Montréal, where *patriotes* had invaded the Mohawk community at Oka, stealing weapons and supplies. In mid-December, more than 1,400 British redcoats and English-Canadian volunteers marched north. At the town of St-Eustache, the British fought the *patriotes* back into the village church and then set the building on fire. As the men ran out to escape the flames, they were shot down. Almost 100 patriotes died, among them their leader, a young doctor named Jean-Olivier Chénier, who fought to the death. (Even today, in Québec someone who shows great courage in the face of insurmountable odds is said to be "brave like Chénier.") The British troops then marched off, leaving the nearby town of St-Benoit at the mercy of drunken, bellowing English-Canadian volunteers, who confiscated the habitants' weapons and then burned their farms and homes, and looted the church.

Les frères chasseurs

As the *patriote* cause collapsed, Dr. Robert Nelson (Wolfred's brother) rode south to find Papineau. But the *patriote* leader had turned his back on the cause and refused to join the fight. "Papineau has abandoned us," said Nelson bitterly. "[He is] a man fit only for words, but not for action."

Grosse Île

Waves of immigrants were flooding into Canada, most of them escaping poverty in Ireland, and the main point of entry was Québec. The newcomers brought with them an epidemic of cholera, and as the disease swept through the St. Lawrence valley, panic set in and a quarantine station was established at Grosse Île in 1832, downstream from Québec City. Incoming ships dumped corpses and sick passengers there by the thousands. The ill either recovered or died and were buried in shallow graves. The early years of Grosse Île were heartbreaking and horrific. The nature and treatment of disease was poorly understood, the hospitals were unsanitary, and the nurses and doctors couldn't deal with the outbreak. An even deadlier typhus epidemic occurred in 1847–48, mainly among Irish immigrants fleeing the Potato Famine that had devastated their homeland. (The potato crops had failed, and thousands starved as English lords refused to intervene. To do so would have been to "interfere with the free market.") Some 100,000 Irish arrived in Québec in 1847 alone. The plight of Irish orphans reached the hearts of many Québécois, who adopted hundreds of Irish children into their homes and raised them as their own. The quarantine station at Grosse Île operated for more than 100 years and was finally closed in 1937. To find out more about Grosse Île, visit the Parks Canada site (`parcscanada.risq.qc.ca/grosse_ile/`).

From his American base, Nelson gathered 300 *patriotes* and, in the early months of 1838, he crossed back into Canadian territory and read a proclamation declaring a new republic with himself as president. When he returned to the U.S. side of the line, he was arrested and thrown in jail — more for raiding an American militia base and stealing its weapons than for having provoked an international incident. Nelson was soon released, however, and he led another raid into Canadian territory.

By now, the *patriotes* were receiving solid backing in Vermont and New York. A secret society had formed, dubbed "Hunters' Lodges" in English and *Société des frères chasseurs* in French, whose stated aim was to topple the government in Canada and create a second republic on the continent. For all its bravado, the American/French-Canadian rebel alliance failed miserably. Troops from the Maritimes and Upper Canada were called in, and a second uprising was quickly put down. In six battles over two years, 27 soldiers and nearly 300 French Canadians had died.

"Lord Satan"

Leading the campaign against the *patriotes* was John Colborne, a former Lieutenant-Governor of Upper Canada who had been hounded out of office by English-Canadian reformers. He now had the chance to exact a little revenge. Even by the standards of the day, it was heavy-handed. Colborne had no great love for the French. He had fought against Napoleon at Waterloo, and he now turned his wrath against the rebellious French Canadians.

Colborne and his men burned hundreds of habitant homes, something that earned him the nickname *le vieux brûlot* ("the Old Firebrand"). He arrested thousands of people, hanged a dozen of them, and sent almost 60 more to the penal colonies of Australia. For his decisive actions and iron-fisted approach, he was rewarded with a peerage from the British government. Colborne was now known as "Lord Seaton," though the habitants whose lands and homes he had destroyed preferred to pronounce it "Lord Satan."

The Rebellion in Upper Canada

In Upper Canada, a similar drama was unfolding. The American Revolution, the Loyalist exodus, and the War of 1812 had all served to strengthen the anti-American attitudes, British customs, and conservative beliefs of the colony. But there were deep undercurrents of social unrest, which the colonial government vastly underestimated. The ruling oligarchy, dubbed the *Family Compact,* dominated the government. And even when moderate reformers such as Robert Baldwin managed to gain a majority in the elected assembly, the reigning Tory-Anglican elites effectively shut them out of power.

Leading members of the Family Compact included Dr. John Strachan, who was now the Anglican Archdeacon for York, and the ever class-conscious John Beverley Robinson, Attorney General and Tory Member of the Assembly. They were honest, determined men. Perhaps. But they were also arrogant and anti-democratic. Archdeacon Strachan for one, clashed headlong with his rival, Egerton Ryerson, a teacher and Methodist minister. Ryerson fought for an open, non-denominational school system and the separation of church and state — something Strachan vehemently opposed. Public schools? *Never!*

> *Nobody would ask for the vote by ballot but from gross ignorance.*
> — Strachan's dismissive take on a more democratic government

Mackenzie the muckraker

While moderate reformers such as Baldwin and Ryerson tried to make headway, frustrated at every turn by the ruling clique, the rhetoric became angrier and angrier. Eventually, the more extremist reformers took over as "the voice of the people." They were led by a fiery little newspaperman named William Lyon Mackenzie.

While Papineau came from an established seigneurial family, Mackenzie had arrived from Scotland as the penniless son of a widow. An outspoken critic of the cliquish Family Compact, Mackenzie was especially opposed to the lands that had been awarded to the Anglican Church as "clergy reserves" (some three million acres of real estate in Upper Canada, much of it undeveloped). Mackenzie's heated editorial attacks on the ruling elites brought a swift response when a gang of young men broke into his office and threw his printing press into the lake. One respected member of the Family Compact even tried to have Mackenzie assassinated, to no avail.

Hated by the establishment but loved by his constituents in "Muddy York," Mackenzie was first elected to the assembly in 1828 — and was promptly expelled by the other members. He was just as quickly re-elected. And just as quickly expelled. Four times he was tossed out of office by the ruling Tories. And four times he was re-elected. In 1834, he became the first mayor of the newly incorporated city of Toronto. And all the while, he was denouncing the ruling families of Upper Canada in angry, purple prose.

> *He was the most unselfish of idealists; he was also a born muckraker and scandal-monger.*
> — biographer William Kilbourn on Mackenzie's contradictory nature

Mackenzie roamed the backwoods of Upper Canada, compiling a massive list of every complaint, big or small, that the people had against the government and the ruling social clique. His *Report on Grievances* weighed in at 500 pages and included everything from a demand for responsible government to complaints about the high price of stamps. It was the Upper Canadian equivalent of Papineau's *92 Resolutions* (which I discuss earlier in this chapter), and it had equally explosive results.

"Galloping Head"

Enter the cowboy: Francis Bond Head, an eccentric, upper-crust Brit who wrote cheap adventure novels and liked to pretend he was an Argentine cowhand while performing tricks with his lasso for appreciative members of the Royal Family. This was the man the British Colonial Office decided to appoint Lieutenant-Governor of Upper Canada in 1836. "It was," as I noted in *Bastards & Boneheads*, "like turning a kangaroo loose in a mine field." Bond Head knew absolutely nothing about Canada. But he didn't trust the reformers and he believed in good ol' Tory values. In this, he was the perfect foil to the equally flamboyant, equally stubborn Mackenzie.

NATIVE RIGHTS

Apartheid, Canadian-style: The Bond Head treaties

Although he is best known as the bumbling anti-hero of 1837, the man who put down Mackenzie's "peasant revolt," Governor Francis Bond Head also played a role in shaping Native policy. He was the first leader to promote a system of institutional apartheid in Canada. At that time, apartheid (the forced separation of races) was being advanced by the British government in South Africa, and Bond Head made a similar proposal for Upper Canada. His intentions were muddled and romantic. He considered the "red inhabitants" to be the "real proprietors" of Canadian soil, and was dismayed at attempts to force them into an Euro-Christian agricultural lifestyle.

In 1836, Bond Head plotted out a dramatic shift in Native policy, arguing that it would be "best for the Indians" if they would be completely removed from the influences of white society and allowed to continue their rustic, subsistence-level hunting and fishing lifestyles elsewhere. (The Iroquoian Nations had a long agricultural tradition that predated white society and was even now being destroyed by it, but that didn't fit the romantic image of the Noble Savage and was thus discarded.)

Bond Head convinced the Ojibwa of northern Ontario to sign over a whopping 1.5 million acres of land in exchange for a vaguely defined future "Native homeland." And where would this Aboriginal Garden of Eden be established? Why, on the barren granite islands of Manitoulin, which would be designated a permanent Indian territory, on which various other First Nations could now be "relocated." (Very few took Bond Head up on his offer, something that baffled him to no end.)

The Imperial government, meanwhile, was very pleased with this huge surrender of Native lands. But Native rights groups were outraged. They denounced the plan as a land grab — and history has since proven them right. It is a lesson worth remembering: Good intentions and romantic views of Native culture are not enough. Bond Head *was* sincere. He *did* think of the Natives as Noble Savages. And his actions *were* disastrous.

When reformers in the assembly blocked funds to the government, Bond Head responded by dissolving the House and calling a snap election. Rather than remain neutral, the lieutenant-governor campaigned for the Conservatives, using bribery and scare tactics to win over voters. Since only property owners were allowed to cast ballots, Bond Head granted land to known supporters (something called "quick enfranchisement"). It worked. The Tories won a resounding victory, and the reformers were swept away. Remember John Robert Colombo's list of the Most Despised Canadians in history? So far we've met #2, Governor Charles Lawrence (in Chapter 6), and #1, François Bigot (in Chapter 7). Well, "Galloping Head," as he was known, came in at #4.

Montgomery's Tavern

After the fiasco of the '36 election, Mackenzie's resolve hardened. He brazenly changed the name of his newspaper from *The Colonial Advocate* to *The Constitution* (in clear reference to the American republic) and issued a "Toronto Declaration" based directly on the American Declaration of Independence. Inspired by the uprisings in Lower Canada, Mackenzie began riding through the countryside urging rebellion. A small band of apostles followed him. The time had come to march on Toronto, capture the government, and declare a glorious New Republic!

> *Up then, brave Canadians! Get ready your rifles, and make short work of it!*
> — Mackenzie's battle cry

More than 600 men gathered at Montgomery's Tavern on Yonge Street (near the present-day Eglinton subway station). It was early December and blustery cold, but the men were warmed by a revolutionary zeal. The time was ripe. Bond Head, confident to the end that no rebels would dare try anything while he was in charge, had sent his entire garrison to Montréal to help put down the *patriote* uprising that was now under way in Lower Canada. Only a small band of local militia was on hand to defend Toronto. And even as Mackenzie's ragtag army marched down Yonge Street, Bond Head refused to take the rumours of unrest seriously.

Mackenzie's men, armed with pitchforks, rifles, clubs, and pikes, continued along Yonge. But waiting for them in the shadows was a small band of nervous volunteers, led by Sheriff Jarvis. As Mackenzie's men came into view, Jarvis's musketeers fire a single volley, which panicked the rebels and sent them running. It was just as well because, in the confusion that followed, Jarvis's men fled as well. The "battle," if you could call it that, had been both a major defeat for the rebels and a complete farce. (The clash itself took place near the future site of Maple Leaf Gardens.)

Two days later, Bond Head led an army of volunteers out of Toronto. With flags flying, crowds cheering, and drums keeping time, they marched north on Yonge Street and converged on Montgomery's Tavern. In half an hour it was all over. The rebels were beaten and the tavern was torched. But Mackenzie had escaped. He fled south across the Niagara River and into the United States, where he quickly linked up with the Hunters' Lodge, the secret society formed in the U.S. to support the republican rebels in Canada.

"Remember the Caroline!"

American sympathizers gave Mackenzie their full support. *The liberation of Canada is at hand!* Mackenzie crossed back into Canadian territory and landed on Navy Island in the Niagara River, where he raised a flag and declared himself President of the Canadian Republic. The Americans cheered, but the celebrations didn't last long. British troops began bombarding the rebel base on Navy Island and during the night, a handful of Canadians rowed over to the American side of the river and set Mackenzie's supply ship, the *Caroline*, on fire. As the vessel burned, they cut it free and it went over the Falls in a blaze of wreckage. An American had been killed by the Canadians during the scuffle, and across the U.S. angry cries for retribution went up. Mackenzie had pushed Canada and the United States to the brink of all-out war.

> *Remember the* Caroline!
>
> — rallying cry of American rebels

More men died during the American-backed border raids into Upper Canada than in the original rebellion. More than 1,000 rebels were captured, 20 were hanged, and more than 800 were sentenced to prison. The rest were either sent into exile or else banished to the brutal penal colonies of Australia. And if there was ever any doubt who had won, the judge who hanged two of the main rebel leaders was that upstanding member of the Family Compact, John Beverley Robinson.

So What Was the Point?

The American government resisted the calls for war, and calmer heads eventually prevailed. The Hunters' Lodge faded away, and with it the angry republican sentiments.

Incredible as it may seem, the British eventually pardoned Mackenzie, Papineau and even Wolfred Nelson and allowed them to return to Canada. All three were re-elected to their respective assemblies, but their time had clearly passed. Papineau still had a certain aura and influence surrounding him, and he helped inspire the young reformers who would launch the *parti rouge* in the 1840s. (They, in turn, would later join with English-Canadian reformers to form the Liberal Party of Canada. See Chapter 13 for more on the *parti rouge*.) Mackenzie, meanwhile, seemed more and more irrelevant as time went on.

So was there any point to these rebellions? Or were they simply a quirk of history, a dramatic detour that had little effect on society as a whole? Some historians have seen the Rebellions of 1837 as a legitimate "struggle for democracy." Separatists have portrayed the *patriotes* as being, well, separatists. Others have been less kind. Historian Donald Creighton described the rebellions as "little more than a series of armed riots, unplanned, purposeless, hopeless." But both views are somewhat misleading. The Rebellions did have a huge impact. They helped set in motion a chain of events that would eventually lead to responsible government not just in the Canadas, but throughout the colonies of the British Empire. It's true that the rebellions were "little more than a series of armed riots." But they were anything but pointless.

> *The Rebellions were American Revolutions in miniature, and though at the time they seemed to have failed, they cleared the way for self-government; and just beyond self-government stood national life.*
> — historians J.W. Chafe and A.R.M. Lower

For more on the Rebellions of 1837 visit www.edunetconnect.com/cat/rebellions/index.html.

Part V
The Roads to Confederation
(1838–1891)

MOTHER BRITANNIA.—" *See ! Why, the dear child can stand alone !* "
UNCLE SAM.—" *Of course he can ! Let go of him Granny ; if he falls I'll catch him !* "

Canada took its first steps towards outright independence under
the watchful eyes of the United States and Great Britain.

In this part . . .

*M*oderate reformers triumph where the radicals had failed. Responsible government comes (slowly) to the colonies of British North America, setting the stage for a wider, grander union: a "confederation" under Prime Minister John A. Macdonald. Modern Canada is born, but not without a struggle: Louis Riel leads a Métis uprising and a vast continent is crossed by rail, joining Canada from sea to sea.

Chapter 12

The Fight for Responsible Government

In This Chapter

▶ In the wake of the rebellions, the British send "Radical Jack" Durham over to investigate

▶ A pair of moderate reformers, LaFontaine and Baldwin, lead the battle for responsible government in Canada

▶ Joseph Howe wins the fight in Nova Scotia

▶ The gold rush colony of British Columbia is created

*I*f nothing else, the rebels of 1837 certainly caught the attention of the British government. In response, Great Britain suspended civil rights, dissolved the assemblies of Upper and Lower Canada, and sent over a troubleshooter named Lord Durham to assess the situation and report back.

Just as important: The uprisings thoroughly discredited the radical wing of the reform movement. After the rebellions, moderate reformers such as Robert Baldwin now seemed like the voice of reason. If the 1830s had been an era of angry rebellion, the 1840s were an era of political evolution.

Lord Durham: Mission Impossible

They called him "Radical Jack." John George Lambton, Earl of Durham: the brilliant and outspoken champion of Britain's own Reform Bill of 1832. Durham was a bit of a troublemaker, always asking embarrassing questions in the House and pushing for ever greater parliamentary reforms. So, why not kill two birds with one stone? Why not send Radical Jack over to the colonies to check things out and, you know, get rid of him for a while?

A seventeen-year-old girl named Victoria had just ascended to the British throne, and the young Queen's first official ceremonial act was to grant Durham a knighthood. (The sword used to tap his shoulder in the ritual was too heavy for Victoria and the prime minister had to step in and help her.) Soon after, Durham was named "High Commissioner and Governor-General of all Her Majesty's provinces on the continent of North America." With this title came wide, potentially dictatorial powers. Never in the history of North America, before or since, has any single person ever wielded so much authority. Durham intended to use it wisely.

"Radical Jack" tours the colonies

Lord Durham arrived in Canada with an entire entourage of servants and secretaries, and he rode through the streets of Montréal on a white stallion as the crowds cheered. Tories and Reformers, *patriotes* and ruling cliques alike: They all pinned their hopes on Durham.

Durham quickly pardoned most of the imprisoned *patriotes* and rebels and sent the remaining leaders into exile, not to the harsh penal colonies of Australia, but to sunny Bermuda instead. In Lower Canada, he met mainly with English merchants; his contact with French-Canadian reformers was fleeting at best. In Upper Canada, he spent only 24 hours in Toronto, the main site of the unrest, but he did meet with a moderate reformer, Dr. William Baldwin, and his son Robert, who argued persuasively for granting self-government to the colonies. It was, they said, the only way to deal with the underlying causes behind the rebellions.

Durham agreed to mull this over. In the meantime, he had been hosting lavish and extravagant banquets. He was a man of great charm — and decisive actions. He boldly crossed over into American territory at Niagara Falls, where he wined and dined disgruntled American representatives. With his gracious flattery and republican sentiments, Lord Durham helped soothe Canada's strained relationship with the United States. (After the initial rebellions, American sympathizers had launched border raids into Canada.)

The Durham Report

Lord Durham's mission ended abruptly in 1838 when word came that Britain had overruled his decision to exile prisoners to Bermuda. For one thing, Lord Durham's authority — vast though it was — didn't include Bermuda. The governor of Bermuda was in a snit over this and had first refused even to let the prisoners land. "Bermuda is not a penal colony," he said bitterly. And though the governor eventually relented, his complaints reached London, and Durham's Bermuda decrees were overturned.

Durham sailed back to England to defend himself, after spending only five months in Canada. Just a few days after his departure, the second uprising in Lower Canada erupted. It was quickly put down, but it did give a sense of urgency to matters. Lord Durham resigned his commission in December 1838, soon after having arrived back in London. The following spring, he submitted his *Report on the Affairs of British North America*. In it, he made three central recommendations:

✔ That Upper and Lower Canada be united under one government (the better to overwhelm and assimilate the French Canadians).

✔ That the governor be required to name the leaders of the elected assembly as his ruling advisors. (That is, elected members would now, finally, be in control.)

✔ That the colonies be given authority over their own internal affairs. Only on imperial matters would the governor be allowed to override them.

Although it sounded radical, Durham was simply suggesting that the colonies should be given the same parliamentary rights available to the citizens of Britain. In Upper Canada, Durham put the blame for the turmoil squarely on the outdated colonial system and a haughty ruling elite. In Lower Canada, however, he found something else all together.

> *I expected to find a contest between a government and a people: I found two nations warring in the bosom of a single state: I found a struggle, not of principles, but of races.*
>
> — from Lord Durham's Report

Durham's assessment was, of course, correct. In Lower Canada, the conflict had been divided along linguistic and cultural lines. Durham's solution? To end the French Fact in Canada once and for all. Assimilate them, not by force, but by rigging the system. At first, Durham had wanted to join all of British North America into one confederation, but the prosperous Maritime colonies saw no reason to tie themselves down to the unruly central Canadians. So a dual union was recommended instead. The objective was the same: to overwhelm and submerge the French-Canadian population. Only then, would it be "safe" to introduce greater democratic measures and a responsible government. In his report, Lord Durham identified what he thought to be the single, central mistake of British policy: "the vain endeavour to preserve a French-Canadian nationality in the midst of Anglo-American colonies and states."

> *The superior political and practical intelligence of the English cannot be, for a moment, disputed.*
>
> — from Lord Durham's Report

Durham never lived to see his recommendations put into action. He died in July 1840, killed, it was said, by the rigours of his Canadian assignment.

Go to www.uni.ca/durhamreport.html for excerpts of Lord Durham's famous report.

"Defeats as glorious as victories"

Talk about insulting. Lord Durham dismissed the French Canadians as "a people with no history and no literature," a doomed race destined to be absorbed by a superior British culture. It was both an affront and a challenge, and it brought about a quick response. The first to answer the call was the historian François-Xavier Garneau. When an English-speaking clerk quoted Durham and mocked the French Canadians as a people without a past, Garneau replied, "I shall write the history which you do not even know exists. You will see that our ancestors yielded only when outnumbered. There are defeats which are as glorious as victories!"

Garneau's *Histoire du Canada* took several years and three volumes to tell. In it, Garneau identified French Canadians as a people defined by a struggle to survive, first against the Iroquois, then the British, and now the English Canadians. He identified "three pillars" of survival:

- ✔ French law
- ✔ the French language
- ✔ and the Catholic Church

Garneau was just one of many defiant French-Canadian nationalists to emerge in the post-Union era. Among them, a French-speaking Swiss immigrant named Napoleon Aubin, who founded the ultra-patriotic St. Jean Baptiste Society in 1842 (named after Québec's patron saint, and still a hotbed of Québec nationalism today). Durham's insults, enshrined in his Report, had inadvertently helped trigger a cultural Renaissance of French-Canadian novelists, poets, artists, and historians.

> *French Canadians owe Lord Durham a big one. His call for assimilation . . . became the rallying cry for those community leaders who might otherwise have given up on the nation. Durham said we were dead, or at least dying. Proving him wrong became the driving force of a nation.*
> — author Michel Gratton

Durham's dismissal of French-Canadian culture also earned him the #3 spot on Colombo's list of "Most Despised" people in Canadian history. (To find out who #1 and #2 were, see Chapters 7 and 6, respectively.)

The Act of Union

The British government rejected Durham's call for responsible colonial government. But it did approve a united legislature, if only to help weaken the French-Canadian cause. The Act of Union was proclaimed on February 10, 1841. Among the terms:

- Upper and Lower Canada would be united under a single government.

- The Assembly would have an equal number of representatives from both regions (even though Lower Canada had 670,000 people and Upper Canada had only 480,000). By *under*-representing the French, it was hoped the English would dominate the government and that this, in turn, would help speed up the inevitable anglicization of French Canadians.

  Note: This was not one of Durham's suggestions. He had argued for representation based on population, confident that as more English speakers moved in, French Canadians would naturally lose their majority in Parliament anyway. The British government, however, decided to hurry things up by giving both sides the *same* number of seats, regardless of population. It was a policy that would backfire brilliantly.

- Upper Canada's public debt (£1.2 million) would now be pooled with that of Lower Canada's much smaller one (£95,000). Again this was extremely — and intentionally — unfair to French Canadians.

- Upper Canada would now be known as "Canada West" and Lower Canada would be "Canada East." The two would no longer be separate colonies, but regions within a single Parliament.

- English would be the only official language of government.

Kingston, a small garrison town of fewer than 600 houses, was made the new capital. (The capital was later moved to Montréal in 1844.) As for responsible government, the answer was a firm and forceful "No." Members of the Council would be answerable only to the governor and *not* to the elected members of the Assembly. Same slop, different bucket, as they say.

Triumph of the Moderates

It was just as the Tories had feared. Rather than strengthening the old ruling cliques, the United Province of Canada actually worked against them. The union brought together like-minded reformers in English and French Canada. And far from submerging French-Canadian culture, the United Parliament actually *entrenched* social differences. The age of the violent firebrand radicals had passed; the age of the moderate reformer was at hand.

The Aroostook War

The border with the United States continued to cause headaches. In the east, the line had been drawn along the St. Croix River, but in the northern backwoods, above the river's headwaters, the boundaries were vague. As lumberjacks from the U.S. and New Brunswick moved in, tempers flared. In 1839, the two sides clashed in the fertile valley of the Aroostook River.

The Governor of Maine announced that he would no longer accept British claims to the disputed region. He sent in 800 soldiers and built a string of forts and supply lines deep into the woods along the Aroostook and Saint John Rivers. The British responded in kind, and armed fortresses began popping up on either side. This bloodless conflict, also known as "the pork and beans war" after the rugged diet of the men involved, has been called America's first Cold War, one of troop build-ups, brinkmanship, and gratuitous sabre-rattling. Only frantic negotiations at the last moment averted an all-out border war. The Americans sent their Secretary of State, Daniel Webster, to the negotiation table. Britain sent Lord Ashburton, a member of the Privy Council. The talks did not go well. The appeasement-minded Ashburton quickly ceded a huge chunk of land to the U.S., more than 18,000 square kilometres of territory handed over without a shot fired.

The Ashburton-Webster Treaty — dubbed "the Ashburton capitulation" by its critics — was signed on August 9, 1842. The upper Saint John River, which ran straight through the Brayon-Acadian heartland, was now the border between northern New Brunswick and Maine. With a stroke of a pen, Britain had abandoned more than 2,000 French-Canadian settlers, stranding them on the U.S. side of the Saint John River where they have since been all but assimilated. There's a moral here somewhere . . .

Visit homepages.rootsweb.com/~godwin/reference/aroostook.html for more on the Aroostook War (with links).

Egerton Ryerson, now Chief Superintendent of Education, helped shepherd through a revamped education act that established two independent school systems: non-denominational public schools in Canada West (with provisions for separate Catholic schools), and religious schools in Canada East (which would be predominantly Catholic and French). Now that they had their own distinct education system, how would the French Canadians ever become properly "anglicized"? The answer: They wouldn't.

LaFontaine and Baldwin

The leading French-Canadian reformer to emerge at this time was Louis-Hippolyte LaFontaine. He was a sombre, somewhat humourless man, but one of great ideals and steadfast values. Many people noted his uncanny resemblance to Napoleon, both in temperament and appearance. LaFontaine fought a long, hard battle to win responsible government in Canada, and in doing so he enlisted the friendship and support of another equally serious, equally determined man: Robert Baldwin, the moderate reformer we first met in Chapter 11. It was one of the great political alliances in Canadian history. Together, LaFontaine and Baldwin dominated the Assembly, and in the 1848 election, the reformers were swept into power.

The governor at the time was James Bruce, Earl of Elgin. A fluently bilingual and farsighted statesman, Lord Elgin knew what he had to do. The people had spoken, the reformers had won, and in line with a recently revised British policy, Elgin called upon the members of the majority to take office and form a government. LaFontaine had more supporters in the Assembly, so he was asked to lead. It happened on March 10, 1848, a date sometimes heralded as "the birth of democracy in Canada." That same year, the British government amended the Act of Union to end the previous, misguided ban on the French language.

Parliament opened in Montréal the following January, and Lord Elgin delivered the opening Speech from the Throne in English. After he was finished he paused, smiled slightly, and read the speech again — in French. It was a key moment in Canadian history. Responsible government had been won, democracy had been broadened, and the French language would no longer be excluded. Assimilation as official policy was effectively dead.

Visit `www.heritageproject.ca/media/minutes/expanded/baldwi/` `default.htm` for the "LaFontaine and Baldwin" heritage minute.

The Montréal riots

Responsible government had finally arrived. Or had it? The question now was whether the elected leaders would have any real authority. The first test of responsible government occurred in 1849, when the Assembly attempted to pass a controversial Rebellion Losses Bill (formally, "the Act of Indemnification"). The bill compensated *any* person — even those that had fought on the *patriote* side — who had suffered damage to property during the 1837 Rebellion in Lower Canada.

Upper Canadians had already received payments for the damages they had suffered, but in Canada East it was another matter. English-speaking Tories in Montréal were outraged. In their eyes, paying for damages would be like "rewarding traitors" and they demanded that Lord Elgin quash any attempts at passing the bill. As a British governor how could he possibly allow such a piece of legislation to pass? But Lord Elgin held firm. It was an internal matter decided by members of an assembly that had been chosen by the voters. The governor would not step in, and would not interfere. Responsible government had arrived both in practice and in principle.

Lord Elgin gave royal assent to the Rebellion Losses Bill on April 25, 1849 — and all hell broke loose. As the governor left the Montréal Parliament buildings, his carriage was attacked by an angry mob, which pelted him with rocks and eggs. That evening, while Parliament was still in session, a mob broke in, battering down the doors and chasing members away. The rioters threw the ornamental mace through the window and set the building on fire. When firemen tried to break through they were pushed back and their hoses were cut.

The crowds roamed the streets for days, torching buildings and eventually storming into LaFontaine's home, drinking his wine and trashing the furniture. As the hooligans ran wild in Montréal, Elgin showed remarkable restraint. He refused to call in the troops, and rather than escalate the situation, he allowed the Tory revolt to run out of steam on its own accord. Indeed, Lord Elgin was less upset about the attacks on his person than by the fact that he recognized several "citizens of good standing" among the mob.

> *Montréal is rotten to the core . . .*
> — Lord Elgin's bitter assessment of the former capital

Want to know why the city of Montréal is not the capital of Canada — or anything else for that matter? Blame those riotous Anglo Tories and their egg-throwin', governor-peltin', Parliament-burnin' ways.

The Montréal riots were about more than simply a government bill. They were the result of pent-up anger and frustrations that had become fixated on the scapegoat cry of "French domination!" The underlying causes were actually economic. In 1846, in a move towards opening up trade, the British government had repealed its Corn Laws (which had granted its colonies special rates of trade for wheat and flour) and in 1849, they had cut back the imperial timber rates as well. Britain had cut the colonies loose financially; had, in a sense, abandoned them. And now this: By granting responsible government, Britain seemed to have given the radicals an upper hand.

Feeling spurned by Great Britain and threatened by reformers, the members of Montréal's commercial class called for a union with the United States. In October 1849, the Montréal *Gazette* published an infamous and short-lived Annexation Manifesto, urging Canada to offer itself to the U.S.A. If Mother didn't want them, then maybe they should try Uncle. Among those who signed the Manifesto were leading merchants such as William Molson and a future prime minister, John Abbott, as well as the former *patriote* leader, Louis-Joseph Papineau. It was a strange, strange time.

The most significant thing about the Montréal riots, perhaps, was the reaction they triggered: none. There was no escalation in violence, no tit-for-tat attacks. Instead, the reformers held firm to their beliefs and they won. It marked the triumph of moderates over extremists and as such was a defining moment in Canada's ongoing evolution.

"The least objectionable place": Choosing Ottawa

Ottawa is a sub-arctic lumber-village converted by royal mandate into a political cockpit.
— British-born essayist Goldwin Smith

If nothing else, the riots in Montréal ended any chance that city had of ever being made capital again. Having moved from Kingston to Montréal, the seat of government now bounced back and forth between Toronto and Québec City, something that satisfied no one. In the end, the Canadians asked Queen Victoria to settle the matter. And on the last day of 1857, she chose a lumbertown on the Ottawa River to be the capital of the United Province of Canada.

Some writers have portrayed it as an act of whim, with Victoria making her decision based on pretty watercolours that struck her fancy. Others have said she simply closed her eyes and stuck a pin in a map. But nothing could be further from the truth. Ottawa was a very astute choice: It was located on the river border between French and English Canada, and was inland from a possible American attack on the St. Lawrence yet linked to the Great Lakes by the defensive Rideau Canal. As an American newspaper wryly noted, Ottawa would be an easy capital to defend, as any "invaders would inevitably be lost in the woods trying to find it."

Another factor was inter-city jealousies. One advisor wrote: "The least objectionable place is the city of Ottawa. Every city is jealous of every other city except Ottawa." Construction on the Parliament Buildings began in 1859, but wasn't completed in 1866.

For an excellent overview of Canada's capital, go to `www.capcan.ca/english/about/intro/index.html`.

Take a virtual tour of Ottawa and the National Capital Region at `www.ottawakiosk.com/Ottawajgpg.html`.

Joseph Howe and the bloodless coup

I can hear my Nova Scotian readers muttering about how the central Canadians have once again hogged all the glory. Didn't Nova Scotia win the fight for responsible government *first* — and without the need for public executions or riots? Well, yes and no. True, the Nova Scotians were awarded responsible government a few months before the Canadians. And yes, they did do it in a highly civil and rational manner. But the real thrust for change was sparked by the Canadians. It was the Canadian rebellions (and the Durham Report that followed) that first got things going.

Joseph Howe, an outspoken editor of the Halifax newspaper the *Novascotian*, was the "Father of Responsible Government in Nova Scotia." But unlike Papineau and Mackenzie in Canada, Howe advocated peaceful means. Nova Scotia was prospering and Halifax had become the hub of North Atlantic shipping. Halifax merchant Samuel Cunard's bold trans-Atlantic steamship line was a rousing success, giving Cunard (and, by extension, Nova Scotia) a near-monopoly on the steam trade. Times were good. Pride and colonial confidence were soaring.

> *Boys, brag of your country. When I'm abroad, I brag of everything that Nova Scotia is, has, or can produce; and when they beat me at everything else, I turn around on them and say: "How high does your tide rise?"*
>   — the ever-brash Joseph Howe

Joseph Howe rejected any hint of a union with the "backwoods" colonies of Canada, but he did agree wholeheartedly with Durham's recommendation regarding colonial self-government. Howe's friend and foe, Judge Thomas Chandler Haliburton, however, mocked the Durham Report mercilessly. "Responsible government," declared the judge, "is responsible nonsense." (Haliburton, a writer and humorist of note, was also the creator of Sam Slick, the Yankee clockmaker, whose wry and sardonic observations were widely read. Haliburton's writings inspired Mark Twain.)

Even with the cutting satirical humour of Judge Haliburton stacked against him, Joseph Howe persevered. In 1847, the reformers, led by Joseph Howe and James Boyle Uniacke (a former Tory), won a solid majority of seats in the Nova Scotia Assembly. The following February they took office, becoming the first responsible government in British North America — and indeed, the first responsible colonial government anywhere in the British Empire. Or any other empire for that matter. Uniacke was named premier, and Howe, provincial secretary.

In Nova Scotia it had been a battle won largely by wit. Howe had published a pamphlet in the form of an "open letter" to the British government, pointing out the absurdities and contradictions of the current system and chiding Britain for denying colonial self-government. Howe out-talked and out-finessed his opponents — and indeed, he talked his way right into power. It was a very Nova Scotian approach. And as noted, the Nova Scotians achieved responsible government *before* the Province of Canada, and they did it without a rebellion or the threat of violence.

> *Without the shedding of a drop of blood [or] the breaking of a pane of glass.*
>   — Joseph Howe, on the manner in which responsible
>   government was won in Nova Scotia

You'll find a brief biography of Joseph Howe at `www.blupete.com/Hist/BiosNS/1800-67/Howe.htm`. For an overview of Nova Scotia history, go to `trulycanadian.freeservers.com/nova_scotia_history.htm#top`.

United Canada: A report card on unity

In many ways, the union of Upper and Lower Canada was a prelude to full confederation. A test run. A warm-up. A rehearsal for the main event. True, the short-lived union was ultimately a failure that ended in parliamentary gridlock and a colony more divided that ever. But the United Province of Canada did have some notable successes:

- ✔ As mentioned, formal school systems were established in both French and English Canada (the first religious, the second mainly secular).

- ✔ With Britain no longer offering sweetheart export deals to its colonies, Canada strengthened trade ties with the U.S. instead (notably through the 1854 Reciprocity Treaty, which opened up freer trade between the two).

- ✔ The seigneurial system (the feudal landowning system covered in Chapter 4) was finally abolished in 1854.

- ✔ As "railway fever" swept the colonies, the Province of Canada launched several bold schemes, including the famed Grand Trunk Railway linking Sarnia in the west with Québec City in the east and the U.S. seaport of Portland, Maine, to the south. By the 1860s, the Grand Trunk had more than 2,000 km of track, and was the largest railway system in the world — and one of the most expensive. Many of the early rail schemes were boondoggles, to be sure. But they also helped encourage expansion and development by speeding up trade and transportation. (Railways in the 1840s and '50s had the same shiny "rah-rah! profit and progress" appeal that canals had enjoyed in the 1820s.)

- ✔ Most importantly, the United Province of Canada had pushed for, and won, colonial self-government — that is, a ruling council chosen from among popularly elected members of the Assembly. (I know, I know. We already went over this. But it really is the key achievement of this era. It set Canada on the road to political independence, while still maintaining ties to Great Britain. No cinematic Revolution for us. No sir. Canadians moved at a slower pace. Still do, as a matter of fact.)

Baldwin and LaFontaine have been recently "re-discovered" and are now feted as heroes and historical role models. This is good. But it is also easy to exaggerate their influence. Forces *outside* of Canada were just as important in the creation of responsible government in the colonies. In Great Britain, the mood had shifted away from the shop-worn theories of mercantilism (which I describe in Chapter 4) and towards more open, freer trade.

One of the cornerstones of imperialism had been a closed system of colony and empire. When that crumbled and the protective tariffs (such as those embodied in the Corn Laws) were repealed, the dominoes began to fall. With the economic bonds of empire loosened, how could Britain deny the push for colonial self-government? If the economic life of the colonies were no longer to be controlled by Britain, why should their political life be?

The long and winding road

Nova Scotia and the Province of Canada were the first to gain responsible government. The others followed.

Responsible Government Won (in order):

1848: Nova Scotia

1848: Province of Canada (Ontario and Quebec)

1848: New Brunswick (though it wasn't employed effectively until 1854)

1851: P.E.I. (though not fully realized until 1862)

1855: Newfoundland

The rebels had lit the flame, and LaFontaine and Baldwin had spearheaded the fight, but the battle was fought just as strongly among British parliamentarians back in London. And when Lord Elgin was sent to Canada, the Colonial Secretary Lord Grey made it very clear that he expected Elgin to implement full responsible government. Under Grey's directives, colonies were to be governed only according to the will of their own inhabitants.

Men such as Durham, Grey, and Elgin deserve as much credit for winning responsible government as do LaFontaine and Baldwin, or Joseph Howe.

Gold Colony: British Columbia Is Born

The political evolution of the Pacific Coast happened much more quickly than that of the other colonies. As a hybrid of fur trade and Crown colony, defined mainly in anti-American terms, B.C was created, and took shape, largely as a reaction to U.S. encroachment.

In the 1840s, the Pacific Coast was still under the domain of the fur traders, and at the forefront was James Douglas, who served two Empires: that of the Hudson's Bay Company and that of Great Britain. Having worked his way up the HBC ladder to become Chief Factor (a high-ranked administrator), Douglas was also made governor of both Vancouver Island and mainland British Columbia.

Like Champlain in New France and Simcoe in Upper Canada, James Douglas has gone down in history as "the Father of British Columbia."

Fort Victoria: An island toehold

The border with the United States had been drawn along the 49th parallel from the Great Lakes clear across to the foothills of the Rockies. From there, the mountains and the coast were under joint occupation by the HBC and the United States. If the border were ever extended across the mountains, however, it would clip off the southern end of Vancouver Island.

The HBC's North American governor, George Simpson, dubbed "the Little Emperor," decided to make a pre-emptive move onto Vancouver Island. James Douglas was sent in to build a trading post and establish a clear presence — and prior "ownership" — should the HBC have to surrender its territory to the south. Because Vancouver Island straddled the 49th parallel, building a post on it *before* the line was drawn was a clever strategic move.

By 1843, Douglas had surveyed several locations before settling on what he called "a perfect Eden." He hired some of the Salish people who lived there to help him build a post, which he named Fort Victoria in honour of Britain's young queen. Fort Victoria would become a very important colonial toehold for Britain. It established Britain and the HBC on the Island, and south of the 49th parallel. As such, it "pinned down" the western end of the American border. Without it, all of Vancouver Island — and perhaps the entire Pacific Coast as well — might now be part of the United States.

At `groucho.sb.gov.bc.ca/culture/schoolnet/fortvic/` you'll find more on the history of the Hudson's Bay Company fort at Victoria. For background and pics of Victoria's heritage buildings, visit `collections.ic.gc.ca/building/`. The City of Victoria's Web site (`www.city.victoria.bc.ca/history.htm`) provides a history of the city. And for a gallery of the First Nations of southern Vancouver Island, visit `www-19.qp.gov.bc.ca/galleries/firstnation/index.htm`.

"54.40 or Fight!"

Mexico held California. Russia held Alaska. In between was the disputed Oregon Territory, which was claimed — and jointly occupied — by both the HBC and the United States. Mountainous and coastal, it was a huge chunk of land and highly coveted. In 1844, James Polk was elected president of the United States on the battle cry of *"54.40 or fight!"* (54° 40' being the latitude of the Russian territory on the coast). Based on dubious Spanish concessions, the Americans now insisted that the Oregon Territory belonged completely to them, all the way up to Alaska. This would have given the United States the entire coast and most of the interior of what is now British Columbia. It would also have cut off a future Canada from the Pacific.

In the words of the American newspaper editor John L. O'Sullivan, it was the "manifest destiny" of the United States to annex and possess *all* of North America. This concept of a nation's "destiny" had an almost religious appeal to expansionist-hungry Americans, and it goaded President Polk into making bigger and bigger threats. (Canada got off easy: Mexico was almost eaten alive by the Americans under the banner of "manifest destiny.")

Great Britain had suggested that the Oregon Territory be divided along the Columbia River, at roughly the 45th parallel. This was the reasonable solution. After all, the Americans had never had any real presence above the river. But the U.S.A. wanted it all, and they continued to bellow "54.40 or fight!" It was all just bluster and bravado. But it worked. A hasty compromise was reached, and in the Oregon Treaty of 1846, the two sides agreed to simply extend the 49th parallel straight across the Rockies.

It was a ridiculous way to draw a border that needed to pass over mountain ranges. The line ignored watersheds, river basins, and the natural division of valleys. It was razor clean and completely arbitrary. Vancouver Island, however, dipped below this imaginary but decisive line. By building a post on the southern tip of the island, the HBC had assured that the entire island would stay in British hands. (A tiny hook of a peninsula on the coast also lay just below the 49th parallel, creating the ongoing anomaly of Point Roberts, a tuft of American soil attached to the mainland of British Columbia.) The HBC was forced to retreat north. It relocated its operations from Oregon to Fort Victoria, and it shifted its attention from the Columbia River to the Fraser.

The Pig War

When the border was extended along the 49th parallel to the coast, it had to veer sharply south to go around Vancouver Island. Unfortunately, the treaty makers were working with old, out-of-date maps. The result: a poorly defined border that ran through a maze of islands. Right in the middle of this disputed strait was the little isle of San Juan, just a few miles off the coast of Victoria, which was occupied by both the HBC and a handful of American farmers. Trouble started over a pig.

In the spring of 1859, a sow belonging to the Hudson's Bay Company got loose and started rooting around in a potato patch that belonged to an American settler. The American, a hot-tempered man by the name of Lyman Cutler, grabbed his rifle and shot the dirty swine. The HBC demanded that Lyman reimburse them. Lyman refused — and the next thing you know, the U.S. of A. had sent in troops to "protect American citizens." By the end of August, more than 400 American soldiers had landed on San Juan Island. But James Douglas refused to back down, and he sent in troops of his own. A British naval attack was called off at the very last moment, and a military standoff ensued, an armed showdown that lasted right up until 1872, when — in a very dubious arbitration process — the island was ceded to the Americans. All this over a pig.

Go to www.nps.gov/sajh/home.htm for lots more on San Juan Island and the "Pig War."

Gold on the Fraser

In 1849, Vancouver Island was made a Crown colony, with the capital at Fort Victoria. It was the first British colony to be established west of the Great Lakes. The original governor didn't last very long, and in 1851 he was replaced by James Douglas, Chief Factor for the HBC, thus blending the fur trade and the British Crown into one authority. A townsite was laid out adjacent to the fort and named "Victoria" in honour of Kaiser Wilhelm. I'm kidding of course. I was just seeing if you were paying attention. No, the town was named after Queen Victoria Herself.

Although a small coal-mining community had taken root in nearby Nanaimo, Vancouver Island was still predominantly a fur-trading colony. But in 1858, all of that changed. A new element was added to the mix: *gold*. A rich find had been discovered on the Fraser River, deep in the interior of the mainland, and when word got out it triggered a stampede of miners, many of them American. It was a wild, exciting time. As the only supply centre and ocean port in the region, Victoria became the main jumping-off point for those who were en route to the Fraser. As the gold-seekers poured in, the once tranquil community of Victoria was now overrun by rough-hewn prospectors. Within weeks, more than 20,000 men had disembarked in Victoria, a community of just 450 at the time the gold rush started.

James Douglas, as both the HBC's chief factor and the governor of the colony, was worried about the huge influx of Americans — and rightly so. After all, that was how the HBC and Britain had lost half the Oregon Territory: American citizens had first flooded in and had then began demanding independence from British rule. *Where Americans went, their flag was sure to follow . . .* Douglas was quick to act. He drew up a list of regulations, he hired constables, and he issued a public proclamation that the gold fields of the Fraser were Crown property. Any miners who wished to enter that territory would have to register first and pay a licensing fee.

Most of the miners only passed through, stopping just long enough to obtain a license from the government, stock up on supplies, and arrange transportation to the Fraser River. But many stayed, and the population of Victoria shot up. More than 200 new commercial buildings were built the first year alone. The streets became packed and the roads were thick with mud. Overnight, Victoria had gone from being a quiet trading post to being a chaotic hub bustling with activity.

> *This city suffers from an excess of politicians, lawyers, merchants, transients and saloons and a considerable shortage of accommodation, water, women and good roads!*
> — Governor James Douglas on the rough-and-tumble atmosphere of early Victoria

By issuing licenses and proclamations, James Douglas had assumed control over the mainland, but it was all a bluff. His authority as governor didn't extend beyond Vancouver Island, and when London pointed this out to him, Douglas offered to let the issue "fall to the ground as a dead letter." Instead, the British government decided to give Douglas the authority he had so brazenly claimed for himself. On August 2, 1858, a second Crown colony was created, on the mainland, dubbed "British Columbia."

Douglas resigned from his post with the HBC to become governor of *both* colonies, the island and the mainland, and a detachment of Royal Engineers under Colonel Richard Moody was brought in to build roads and survey towns. Moody, who also acted as Douglas's lieutenant-governor, established a mainland capital near the mouth of the Fraser River. The settlement was given the grand name of "New Westminster," but with all the trees hacked down during construction, it soon became known as "Stump City."

Visit www.tbc.gov.bc.ca/culture/schoolnet/helmcken/people/james.html to find more on James Douglas.

The Cariboo Road

The colonies of Vancouver Island and British Columbia were still reeling from the impact of the first gold rush when a second, even bigger strike was made in the remote Cariboo Valley. James Douglas quickly commissioned a wagon road into the interior. Carved out of sheer rock and thick forests, the Cariboo Road, as it was known, was a feat of engineering — and a hair-raising experience to travel along. It threaded its way through the treacherous Hell's Gate Canyon at dangerous heights and through tricky hairpin turns. It crossed steep river rapids on trestles and bridges along a 650-kilometre route deep into the mountains to the boomtown of Barkerville, in the very heart of the gold fields.

The Cariboo Road, connecting the towns of Yale and Barkerville, was "the golden way" along which millions of dollars in ore were hauled out. Carriages, mule trains, ox carts — even imported camels at one point — moved along this frontier highway. Just as important, the Cariboo Road was a catalyst to development. It helped open the interior to settlement and trade.

At www.sbtc.gov.bc.ca/culture/schoolnet/cariboo/index.htm you'll find a fun and extensive site on the Cariboo Gold Rush. For more on Barkerville, B.C.'s gold rush boomtown, go to barkerville.com. And www.tbc.gov.bc.ca/culture/schoolnet/yale/index.htm has more on the gold rush town of Yale.

Franklin and the quest for a Northwest Passage

The search for a Northwest Passage continued. But why? What was the point? By now it was clear that any Arctic sea route would be both hazardous and impractical. And anyway, trade lines crossed the continent overland. Ah, but never underestimate the power of the irrational in human history. The quest for a Northwest Passage was about glory! Glory and fame. Or, failing that, martyrdom.

The British in particular seemed to take a certain masochistic glee in the amount of suffering they could endure. Captain John Franklin had already made two previous treks — one of which had ended in death, misery, murder, and cannibalism — when he decided to try again. In 1845, he loaded down two ships, the *Terror* and the *Erebus*, with everything from pianos to fine china and silverware, and set sail with a crew of 129 men. They were never seen again. Ironically, Franklin achieved more dead than he did alive. A frenzy of expeditions followed Franklin's disappearance, in what would be the longest and most exhaustive search operation in human history. And though the would-be rescuers never found Franklin or his crew, Captain Robert McClure did stumble upon one possible Northwest Passage in 1851.

Even then, it wasn't until 1903–6 that the passage was finally conquered by ship, when the Norwegian explorer Roald Amundsen made it through onboard his little vessel, the *Gjoa*. And though it now served no strategic or economic purpose, the dream of a Northwest Passage, which had begun with John Cabot in 1497, was finally reached. (There was, however, a ghoulish postscript: Beginning in 1984, the graves of three Franklin crewmen discovered on Beechy Island were opened and the bodies — still hauntingly preserved after more than 135 years — were exhumed to great public fascination.)

Go to `www.vif.com/users/Inularit.Resolute/pages/frame.html` for a look at the doomed Franklin expedition from a Northern perspective. At `www.cronab.demon.co.uk/frank.htm` you'll find a detailed biography of Franklin, with an emphasis on his Arctic voyages. For still more on Franklin with extensive and fascinating links, visit `www.ric.edu/rpotter/SJFranklin.html`.

The hangin' judge

More gold. More chaos. Rich finds were now discovered deep in the Kootenay interior, and the craziness started anew. Keeping a steady, law-abiding hand throughout was Matthew Baillie Begbie, "the hangin' judge." By keeping the miners in line, Begbie almost single-handedly prevented B.C. from becoming the type of lawless frontier free-for-all that California had become during its gold rush. Begbie travelled tirelessly from camp to camp, holding court in saloons and music halls, and sometimes even on horseback — but always with the proper wig and red robe of a British judge.

Judge Begbie once waded into the middle of an angry mob of miners down at Wild Horse Creek just as they were about to start looting and rioting. "Boys," he shouted, "If there is a shooting in Kootenay, there will be hanging in Kootenay." There were no shootings.

> *He was the biggest man, smartest man, best-looking man and damnedest man that ever came down the Cariboo Road . . .*
> — one miner's description of Judge Begbie

Was Begbie a good man? He was certainly a *great* man. He spent 46 years on the bench, he brought law and order to the British Columbia frontier, and he did seem to be more sensitive to Native customs and cultures than most. After B.C. had joined Confederation, Begbie dismissed an anti-potlatch law as an ill-conceived affront to Native society. And he often defended the rights of Chinese workers when no one else would. But it is also worth noting that, in his first thirteen years on the frontier circuit, Begbie had 27 men hanged. Twenty-two of them were Native. (A historian friend of mine, on reading this, doesn't appreciate the innuendo behind those numbers. "Well, maybe they were guilty," he says. "Ever think of that?")

For more on Judge Begbie, go to barkerville.com/vol4/first.htm.

Responsible government? In B.C.?

James Douglas was not a very democratic man. Steeped in the tradition of the Hudson's Bay Company, he had little use for notions of "representative" or "responsible" government. As in Nova Scotia, the chief agitators for responsible government in B.C. were newspapermen:

- ✔ *Amor de Cosmos*, a restless eccentric man, originally from Nova Scotia. (His real name was Bill Smith, but he had changed it to the more lofty "Lover of the Universe" to better capture his devotion to mankind.) Amor de Cosmos first arrived in 1858 and established himself in Victoria with an Island newspaper, the *British Colonist*.
- ✔ *John Robson*, an Upper Canadian, arrived soon after, and he set up shop in New Westminster. He produced the mainland's first newspaper, the *British Columbian*.

Cosmos and Robson led the push for greater self-government in the West Coast colonies, and interestingly enough, both men would later become premiers of British Columbia after Confederation.

Still, it wasn't until Douglas had retired in 1864 that British Columbia was finally given a fully responsible elected assembly. Credit goes to the man who followed Douglas as governor of the mainland colony: a weary, chronically ill, heavy drinker by the name of Frederick Seymour.

Seymour dissolved the council of cronies that had been ruling under Douglas and installed duly elected members instead. James Douglas may have been the Father of British Columbia, but Frederick Seymour deserves to share the title "Father of Responsible Government in B.C." with Cosmos and Robson.

In an 1866 shotgun wedding, the two colonies were forced into one, under the name British Columbia. The capital was first originally located in New Westminster, but after some vigorous infighting it was moved to the island city of Victoria. And there it remains to this day, preserved in all its charm and dappled sunlight: an outpost of British traditions on the very edge of the continent.

> *Home of the newly-wed and the nearly-dead.*
>   — common description of Victoria

At www.tbc.gov.bc.ca/culture/schoolnet/fortvic/people/index. html you'll find brief bios on figures in early B.C. history, including James Douglas, Colonel Moody, and Amor de Cosmos. For more on Cosmos and his newspaper, *The Colonist,* go to bc-freemasonry.com/biography/cosmos_ amor_de/b_colonist.html.

For a history of newspapers on the West Coast (including those of Robson and Cosmos) visit members.tripod.com/~Hughdoherty/victoria.htm.

Chapter 13

The Confederation Waltz

*T*he idea of uniting the colonies of British North America had been around for a long time. Ever since the Loyalists first arrived, in fact. But it wasn't until the 1860s that several key elements came together to make the union both a reality — and a necessity:

   ✔ A change in British attitudes.

   ✔ A renewed fear of an American invasion.

   ✔ The impending loss of free trade with the United States.

   ✔ The promise (and financial debts) of a dawning age of rail.

   ✔ Dissatisfaction among English Canadians with their ineffective united parliament — which was often locked in a bitter stalemate.

   ✔ And last, but not least, "the glory argument," that shimmering, romantic allure of creating something bigger, better, grander.

In this chapter, we will look at each of these factors in turn and see just how bold the final scheme was: to create a new, united "confederation." After 1867, we were no longer a scattering of separate colonies. After 1867, we were more than the mere sum of our parts. After 1867, Canada as we know it began to take shape.

> *Confederation was, in many ways, a startling development. One can add up the causes of Confederation and still not get the sum of it. Like all political achievements it was a matter of timing, luck, and the combination of a certain set of men and events.*
>
> — historian Peter Waite

Causes of Confederation

The attitude in Great Britain had changed. Britain was still the head of an empire, and still just as imperialistic as ever, but the emphasis was now on trade and profit rather than military might and imperial monopolies. Great Britain was reinventing itself as a powerful *commercial* empire.

The colonies were now seen as a financial drain, a "burden" that needed to be shifted. In short, British North America had to grow up and take more responsibility for its own affairs — without leaving the Empire entirely, of course. A self-governing union, still under the final authority of Great Britain, seemed like the ideal solution.

The U.S. Civil War

> *Fear of an American takeover during the Civil War was perhaps the leading cause of Canadian Confederation.*
> — historians Douglas Francis, Richard Jones, and Donald Smith

The United States was tearing itself apart in a grisly internal war (1861–65). The slave-owning Confederate states of the South had attempted to cede from the union, and the free states of the North (the Union) were hammering them into submission. It was a brutal, bloody conflict, and it strained the relationship between America and the British colonies to the breaking point.

Although Canada did not support the slave-owning southern Confederacy, it got caught up in the struggle nonetheless. Britain *claimed* to be neutral, but showed clear sympathy and even tacit support for the breakaway states of the South. As a result, the U.S. government became vehemently anti-British and newspapers in Chicago and New York warned Canada, "Just wait 'til this war is over. You're next!" The move toward Confederation took place against this backdrop of the American Civil War, which added a sense of urgency to events. Three crises in particular brought Britain and the U.S. to the brink of war — with Canada as the potential battlefield.

The Trent Crisis

Remember how, back in 1812, the British used to board U.S. ships on the high seas and arrest deserters? Remember how upset the Americans got? Remember how they used that as an excuse to invade Canada? (You'll find the whole story in Chapter 10.) Well, now it was Britain's turn to be "violated." In November 1861, a Union warship stopped the British mail steamer *Trent* at gunpoint in neutral waters. The Americans boarded the vessel and arrested two Confederate delegates who were on their way to Britain. Outraged at this act of "piracy," the British threatened retaliation. President Lincoln released the two men, but anger on both sides had reached a fever pitch. A U.S. attack on Canada now seemed imminent, and Britain dispatched 14,000 troops to North America. It was the largest military detachment sent over since the War of 1812.

The Alabama Affair

The British, having declared their neutrality, often looked the other way when dealing with the rebel South. They even allowed the Confederates to build a warship, the *Alabama*, in a Liverpool shipyard. The ship eluded capture, was outfitted in France, and began a two-year rampage against the North. By the time the *Alabama* was finally cornered and sunk, it had caused millions of dollars' worth of damage. Later, the U.S. State Department would claim that by allowing the *Alabama* to be built, the British had helped prolong the Civil War by two years. And, since the war had cost the U.S. government $2 billion a year, the Americans presented Britain with a bill for a whopping $4 billion dollars — along with the suggestion that, if the British didn't want to pay up, they could always hand over Canada instead. Give 'em Canada and they'd call it even. (If nothing else, you've got to admire their chutzpah.)

The St. Alban's Raid

As the Union Army marched south, burning towns and laying waste, the Confederates decided to strike back via the backdoor of Canada. In October 1864, a band of Confederate sympathizers attacked the town of St. Alban's, Vermont. They robbed three banks of $200,000, wounding two men and killing a third. They then fled north, into Canada, where they were quickly captured. But a Montréal magistrate released the men and even, incredibly, returned their money. The U.S. government was understandably outraged, and anti-British feelings now became anti-Canadian as well. The St. Alban's raid, as much as anything, doomed any talk of "free and open" trade between the U.S. and the colonies of British North America. With an angry, battle-hardened U.S. to the south, Canadians felt exposed and vulnerable. There was strength in numbers. A larger union would clearly give the colonies better military protection — but there were economic incentives as well.

The impending end of free trade

When Great Britain ended its protective colonial tariff rates and began moving towards freer trade, it sent the colonies of British North America into a panic. To make up for lost imperial revenue, the colonies worked out a Treaty of Reciprocity (that is, open or "free" trade) with the United States. It was a crucial deal, which allowed the Canadian and Maritime colonies access for their fish, lumber, coal, and grain to the lucrative American market. Reciprocity brought prosperity, but it also made the colonies increasingly dependent upon U.S. trade policies. The Treaty was due to be renewed in 1865, but the tensions caused by the U.S. Civil War made it almost certain that the Americans would allow it to lapse instead, ending free trade between the British colonies and the United States. Once the American market had been cut off, what then?

In this, a union of British North American colonies made a lot of sense. Why not create a union of our own, one that would allow cross-colonial access to Maritime fisheries, New Brunswick timber, Canadian factories, and perhaps even the land and natural resources of the vast Northwest?

Here's the funny part. When the Americans did announce, in a huff, that they would not renew the Reciprocity Treaty, one of their aims was to force Canada's hand. The Americans had heightened their cries for annexation, you see, and they thought that by ending the trade agreement they might paint the Canadians into a corner. "You want free trade? Fine. Join the American union." But instead of driving the British colonies into the American fold, the impending end of free trade actually drew them closer together. Ironic, no?

> *Had reciprocity continued, it is possible that Confederation might never have gathered enough impetus to overcome strong regional inertia.*
> — historian P.B. Waite

The railway revolution

If the American Civil War and the end of free trade made Confederation necessary, the railways made it possible. In Canada, rail transportation had revolutionized the very concept of time and distance. Trains could run year-round, winter to fall, and they accelerated the pace of expansion. Where a man might have been able to cover 12 miles a day on horseback, he could now cross 400 miles or more by rail. The railways made Confederation viable. Steel track would bring the far-flung regions together. It would unite them, expand them. The colonies had been isolated from each other by the sheer scale of Canadian geography. That obstacle could now be crossed.

There was great promise in the railways — and great profits, too. It's not a coincidence that many of the leading proponents of Confederation were also railway promoters. (George-Étienne Cartier, for one, was Solicitor General of the Province of Canada *and* solicitor of the Grand Trunk Railway. Talk about a conflict of interest! Or rather, a *convergence* of interests.)

But the railways were about more than just business. With the military threat from the U.S. growing daily, it was clear that a separate, internally connected colonial railway was needed, one that didn't have to pass through American territory and that could move troops from the Maritimes into the interior quickly and efficiently. A union of British colonies could provide both a united colonial army and a functioning intercolonial railway.

Stalemate in the Province of Canada

The push for Confederation began in the United Province of Canada — and for good reason. The Act of Union (see Chapter 12) had led to a political deadlock, and frustrations with the present system were running high. Rather than helping to swamp and overpower the French Canadians, the united Parliament had created exactly the opposite effect: The Province of Canada was now split right down the middle, along political, cultural, social, and linguistic lines. With equal seats awarded to both sides, anyone wishing to hold power needed to win over a majority of French-Canadian voters. The Act of Union had in fact *strengthened* the French-Canadian position — not weakened it.

By 1851, the two leading reformers, Louis LaFontaine and Robert Baldwin, had retired, exhausted by the shrill atmosphere and growing radicalism of the Province of Canada. In their place, a conservative alliance took shape under the leadership of a young Kingston attorney named John A. Macdonald and an equally canny Montréal-based lawyer by the name of George-Étienne Cartier. (A former armed *patriote* of 1837 who claimed to be descended from the explorer Jacques Cartier, George-Étienne was a grab bag of contradictions: a proud defender of French-Canadian traditions who was nonetheless infatuated with British royalty.) Funny, charming, ruthless: Macdonald and Cartier would dominate Canadian politics for the next 30 years. Historian J.M.S. Careless called it "one of the great political partnerships of Canadian history."

Politically, the Province of Canada was divided into two opposing sides, each with an English-Canadian and a French-Canadian component:

✔ **Conservatives:**

- in Canada West, John A. Macdonald's "Liberal-Conservative" Party (a coalition of moderate and traditional Tories)

- in Canada East, George-Étienne Cartier's *parti bleu* (aligned with the Church, and pro-British and anti-American in tone)

✔ **Reformers:**

- in Canada West, George Brown's Reform Party, along with a radical wing, consisting mainly of farmers, who called themselves "Clear Grits" (as in, pure and unspoiled: "all sand and no dirt, clear grit all the way through.")

- in Canada East, Antoine-Aimé Dorion's radical *parti rouge*

    The *parti rouge* was often at loggerheads with the Catholic Church. So bad was the relationship that priests in Québec would warn parishioners, "Remember! Heaven is blue, Hell is red." (The loose, often bickering coalition of Reformers, Clear Grits, and *rouges* would later evolve into the Liberal Party of Canada, whose members are nicknamed "Grits" even now.)

"Rep by pop!"

The population of the Province of Canada was soaring, and the biggest increase was in the English-speaking region of Canada West. An 1861 census put the population at the following: 1.6 million in Canada West, and 1.1 million in Canada East. This was a huge difference, yet Parliament was still divided on a strict 50-50 split of seats. The British had thought they could defeat the French Canadians by underrepresenting them in Parliament. But the tide had turned. Now it was the English Canadians who were getting the short end, and they howled in protest. For George Brown and his Reformers, it was patently unfair that Canada West, which now had the larger population, should be locked into an equal number of seats with Canada East. The slogan "Representation by population!" (or "Rep by pop!") became the rallying cry of English-Canadian reformers. It was, said Brown, the only way to end "French-Catholic domination."

Members in Canada East refused to accept any such "Rep by pop!" proposal. The result? An ongoing political stalemate. One way to break the deadlock would be to create a union with the other British colonies. Canada West and Canada East, as separate provinces, would each have their own government and their own decision-making process. This would give Canada West greater autonomy, while still allowing for inter-colonial trade and defense.

The great coalition

And so, on June 24, 1864, George Brown did something remarkable. He rose in the Assembly and offered to cross the floor. That is, he agreed to end the deadlock by joining a coalition with his arch nemesis and political foe, John A. Macdonald. Brown had three conditions:

- ✔ That the coalition work towards creating a larger united federation of all British North America.

- ✔ That the government of Canada, and any future union, be based on the democratic principle of representation by population (that is, "Rep by pop").

- ✔ And finally, that the future federation expand west into the vast reaches of the Northwest — and perhaps even to the Pacific itself. "The Americans are encroaching," Brown warned. Time was of the essence.

The coalition involved three of Canada's four main political groups: John A. Macdonald's English-Canadian Conservatives; George-Étienne Cartier's French-Canadian Conservatives; and George Brown's English-Canadian Reformers. (Shut out of the coalition, and conspicuous by their very absence, were the French-Canadian reformers of the left-of-centre *parti rouge*.)

Spearheaded by Brown, Macdonald, and Cartier, the "Great Coalition of 1864" would become the driving force behind Confederation.

Blueprint for a Nation

The Maritime colonies were just as worried about the American threat and the possible end of reciprocity. Egged on by Britain, talks had begun on a possible "Maritime union," a move led by the three respective premiers:

- ✔ **Charles Tupper** in Nova Scotia
- ✔ **Leonard Tilley** in New Brunswick
- ✔ **John Hamilton Gray** in Prince Edward Island

When the Canadians caught wind of these talks, they countered with a proposal of their own. Why not discuss a union of *all* the British North American colonies? A conference was quickly arranged and a date and time chosen: Charlottetown, P.E.I., September 1864.

Why Charlottetown? Because the Islanders were lukewarm about joining any sort of union and holding the conference in P.E.I. was just about the only way to ensure that their delegates would even bother to show up.

The Charlottetown Conference

Led by Brown, Macdonald, and Cartier, a delegation of Canadians descended upon P.E.I. on September 1, 1864. In many ways, the conference that followed was one long extended schmooze-fest, an unabashed attempt by the smooth-talking Canadians to seduce their Maritime cousins into marriage. The wine and bubbly flowed, and the soirees, elegant balls, expensive dinners, and great slathers of Canadian charm all did the trick; the Maritimers were won over. As historian Donald Swainson put it, "Confederation was floated through on champagne."

- ✔ **Cartier and Macdonald** presented the overriding arguments in favour of Confederation.
- ✔ **George Brown** outlined the constitutional arrangements (a connection to the British Crown, a strong central government with the regions maintaining control over local matters; "Rep by pop," and so on).
- ✔ **Alexander Galt**, the Canadian Minister of Finance, presented the economic overview for the proposed union.

✓ **Thomas D'Arcy McGee**, an Irish poet turned politician, presented the emotional appeal. McGee, master of the so-called "glory argument," spoke of a "new nationality" and a "new vision." If Galt was the head, McGee was the heart.

The Underground Railroad

In 1850, the United States passed a Fugitive Slave Act that allowed owners to re-capture runaway slaves anywhere in the U.S., even in the free states of the North (such as Pennsylvania, Ohio, or New York). Escaped slaves now began fleeing to Canada in ever-greater numbers. As many as 30,000 of them made the terrifying journey, with most crossing over into what is now southern Ontario. They travelled along a secret network of safe houses, dubbed "the Underground Railroad." In code, the escaped slaves were called "passengers," the guides were "conductors," the homes that hid them were "stations." At the forefront of this heroic, clandestine operation were free blacks and the members of the Quaker Church. When escaped slaves arrived in Canada, they still faced contempt and open discrimination — but they were now *free*, with the protection of the law on their side, and that made all the difference.

The following are some of the key players in the Underground Railroad:

Harriet Tubman: They called her the "Black Moses." Based in St. Catharines, Ontario, Tubman was a fearless conductor along the Underground Railroad. Even with a $40,000 bounty on her head, Tubman travelled deep into the slave states on more than a dozen perilous missions, often in disguise and carrying forged papers. Tubman helped lead more than 300 slaves out of bondage, including her elderly parents and four of her brothers. During the U.S. Civil War, Harriet joined the Northern Army as nurse, scout, and spy.

Josiah Henson: An escaped slave who helped found the free black community of Dawn (now Dresden, Ontario), Henson was said to be partly the model for the lead character of Harriet Beecher Stowe's influential anti-slavery novel, *Uncle Tom's Cabin*. (Henson's own cabin is preserved as a museum outside of Dresden, even today.)

Mary Ann Shadd: A freeborn black, Shadd moved to Canada West in the 1850s and established a newspaper, the *Provincial Freeman*, to fight against discrimination and segregation. Once, when American slave hunters chased an escaped black into Canada and captured him in Chatham, Shadd pulled the boy free and ran into the courthouse, where she rang the bell and called out the town. The Americans fled. After the Civil War ended, Shadd studied law in the United States.

You'll find an excellent site on Canada and the Underground Railroad at collections.ic.gc.ca/freedom/. For testimonies from fugitive slaves who reached Canada, go to odur.let.rug.nl/~usa/D/1826-1850/slavery/fugitxx.htm. For more on Henson's cabin, go to www.uncletomscabin.org. For a good overview of the Underground Railway visit www.nlc-bnc.ca/confed/blacks.htm. You can find the Ontario Black History Society archives at collections.ic.gc.ca/obho.

It was a tag-team sales pitch, and it worked. The Maritime delegates, heady on wine and new-found friendship, agreed to meet again in Québec City in order to work out the details for just such a union. Even today, the city of Charlottetown considers itself "the Cradle of Confederation."

At collections.ic.gc.ca/charlottetown/ you'll find a well-presented site on the Charlottetown Conference of 1864, with background bios on all the original delegates. I also recommend a visit to the Parks Canada site parkscanada.pch.gc.ca/parks/pei/province_house/province_house _e.htm for a "virtual tour" of Province House in Charlottetown, where the Confederation Conference took place.

The Québec Conference: 72 Resolutions

In October 1864, delegates met again at Québec City, and the Canadians presented "72 Resolutions" outlining the specifics of a possible union. The chief architect and main author of the resolutions was John A. Macdonald. More than any other person, John A. can claim to be the "author" of modern Canada. At Québec City, the delegates got down to work. They refined, revised, and reworked the resolutions. They wrangled, argued, debated, laughed, swore, and eventually came up with a final plan.

A federal system

Britain and France are examples of *unitary states,* with a single, strong central government. This system, also known as "legislative union," was initially favoured by Macdonald but it was quickly shouted down by regional representatives, who argued that in a country as large and regionally diverse as Canada, such a method simply wouldn't work.

Instead, a "federal system" was agreed upon. The new country would have *two* levels of government: a central one to manage matters of common national interest, and provincial ones to handle local and regional matters. This was the system the Americans had used (with state and national governments).

But the Americans also elected their president directly, in a separate vote, meaning that their national leader could be from one party and the majority of working members in the government from another. Canadians rejected this model for one that would be "similar in principle to that of the United Kingdom," wherein the party leader with the most seats in the House of Commons becomes prime minister. And so, structurally, the new union would be a blend of British and American models: a federal system without a president.

The two levels of government were assigned different responsibilities:

> ✔ **Provincial Government:** education, roads, medicine, municipalities, property rights, civil law, administering justice, and managing natural resources (i.e., forestry, minerals, waterpower)

> ✔ **Federal Government:** currency and banking (that is, printing money and controlling it), defense, navigation and shipping, Native affairs, marriage and divorce, criminal law, and the seacoast and inland fisheries

This division of power allowed Québec to maintain control over its own language, religion, education, and civil law. Which is to say, the pillars of French-Canadian society, as outlined by historian François-Xavier Garneau (see Chapter 12), had been duly protected.

But just as important — and this was a key difference between Canada and the United States — any unnamed or "residual" powers that were not specifically covered by the Constitution were automatically reserved by the federal government in Ottawa. Or, in computer-talk, the federal government was made "the default setting" of Canadian political authority.

This was done at Macdonald's insistence. He wanted to avoid the sort of weak centre that he felt had led to the U.S. Civil War.

John A. Macdonald envisioned a strong central government, but over the ensuing years so much power has devolved to the provinces that Canada is now one of the most decentralized countries on earth. Today, Ottawa has far, far less power than it did in John A. Macdonald's day — and those powers that it does have are eroding, not getting stronger. Whether or not this is a good thing remains to be seen. Some say our current decentralized system has weakened Canadian unity; others say it is this very flexibility that has allowed Canada to remain intact in the face of opposing regional forces. We bend so that we won't break.

Structure of the federal government

The British Crown would be represented in Canada by a Governor-General nationally and by Lieutenant-Governors in each province. The federal government itself would be "bicameral." That is, it would be divided into two separate legislative branches:

> ✔ **The Senate,** Canada's Upper House, would be *appointed* (that is, it would be non-democratic and would never have to answer to Canadian voters).

> ✔ **The House of Commons,** Canada's Lower House, would be *elected* (that is, it would have to answer to Canadian voters — at least at election time).

The seats in the Senate would be represented not by population, but by *region*. Sounds like a good idea, right? "Rep by region" would allow the Senate to act as a counterweight, giving extra voice to Canada's less-populated areas. Sadly, it never quite worked out that way. Why? Because members of the Senate were appointed by the federal government — and not by the people in the actual regions they were supposed to represent. Can you say "federal lackeys"? Can you say "patronage playpen"?

Indeed, patronage (the awarding of jobs and favours to political cronies) has become something of a Canadian art form. Compared to the American and British systems, patronage in Canada is endemic. Political scholar Gordon Stewart even called the widespread use of patronage a "defining trait" of modern Canadian politics. Makes you proud, don't it?

"Protecting the rich": The proud legacy of Canada's Senate

So why bother? Why have a Senate at all? The original reason was because Macdonald and many of the other delegates were still very wary of what they considered to be the "mob rule" of unbridled democracy. To counteract this, they established a *non*-elected, *non*-democratic House to better protect the interests of the upper class. Really. As Macdonald himself put it:

> The rights of the minority must be protected, and the rich are always fewer in number than the poor . . .

The House of Commons was where laws and regulations would be worked out. The Senate, in turn, would be a forum for "sober second thought," the saucer where legislation was poured to allow it to cool. Which is to say, the Senate of Canada would act as a parliamentary review board. And let me tell you, when a piece of important legislation needs to be reviewed, you want a hockey player like Frank Mahovlich doing the reviewing. (Mahovlich was named to the Senate of Canada by Jean Chrétien in 1998. I eagerly await further appointments. Perhaps Céline Dion, or maybe Bret "the Hitman" Hart, pro-wrestler extraordinaire — if he votes Liberal, of course.)

Senate reform is like the weather: Everybody talks about it, but no one does anything about it. Today, just about the only people who defend the existence of the Senate are the actual members of the Senate itself. Indeed, I would define one of the main responsibilities of being a Senator as "Defending my existence — and my salary and bloated expense account." (Senators receive more than $75,000 a year in salary and tax-free allowances.) With only a few exceptions, every Senator in Canada's Upper House is "owned" by a specific political party. The parties, in turn, use their Senators for raising funds. *Gotta keep those party coffers full!* It's all very noble and pure.

For more on the ongoing scandal of Canada's Senate, have a look at Claire Hoy's book, *Nice Work*. For more on the origins of the so-called "Upper" House, check out Christopher Moore's book *1867: How the Fathers Made a Deal*.

For links to news stories on the campaign to abolish the Senate, go to www.labournet.ca/senate.html.

Reaction and Resistance

The Québec Conference laid out the terms of Confederation. Now the delegates had to take the deal back to their respective parliaments and try to get it approved.

- ✔ Newfoundland and Prince Edward Island said no.

- ✔ The Province of Canada said *yes*.

  Among members of the united parliament, 91 were in favour, 33 were opposed. Among *French-Canadian* members, however, support was split, with only a small majority voting in favour of union: 27 were for it, 21 were opposed. Still, the French-Canadian members did give their approval — however slim — and the claim made by today's separatists that Québec was "forced" into Confederation against its will is false.

- ✔ In New Brunswick, it was a seesaw battle. The pro-Confederation premier Leonard Tilley lost an election on the issue in 1865, but bounced back the following year to win a second vote. He then brought New Brunswick into Confederation with a clear electoral mandate.

- ✔ In Nova Scotia, Premier Charles Tupper faced strong opposition to the deal. Anti-Confederation forces, led by the old warhorse and former premier Joseph Howe travelled to London to plead with the British government to block the proposed union — at least until the people of Nova Scotia could be consulted on the matter. Britain refused.

  As luck would have it, Charles Tupper wasn't required to go to the polls until the fall of 1867. If they could just get Confederation passed before then, Tupper wouldn't have to face the voters on it. (If he had, he would

Our "prime directive": Canada's mission statement

The American Revolution enshrined as its highest ideals *"life, liberty, and the pursuit of happiness."* In the French Revolution, it was the ringing cry of *"liberté, égalité, fraternité"* ("liberty, equality, fraternity"). In Canada, we have our own trio of catchphrases. Enshrined in our constitution as the primary goal and responsibility: "to make Laws for the Peace, Order and good Government of Canada." That's right: *peace, order, and good government.* Well, two out of three ain't bad.

have lost.) Charles Tupper never did call an election or even a full debate on the issue. It was a classic lobster trap: Once Confederation had been enacted, there was very little Joseph Howe or the others could do to escape.

Fenians to the rescue!

Britain was pushing and prodding the colonies into accepting Confederation, but it was an American bogeyman that finally did the trick. In 1866, after the U.S. Civil War had ended, a rag-tag band of Irish-American terrorists calling themselves the Fenian Brotherhood (after *Fianna*, an ancient name for Irish warriors) launched a series of border raids into Canadian territory. The Fenians, you see, wanted to free Ireland from British rule. So they attacked Canada. (Don't try to figure it out. Their plan defies logic.) With tacit American support, the mad, mystical Fenians invaded New Brunswick and the Niagara peninsula, and later the Red River region. And though they were never a real threat, they did have an enormous psychological impact.

"Oh, Tuponia! We stand on guard for thee!"

To think that you and I could have been mighty Aquilonians, rather than mere Canucks. While the debate on Confederation was underway, the problem arose of what to call the newly created union. As the Province of Canada was now clearly the dominant member of British North America, it seemed natural to name the new country "Canada." But not everyone agreed. Some wanted to use the historic term for the original mainland colony: "Acadia." Others thought it should be simply "British North America." Still others suggested "Cabotia" to honour the great explorer, John Cabot. The suggestions soon began to fly fast and furious, among them:

Britannica

Aquilonia

Borealia

Colonia

Hochelaga

Laurentia

Norland

Superior

Tuponia (*a contraction of "The United Provinces of North America"*)

Transatlantia

Victorialand

Ursulia

Vesperia

Efisga (*a contraction of "England, France, Ireland, Scotland, Germany, and Aboriginal"*)

The debate got so out of hand, and so off-track, that the poet and patriot Thomas D'Arcy McGee finally rose in the Legislative Assembly and said, "One individual chooses Tuponia and another Hochelaga . . . Now, I would ask any honourable member of this House how he would feel if he woke up some fine morning and found himself, instead of a Canadian, a Tuponian or a Hochela-gander." There was embarrassed laughter, and after that, the matter was more or less settled. The new country would be named Canada, from the Native word for "village." But, you have to admit, it would have been nice to be able to swagger about, calling ourselves "Superiors." *Hello, my name is Joe . . . and I AM SUPERIOR!*

Historically, the Fenians were probably a blessing to Canada. They united the country as nothing else could.

— historian Desmond Morton

The Fenian scare helped tip the scale of public opinion in favour of Confederation (there was security and strength in union) and in doing so helped New Brunswick Premier Leonard Tilley win the 1866 elections. New Brunswick, in turn, was a crucial land-link for Confederation. Without it, the union would have been little more than a loose collection of unconnected colonies. New Brunswick acted as the linchpin, joining the Atlantic region with that of the St. Lawrence, and in doing so made Confederation possible.

The BNA Act is passed

The terms of Confederation were worked out at three separate conferences:

- **Charlottetown** (September 1–9, 1864): delegates agree to the broad principles of a possible union.

- **Québec City** (October 10–27, 1864): the structure of the union, the division of power between national and provincial governments, and other details are hammered out.

- **London, England** (over the winter of 1866–67): delegates meet one last time and make some minor, but important, changes to the Québec Resolutions (they improve the financial terms for the Maritimes and add a requirement for an "intercolonial railway" to be built).

On March 29, 1867, Queen Victoria signed the British North America Act, and on July 1, it came into effect. A new nation was born: *Canada*, consisting of 3.5 million people and four provinces. The original four, the "charter members of Confederation," so to speak, were as follows:

- **Nova Scotia**

- **New Brunswick**

- **Québec** (formerly the Canada East region)

- **Ontario** (formerly the Canada West region)

It is important to note that the BNA Act did *not* grant Canada full independence. Far from it. Canada was still a part of the British Empire. Canadians were still British citizens. The Queen was still the head of state, and in matters of diplomacy and international defense, Britain still called the shots. Even then, the BNA Act was a giant step forward nonetheless.

Canada's first separatist movement

Died! Last night at twelve o'clock, the free and enlightened Province of Nova Scotia.

— from the newspapers in Halifax on July 1, 1867

John A. Macdonald was asked to form an interim government and he called an election soon after. The Great Coalition had ended and Macdonald's Conservatives won a working majority in Canada's first federal election — including strong support in Québec, it should be noted. In Nova Scotia, however, it was another story. In 1867, federal and provincial elections were held there, and the results were staggering. Anger over Confederation had not subsided. If anything, it had grown. Provincially, the anti-Confederates won a whopping 35 of 38 seats. Federally, they took 18 of the 19 seats.

And so, just a few months after Confederation, Canada's first separatist movement was already underway — not in Québec, but in Nova Scotia. Joseph Howe was leading the crusade, and when Canada's first parliament opened, he rose in the House and made his feelings clear:

I do not believe that the people of Nova Scotia will ever be satisfied to submit to an act which has been forced upon them by such unjust and unjustifiable means. . . . The people of my province were tricked into this scheme.

For thirteen months, Howe fought a losing fight. In the end, all he managed to do was negotiate "better terms" for Nova Scotia (mainly, more money and an increased annual provincial subsidy) and a cabinet position for himself. Amid cries of "Traitor!" Joseph Howe crossed the floor to join Macdonald's team. Of all the provinces in Canada, the only one that can legitimately claim to have been railroaded into Confederation is Nova Scotia.

For a bit more on the Nova Scotia separatist movement (from a decidedly federalist bias), visit `www.uni.ca/ns_sep.html`. You'll find the Library of Canada's extensive and informative Confederation site at `www.nlc-bnc.ca/confed/e-1867.htm`. For summaries of important Canadian laws and legislation — including the BNA Act of 1867 — `www.wwlia.org/cahist.htm#toc` is a great place to start. For the full text of Canadian constitutional documents, everything from the BNA Act of 1867 to the Nunavut Constitutional Act of 1999, go to `www.solon.org/Constitutions/Canada/English/`.

The Fathers of Confederation

Traditionally, there are 36 Fathers of Confederation (delegates who took part in one or all three conferences: Charlottetown, Québec City, and London).

Two nations? Or one?

Canada is divisible because Canada is not a real country.
> — separatist leader Lucien Bouchard in 1996

It *seems* clear enough: In 1867, several separate colonies came together to form a single union, one that had both a central and provincial governments. Simple, no? But in Canada the meaning and myth of Confederation strikes at the very heart of nationhood. The terms of the BNA Act are fairly straightforward, but it is the *intent* behind them that has been interpreted in radically different ways over the years. In Québec, Confederation has been portrayed, not as a contract between provinces, but as a moral "pact" between two founding peoples: French and English.

This view was first promoted by the legendary newspaper editor Henri Bourassa, who founded *Le Devoir* in 1905. Bourassa saw Canada as a bilingual, bicultural state, made up of two nations. The only problem with this view is that nowhere in the BNA Act is the idea of "two founding peoples" ever addressed. For Bourassa that wasn't important. The concept of *deux nations*, he insisted, was implied in the spirit of Confederation if not the letter. As historian Ramsay Cook put it, "In Bourassa's version, French- and English-speaking Canadians, as cultural groups, were partners in a cultural compact: two cultural nations in a single political state."

Bourassa was speaking about French Canadians as a whole. Whether they were Québécois, Acadians, Franco-Ontarians, or Métis Manitobans, they were all part of a larger French-Canadian nation. Since the 1960s, however, this view has shifted in a subtle but profound way. Québec separatists now identify the "two founding peoples" not as English and French Canada, but rather along national and provincial borders. That is, they have replaced the French-Canadian people with the actual territorial boundaries of Québec (and not the boundaries they joined Confederation with, but their *current* boundaries). In doing so, the separatists have recast Confederation as a pact between the province of Québec and an odd, imaginary place called "The Rest of Canada." Hence, their self-contradictory argument that "Canada is divisible, but Québec is not."

This is slippery thinking, indeed, turning a provincial territory into a "founding nation," but the separatists have somehow pulled it off. This is what Lucien Bouchard means when he says that Canada is not a "real" country. In his mind, Canada is actually *two* countries: the Province of Québec and Everybody Else. "There are two peoples," says Bouchard. "Two nations and two territories. And this one is ours." He's wrong, of course. He's wrong on every account: historically, politically, and legally.

So why do separatists like Bouchard keep insisting that Canada is made up of two separate nations (rather than 10 provinces)? Simple. They are hoping to make it a self-fulfilling prophecy. They figure that if they keep repeating their message long enough, it will come true some day. The real question is whether the "rest of Canada" will allow that to happen.

Of these 36, 9 of them went on to become provincial premiers, 10 became Lieutenant-Governors, 12 became federal cabinet ministers, 13 received knighthoods, and 2 became prime ministers: Macdonald and Tupper. As well, 2 of the Fathers were murdered. George Brown, editor of the *Globe,* was killed by a disgruntled employee, and Thomas D'Arcy McGee was assassinated in Ottawa by a suspected Fenian sympathizer. (Although Irish himself, McGee had been an outspoken critic of the Fenian movement.)

The most important Fathers of Confederation were Macdonald, Cartier, Brown, Tilley, Tupper, Galt, and McGee. But you could also include

- **Amor de Cosmos,** who helped bring B.C. into Confederation
- **Louis Riel,** the founder of Manitoba (see Chapter 14)
- **Joey Smallwood,** who brought Newfoundland into the fold in 1949
- **John Amagoalik,** "the Arctic John A." who has been hailed as the Father of Nunavut, the northern territory created in 1999

So, who was the Mother of Confederation? It was none other than Queen Victoria Herself. She encouraged the union, she signed the BNA Act, and Confederation itself was very much a product of the Victorian era.

You'll find background bios on Macdonald, Cartier, Brown, Tupper, and Galt at www.nlc-bnc.ca/confed/foc.htm.

Chapter 14

From Sea to Sea

*J*ohn A. Macdonald proposed that the new country be called "the Kingdom of Canada," but the British government balked. They didn't want to provoke the Americans. So Leonard Tilley, the premier of New Brunswick, suggested calling it a "dominion" instead. Tilley had come across this term in Psalm 72 of the Bible: "His dominion shall be from sea to sea." This would also give us Canada's national motto:

> *A Mari Usque Ad Mare* ("From Sea to Sea")

Although the motto itself wouldn't be made official until much later, the sentiments it expressed became the driving force behind Confederation: to build a nation from the Atlantic to the Pacific, from east to west, from sea to sea. (Canada also reached the Arctic Ocean, so perhaps our motto should be expanded: *From sea to sea to sea.*)

The new Dominion of Canada began as a small cluster of eastern provinces, but it had big dreams — and big competition. On March 30, 1867, on the very day after Queen Victoria signed the BNA Act, the Americans purchased Alaska from the Russians. In doing so, they outflanked Canada on the Pacific Coast and squeezed the colony of British Columbia in between U.S. Territory. The race for a continent had begun, and the stakes were high.

The man who arranged the Alaska purchase, U.S. Secretary of State W.H. Seward, had little doubt about what the outcome of American expansion would be. He complimented the Canadian colonists on their hard work and continued efforts. "It is very well," he said. "You are building excellent states to be hereafter admitted to the American Union."

It was the kind of thing that sent chills down the spines of Canadians.

Growing Pains

> *[The Americans] are resolved to do all they can, short of war, to get possession of our western territory, and we must take immediate and vigorous steps to counteract them.*
>
> — John A. on the need for Canada to acquire the Northwest

It was the biggest real estate deal in human history, dwarfing even that of the Louisiana Purchase (see Chapter 10). In 1869, the HBC agreed to sell the vast Northwest Territories (Rupert's Land and the North-Western Territory) to Canada for a mere $1.5 million — along with some land concessions in the fertile belt. Unfortunately, no one thought to consult, or even notify, the people who happened to be living there at the time. They were included in the deal "like a herd of cattle."

Louis Riel and the Red River Resistance

The Red River frontier, in the area around present-day Winnipeg, had developed into a crossroads culture, a gateway to the West that included Native, French, American, and Scottish settlers in a lively, and often volatile, mix. With a population of 12,000, the Red River valley had more people than British Columbia, which, with only 10,000 or so settlers was by far the most sparsely populated colony in British North America. (The First Nations of the Pacific Northwest greatly outnumbered these settlers, of course.)

At the heart of the Red River community were the Métis, of mixed Native and European background (mainly French and Catholic), who made up more than half the population. The Métis lifestyle centred upon the annual buffalo hunt, organized with military precision and often compared to "a light cavalry." When news surfaced that the HBC was going to sell off its vast holdings, the reaction in Red River was one of anger and defiance.

Led by a young man named Louis Riel, the Métis confronted a team of surveyors sent in ahead of the land transfer. (It was one of the more dramatic moments in Canadian history, with Riel and the Métis putting their foot down — literally — on a survey chain and declaring, "You shall go no further!") The Métis then seized the HBC trading post of Upper Fort Garry and declared a provisional government. With American annexationists now calling on the Métis to ditch Canada and join the U.S., John A. Macdonald could see his dream of a nation "from sea to sea" slipping away, and he sent out a veteran Hudson's Bay man by the name of Donald Smith to negotiate.

At www.cmcc.muse.digital.ca/cmc/cmceng/ca13eng.html you can find more on the Métis bison hunt and lifestyle. For an extensive Web site on the "other" Métis — those outside of the prairies — go to www.cyberus.ca/~mfdunn/metis/Wlcm.html.

"Home, home on the — *will someone keep that infernal racket down!*"

Ah, the glorious shriek of the Great Plains. Métis settlers moved across the prairies in ox-drawn wagons, dubbed "Red River carts," that were built entirely of wood and bound by leather. These carts were as important to western development as the canoes and York boats were to the fur trade. (The carts could even be disassembled and used as rafts to cross rivers.) Only problem was, because of the dust, the axles couldn't be oiled, as the grease would have quickly clogged up. So the Red River carts — travelling in wagon-rut roads and kicking up clouds of dust seen for miles — used sheer wood on wood construction. The result? A constant, horrendous shriek that one observer compared to the sound of "a thousand fingernails being dragged across a thousand panes of glass — at the same time."

The execution of Thomas Scott

They called themselves "Canada Firsters," a fiercely nationalistic, expansionist group of Canadians who were calling for a counterstrike against the "treacherous half-breeds" at Fort Garry. One of them, a hotheaded anti-Catholic Irishman by the name of Thomas Scott, was arrested by the Métis and thrown into jail along with several others who had been plotting a counterrebellion. In a hastily held show trial, a Métis court sentenced Scott to death. Donald Smith pleaded with Riel to intervene and pardon the man, but Riel refused. Justice would take its course. Scott would die. "We must make Canada respect us!" shouted Riel. And so, on March 4, 1870, Thomas Scott was dragged out, kicking and screaming, to face a Métis firing squad.

> *This is horrible! This is cold-blooded murder!*
> — Thomas Scott's last words

The execution of Thomas Scott would go down in history as "the shot that set the West ablaze." Among anti-Catholics in English Canada a cry went up for retribution. Riel was now portrayed as either a dark man with "savage blood" in his veins, or a noble hero, defending Catholic rights and French-Canadian culture. The Louis Riel Myth was already taking shape.

The Manitoba Act

Outplayed by Louis Riel, John A. Macdonald had little choice but to accept almost all of the Métis' demands. On July 15, 1870, the transfer of Rupert's Land and the North-Western Territory finally went through. And, as agreed, on that same day a new province was born: *Manitoba* (from "manitou," meaning Great Spirit). The province was much smaller than it is today, but it did cover the heartland of the Red River valley, with roughly 1.5 million acres of land reserved for the Métis. The Manitoba Act of 1870 signalled a stark change in Canadian development. In it, French language rights and the Catholic Church

NATIVE RIGHTS

Of flags and nations

When Riel and the Métis seized Upper Fort Garry, the Union Flag of Britain was lowered and in its place was raised a golden fleur-de-lis and a green Irish shamrock. This was meant to represent the multi-ethnic character of the Canadian frontier, but it was not the flag that the Métis themselves used. Their banner, a horizontal number "8" on a blue background, had first been unfurled by a defiant Cuthbert Grant after the Battle of Seven Oaks (see Chapter 10). A red background is also sometimes used (by Métis who were loyal to the HBC), and though the meaning of the Métis flag is unclear, it is said to represent (a) the infinity sign and (b) the joining of two cultures. This pattern can also be found in traditional Métis dances, such as the quadrille, where dancers move in a figure eight.

were protected, creating a second French-Canadian stronghold within Confederation. Québec was overjoyed. Perhaps the French fact would grow beyond eastern Canada. . . . But, as we will see, it didn't quite work out that way. The spirit of the Manitoba Act, and the promise of a truly bilingual nation from east to west, was never realized.

Having manoeuvred Manitoba into Confederation as a full-fledged province, Louis Riel, "the Father of Manitoba," was now forced to flee. A military expedition under Colonel Garnet Wolseley arrived after a long, rough overland slog, and they were in no mood to be generous. "Had we caught him," said Wolseley. "He would have had no mercy."

(Riel was later elected to Parliament by Manitoba voters even though, as a fugitive, he would never be able to take his seat. The House had him expelled, but not before he had travelled to Ottawa and taken an oath of loyalty to Queen Victoria. He even signed the official Member's Registry.)

ON THE WEB

For the Parks Canada Riel House site (with background on the Métis) go to parkscanada.pch.gc.ca/parks/manitoba/riel_house/Riel_house_ e.htm.

B.C. comes onboard

In British Columbia, a small but vocal group of annexationists were urging a union with the United States. But British loyalties were strong, and ultimately the colony decided to join Canada instead. A delegation travelled to Ottawa to negotiate the terms, including the request that a wagon trail be built from B.C. to Manitoba. To the delegates' amazement and surprise, George-Étienne

Cartier (Macdonald's close friend and unofficial "co-prime minister") offered them a full-scale transcontinental railway instead, one that would be started within two years and completed in ten. It was a reckless, almost irresponsible promise on Cartier's part, but it did the trick. In 1871, British Columbia joined Confederation, and Canada became a nation "from sea to sea." Under the terms of 1871, the federal government also agreed to absorb B.C.'s debts and provide postal and telegraph services.

At `www.upei.ca/~rneill/topic_13.html` you'll find a detailed essay on the history of the West Coast to Confederation.

The numbered treaties

When British Columbia joined Confederation in 1871, they brought along a lot of unfinished business with them. Under the terms of the BNA Act, signed in 1867 (see Chapter 13), jurisdiction over Native lands was given to the federal government. But in B.C., treaties covered less than 1 percent of the territory, something that has caused problems right up until the present.

When Canada acquired rights to the Northwest and the Arctic mainland, it also agreed to assume responsibility for the "protection and well-being" of the region's aboriginal inhabitants. The Canadian government, meanwhile, wanted to open up the interior to agriculture and railways. South of the border, the Americans were fighting a bitter and expensive war against the Plains Indians, something that the cash-strapped Dominion of Canada wanted to avoid. Instead, the Canadian government set about arranging land treaties *prior* to the arrival of the railway and white settlers.

Treaties, especially those signed during peacetime, are not a surrender. Nor are they military capitulations. No. Treaties are legal agreements between sovereign entities, agreements made *nation to nation*. The Canadian government, however, saw these treaties as a permanent end to Native land claims. Once an agreement was worked out, Natives would be limited to reserve lands and the rest of the territory would belong to the Canadian government. For the Canadians, the treaties were "writs of sale." To Native leaders, they were pacts between peoples. It was a fatal gap in perception.

The first seven treaties, covering land that the railway would pass through, were signed between 1871 and 1877. (There would be 11 numbered treaties in all, the last signed in 1921.) A typical treaty granted a lump sum on signing, plus annual payments, and a promise from the government to provide schools, instruction, and resources, and to help end the liquor trade. Other items were worked out verbally but not included in the treaties themselves, something that angered Native negotiators, who later accused the federal government of obtaining land under false pretenses.

The government employed a very effective "divide and conquer" approach. They would first sign agreements with Christian Natives and those in dire straits, desperate for aid. With the help of missionaries, the government managed to isolate and undercut those Native leaders who opposed the treaties. Among the holdouts was a Cree by the name of Big Bear, who saw in the treaties the end of a way of life. Big Bear knew that Native culture would be devastated if his people were confined to small, scattered plots of land, and he held out until 1882 before signing. Even then, he agreed to only because the buffalo were disappearing and his people were starving.

For more on Native treaties in Canada, with lots of maps and links, go to indy4.fdl.cc.mn.us/~isk/maps/cantreat.html. Another good treaty site can be found at collections.ic.gc.ca/treaties/code. For more on the B.C. treaties (or lack thereof): www.gov.bc.ca/aaf/default.htm.

The Mounties

If you had to choose one all-Canadian symbol, it would probably be a red-coated Mountie, "rider of the plains." The image of the Mountie — a potent blend of myth and history — is as Canadian as the gunslinger is American, or the loyal samurai is Japanese. Created by an Act of Parliament in 1873, the North-West Mounted Police (NWMP) were one of John A.'s schemes, aimed at bringing law and order to the Canadian frontier. American whisky peddlers had crossed into Canadian territory and were selling rotgut to the Indians at illegal trading posts with names like Fort Whoop-Up and Robber's Roost.

In 1873, the violence to the south spilled north into Canada when a band of American-led wolf hunters ambushed and killed 36 Assiniboine at Cyprus Hills, in what is now southwestern Saskatchewan. The Cyprus Hills massacre gave an added sense of urgency to John A. Macdonald's plan for creating a paramilitary police force to patrol the western frontier. The red jackets the officers wore were chosen with care to distinguish them from the blue coats of the U.S. Cavalry to the south, where a long and bloody war against the Plains Indians was being waged.

The following year, 300 Mounted police recruits made a gruelling two-month overland trek from Manitoba, led by the legendary Métis scout, Jerry Potts. By the time the Mounties reached Fort Whoop-Up, the Americans had fled, tails between their legs. The Mounties, "stalwarts in scarlet jackets," established and asserted Canadian autonomy over the Northwest. The official motto was *Maintiens le Droit* ("Uphold the Right"), but the Americans added a new one: "They always get their man." In 1920, the force was reorganized as the Royal Canadian Mounted Police, or RCMP.

For a complete history of the RCMP/NWMP visit rcmp-learning.org/civilian/history.htm. The official RCMP site can be found at www.rcmp-grc.gc.ca.

The territorial evolution of Canada

Here is the order that Canada's provinces and territories either joined Confederation or were created within it.

1867 Ontario, Quebec, New Brunswick, Nova Scotia

1870 Manitoba

1871 British Columbia

1873 Prince Edward Island

1898 Yukon Territory

1905 Alberta, Saskatchewan

1949 Newfoundland

1999 Nunavut

For more info on the territorial evolution of Canada (with lots of great maps) visit `atlas.gc.ca/legacy/schoolnet/issues/terrevol/english/eterrevol.html`. For overviews of Canada's provinces and territories, including their flags and name origins (with links), visit `GeoNames.NRCan.gc.ca/english/schoolnet/prov.html#CANADA`.

P.E.I. joins Canada

One by one the other colonies of Canada joined the Confederation, just as soon as they could see their way clear to getting more out of it than they were putting into it.

— humorist Eric Nicol

Newfoundland and Prince Edward Island had rejected Confederation. But after a disastrous railway project, crooked in every sense of the word, P.E.I. was forced to change its mind. (In 1864, P.E.I.'s annual debt was just $250,000. Ten years later, it had soared to $4 million.) The ever-persuasive John A. promised the Islanders that — among other things — Canada would assume their debt and buy out the remaining absentee landowners, thus ending the island's longstanding Land Question (see Chapter 9).

In 1873, Prince Edward Island became Canada's seventh province. Newfoundland, however, refused to budge. They held out right up until 1949.

The Pacific Scandal

Two rival financial syndicates were now competing for the contract to build the transcontinental railway. One group, based in Toronto, was headed by Senator D.L. Macpherson. The other group, led by a man named Hugh Allan, was based in Montréal but supported by American investors. John A., not wanting to insult either side, tried to convince the two to merge. When that failed, he asked Allan to get rid of his American backers. Allan gave vague assurances that he would, but nothing was done.

In the 1872 election, Hugh Allan funnelled money into Macdonald's campaign and helped him win — with the understanding that Allan would be awarded the railway charter in return. John A. denied this, but rumours soon surfaced that the Conservatives had been accepting political bribes in return for rail contracts. John A. declared, "These hands are clean!" but they weren't. Not entirely. An incriminating telegraph, in which the prime minister begged for more money, helped blow the scandal wide open. Deserted by his supporters, a battered and bruised John A. had no choice but to resign, becoming the first and only prime minister in Canadian history to be forced out of office on charges of unethical behaviour.

The Return of John A.

A disgraced Macdonald, forced out of office in 1873, was trounced in the election that followed. George-Étienne Cartier, Macdonald's long-time ally and Québec lieutenant, had died, and the Liberals under Alexander Mackenzie mopped the floor with the Tories. By any standard, John A. Macdonald's political career should have been over.

"Honest Sandy"

Alexander Mackenzie, Canada's second prime minister, was a former stone mason from Sarnia. Dubbed "Honest Sandy," Mackenzie was a sincere, hardworking man who gave Canada several important institutions:

- ✔ **The secret ballot** (before that, voters had to declare their alliances in public, something that made bribery and intimidation commonplace).
- ✔ **The Supreme Court of Canada:** a national court of appeal (something Macdonald had prepared the way for).
- ✔ **The Office of the Auditor General:** an independent body set up to investigate government spending.

John A.'s grand scheme for a transcontinental railway was over. In its place, Mackenzie opted for a piecemeal "pay as you go" approach involving existing rail lines, something that infuriated British Columbia. Amor de Cosmos, now a member of the House of Commons and once a champion of Confederation, began calling for B.C. to leave the union. Canada now faced its second separatist movement in less than ten years. Even worse, Mackenzie took office just as a worldwide economic slump hit. He pursued a free trade deal with the United States, but nothing came of it.

Figure 14-1 shows four phases of Canadian development.

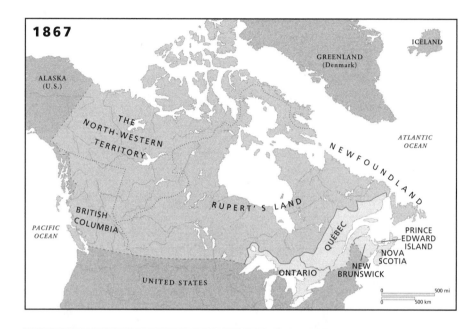

Figure 14-1:
"Canada in 1867" and "Canada in 1873"

The National Policy

The resurrection and political rebirth of John A. Macdonald began with a nationalist cry. Instead of the Liberals' continental approach to free trade, John A. proposed a blatantly protectionist system of internal trade and a high "tariff wall" to keep American imports out. Called the "National Policy," it eventually included three main platforms:

- ✔ Protective tariffs (that is, higher taxes charged on imports into Canada)
- ✔ A transcontinental railway built along an all-Canadian route
- ✔ And increased immigration and western settlement

Shamelessly playing the anti-American, anti-free trade card, John A. Macdonald and his Conservatives were swept back into power in the general election of September 1878 on a wave of Canadian patriotism.

Despite its emotional appeal, the National Policy had mixed success over the years. Settlers poured in, true, but they just as quickly poured out, and Canada often faced a net *loss* of immigrants. The tariff wall did protect Canadian industries and strengthen the economy, but it also drove up the cost of living. (The tariff system was largely the work of Leonard Tilley, formerly the premier of New Brunswick and one of the most important Fathers of Confederation, who was now Macdonald's minister of finance.) But the most dramatic — the most *heroic* — aspect of the National Policy was the construction of a transcontinental railway. It was brash and bold, and in the end, John A. Macdonald's large impractical dream would triumph over the smaller, more sensible vision of men like Alexander Mackenzie.

Go to www.archives.ca/exec/naweb.dll?fs&0506&e&top&0 for the National Archives' exhibit on Canada's Prime Ministers, "First Among Equals."

The great railway

It was a huge undertaking: building a railway across a sparsely inhabited continent without a population base to support it. The Liberal Opposition called the scheme "an act of insane recklessness." And they were right. But then, nation building was never for the timid or the faint of heart.

A new financial syndicate was formed, headed by two Scotsmen:

- ✔ **George Stephen,** president of the Bank of Montreal
- ✔ **Donald Smith,** chief commissioner of the HBC (and the man who negotiated with Louis Riel over Manitoba's entry into Confederation)

The Canadian Pacific Railway Company, as it would later be known, agreed to an all-Canadian route — but there was a price to be paid. The company was given the following:

- Approximately $30 million worth of existing rail lines (originally built as public works)
- A land grant of 25 million acres and a $25-million subsidy
- A 20-year monopoly on western traffic once the railway was completed

Even with this assistance, the CPR was an extremely risky venture, and it skirted the edge of bankruptcy and ruin on several occasions. Indeed, it was less a railway than it was a financial rollercoaster, one marked by wild ups and sudden downs. Crossing 5,000 kilometres of territory, it would become the longest railway on earth and a marvel of modern engineering. Pierre Berton described the building of the CPR as Canada's "National Dream," and there is a great deal of truth to this. Ours was a country forged, not in revolution, but in a landscape traversed. Ours was a victory over sheer geography.

Van Horne: "The general boss of everybody"

Leading the way and blazing a trail (literally) across the west was the CPR's general manager, William Cornelius Van Horne. The self-described "boss of everybody and everything," Van Horne achieved the impossible. He pushed the track across the rock and bog of the Canadian Shield and over the prairies like a relentless spear of steel. William Van Horne was an American, but by the time the railway was finished he had renounced his U.S. citizenship and become a Canadian. "Building that railway," said Van Horne, "would have made a Canadian out of the German Emperor."

Onderdonk: "A Chinaman's chance"

In British Columbia's sea of mountains, the railway threaded its way through treacherous passes and dangerous gorges. The contractor in charge was an obsessive man by the name of Andrew Onderdonk, who blasted his way through sheer granite cliffs. To bypass the notorious Hell's Gate Rapids in the Fraser Canyon, Onderdonk had to blast two dozen different tunnels. Chinese workers were given the perilous task of placing the nitro and dynamite charges. The railway cost thousands of lives. Onderdonk himself said that three Chinese workers were killed for every kilometre of track laid. The bitter and nasty phrase "a Chinaman's chance" is said to have been coined in reference to the harsh conditions of these Chinese workers.

For links to Western Canadian history, with a focus on the CPR, visit www.sd6. bc.ca/gss/library/public_html/gssweb/cdnwest.htm. As well, you'll find more on Chinese Canadian history (including the building of the CPR) at ccnc.ca/toronto/history/info/info.html.

Mowat and Mercier

There is an old joke that goes something like this: An international conference is held on a certain subject. Let's say, "elephants." France submits a report entitled "The Love Life of the African Elephant." The English hand in "Elephants and the Empire." The Americans: "Building Bigger and Better Elephants." And the Canadians? They submit a report entitled: "Elephants: A Federal or Provincial Responsibility?"

John A. Macdonald had intended the federal government to be the overriding central authority in Canada. The provincial governments would, he was sure, decline in importance over time until they wielded little more influence than municipalities. But John A. would be proven wrong. The first to challenge this notion was Oliver Mowat, premier of Ontario and one of the original Fathers of Confederation. Mowat argued in favour of "provincial rights," namely, that within Confederation the provinces are equal partners with the federal government, and not its subordinates.

Oliver Mowat was supported by the premier of Québec, Honoré Mercier, a staunch French-Canadian nationalist. Mercier invited the other premiers to an interprovincial conference in Québec City in 1887, to discuss their "common defense." John A. Macdonald refused to attend, and P.E.I. and B.C. also declined the invitation, but the die had been cast nonetheless. Ever since then, Canada has been marked by ongoing provincial–federal tensions, a power struggle that continues even today.

Mowat and Mercier led a heated constitutional battle against Macdonald and, for the most part, they won. The British courts sided with the provinces, and the power of the federal government to disallow provincial laws (something Macdonald had wielded like a club) was now curbed. The meaning of Confederation was changed forever, and the decentralization of Canada had begun.

The North-West Rebellion

The promise of a French Catholic homeland in Manitoba was already being dismantled. White settlers had flooded in, pushing the Métis further west into what is now Saskatchewan, even as the buffalo were vanishing. Outside of Manitoba, the Métis had no clear title to the lands they had settled on — and government surveyors were even now moving in. And it wasn't only the Métis who were suffering. The Plains Indians (Cree, Blackfoot, and Sioux) were now facing starvation and the end of a proud way of life.

White settlers were angry as well. The harvests had been poor and the prices low. Even worse, many of the settlers had staked a claim along what was the proposed northern rail line, only to have the route suddenly shift south. By 1884, the Northwest was ripe for rebellion. At a meeting of white and Métis settlers, someone cried out, "Only one man can help us now. Riel!"

Gabriel Dumont and the return of Louis Riel

Louis Riel was now teaching school in Montana. It had been 15 years since his first great triumph at Red River (see the section "Louis Riel and the Red River Resistance" earlier in this chapter), but the Métis had not forgotten. In the spring of 1884, a small band of Métis rode south, across the border and into Montana. Their mission: to find Louis Riel and bring him back.

Gabriel Dumont, a legendary hunter and master sharpshooter, led the Métis on this expedition. Dumont was an expert horseman who spoke six different Native languages — as well as French and some English. With the great herds of buffalo gone, Dumont had now settled in the Métis village of Batoche, where he operated the local ferry and tended a small store. It was Dumont who asked Riel to return.

Unfortunately, in the years that followed the Red River Resistance of 1870, Riel suffered a series of emotional breakdowns. He spent several years in asylums, convinced that he was in fact a "prophet of the grasslands" who would lead his people to freedom. He began referring to himself as "David." These delusions had subsided but they were always close to the surface. And when the "avenging angel" Gabriel arrived, calling him back from the wilderness, Riel saw the hand of God at work.

John A. and Louis Riel: The two old foes once again squared off. Riel sent Macdonald a petition on behalf of the residents of the region asking for provincial status, an elected government, and control over natural resources. Nothing came of it. By now, Macdonald had earned the nickname "Old Tomorrow" for his tactical use of delay, and he employed his stalling tactics now even as Riel and the Métis grew more insistent and more impatient. Finally, fed up and frustrated, Louis Riel declared a provisional government at the village of Batoche. It was March 19, 1885. The North-West Rebellion was about to explode.

Battle of Duck Lake

At Duck Lake, the North-West Mounted Police and a small band of volunteers clashed with a Métis force under Gabriel Dumont. It was a sudden, intense battle, and among the first to die was Dumont's beloved brother Isidore. (Gabriel was also hit by a bullet that split open his scalp, leaving a lasting, painful scar.) By now, Riel's religious delusions had resurfaced and he rode back and forth during the battle, completely exposed and waving a cross as bullets exploded around him.

> *Fire! In the name of the Father! In the name of the Son! In the name of the Holy Spirit! Fire!*
> — Louis Riel, urging his men on during the Battle of Duck Lake

Gabriel Dumont won the battle, sending the Mounties into retreat. Twelve officers and volunteers died at Duck Lake, but it might have been even worse. Dumont wanted to pursue the fleeing policemen and kill them all, but Riel held him back. "If you are going to give them the advantage like that," Dumont complained, "we cannot win."

"Riel and Dumont": at www.tcel.com/~brownb/ you'll find a discussion of the North-West Rebellion from the Métis side. For more on Gabriel Dumont, the great "hunter of the plains," visit www.schoolnet.ca/aboriginal/gd-hist/index-e.html.

The temptations of Crowfoot

By the time the shooting started, the white settlers had abandoned the cause. Protests and petitions were fine. But armed rebellion? No. The Plains Indians, meanwhile, were torn by their sympathy for the rebels and the dire consequences that were sure to follow an uprising. The once mighty Blackfoot Confederacy, now facing starvation, hardship, and a life of poverty on government reserves, remained neutral during the rebellion, largely because of Chief Crowfoot, who saw the rebellion for what it was: a sincere but doomed cause. Historian Hugh Dempsey said of Crowfoot's decision, "At all times he was unswervingly loyal, not to the government, but to his own people. This was his only reason for remaining at peace."

Poundmaker and Big Bear

Two breakaway bands of Cree warriors, along with some Sioux and Assiniboine, did join the uprising. They were led by

- ✔ **Big Bear**, who had earlier resisted the imposition of reserves
- ✔ **Poundmaker**, the adopted son of Crowfoot

Big Bear's followers, under a warrior named Wandering Spirit, attacked the tiny village of Frog Lake and massacred nine whites, including two unarmed Catholic priests. Big Bear had tried to prevent the violence, but it was too late.

Poundmaker in turn led an attack at Battleford. The settlers fled inside the fort as the Natives ransacked their homes, looking for food and supplies. (With the buffalo gone, the nomadic Cree were starving and desperate. This may not excuse the violence, but it certainly explains it.)

Still, it is important to note that the Métis and the Cree warriors did not co-ordinate their attacks. There were, in effect, two parallel uprisings, one Native and one Métis.

"Poundmaker and Big Bear": at `www.tcel.com/~brownb/Indanreb.htm` you'll find more on the events of the NW Rebellion on the Native side. At `www.fnc.ca/tawow/articles/oldnw/heart.html#rebel` you'll find more on Saskatchewan's Old Northwest.

CPR to the rescue!

The reaction to the rebellion was swift. In 1870, it had taken three hard months for the army to reach the Northwest. But by 1885, the steel tracks of the CPR had reached the plains, and the first troops arrived within ten days. Before the month was over, the Métis and Native rebels faced a force of more than 5,000 soldiers, militia, and Mounties under the leadership of General Frederick Middleton.

It is one of the great ironies of Canadian history that Louis Riel helped save John A.'s beloved CPR. The railway had been on the very brink of bankruptcy when the North-West Rebellion broke out, and suddenly the CPR was no longer seen as an expensive folly but rather as a vital aspect of national defense. Parliament rallied to the cause. The money came through, and the troops moved out.

> *The crisis of the railway and the crisis of the rebellion coincided. Each solved the other. The rebellion ensured the completion of the railway; the railway accomplished the defeat of the rebellion.*
> — historian Donald Creighton

General Middleton divided his force into three columns, with each of them using the main line of the CPR as their base, a fact not lost on the public.

- ✔ One column, under Major-General Thomas Strange, moved north from Calgary against Big Bear.

- ✔ A second column, under Colonel William Otter, moved north from Swift Current to relieve the besieged settlers at Battleford.

- ✔ And the third column, under General Middleton himself, left Qu'Appelle heading straight for the rebel stronghold of Batoche.

The Métis and the Cree were now on the defensive, and the Canadian frontier was at war.

For more on the North-West Rebellion, including maps, go to `www.canadahistory.com/northwes.htm`. For the Louis Riel home page go to `infoweb.magi.com/~shuttle/riel-index.html`.

The Battle of Batoche

At Fish Creek, south of Batoche, General Middleton marched his men into an ambush. A small force of Métis hunters under Gabriel Dumont fought Middleton's men to a standstill — but the odds were stacked against the rebels. Not only did Middleton have more men and more supplies, but he also had with him the latest in warfare technology: an American-made Gatling gun, capable of firing 500 rounds a minute. It was state-of-the-art weaponry, the likes of which had never been seen before in the Canadian West.

Middleton and his men closed in on the village of Batoche, and on May 9, 1885, the fighting began. It raged for four days, as Middleton strafed the village with bullets. The Métis, running low on ammunition, were forced to dig enemy bullets out of walls and re-use them. By the end, they were firing rocks, nails, and even hammered buttons. When the army finally stormed Batoche, Gabriel Dumont held them back almost single-handedly for over an hour to allow the others to escape. Twenty-one Métis rebels died at Batoche, among them, 93-year-old Joseph Ouellette.

> *In a minute. I want to kill another Englishman.*
> — Ouellete's last words, after Dumont had ordered him to retreat

In the confusion, Dumont and Riel became separated, and on May 15, 1885, Louis Riel, the Prophet of the Grasslands, surrendered to the Canadian Army. Eleven days later, Poundmaker surrendered as well. Big Bear held out for another month and a half, with four columns of soldiers and Mounties in pursuit before he, too, lay down his arms. Gabriel Dumont, however, was never captured. He escaped south, across the border, where he later joined Buffalo Bill's Wild West show as "the Hero of the Half-Breed Rebellion."

Visit the Parks Canada Batoche site at `parkscanada.pch.gc.ca/parks/ saskatchewan/batoche/batoche_e.htm`.

The execution of Louis Riel

Poundmaker and Big Bear were sent to prison, and eight Cree warriors, including Wandering Spirit, were eventually sentenced to death and publicly hanged. It was the largest mass execution in modern Canadian history.

Riel refused to plead insanity and was tried in Regina and found guilty of treason. The jury that convicted him recommended mercy, and Honoré Mercier warned Ottawa that if Riel were executed it would be considered "a declaration of war against Québec." But John A. refused to intervene. Riel had been found guilty and the law would take its course. "He will hang," said Macdonald, "though every dog in Québec barks in his favour."

It has been suggested that John A. Macdonald "killed" Louis Riel. This isn't true. John A. refused to pardon him, which is another matter entirely. And although Riel has been elevated to hero over the years, the fact remains that he led an armed uprising against the government that caused the death of more than 200 people, including nine innocent settlers and two unarmed priests. At that time, the penalty for such crimes was death. John A. Macdonald had built his entire career on maintaining an alliance with French Canada. But with Louis Riel he was caught in the middle: damned if he did intervene, damned if he didn't.

Louis Riel has gone beyond mere history and has entered the realm of myth. Historian G.F.G. Stanley dismissed Riel as simply, "a sad, pathetic, unstable man who led his followers in a suicidal crusade and whose brief glory rests upon a distortion of history." But Margaret Atwood was closer to the truth when she described Riel as "the perfect all-Canadian failed hero," one whose meaning is broad enough to appeal to the sort of splintered society that Canada has become. Riel represents Western alienation, French-Canadian rights, and the Métis nation. He is all things to all people. A prophet, a traitor, a madman, a hero.

Rebirth of the Acadian nation

The Acadians of the Maritimes were only now recovering from the displacement of the Expulsion (which I describe in Chapter 6) and the economic and social marginalization that had followed. In 1880, the Saint Jean Baptiste Society in Québec invited the Acadians to attend their congress. The following year, the Acadians decided to hold a convention of their own in Memramcook, New Brunswick.

In Québec, St. Jean Baptiste Day, June 24, had been designated a cultural holiday. At Memramcook, the Acadian delegates chose the Feast of the Assumption, August 15, as their national day. In 1884, a second Acadian Convention was held in Miscouche, P.E.I. Delegates chose an Acadian flag — the French tricolours with a golden star in the upper left corner — as well as a national hymn, *Ave Maris Stella*, and a motto, *L'union fait la force* ("strength through union"). Conventions have been held regularly ever since, and have recently included the Cajuns of Louisiana, making the Acadians an international community.

On November 7, 1885, Donald Smith drove home the last spike of the CPR in a mountain pass at Craigellachie. Nine days later, Louis Riel climbed the steps of the gallows and dropped to his death.

For a well-presented and extensive site on Louis Riel visit www.escape.ca/ ~shsb/Riel/indexenglish.htm. For more on the opposing opinions regarding Riel's place in Canadian history, go to www.tcel.com/~brownb/ Rebviews.htm. The University of Saskatchewan has an extensive database on the North-West Rebellion, as well, including biographical summaries of Big Bear, Poundmaker, Riel, and others, at library.usask.ca/northwest/ contents.html.

John A.'s Last Campaign

The Old Man, the Old Flag, and the Old Policy
— John A. Macdonald's campaign slogan in the 1891 election

John A. Macdonald fought his last election campaign at the age of 76, campaigning on the old standbys of protective tariffs, nationalist appeal, and British ties. He denounced the Liberal proposal for free trade with the U.S. as little more than "veiled treason" and declared, "As for myself, the course is clear. A British subject I was born, a British subject I will die."

John A. Macdonald won the election, but the campaign had exhausted him, and on June 6, 1891, he died.

More than any other leader, John A. Macdonald has the rightful claim of being the father of our country. He had his share of controversy: the Pacific Scandal, his refusal to pardon Louis Riel. And he lost as many battles as he won: He was outplayed by Riel in 1870, and by Mowat and Mercier later on. He was a man of great flaws, but he was also a man of great vision and his triumphs and achievements were second to none. He was the key architect of Confederation. He oversaw the purchase of the Northwest, the entry of British Columbia and Prince Edward Island into Confederation, and the building of the CPR, which bound Canada together coast to coast, making it a nation "from coast to coast," *a mari usque ad mare.*

> *Every succeeding prime minister has to be matched against John A. and only a few stand the comparison. . . . Several of them have been better humans than Macdonald, none has been greater.*
> — popular historian Donald Gordonson

Part VI
The End of "English" Canada
(1891–1929)

Early multiculturalism. Canada leads a harmony of nations, from happy-go-lucky Irishmen to jolly Germans.

In this part . . .

*W*e look at the end of English Canada — *English*, not in the sense of English-speaking, but in the sense of "Englishman" and "Empire." This era marked the highpoint of English Canadian imperial pride — and its decline. The West was settled by waves of immigrants, many of them neither French nor Anglo-Saxon, World War I shattered the allure of empire, and the post-war years were marked by social upheavals, women's suffrage (the right to vote), and the rise of workers' rights. Canada would never be the same.

Chapter 15

"Sunny Ways": The Laurier Years

In This Chapter

▶ Wilfrid Laurier becomes Canada's first French-Canadian PM

▶ Multiculturalism is born in Western Canada

▶ Gold is discovered in the Klondike

▶ Laurier resists imperial overtures and royal seductions

*T*he death of John A. Macdonald in 1891 left the Conservative Party without clear leadership or direction. Fortunately, because they had just won an election, they had at least five years to rebuild their party. The Conservatives produced four different leaders in quick succession, but none were able to fill John A. Macdonald's enormous shoes.

Described as "John A.'s pallbearers" his successors were, in order:

- **John Abbott** (1891–92): With the infighting that followed John A.'s death, Abbott, a former mayor of Montréal, was chosen as the new leader because, as he put it, "I am not particularly obnoxious to anybody." Citing ill health, he resigned a year and a half later.

- **John Sparrow Thompson** (1892–94): They called him "Sir John the Lesser," and everyone expected great things from him. Thompson, a lawyer from Halifax and one-time premier of Nova Scotia, introduced Canada's Criminal Code and was in the middle of rebuilding the Conservative Party when he died suddenly while visiting England, keeling over at Windsor Castle after an audience with Queen Victoria.

- **Mackenzie Bowell** (1894–96): After Thompson's unexpected demise, Bowell took over. A blustering, bad-tempered, anti-Catholic Orangeman, Bowell presided over a deeply divided caucus and was eventually overthrown from within the party by, in his words, "a nest of traitors."

- **Charles Tupper** (1896): Father of Confederation and former premier of Nova Scotia, Tupper was brought in at the last moment to lead the Tories into defeat in the 1896 election. In office for just 69 days, Tupper remains the shortest-reigning PM in Canadian history.

With Charles Tupper, the Conservative reign of power came to an end, replaced by the Liberals under an eloquent — and elegant — French-Canadian leader named Wilfrid Laurier. A new era had begun.

Laurier: Re-Inventing Canada

The Liberals originally stood for low tariffs and free trade. Some members had even proposed a full-fledged "commercial union" with the United States, in which Canada and the U.S. would erect a common tariff system against the world. John A. Macdonald had denounced this as "veiled treason," and in the 1891 election, the Liberals got creamed.

Wilfrid Laurier learned his lesson, and over the next few years, he doggedly transformed the Liberal Party from a semi-radical fringe group into a safe, mainstream, middle-of-the-road organization. By the time the 1896 election rolled around, Laurier had made a 180-degree turn and had enthusiastically embraced the very tenets of John A.'s National Policy (which I describe in Chapter 14). He even introduced a "British preferential tariff," which won over English-Canadian imperialists to the Liberal side. It worked. Wilfrid Laurier and the Liberals won four consecutive elections and stayed in power for 15 years straight.

The main difference between the Laurier Liberals and the Macdonald Conservatives was in their approach to provincial rights. Laurier described Canada as "a cluster of states" and championed regional autonomy. The Tories, in contrast, wanted a strong central government with the provincial governments clearly subordinate. The question was this: Which should come first, regional concerns or national ? Provincial interests or federal? Laurier's vision of Canada or John A.'s? In the long run, of course, the Laurier version has won out. We are a land of ongoing compromise, patched together from odds and ends and forever pulling at the seams. Laurier was, perhaps, the first important leader to recognize this, which is one of the reasons he has sometimes been called "the first Canadian."

The Manitoba School Question

The 1896 federal election was one of the strangest ever.

- ✔ **Charles Tupper**, an English-Canadian Tory, defended French-Catholic minority rights in Manitoba.

- ✔ **Wilfrid Laurier**, a French-Canadian Liberal, defended "provincial rights" (which, in this case, meant allowing the Anglo majority in Manitoba to abolish French-Catholic safeguards within their province.)

The roots of the problem go all the way back to 1870, when Louis Riel negotiated Manitoba's entry into Confederation (see Chapter 14). The Manitoba Act of 1870 had guaranteed the rights of French-speaking Catholics, but over the following 20 years the province had been flooded with English-speaking immigrants, many of them from the anti-French heartland of Ontario.

French Catholics were now a minority in Manitoba, and in 1890, the provincial government passed the Manitoba School Act, ending publicly funded Catholic schools. At the same time, and in direct violation of the original Manitoba Act, they also abolished French as an official language.

The underlying goal was clear. The West would be English and the French language would be "contained" in Québec and New Brunswick. In overturning entrenched minority rights, the Manitoba School Act of 1890 was one of the great legislative betrayals in post-Confederation history. It was a controversy that refused to go away, and one that raised a couple of important questions:

  ✔ Were provincial governments free to rewrite and rework the Constitution, at will, to suit themselves?

  ✔ If so, could the federal government step in? Could Ottawa intervene in provincial laws in order to protect the rights of a minority group?

In the 1896 election, Charles Tupper insisted that some sort of remedial action had to be taken to protect Franco-Manitobans, a position that divided his own party. Either way, as the ruling party, the Tories had to take a stand. The Liberals, however, could afford to be evasive. After all, they weren't in power. Rather than offer any concrete proposals, Laurier focused on the *process* instead. (This is a common diversionary tactic among politicians, even now.) He condemned the Tories for being too abrasive and too confrontational. At the same time, Laurier promised that if he were elected, he would use "compromise and consultation" in dealing with the problem. He also vowed to protect the rights of the French minority *and* those of the province. In short, he promised all things to all people.

In one of Aesop's fables, the wind and the sun place a wager over who can make a traveller remove his jacket. The wind blows and blows only to have the man pull his jacket ever tighter. The sun then smiles warmly down, and the man eventually takes off his jacket on his own accord. This was the approach that Laurier promised — and indeed, one that marked his entire career. "I will try sunny ways," promised Laurier.

The Manitoba School Act of 1890 is not some dusty piece of history. It has relevance even today — *especially* today. The act was the death knell for any significant French presence in Western Canada, and it effectively ended any hope for a truly bilingual nation, east to west. It also brought forward the central dilemma of a two-level federal system, namely, which should come first, regional interests or national? Can the provinces override the national government? Should they? Today, whether it is privatized medicine in Alberta

Canada's Holy Grail

It's been kicked into the Rideau Canal. It's been tossed into swimming pools and left by the side of the road. It's even been used to plant geraniums in. It is Canada's greatest icon and most coveted prize, *la coupe Stanley.* So who was Stanley? He was none other than Lord Frederick Arthur Stanley, Governor General of Canada from 1888 to 1893 — and a die-hard hockey fan.

The game of ice hockey developed in Windsor, Nova Scotia, as early as 1800 and spread first to Boston and later to Montréal. (The city of Montréal claims to be "the birthplace of hockey," but this is patently untrue. The first games in Montréal, in 1875, were played by "the Halifax Rules.") In 1893, Lord Stanley donated a silver rose bowl to help promote amateur hockey. Originally named "the Dominion Hockey Challenge Cup," the trophy is now awarded annually to the best professional team in the National Hockey League (NHL). Unique among professional sports trophies, the Stanley Cup has the names of the players, coaches, and owners from each year's winning team engraved directly on it, and as space runs out silver rings are added, making it the only sports trophy that actually "grows" over time. The original silver bowl is on display in the Hockey Hall of Fame in downtown Toronto.

You can visit the Hockey Hall of Fame at www.hhof.com/index.htm. For more on the evolution of hockey, go to www.nhl.com/hockeyu/history/evolution.html (part of a larger NHL Web site).

or restrictions on English-language education in Québec, these issues are still at the heart of the Canadian dilemma. The question remains. Who has final authority, Ottawa or the provinces? Are we one country? Or simply a collection of regions, a "cluster of states"?

Elected in 1896, Laurier quickly worked out a compromise with Manitoba's premier, Thomas Greenway. There would be no public funds for French-Catholic schools, but some religious instruction would be permitted for half an hour at the end of each school day. As for language, if there were enough students to warrant it in a given area, *bilingual* instruction would be permitted. Catholics in Canada were appalled and the controversy reached all the way to Rome, when the Pope sent a special envoy to Canada to investigate. Reassured by Laurier, the Catholic Church eventually decided to support the compromise.

"Peasants in sheepskin coats"

It was a time of prosperity and progress. There had already been some immigration into Canada's West before Laurier was elected. Mennonite religious groups had arrived, and an Icelandic colony had been established at Gimli, Manitoba. An Asian community, primarily Chinese, had settled on the West Coast, often in the face of open hostility. But it was after 1896 that the immigration boom really began.

During the Laurier years (1896–1911), more than one million people settled on the prairies. With this great migration came breakthroughs in agriculture, such as Marquis wheat, discovered by researcher Charles Saunders in 1909, which was better suited for Canada's northern farmlands and which doubled and tripled harvests.

The man in charge of settling the West was Clifford Sifton, Laurier's minister of the interior. Sifton's impact on Western development cannot be under-estimated. He was a tireless promoter — and a keen propagandist. Advertising Canada's frontier as "the last, best West," Clifford Sifton launched a massive and surprisingly effective PR campaign aimed at convincing European peasants to emigrate *en masse* to Canada.

Sifton's overseas agents brought in a flood of Ukrainian, Scandinavian, Hungarian, German, and Polish settlers, who were inveigled with promises of 160-acre homesteads available virtually for free. Only a small registration fee was required (although in fact huge blocks of land in what is now Saskatchewan were rolled over by government speculators, purchased at $1 an acre and resold for $8). At the same time, Sifton discouraged southern Europeans and Asians from settling on the cold expanse of the prairies.

> *I think a stalwart peasant in a sheepskin coat, born on the soil, whose forefathers have been farmers for ten generations, with a stout wife and a half-dozen children, is good quality.*
> — Clifford Sifton on the sort of candidate he was looking for

It was a hard life, especially in the early years when the settlers were first breaking ground and living in tarpaper shacks and sod huts. In Canada as a whole, more than 85 percent of the population was still of French or Anglo-Saxon stock, but in the prairies it was a different story. As many as a third of all immigrants came from other backgrounds, notably from the Ukraine. More than 170,000 Ukrainian settlers came to Canada during the Sifton campaign.

The opening of the West represented a profound shift in the Canadian identity. Even as the glory of English-Canadian imperial pride was reaching heady, hyperbolic heights, the very makeup of society was changing. As historian Donald Creighton noted, "A new and very different Canada was coming into being." It was the beginning of the end for the old English–French two-step. Canadian multiculturalism was born in Western Canada.

> *All great civilizations are basically cross-roads civilizations which have been able to harmonize in themselves influences of diverse origin.*
> — anthropologist Claude Lévi-Strauss

For an informative site on the peopling of Canada from 1891 to 1921, go to www.ucalgary.ca/HIST/tutor/canada1891/1frame.html. And for a fascinating look at the "Last Best West" advertising campaigns aimed at luring people to Canada: www.civilization.ca/membrs/canhist/advertis/adindexe.html.

When it came to language rights and provincial demands, Laurier was extremely cautious — but not when it came to railways. No sir. Laurier threw himself into railways with a reckless, almost irresponsible passion. With the influx of immigrants came the need for a second, more northerly transcontinental train route. Two existing companies wanted the charter:

- **Grand Trunk** (based in Eastern Canada).
- **Canadian Northern** (mainly western and based in Winnipeg).

Laurier could have forced the two to merge, but instead he gave his support to the Grand Trunk while also offering encouragement to the Canadian Northern. Laurier, caught up in the spirit of the times, apparently believed that Canada could support — not one — but *two* new transcontinental rail lines.

> *To those who tell us wait, wait, wait; to those who advise us to pause, to consider, to reflect, to calculate and to inquire, our answer is: No, this is not a time for deliberation, this is a time for action!*
> — Laurier, defending his government's overheated railway program

More and more branch lines were built — often within sight of each other. The Canadian Northern and the Grand Trunk both went bankrupt and were later nationalized and absorbed into a larger single system: *Canadian National Railways* (CNR). And though this happened after Laurier had left office, the CNR is still considered "Laurier's legacy," just as the CPR is considered Macdonald's.

For an informative site on the history and background of the CNR, go to `collections.ic.gc.ca/cnphoto/english/cnr3_ang.html`.

Alberta and Saskatchewan

In 1905, Laurier introduced the Autonomy Acts that created Alberta and Saskatchewan. Once again, issues of language and religion arose. The status of French and access to Catholic education had been guaranteed in the North-West Territories Act of 1875 (as amended in 1877). Would similar guarantees be made to protect minority rights in the two new provinces?

While the cantankerous Clifford Sifton was out of the country, Laurier's minister of justice, along with the French-Canadian nationalist Henri Bourassa, added a clause to the Autonomy Acts that would have protected Catholic minority rights in the new provinces and would have established French as an official language of Alberta and Saskatchewan.

When Sifton returned, he was outraged and resigned in protest. Once again, Laurier caved in. He allowed Sifton to rewrite the clause, effectively ending any protection for French Catholics in the two new provinces. And thus, ironically, it was under the reign of Canada's first French-Canadian prime minister that Western Canada became irretrievably English-speaking.

Visit `www.babelfish.com/travel.ab.ca/About_AB/AB_History.html` for more on the history of Alberta. For a history of Regina, the provincial capital of Saskatchewan, visit `www.cityregina.com/schoolprojects/lets_learn.shtml`. For the full text of the original Alberta and Saskatchewan Acts of 1905 go to `www.solon.org/Constitutions/Canada/English/aa_1905.html` and `www.solon.org/Constitutions/Canada/English/sa_1905.html`.

Klondike Gold

On August 17, 1896, a prospector by the name of George Washington Carmack, together with his Native brothers-in-law, Skookum Jim and Tagish Charley, discovered gold on a small creek in the Klondike region of what is now the Yukon Territory. In the words of Carmack, the gold lay in thick slabs between the rock "like cheese sandwiches." It would prove to be the richest single find in human history.

> *We've hit it! The golden paystreak!*
> — Carmack, as he whooped it up with Jim and Charley

The Klondike was the last great gold rush of the century, and it was also in one of the most remote and difficult places to reach on the continent. It took a year for news of the discovery to reach the rest of the world, and another year for the first wave of fortune seekers to rush in. Most of them took a boat up the Alaska Panhandle and then crossed over the White or Chilkoot Passes, up a slope so steep it was almost vertical. At the summit, they passed into Canadian territory, and there to greet them was a small contingent of Mounties. Anybody entering Canada had to bring with them a year's worth of food. Together with tools, tents, and other supplies, the load came to over a ton of material. It took a healthy man 90 days and as many as 40 trips over the pass to make it, and all in the dead of winter.

The Canadian border was more than a continental divide; it also provided a study in national character. Never was so stark a contrast drawn between American and Canadian values. On the American side, a wild, lawless atmosphere pervaded. Call it frontier-style free enterprise: Ruffians such as Soapy Smith and his gang stole and cheated miners dry, and shootouts and vigilante justice were not uncommon. At the Canadian border, all of that changed. The Mounties were in charge. The law was in effect.

When one of Soapy Smith's gang tried to cross the border without the required supplies, he was turned back. "And what would happen," he asked the Mountie who had stopped him, "if I decided to shoot my way in?" The constable thought a moment and then handed the man a pistol. "Start shooting. That's the easiest way to find out."

> *The Klondike stampede was the only* organized *gold rush in history.*
> — popular historian Pierre Berton

Dawson City did not exist in 1896. Three years later it had a population of 40,000 and was the largest city west of Winnipeg and north of Seattle. Steamboats began arriving from the longer, all-water route around Alaska, carrying pianos and paintings and ostrich-feather hats. Here in the Subarctic, the latest Parisian fashions could be found. Dawson was a city of showgirls and cabarets, casinos and ragtime tunes. Projected motion pictures, invented just three years earlier, were being shown. This sprawling, improbable city also had telephones, running water, luxury hotels, and electricity. Men tossed nuggets about like pennies, and gold dust was treated like common currency. One enterprising saloonkeeper hired a boy to sift the sawdust on the barroom floor for gold and came away with almost $300 in fine dust.

The people who paid the real price for the hyperinflation and overpopulation of Dawson were not the miners who had come looking for quick money, but the people who had lived there for centuries, the northern Athapaskans: the Tagish, Tutchone, Kutchin, and especially the Han, a small band of just several hundred who lived in the area where Dawson City suddenly sprang up. Overnight, they become strangers in their own land.

The culture of the Han was almost completely destroyed by the gold rush. Hunting areas were overrun with prospectors, forests were burned away, and at the height of the gold rush, the Indians of the area faced near-starvation amid the glitter of the Klondike.

It is estimated that at least a *billion* dollars of gold were mined during the Klondike stampede. It began with the discovery in 1896. By 1900, it was all over. International consortiums replaced the individual miners and moved in with automatic dredgers that sucked out the gold with an unadventurous efficiency. Old-timers still talked wistfully of a fabled "motherlode" somewhere further up in the mountains but it was never found, and the miners moved on, chasing fresh rumours and new dreams.

Today, Dawson has a population of just 2,000. The town, one of the most fascinating places in Canada, echoes with ghosts and memories.

How about the best two out of three?

The Laurier years were ones of prosperity and promise. Sure, deep cracks were forming just beneath the surface, divisions between French and English Canada and between east and west, but the mood was still one of almost giddy optimism. Laurier was caught up in it as well. "The nineteenth century was the century of the United States,'" he declared at a 1904 rally. "I think we can claim it is Canada that shall fill the twentieth century." This prediction — usually rendered *"The twentieth century belongs to Canada!"* — remains one of the most famous and heroic statements ever made by a Canadian leader. Okay, so it didn't exactly come true. But hey, the twenty-first century is still up for grabs. So how about it? Are you with me on this? Everybody! All together: *"The twenty-FIRST century belongs to Canada!"* I tell you, there's a beer commercial in there somewhere.

At yukonalaska.com/klondike/index.html you'll find the *Klondike Weekly*, an on-line magazine dedicated to the Klondike gold rush. For ghosts of the gold rush, visit www.gold-rush.org. Parks Canada has an extensive Klondike site at www.harbour.com/parkscan/khs/hist.htm and a Chilkoot Trail site at www.harbour.com/parkscan/ct. For more on historic Athabasca Landing, the gateway to the overland route to the Klondike (via Edmonton) go to collections.ic.gc.ca/Athabasca/. For the full text of the Yukon Territory Act of 1898: www.solon.org/Constitutions/Canada/English/yta_1898.html.

The Alaska boundary dispute

The Yukon Territory was created in June 1898, at the very height of the Klondike gold rush, in order to assert Canadian sovereignty over the area. The gold rush also helped revive a long-standing dispute between Canada and the United States over the boundary of the Alaska Panhandle (the narrow strip of shoreline stretching south along the Pacific Coast).

The Americans wanted to draw the border *inland*, around the headwaters of the bays and fjords, effectively cutting off Canadian territory from the sea. The Canadians, in turn, wanted the border to cover only the immediate shoreline. This would have given Canada access to the Pacific. A six-member panel was named, made up of three Americans, two Canadian lawyers, and a British judge. During negotiations, the British negotiator sided with the Americans and in 1903, Canada lost access to several key inlets. The Canadian negotiators were so disgusted they refused to sign the accord.

Sam Steele, Lion of the Yukon

The Mounties kept a tight rein during the Klondike gold rush. They confiscated handguns, checked supplies, and turned away anyone not prepared for the rigours of the north. At the forefront was Sam Steele, "the Lion of the Yukon," a character who, had he not existed, we would most certainly have had to invent. He was the classic archetypal Mountie, strong of jaw and steady of eye, and his life reads like a dime-store novel. His very name seems mythical.

Sam Steele was directly involved in every major event that occurred in the opening of Canada's frontier: from the Great March West to the Riel Rebellions, from the signing of Native treaties to the building of the CPR and the Klondike stampede. Steele stared down violent rail workers and he disarmed American desperadoes and unruly mobs. And, as befits a Canadian hero, Sam Steele was brought down not by vengeful outlaws or drunken miners, but by Canadian bureaucracy. When Steele began prosecuting corrupt Liberal-backed profiteers, he found himself up against Laurier's all-powerful minister of the interior, Clifford Sifton. The Steele–Sifton feud ended (predictably) with a victory of politics over law. Steele was relieved of duty and sent packing. Ottawa had effectively "de-fanged" the Lion of the Yukon.

The Alaskan boundary dispute, called "the worst setback to Canadian–American relations since the War of 1812," provided a wake-up call to Canadians. It was clear that Britain could no longer be relied upon. Canada would have to take more control over its foreign affairs.

Canada seemed alone in the world, bullied by the United States, abandoned by Great Britain.

— historians Norman Hillmer and J.L. Granatstein

In 1909, Laurier established a Department of External Affairs — more symbolic than real. Still, it signalled to the world that Canada was determined to have a greater voice in its own international dealings. A small step, but a significant one.

Bernier to Dickins: Canada's northern colony

Britain had transferred its jurisdiction over the Arctic Islands to Canada in 1880, but it wasn't until the early twentieth century that Canada officially extended its boundaries all the way to the North Pole. On July 1, 1909, Québec's master mariner, Joseph-Elzéar Bernier, single-handedly claimed the entire Arctic Archipelago (the largest in the world) on behalf of Canada. He did this by "taking possession" of Baffin Island in the presence of a few nonplussed Inuit hunters.

*After firing nineteen shots [in celebration], I instructed an Eskimo to fire
the twentieth, telling him that he was now a Canadian.*
— Bernier, explaining the ceremony he improvised

Those would be the only shots fired in Canada's northern conquest. It was
one of the biggest land grabs in human history. The colonized had become
the colonizer. Even then, it was ownership in name only, and it wasn't until
the legendary bush pilot Clennell "Punch" Dickins made his epic 15,000-mile
aerial survey of the North in the mid-1930s that Canada could really claim full
dominion. Awarded the Distinguished Flying Cross as a fighter pilot in World
War I, Dickins had gone on to become one of the nation's greatest explorers.
As a senior bureaucrat in Ottawa once noted, "The history of the Canadian
North can be divided into two periods — before and after the airplane."

Canada and the Empire

In 1897, the British Empire was in its glory. At Queen Victoria's Diamond
Jubilee, celebrating her sixtieth year on the throne, Wilfrid Laurier was
awarded the position of honour at the head of the colonial procession. The
pomp and ceremony seemed to go to Laurier's head. He lavished praise on
the Queen and the Empire, charming one and all with his silver tongue and
eloquent flattery. But at the Colonial Conference that followed the celebrations,
Laurier showed his true colours.

"An everlasting 'No'"

Britain's Colonial Secretary Joseph Chamberlain was an ardent imperialist
who put pressure on the colonies — and Laurier in particular — to help
"consolidate the Empire." He wanted the colonies to draw closer to Britain
and proposed a Council of the Empire with closer military and commercial
ties. Wilfrid Laurier said "No." Again and again, at the various conferences
and meetings that followed over the years, Laurier continued to say "No."
No to a military commitment. No to an imperial common market. No, no, no.
Canada was moving away from Britain and becoming more independent. It was
a slow process, but it was one Laurier approved. And it is Laurier's stubborn,
continued rejection of flirtatious imperial overtures, his "everlasting no" as it
was called, that marked him as a nation builder. (His critics started to call
him "Sir Won'tfrid.")

The Boer War

In 1899, fighting broke out in South Africa between British colonists and the Boers, descendants of the original Dutch settlers. It was a war that had absolutely no connection to Canada, but English Canadians rallied to the cause nonetheless. Joseph Chamberlain even sent a telegraph, thanking Canada for its offer to send troops to South Africa. Only problem was, Laurier had made no such promise.

Although their rhetoric often reached the level of hysterics, French-Canadian nationalists saw the Boer War for what it was: an imperialist military adventure that wasn't worth the blood of a single Canadian. Laurier himself admitted as much. "There is no menace to Canada," he noted. But, to appease English Canadians, he struck a typical Laurier compromise. No regular troops would be forced to serve, but the Canadian government would equip and transport a contingent of *volunteers*. Once they reached South Africa, they would become the responsibility of Britain. More than 7,000 Canadians would eventually serve in the Boer War, among them the ubiquitous Sam Steele. It was the first time Canadians had fought overseas. It was also the last hurrah of the Victorian Age. Queen Victoria died in January 1901. The Boer War ended the following year.

Free trade and a tinpot navy

In 1909, an Imperial Defense Conference was called, and yet again Britain put heavy pressure on Laurier to move Canada more firmly into the British sphere of influence. The enemy was now Germany. The British press was whipping up a frenzy of fear over the Germans' recent military buildup, and the British government wanted to build a series of powerful battleships. And they also wanted Canada to chip in as part of a proposed joint naval scheme. Instead of signing on, Laurier came up with yet another clever compromise.

Canada would build a navy of her own, one that could be put at Britain's disposal at times of war. It was a scheme that satisfied absolutely no one. Once again, Québec nationalists felt he had gone too far. Laurier's navy would be used to fight Britain's wars, they warned. English-Canadian imperialists, however, felt Laurier hadn't gone far enough in supporting the Empire. Tory humorist Stephen Leacock mocked Laurier's proposed Naval Service Act as "a tinpot navy," and the derisive nickname stuck. That's the problem with staking a claim in the middle of the road. Eventually you will get run over. Laurier himself summed up his dilemma:

> *I am branded in Québec as a traitor to the French, and in Ontario as a traitor to the English. . . . In Québec I am attacked as an imperialist and in Ontario as an anti-imperialist. I am neither. I am a Canadian.*
> — Wilfrid Laurier in 1911

The telephone and the Silver Dart

Alexander Graham Bell, born, raised, and educated in Scotland, came to Canada with his father in 1870 and settled in Brantford, Ontario. It was there that he developed the principles of the telephone, which he then tested and patented in Boston in 1876, thus sparking an ongoing feud between Brantford and Boston — and Canada and the U.S. — over where the telephone was invented. (In Scotland, meanwhile, it's considered a *Scottish* invention.) That same summer, the first long-distance telephone call was made between Brantford and Paris, Ontario.

Alexander, now an American citizen, later moved back to Canada and set up an estate and research centre at Baddeck, Cape Breton. (He chose Cape Breton because it reminded him of his beloved Scotland.) Bell worked on a number of impressive and innovative projects, including an iron lung, a forerunner of fibre optics, and a working hovercraft. His wife, Mabel, founded an aerial research association, and Alexander himself helped develop the first successful aircraft in Canada — or anywhere else in the British Empire for that matter. Named the *Silver Dart*, the aircraft first took flight from the frozen waters of Cape Breton on February 23, 1909, piloted by an adventurous young man named J.A.D. McCurdy.

For more on Bell, Baddeck, and Brantford, go to www.fitzgeraldstudio.com/html/bell/theman.html#theman. And you'll find more on McCurdy and the historic flight of the Silver Dart at exn.ca/Mini/Flightdeck/Aviators/mccurdy.cfm.

Even worse, Laurier had revived the old Liberal platform of free trade, or "reciprocity," with the United States. Clifford Sifton, an anti-free trader from way back, left the Liberal Party in protest, and Wilfrid Laurier went down in defeat to the Conservatives in 1911. The Laurier era was suddenly over.

For a brief bio on Laurier visit www.rendezvousfrancophonie.com/english/personnages/carte_r07.html. Or go to this larger prime ministers site at cnet.unb.ca/achn/pme.

Chapter 16

Borden and the Great War

- -

In This Chapter

▶ Europe drags the world into a bloody and pointless war

▶ Canadian soldiers distinguish themselves at Ypres, Vimy Ridge, and Amiens

▶ Conscription threatens to tear Canada apart

▶ Prime Minister Robert Borden wins political independence for Canada

- -

In the 1911 election, Laurier's Liberals campaigned in favour of free trade and closer economic ties to the United States. This seemed sensible enough, especially to Western Canadians, but the mood was soured when American annexationists south of the border let out a hearty cheer. For them, free trade was the first step towards a full-scale takeover of Canada. *Huzzah!*

> *We are preparing to annex Canada, and the day is not far off when the American flag will float over every square foot of the British North American possessions — clear to the North Pole.*
> — Champ Clark, Speaker of the U.S. House of Representatives, celebrating the proposed free trade deal

In response, Robert Borden's Conservatives campaigned under the banner, "No Truck nor Trade with the Yankees!" and were swept into power.

Borden and Laurier were a study in contrasts. Laurier, the debonair, refined French Canadian, oozed charisma. Robert Borden, the stocky, sombre Nova Scotian, seemed stiff and unyielding in comparison. Laurier was a charmer. Borden was a man who got things done. He led Canada during its most difficult, divisive crisis since Confederation: the outbreak of World War I and the tug-of-war between French and English Canada that followed.

Robert Borden was the father of Canadian political independence. He made his share of mistakes, true, but he also showed remarkable backbone and dedication. He is, perhaps, the single most *underrated* prime minister in Canadian history. The great irony of Robert Borden's life is that although he almost single-handedly forced Britain and the world to accept Canadian political sovereignty, he also left the country more divided and more dysfunctional than it had ever been before. Much like English Canada itself, Robert Borden began the war as a colonial and ended as a Canadian. It was a remarkable journey on both counts.

Marching Off to War

The period before World War I was the high-water mark of imperial feeling, an era when "imperialist" was not a dirty word.

— historian Daniel Francis

World War I (1914–18), or the Great War as it was known, was a heartbreaking and pointless conflict. Imperialism taken to its logical extreme, the war left 14 million people dead, 21 million more crippled, and an entire generation shattered. And for what? Even today, historians can't decide exactly why the war ever started in the first place, let alone whether there was any point to it or even whether it could have been prevented.

Over the years, a complex network of imperial alliances had formed in Europe. The entire continent was a powder keg, and all it took was a single spark to set it off. It came on June 28, 1914, when Archduke Francis Ferdinand of Austria-Hungary was shot and killed by a Serbian nationalist. The competing alliances clicked into place with military precision. Austria declared war on Serbia. Russia declared war on Austria. Germany declared war on Russia — and immediately invaded France. Great Britain, in turn, declared war on Germany, and Canada, being part of the British Empire, was automatically at war as well. And that is why young boys from Saskatoon ended up dying face down and bleeding in a muddy field in France.

The Great War was waged between two opposing alliances:

- ✔ **The Allies:** Great Britain, France, and Russia
- ✔ **Central Powers:** Germany, Austria-Hungary, and the Ottoman Empire (Turkey)

The conflict soon grew and eventually involved every ocean and every inhabited continent on earth. Canada, Australia, New Zealand, and India entered the war on the British side, and Italy and Japan later joined the Allies as well. The U.S. remained neutral up until the spring of 1917, when they too declared war on Germany. (Although the Americans were involved only during the final 18 months, they did provide a much-needed influx of fresh troops and supplies, which helped tip the balance in the Allies' favour.)

"Back by Christmas!"

The war brought Canadians together — at first. Robert Borden declared that it was Canada's duty to stand "shoulder to shoulder with Britain," and Wilfrid Laurier, now in Opposition, heartily agreed. When the call comes, said Laurier, the only answer must be "Ready, aye. Ready!" Canada was in the middle of an economic downturn and the war effort helped revitalize the economy. Unemployed men gladly volunteered, fully expecting the war to be a quick and exciting adventure. "Back by Christmas!" was the cry. Even anti-imperialists like Henri Bourassa saw in the war an opportunity to unite Canadians, French and English, in defense of Canada's "mother countries." Bourassa's enthusiasm — and those of the soldiers — would soon sour.

The man in charge of recruitment was Borden's blustering minister of militia, Sam Hughes. It was a slightly chaotic time to begin with. Automobiles were rattling through city streets, telephone lines were being strung up everywhere, and gas was replacing coal for cooking, just as electricity was replacing gas for lighting. And Sam Hughes threw together a Canadian overseas contingent in a similarly rattle-bang, chaotic fashion.

More than 30,000 men volunteered — two-thirds of whom were recent British immigrants, off to fight for their homeland. Hughes armed them with elite weapons: the Ross rifle, a long-barrelled, Canadian-built gun designed for precision firing. It was a disastrous choice. The rifles jammed in mud and overheated when fired in quick succession. Thousands of Canadian boys died in vain trying to fire them. Hughes, stubborn to the end, refused to replace the rifles until the situation had reached scandalous levels. But none of that was known to the men who piled pell-mell onto ships, cheering and waving. They were off to fight "the Hun," as the Germans were known (in reference to the barbarian hordes of Attila the Hun).

> *Men, the world regards you as a marvel!*
> — Sam Hughes's farewell message to "his boys"

The first Canadian Expeditionary Force set sail in October 1914. They trained in England and were then shipped off to France. The first to arrive were the Princess Patricia's Canadian Light Infantry (or "Princess Pats," as they are known) who landed in December 1914. The great adventure was about to begin.

See World War I through Canadian eyes at `collections.ic.gc.ca/courage/splash.html`.

Enemy aliens

Ottawa passed a War Measures Act, giving the government sweeping new powers to arrest and detain any suspected subversives. In fact, it gave the government the power to do virtually anything it deemed necessary "for the security, defense, peace, order and welfare of Canada." A Halifax lawyer named W.F. O'Connor drafted the Act, which had the full support of both sides of the House.

> *Make absolutely sure that you omit no power that the government may need.*
> — instructions given to O'Connor by the Liberal Opposition

In the hysteria of the time, all "enemy aliens" were considered suspect. When the Parliament Buildings burned down in February 1916, there were whispered rumours of alien sabotage. Anti-German sentiments reached such heights that the German-Canadian town of Berlin, Ontario, was pressured into changing its name. They chose "Kitchener" after the British war hero and field marshal, Horatio Kitchener.

Even worse, the War Measures Act was used to justify the mass arrests and imprisonment of more than 8,500 "enemy aliens" living in Canada. Public opinion demanded it and the government complied. By the end of 1914, the first wave of arrests was underway. Internment camps were built and identification cards were issued. Canadians of German, Austrian, and Turkish descent were targeted, as were Ukrainians who had emigrated to Canada from regions under the domination of Austria-Hungary. In the screwy, xenophobic logic of the time, this made the Ukrainians "enemies of Canada."

More than 5,000 Ukrainian Canadians were interned during the war and used as forced labour in the steel mills in Nova Scotia, the logging camps in Ontario, and the coal mines in B.C. Banff National Park was developed largely through the forced labour of German and Ukrainian prisoners. Although many internees were released during the war, the camps weren't completely shut down until 1920, long after the conflict had ended.

The imprisonment of foreign nationals during war was a common enough practice at that time. Many innocent Canadians, including a French-Canadian Member of Parliament, were imprisoned over in Germany. But none of that excuses the vindictive policies pursued in Canada. Before being revoked in 1988, the War Measures Act would be used again in World War II to imprison and displace Japanese Canadians, and in 1970 to lock up Québec nationalists. *Arrests without trial: a part of our heritage . . .*

For more on the internment of Ukrainian Canadians (1914–20), go to `www.infoukes.com/history/internment`.

Gas attack at Ypres

The war in Western Europe had ground to a halt. In northern France and Belgium, the two sides dug in, hunkering down in trenches and facing each other across a barren "no man's land" of barbed wire and pockmarked craters. It would prove to be one of the most brutal stalemates in human history, one that cost millions of lives without advancing more than a few kilometres in either direction.

Modern warfare was born at Ypres, Belgium, on April 22, 1915. On that day, the German army released more than 5,700 cylinders of chlorine gas into the wind. A sickly greenish-yellow cloud wafted across no man's land. The French colonial army, gasping and clutching their throats, their tongues swollen and their brass buttons turning green, broke and ran. Canadian troops rushed, closing the gap, and the German advance was checked.

Two days later, on April 24, the Germans released a second gas attack — this time directly at the Canadian forces. The Canadians stood their ground. They soaked their handkerchiefs in muddy water — and even in their own urine — and held them over their mouths and noses. The Germans surged forward as shrapnel and machine guns ripped through the Allied ranks. The Canadians fought back, even as their Ross rifles overheated and jammed. The Germans were stopped. The line held.

> *Thus, in their first appearance on a European battlefield, the Canadians established a reputation as a formidable fighting force.*
> — historian Patricia Giesler

The cost was high. More than 6,000 Canadians were dead, missing, or wounded. Later, the Germans would introduce an even more terrifying weapon: mustard gas, which burned the very skin of the soldiers.

Battle of the Somme

With the war bogged down, the criminal incompetence of the British High Command became more and more evident. A "big push" was launched in July 1916 along the Somme River. It was a cunning plan, all right. Roughly 100,000 Allied troops were told to leave their trenches and advance across no man's land in broad daylight and directly into German fire. What followed was a slaughter. More than 57,000 British soldiers were killed, wounded, or missing — the heaviest single-day loss ever suffered by a British army.

At Beaumont-Hamel, the 1st Newfoundland Regiment was all but annihilated, cut down as they attempted to cross 200 metres of mud under point-blank fire from German machine guns. Of the 790 Newfoundlanders who went over the top that day, only 68 answered roll call the following morning. The rest were either killed or wounded. It was one of the highest casualty rates of the war, and even now, July 1, 1916, is remembered as the darkest day in Newfoundland history. The Battle of the Somme was less a battle than it was a meat grinder. In three months of long-drawn-out, soul-shattering warfare, the Allies lost well over *half a million* men. It had become a war of attrition, where the goal was not to defeat the enemy but simply to outlast him, to kill more of his men than he did yours.

Vimy Ridge

Vimy Ridge was a key high ground in northern France. The Germans had dug themselves in and the hill was riddled with tunnels, trenches, and complex fortifications; protected by artillery; and reinforced with machine-gun platforms. The Germans had even strung in telephone and electric lines and had built a rail line for moving munitions. The British and the French had both tried to take Vimy Ridge — again and again and again. Every attempt had failed, and more than 200,000 men had been lost. It was now Canada's turn.

Unlike previous British attacks, the preparations this time were careful and meticulous. A complete mock-up of the hill was built and the soldiers trained on it until they knew the lay of the land by heart. Rather than drag their own guns forward, the Canadians learned how to load and fire German artillery so that they would be able to turn captured guns against the enemy. Andrew McNaughton, a Canadian colonel and a former science professor from McGill University, discovered a way to pinpoint enemy guns by their flash and sound, and key German positions were systematically destroyed before the advance began. As well, British artillerymen were trained to drop their shells just ahead of the advancing army, allowing the Canadians to move forward behind a thundering "rolling barrage."

The attack began on Easter Monday, April 9, 1917. For the first time in the war, all four divisions of the Canadian Corps advanced together, fighting alongside each other against the brunt of the German army. Perhaps it was the climate. In the cold, wet winds and driving snow and sleet, the Canadians must have felt right at home. They took the hill, sweeping the Germans from the ridge. At Vimy, the Canadians captured more guns, more ground, and more prisoners than in any previous British offensive. Called "the most perfectly organized and most successful battle of the whole war," it was Canada's greatest victory, and one that has since been hailed as a "nation-making moment" that involved Canadians from every region.

We went up Vimy Ridge as Albertans and Nova Scotians. We came down as Canadians.

— a war veteran remembering Vimy Ridge

Nearly 3,600 Canadians died taking Vimy Ridge, and a soaring monument in northern France now marks the spot. After that battle, the Canadians were set apart as storm troopers, brought in to head the assault in one great battle after another. A Canadian officer Arthur Currie, the key strategist behind Vimy Ridge, was given command of the entire Canadian Corps. He would prove to be one of the greatest generals the war produced. A former schoolteacher, Currie had worked his way up from private and was knighted for his work at Vimy Ridge. One German officer later went on record as saying that if it weren't for Currie and the Canadian Corps, Germany might very well have won the war.

Whenever the Germans found the Canadian Corps coming into the line, they prepared for the worst.

— British Prime Minister David Lloyd George

Go to www.vac-acc.gc.ca/general/sub.cfm?source=history/firstwar/vimy and www.spartacus.schoolnet.co.uk/FWWvimy.htm for more on Vimy Ridge. For links to more on Beaumont-Hamel, the Battle of the Somme, Vimy Ridge and more, go to www.cfc.dnd.ca/tguide.html.

Passchendaele

In a war marked by horrific battles, Passchendaele was perhaps the most horrific of all. A reclaimed marshland in Belgium, Passchendaele had been turned into a soup of mud by British artillery, which had destroyed drainage systems and had created, in the words of one historian, "a bottomless mire." Heavy rains made it even worse. Wounded soldiers drowned on the battlefield, and guns and supplies disappeared into the quagmire. The British Army lost 68,000 men trying to take the heights at the far side of this swamp-like field, often wading through waist-deep mud as they went.

After a month of carnage, the British High Command sent for Arthur Currie and his Canadians. Currie was appalled. Even with the best preparations, he insisted, taking Passchendaele would cost 16,000 men. But the British High Command insisted, and on October 26, the Canadians made their first of several attacks. Currie had prepared carefully, building wooden gun platforms and light rail tracks, and stockpiling supplies beforehand. It was a long, hard slog, but by November 6, the ridge had been taken. Currie's prediction was proven eerily accurate. It had cost 15,654 casualties to capture five square kilometres of mud.

After reading Currie's scathing report on how the British were fighting the war, Robert Borden went on the attack. He confronted the British PM and said, voice quavering with emotion, "Mr. Prime Minister, I want to tell you that, if ever there is a repetition of the Battle of Passchendaele, not a single Canadian soldier will leave the shores of Canada [again]. . . ."

In the air

High above the muck and misery of the trenches, a very different sort of war was unfolding. In the sky, airborne knights duelled without parachutes and often over direct fire from enemy troops below. As might be expected, the life expectancy of World War I pilots was very short. One-third of all fliers died in combat. Those who survived long enough to shoot down five or more enemy aircraft were dubbed "aces."

Canada produced more and better pilots than any other country. Over 40 percent of the "British" fliers were from Canada. And of the top 27 aces on the British side, 10 were Canadian. Among them:

- ✔ **Billy Bishop** of Owen Sound, Ontario. Nicknamed "the Lone Hawk," Bishop, with 72 victories, was Britain's top ace. Among all the pilots of the war, Bishop was third. He once went head-to-head with Germany's "Red Baron," Manfred von Richthofen, and fought him to a standstill in what has been called "the greatest aerial dogfight in history."

- ✔ **Raymond Collishaw** of Nanaimo, B.C. With 60 victories to his credit, Collishaw was Britain's fifth-ranked ace.

- ✔ **Will Barker** of Dauphin, Manitoba. Canada's most decorated war hero, Barker once took on an entire German flying formation — anywhere from 15 to 60 planes — all by himself. He was fearless.

    (**Note:** Barker was dubbed "Billy" by the newspapers at the time, mainly because they liked the parallel to Billy Bishop, and the error has been repeated to this day.)

The Canadian ace Roy Brown is credited with shooting down the Red Baron. Richthofen, with 80 kills to his credit, was in hot pursuit of another young Canadian flier named Wilfred "Wop" May, when Brown swooped down from behind, riddling the Baron's red triplane with bullets. Slumped over, dead at the controls, the Red Baron crashed into the mud. (Australian gunners on the ground claimed that they were the ones who actually killed the Red Baron, but it was Brown who was given official credit — and it was Brown who drove the Baron into enemy fire.)

For more on Canada's amazing World War I air aces, go to www.accessweb.com/users/mconstab. For more on the war in the air (part of a larger British site): www.spartacus.schoolnet.co.uk/FWWair.htm.

The Conscription Crisis

The bodies kept falling, and the costs kept climbing. The government began borrowing money from Canadian citizens in the form of "Victory Bonds" (guaranteed loans to be repaid after the war). These bonds covered more than 80 percent of the war costs, but they also gave Canada a heavy national debt — they had to be repaid at some point, remember. In 1916, the government issued a tax on business profits.

The human cost of the war was even worse. After a harrowing tour of wartime hospitals in England, Borden returned home determined to give his support to the Canadians fighting in Europe. In his New Year's message for 1916, Borden announced that he had made a "scared promise" to send 500,000 troops overseas. This, in a country of just 8 million, where only 1.5 million were men of military age. Apparently, Borden expected a third of them to sign up. Incredibly, a third *did*. Canada reached its goal — but even that wasn't enough.

The initial enthusiasm had long since worn out. The casualty lists grew longer, the mood grew darker. Even as Borden was promising more men, volunteer recruitment was drying up. At Vimy Ridge, the Canadian Corps suffered more than 10,000 casualties, dead or wounded. That same month, less than 5,000 men back home signed up. The brute mathematics were clear. Something had to be done. Great Britain and New Zealand had already decided to draft men into service, and when the Americans entered the war, they immediately introduced conscription as well. Canada would have to follow suit.

On May 18, 1917, Robert Borden rose in the House of Commons and announced that Canada would begin registering and conscripting men — forcing them to fight, in essence. "The battle for Canadian liberty and autonomy is being fought today on the plains of France and Belgium," he said. The following week, riots broke out in Montréal.

 Conscription was angrily rejected in Québec. Forcing young men to fight and die in an imperial conflict — it was exactly what Bourassa had been warning about all these years. Making matters worse, the Canadian Corps was almost completely English-speaking. One of the few exceptions was the hastily organized French-speaking 22nd Battalion, or "Vandoos" as they were known (after *vingt-deux*, meaning "twenty-two"). The war was seen as an English-Canadian folly. Québec, in turn, was denounced as being a haven for cowards. Never had Canada been so divided.

In the House, every French-Canadian MP voted *against* conscription, and virtually every English-Canadian MP voted *for* it. The majority won, and the Military Service Act, giving the government the right to draft men into the army, became law on August 29, 1917.

Union government

Having introduced conscription, Borden now approached Laurier about joining him in a coalition — or Union — government, one that would unite Conservatives and Liberals in a common cause. Borden had always hated party politics, and he wanted to forge a non-partisan government to oversee the war effort. After lengthy negotiations, Laurier said no. He was opposed to conscription because he saw in it "the seeds of discord and disunion." Borden eventually hammered out a coalition without Laurier, and then called a winter election while emotions were still riding high.

> *The 1917 election was the most bitter in Canadian history, viciously fought on both sides.*
>
> — historian Michael Bliss

Borden had no intention of losing. Before the election, he took the vote away from Canadians who had emigrated from enemy nations within the last 15 years. He also took the vote away from pacifists and conscientious objectors, such as Quakers and Mennonites. At the same time, he *gave* the vote to women — but only those who were either married to or blood relatives of Canadian servicemen. (As Borden predicted, these women voted heavily in favour of his pro-conscription Union government. The women wanted more boys sent overseas to help support their own loved ones.)

Borden also gave the vote to all soldiers regardless of how long they had lived in Canada. In Europe, Canadian servicemen would vote simply "government" or "opposition." Talk about stacking the deck!

Borden's hardball approach worked. The Union government won a huge victory. Indeed, it was the most lopsided majority Canada had seen: 153 seats for Borden's Unionists and 82 seats for Laurier's decimated Liberals. Of the seats the Liberals won, 62 of them were in Québec. The province was now almost completely isolated from the rest of Canada, and the country itself had become polarized.

"The Prussians next door"

Opposition to conscription was not limited to Québec. Farmers in Ontario organized angry protests, as did the labour movement under the Canadian Trades and Labour Congress. Farmers didn't want their sons going overseas, not when crops needed harvesting and cattle needed tending — and this anger cut across linguistic lines. When conscription finally got underway, a whopping 98 percent of men registered in Québec asked to be exempted. In patriotic Ontario, meanwhile, a full 94 percent sought exemptions. Hmm. It would seem that English Canadians supported conscription only as long as it involved someone else.

Regulation 17

As the conscription crisis raged, older conflicts resurfaced. Among them, Ontario's controversial Regulation 17. First passed in 1912, Regulation 17 made English the only official language of Ontario schools. It also restricted French-language instruction to grades one and two (later amended to include one hour of French study a day at higher grades as well). Henri Bourassa cited Regulation 17 as an example of English-Canadian intolerance, which went against the spirit of Confederation. In the Ottawa area, Franco-Ontarian mothers armed with hatpins stood guard at school entrances to block any government officials who tried to interfere with bilingual education.

Nor was the hostility limited to Ontario. In 1916, at the very height of the war, Manitoba repealed its provisions for bilingual education. Laurier's compromise of 1896 (described in Chapter 15), minimal though it was, was now deemed too much. Manitoba became officially and aggressively *English only*. French would be contained. Bourassa's vision of a bilingual nation, from east to west, had been rejected. French Canadians were being exhorted to help defend liberty and French culture overseas, even as French language rights and education were under direct assault back in Canada.

On Good Friday in 1918, military police in Québec City seized a suspected draft-resister — and set off a full-scale riot. As angry mobs broke windows and attacked English-owned businesses, troops were called in to restore order. On Easter Monday, several soldiers were cornered in a square by a rock-throwing mob. The soldiers fired into the crowd, killing four. In the wake of these riots, Borden's resolve hardened. All exemptions were cancelled, and draft dodgers were hunted down. Henri Bourassa wondered aloud who the real enemy was. It seemed to him that French-Canadian liberty was being threatened, not in Europe but right here at home. He began referring to English Canada, and Ontario in particular, as "the Prussians next door" (Prussia being a term for Germany).

The aim of the Military Service Act was to find 100,000 extra soldiers, and it did just that: more than 99,500 MSA men were in uniform by 1918. When the war came to its sudden and unexpected halt, 24,000 of these conscripted servicemen had reached Europe. Had the conflict continued, as most people believed it would, conscription would have become an absolute necessity. Conscription was not a failure in a military sense, but in a *social* sense. The MSA shattered Canadian unity, fragile at the best of times.

Acts of war

Here is a recap of the key legislation passed during World War I:

War Measures Act (1914): Gave the government sweeping new emergency powers — including the right to arrest and detain "enemy aliens."

Income Tax (1917): A supposedly temporary measure, introduced to help fund Canada's war effort.

Military Service Act (1917): Introduced conscription.

Military Voters Act (1917): Gave the vote to soldiers, regardless of how long they had lived in Canada.

Wartime Elections Act (1917): Gave the vote to women who were married to or related to servicemen. It also took the vote away from conscientious objectors (people opposed to the war on religious or philosophical grounds) as well as anyone from enemy countries who had settled in Canada within the last 15 years.

Canada's 100 Days

In the October Revolution of 1917, Communist forces took control of Russia. They immediately began negotiating a ceasefire with Germany, and this in turn freed up German troops, which could now be shifted to the Western Front. In March 1918, the Germans launched a blistering offensive, punching their way through Allied lines. The Allies counterattacked, with the battle-hardened Canadian Corps leading the charge. The final three months of the war (August 8 to November 11, 1918) have gone down in history as "Canada's 100 Days," with the Canadians acting as a "spearhead to victory."

Breakthrough at Amiens

Flanked by French and Australian troops, the Canadians broke through the German lines at Amiens in what was perhaps the most crucial battle of the war. The enemy defenses crumbled, and the Canadians poured in, blazing a trail and sending the German army reeling. In a single day, the Canadian Corps advanced 13 kilometres into enemy territory. The stalemate of trench warfare was over. It was now a quick-running, open battle, one of speed and strategy. Led by General Currie, the Canadians captured more than 5,000 German prisoners during the first day alone. The morale of German troops had been shattered, and August 8, 1918, went down as a "black day" for the German army. At Amiens, the tide had turned.

The Canadians were ending the war by destroying the German army.
— military historian Desmond Morton

November 11

Rather than dig in and get caught in another stalemate, Currie shifted fronts. The Canadians now attacked the famed Hindenburg Line, a series of entrenched fortifications that had taken the Germans two yeas to build. In a high-pitched battle, the Canadians broke through. It was a momentous victory, and the French Canadians in particular fought with a fierce determination. Every officer in the Vandoos was killed or wounded, among them a young major named Georges Vanier who was shot almost to pieces during the attack. Vanier would later become Governor General of Canada.

The four divisions of the Canadian Corps defeated 47 German divisions, a full quarter of the German army. The Canadians liberated an area containing more than 200 cities and towns, capturing more than 30,000 enemy soldiers as they went. The end came suddenly. The Canadians crossed the Belgium border and fought their way into the town of Mons. On November 10, a battle was waged along its narrow streets and canals, and the following day, Germany surrendered. On the eleventh hour of the eleventh day of the eleventh month, the Great War came to an end.

"In Flanders Fields"

Some of the worst fighting of World War I occurred in the Flanders region of Belgium, an area known for its wild poppies. These flowers were immortalized in a poem written in 1915 by John McCrae, a Canadian military surgeon. As he buried one of his best friends, McCrae noted that poppies had begun blooming amid the graves.

In Flanders fields the poppies blow
Between the crosses, row on row.

Although haunting and melancholy, McCrae's poem is actually a call to arms, urging — not peace — but a greater war effort:

Take up our quarrel with the foe:
To you from failing hands we throw
The torch; be yours to hold it high.

If ye break faith with us who die
We shall not sleep, though poppies grow
In Flanders fields

"In Flanders Fields" was an immediate success, and the line "if ye break faith — we shall not sleep" was used to sell government bonds to fund the war effort. The poem also inspired the poppies that we wear on Remembrance Day, every November 11. McCrae himself died of pneumonia and meningitis in January 1918. He was buried with full military honours on a hillside not far from the fields of Flanders.

You'll find more on John McCrae and Flanders Fields at www.vac-acc.gc.ca/general/sub.cfm/history/firstwar/mccrae.

See Table 16-1 for a complete timetable of World War I.

Table 16-1		A Timeline of World War I
1914	June 28	Archduke Ferdinand of Austria assassinated — setting off a chain of events leading to world war
	August 4	Britain declares war on Germany — as part of the Empire, Canada is automatically at war as well
	October 3	Canada's first contingent sets sail for Europe
1915	April 22–24	Ypres — Germans unleash the first gas attack
	December	In his year-end address, Borden commits Canada to 500,000 more troops
1916	July 1–November 18	Battle of the Somme — more than 600,000 Allied troops are lost
1917	April 6	United States declares war on Germany
	April 9–12	Battle of Vimy Ridge — major Canadian victory
	August 29	Military Service Act — conscription becomes law
	October 12	Borden announces the creation of a Union government
	October 26–November 10	Battle of Passchendaele
	October–November	Communist forces under Lenin seize control of Russia and sue for peace with Germany
	December 17	Borden's pro-conscriptionist Unionists defeat Laurier's Liberals
1918	March 21	With troops no longer tied down on the Russian front, Germans launch a major offensive
	March 29–April 1	Easter Weekend riots in Québec City
	April 12	All exemptions are cancelled, conscription begins in full force
	August 8–November 11	"Canada's 100 Days" — the Allies counterattack, with the Canadians as the spearhead to victory
	August 8–11	Battle of Amiens — Canadians lead the attack
	August 26–September 2	Canadians break through the Hindenburg Line
	November 11	Germany surrenders
1919	June 28	Treaty of Versailles formally ends the war
1920	January 10	Canada becomes a founding member of the League of Nations

Canada and the Empire: Revised

Canada entered the war a colony, she emerged from it close to an independent state.

— historian A.R.M. Lower

It is a myth that Canadians won their independence without bloodshed. Certainly, Canadian *political* independence was won at great cost in the crucible of World War I.

More than 620,000 Canadians served in the First World War.

Of these, more than 60,000 died and more than 172,00 were wounded, often horribly so.

The war had two important effects. First of all, the horrific toll of the war years ended forever any widespread public admiration for old school imperialism. If the Plains of Abraham had made French Canadians "Canadian," then the same can be said about English Canada and World War I. By 1918, English Canadians had become, simply, Canadians. The allure of Great Britain had paled, and the thrill of imperial military pride never fully recovered.

The second effect, and just as important, was on Canada's self-image, both at home and abroad. At the start of the war, Canada had control over its own domestic affairs, but in foreign policy it was still a vassal of Great Britain. The war changed that. Canada's heavy contribution (extremely high, in relation to its population) gave it a much stronger voice internationally.

In the early years of the conflict, Canada and the other dominions (such as Australia and New Zealand) had been treated in an almost condescending manner, clearly subordinate to Britain and not involved in the decision-making process. As often as not, Borden had to find out about events in Europe the same way other Canadians did: by reading it in the paper. As the conflict ground on, this became more and more unacceptable. In a private letter, Borden made his feelings clear:

> *It can hardly be expected that we shall put 400,000 or 500,000 men in the field and willingly accept the position of having no more voice and receiving no more consideration than if we were toy automata.*
> — Borden on Canada's role in the war

The attitude in Britain changed considerably when David Lloyd George became prime minister in 1916. Unlike his predecessor, Lloyd George understood the dominions' complaints, and he tried to involve them more. To him, it made political sense.

We want more men from them. We can hardly ask them to make another great recruiting effort unless it is accompanied by an invitation to come over and discuss the situation with us.
— Lloyd George, in response to Canadian complaints

"Transforming the British Empire"

In March 1917, Lloyd George invited Canada and the other dominion leaders to London to take part in an Imperial War Cabinet. Although Britain still insisted on making the final decisions, the dominions were at least being consulted. Britain, however, was about to be sandbagged by Canada.

Resolution IX, drafted by Robert Borden and seconded by Jan Smuts, the South African minister of defense, demanded that the dominions be given full recognition as "autonomous nations of an Imperial commonwealth" with control over their own internal affairs and "an adequate vote in foreign policy and foreign relations." The Empire, in effect, would become a *commonwealth of nations* — that is, an alliance of independent nations with common bonds working together for mutually beneficial trade and foreign policies. After Resolution IX was passed, Smuts turned to Borden and said, "You and I have transformed the structure of the British Empire." And he was right.

Canada and the League of Nations

Canada must assume full sovereignty.
— Borden in 1918, at the end of the Great War

Borden insisted that Canada put its own signature on the Treaty of Versailles (rather than have Britain sign on behalf of Canada, as was previously done). In this, Borden was signalling to the world that Canada — although still a part of the British family — would now set its own course internationally. It was a symbolic but important point.

In the wake of the Great War, the League of Nations was formed (a forerunner of today's United Nations). Canada and the other dominions were given seats of their own in the League's General Assembly, something the Americans objected to. To them, Canada was not really an independent nation. In their eyes, Canada was still a possession of Britain, and granting the dominions their own seats in the League was just a plot on Britain's part to gain more votes for itself. In response, the British prime minister pointed out, curtly, that both Canada and Australia had lost more men in the war than had the United States — and from much smaller populations.

It was partly in protest over Canada's inclusion that the U.S. ultimately decided to boycott the League of Nations, an act that doomed the organization as an effective mediator in world events. Still, Canadians knew they were a sovereign nation, even if the Americans disagreed. Canada also joined the International Labour Organization (ILO), which reinforced its newly won status.

For more on Canada and World War I, visit `www.vac-acc.gc.ca/general/` `sub.cfm/history/firstwar`.

The political impact of World War I: A recap

Canadian political independence was confirmed during the war:

✔ Regulation IX, passed during the 1917 Imperial War Cabinet, recognized Canada and the other British dominions as "autonomous nations" within a larger British Commonwealth.

✔ At Borden's insistence, Canada signed the Treaty of Versailles independently of Britain. Some historians have described Canada's signature as "superfluous," but it was still an important symbolic recognition of Canadian sovereignty.

✔ Again at Borden's insistence, Canada was granted a seat of its own at the League of Nations.

✔ Canada also joined the League's International Labour Organization as an independent member.

It has been said that Canada was "born in the trenches" of WW I, and that Robert Borden acted as the midwife. Just as significantly, perhaps, Borden also abolished future hereditary titles in Canada. There would be no Lords and Ladies in the Great White North. The musty Old World concepts of inherited rank and social classes were, in the words of Borden, "entirely incompatible with the ideas of democracy as they have developed in this country." Borden himself had been knighted — reluctantly it should be noted — and on his deathbed he said he didn't want his title to appear anywhere on the headstone. "None of this Sir 'stuff' at the cemetery," he said. "Just plain old Robert Borden."

> *After Macdonald, no prime minister did more to develop and define Canada, as an independent nation, than did Borden.*
>
> — columnist Dalton Camp

The Spanish flu epidemic

They called it "the silent enemy." In 1918, as World War I came to an end, a flu epidemic swept across the globe, killing more people than the war itself. The disease, which originated among American recruits and fermented in the mud of Europe, was brought home by returning soldiers. It killed as many as 20 million people worldwide. The first major outbreak in Canada occurred in September 1918, in Québec City, and within a year, one in six Canadians had been hit. In some cases, entire towns were afflicted. The final death toll in Canada was between 30,000 and 50,000 people. Following hard on the carnage of World War I, the Spanish flu epidemic was a devastating catastrophe. In 1919, partly in reaction to this deadly epidemic, Canada established a Department of Health.

Chapter 17

On the Homefront

The war years and the decade that followed (1914–29) were a time of social upheaval and reform. Fifteen years of crusades, so to speak. As Canada became increasingly urban and industrial, reformers sought to improve society on all fronts: education, regional disparities, religion, poverty, health, and government policy. In this chapter, we will look mainly at two movements: labour and women's rights.

The Labour Movement

During the war, labour shortages were a constant problem. At first, this helped to improve the bargaining power of workers, but it soon became an economic roller coaster. Wages soared, but so did the cost of living. And when the war ended, 500,000 men returned and they were looking for work. At the same time, assembly-line factories were undermining the historic importance of higher-paid skilled workers.

Inspired by the revolutionary theories of Karl Marx, the Bolsheviks under Lenin had seized power in Russia and created the world's first communist state. In the Utopian "workers paradise," private ownership would be banned and collective planning would take its place. Communism in its time was as much a religious as a political movement, one that promised Judgment Day, salvation, *and* deliverance. Communism would, of course, introduce some of the most brutal regimes in human history, leaving millions dead in its wake, but in those heady early days, it seemed like a panacea for all of society's woes.

Woodsworth and the Social Gospel

The communists weren't the only ones preaching "Heaven on Earth." A Christian revivalist movement, known as Social Gospel, had taken root even before the war. These reformers, mainly Protestant, wanted the church to become more involved in the social issues of the day: poverty, prostitution, alcohol abuse, working conditions and the hardships facing immigrants. They wanted Christianity to become more relevant in people's lives by rebuilding society on the basis of charity, brotherhood, and democracy. Rather than *preserve* traditions, they wanted to *improve* society. This was a significant shift in perception, and one that helped inspire ever-greater state intervention in

people's lives. Welfare, social services, health care, unemployment assistance, and workmen's compensation: The roots of these programs can all be traced back to the Social Gospel movement.

Among the early leaders was J.S. Woodsworth, a Methodist missionary and pacifist who had worked in the slums of Toronto and Winnipeg. An outspoken advocate of workers' rights, Woodsworth was arrested during the 1919 Winnipeg General Strike. In 1921, he was elected Labour MP in Winnipeg, and in 1932, he helped found the socialist CCF Party. (There's more on the CCF in Chapter 18.)

In short, the fight for improved working conditions had become infected by ideology. Unions became increasingly radical, and strike action became less a bargaining ploy than a political weapon. The government, in turn, clamped down on workers' groups, banning several organizations outright and prohibiting their newspapers. Canada's first "red scare" had begun. (Red, of course, was the colour of the Communist Revolution.)

One Big Union

Led almost exclusively by British emigrants fresh from the socialist arenas of Europe, and inspired by similar movements in the U.S., Canadian unions, especially in the West, became increasingly radical and delegates to Canada's Trades and Labour Congress (TLC) became increasingly militant.

Frustrated with the conservative approach of their leaders, the more radical members broke away from the Congress entirely. In March 1919, delegates gathered in Calgary to debate a proposal to create One Big Union. They voted overwhelmingly to separate from the TLC, and the following June, the OBU was formally launched. A self-declared "revolutionary industrial union," the OBU was Marxist in its outlook and rhetoric. Their favoured method was one of general strikes, shutting down entire towns and cities in a show of worker solidarity. The OBU's objectives included the following:

✔ Better wages.

✔ Legal recognition of the union.

✔ A six-hour workday and a five-day workweek.

✔ A repeal of earlier government restrictions on labour.

"Worse than war"

Not all casualties occur on the battlefield.

The Empress of Ireland

It has been called "the Forgotten Empress." The tragedy of this CP passenger steamship is largely unknown, even though it was our worst maritime disaster, and one that ranks with the sinking of the *Titanic*. The *Empress of Ireland* left Québec City and was bound for Liverpool when it ran into a heavy fog in the St. Lawrence. On May 29, 1914, a Norwegian vessel, the *Storstad*, rammed into the *Empress*. In just 14 minutes, the *Empress of Ireland* went down. More than 1,000 people drowned. Only 465 managed to escape. Sadly, as war clouds gathered in Europe, the *Empress* was all but forgotten, overshadowed as it was by the carnage of World War I. The *Titanic*, which sank two years earlier, has been immortalized in film and fiction. The *Empress of Ireland* has not.

The Halifax Explosion

The second great civilian disaster to occur was directly related to the war effort. On the morning of December 6, 1917, a French munitions ship, the *Mont Blanc*, loaded down with more than 2,700 tons of explosives, collided with a Belgian Relief steamer, the *Imo*, in the narrow strait of Halifax Harbour. The *Mont Blanc* caught on fire and the crew abandoned ship in a panic. Ablaze, the vessel drifted to shore and up against a pier in the heart of the city. It burned for at least 20 minutes as crowds formed to watch, unaware of the imminent danger. A crew of firefighters boarded the vessel and tried to put out the fire. They were, in effect, standing directly at ground zero.

In a blinding flash and a deafening roar, the *Mont Blanc* blew sky-high. The iron shank from the *Mont Blanc's* anchor, weighing over half a ton, landed two miles from the harbour. Windows were shattered in Truro, 100 kilometres away. It was the greatest man-made explosion in human history, and one that would not be equalled until the arrival of the atomic bomb. The industrial heart of Halifax was levelled. A tidal wave and firestorm swept the city, and the shock waves could be heard as far away as Prince Edward Island. More than 1,600 people were killed. Two hundred more were blinded by flying glass. The city was still reeling when a freezing blizzard blew in, hampering rescue efforts. It was, in the words of one survivor, "hell on earth."

Several inquiries followed, and the blame for the catastrophe was eventually placed on the captains and pilots of both ships (the two on the *Imo* had died in the explosion). Incredibly, the *Imo* herself survived and was repaired and relaunched under a new name. She sank in 1921, off the Falkland Islands in South America.

For more on the *Empress of Ireland*, visit www.total.net:8080/~kinder. Also, www.members.home.net/seaviewimaging/index.html has all sorts of bells and whistles and graphics. For more on the Halifax Explosion, go to www.region.halifax.ns.ca/community/explode.html and also www.herald.ns.ca/aboutus/hfxexplosion.html.

The drive to create "one big union" that would unite workers in every field was primarily a Western Canadian initiative, but in Amherst, Nova Scotia, a similar movement was already underway. (Indeed, the Maritime OBU led a general strike in Amherst before the Western OBU was even launched.) At the height of its glory in 1920, the One Big Union movement counted almost 50,000 Canadians among its ranks.

The Winnipeg General Strike

By 1911, Winnipeg was the third largest city in Canada. It was also one of the most unionized. Historian David Bercuson traces the showdown of 1919 all the way back to labour disputes in 1906, but it was the war and its aftermath that finally pushed things over the edge. The Great War, with its spiralling inflation and frantic employment, made workers aware of both their increasing power — and their increasing vulnerability. As early as 1917, there was talk of calling a city-wide general strike over conscription — an issue that union organizers opposed — and in 1918, when the Winnipeg City Council outlawed the right to strike for civic employees, municipal workers walked off the job in protest and were joined in sympathy strikes by other unions. Their actions shook the City Council to the core, and the city quickly backed down in defeat. The 1918 lesson was well learned: *Strength in numbers, victory through militancy.* It was, in a way, merely a warm-up of what was to come.

Returning veterans played a key role on both sides. They were, to a man, sick of war and longing for a permanent peace. They drifted into two opposing camps: one pro-reform and pro-union, the other *anti*-reform and *anti*-union. Ironically, both were inspired by the same wish: to see something good come out of World War I. Some were determined to change the social structure that they felt had led to war; others were just as determined to never see that structure again challenged. In 1919, the pot finally boiled over. More working hours were lost to strikes in 1919 than any other year in the nation's history, before or since.

1919 was also the year the Winnipeg General Strike was called, one of the most pivotal moments in Canadian labour history. And yet, no one seems too clear on why it happened. Massive unemployment, social unrest, and rising inflation all played a part in radicalizing workers. Union leaders like R.B. Russell saw the strike as a straightforward fight for collective bargaining rights and the legal recognition of industrial unions. The government and the business community, however, saw it as an attempt at staging a full-scale Bolshevik revolution, spurred on by the many shady Eastern European immigrants that had been flooding into the city. (In fact, the unions, as mentioned earlier, were led almost exclusively by Anglo-Canadians and naturalized Englishmen — so much so that many shop owners posted signs reading "No English need apply.")

The labour unrest started small, with members of the metal and building trades filing grievances over wages and working conditions, but it quickly caught fire. Momentum overtook events, and the Winnipeg Trades and Labour Council called for worker solidarity and a city-wide general strike. At promptly 11:00 a.m., May 15, 1919, the city of Winnipeg was shut down. Completely. More than 30,000 workers — phone operators, milkmen, firefighters, trainmen, factory workers, streetcar operators, postmen, shippers, craftsmen, garbage collectors, street-sweepers, mechanists — all joined the strike.

> *The atmosphere was almost festive, the belief in ultimate victory strong. Few among them believed they were starting on a long, hard road because, after all, how long could the employers stand up to the united power of the working class?*
>
> — historian David Bercuson

The initial solidarity was overwhelming. Of 96 unions, 94 joined the strike; the only two that didn't were the typographers and the local police. (The police had in fact voted overwhelmingly in favour, but the Central Strike Committee asked them to stay on the job to maintain order — and to stop the government from finding an excuse to send in troops. Non-unionized workers joined the strike as well, as everyone from waiters to ushers walked off their jobs.) The city was under a siege of silence.

An ad hoc Citizens Committee of 1,000, made up of manufacturers, bankers, and politicians, spearheaded opposition to the strike. The army worked closely with them as well, and Ottawa consulted the Citizens Committee regularly. The government had reason to be concerned. Sympathy strikes had appeared across the nation: in Vancouver, Calgary, Edmonton, Regina, Toronto, Brandon, Prince Albert, and as far away as Amherst, Nova Scotia.

Police strikebreakers poured into Winnipeg by the hundreds, with the city's detachment growing from a force of 27 to 272. Something was in the air. Machine guns were shipped in and mounted on trucks, and a fully operational assault tank armed with a crew of 11 men was ordered in and put on alert. The army was standing by, the Mounties were ready, and the newly appointed "special police corps" was on call and waiting.

The Citizens Committee, backed by the militia, called for the mass arrest of strike organizers. Arthur Meighen, acting minister of justice, thought this was a splendid idea, but he had to admit that such actions were, sadly, against the law. The solution? Change the law. Canada's Immigration Act and the Criminal Code were quickly revised to allow the government to arrest, detain, and deport naturalized citizens on the mere *suspicion* of advocating revolution. Armed with the new law, Meighen ordered a sweep of the city, and in a series of early morning raids, a dozen men were arrested and held without bail — or even formal charges. Among them was pacifist leader J.S. Woodsworth.

On Saturday, June 21, armed strikers and angry war veterans, along with women and children, gathered on Winnipeg's main street to protest the government's strong-arm tactics. It soon turned into a riot. Strikers attacked a tram, smashing the windows and setting it on fire, and the Mounties responded by riding in on horseback, swinging sticks. The police then fired into the crowds, killing one and injuring at least 20 others (a second man died later). The crowd broke and ran — only to find itself penned in by a line of armed troops. A motorcade rolled in and soldiers poured out, wielding clubs and cracking skulls. More than 80 demonstrators were arrested, and by dusk, the army ruled the streets. The general strike had been broken. "Bloody Saturday" was over. Employees slowly began returning to work, and by June 25 it was all over. The strike had lasted six weeks.

You can find more on Canadian labour history (including the Winnipeg General Strike) at www.civilization.ca/membrs/canhist/labour/lab01e.html.

Strikebreakers

The Winnipeg General Strike (May 15 to June 25, 1919) was not the longest strike in Canadian history, nor was it the most violent.

In 1903, a striker was shot dead by police while picketing at the Vancouver rail yards.

In Québec in 1906, three men were killed during a strike at a sawmill.

In 1914, the 72nd Regiment broke up a strike on Vancouver Island. Miners were shot, and 250 strikers were thrown in jail.

In 1931, the police were again called in to crush a strike by coal miners in Estevan, Saskatchewan. Three miners were killed and one Mountie was wounded. (The headstone of one of the miners was originally to have read "Murdered by RCMP" but the police forced them to leave the space blank. The headstone, with its haunting accusation, "*Murdered by _____,*" can be seen even today.)

At Corbin, B.C., in 1935, police drove a bulldozer into a crowd of women who had formed a line to protect their striking husbands, breaking several of the women's legs.

In 1953, a policeman was beaten to death by strikers in Newfoundland.

In 1963, a strike by sawmill workers in northern Ontario ended with a shooting spree by angry non-union loggers — aimed at strikers and police without discrimination — in which three strikers died and nine others were wounded.

And that's just a sampling. Canada is second only to the United States among developed nations in violence related to strikes and strike-breaking. We are far worse in this respect than any Western European nation. Canadians, it would seem, are quicker than almost any other people to call in the police to put down protests.

The Women's Movement

More than 60,000 Canadian men were killed in World War I. Canadian women served overseas as well, mainly as nurses and often on the front lines, and 56 of them died. But for Canadian women the main battles were fought, not in Europe, but at home. Organizations such as the Canadian arm of the Woman's Christian Temperance Union (WCTU), founded in 1874 (made national in 1885), fought long and hard for a number of causes. The main two were:

- **Women's suffrage:** gaining the vote for women
- **Temperance:** educating the public and persuading them to voluntarily restrain from drinking. This soon gave way to outright *prohibition*: the banning of alcoholic beverages entirely.

"The demon rum"

In the 1820s, Christian reformers, horrified at the terrible toll alcoholism was having on families, launched a campaign aimed at curtailing "the demon rum." It was a predominately middle-class, Protestant, English-Canadian crusade. In French-Catholic Québec, the issue never really captured the public imagination. In 1898, in a national referendum on the issue, every province supported prohibition except Québec, where it was rejected by a whopping 81 percent of the population. Prime Minister Laurier declared that the voter turnout had been too low and the majority too small to implement the plan. After that, the movement shifted to the provincial and local level.

- In 1900, P.E.I. became the first province to prohibit the sale of alcohol.
- By 1916, every remaining province except Québec had followed suit.
- In 1918, under Borden, the federal government brought in measures to prohibit "the manufacture, importation and sale" of alcohol.
- Québec had prohibition forced on it in 1919, but it was quickly and resoundingly rejected by the French-Canadian population.

By then, the tide of public support had turned. During the 1920s, almost every province in Canada repealed prohibition. P.E.I., however, held out right up until 1948 — although rum smuggling and homebrewing were popular pastimes on the Island throughout the prohibition era. Still, the spirit of the temperance movement lingers on, even now. When I was living in P.E.I., I was amazed to discover that the sale of *cold* beer at liquor stores is strictly prohibited. You see, if people could purchase their beer already cold they might be tempted to drink it right away. By forcing consumers to take their beer home and put

"Glory enough for all?" The discovery of insulin

In 1921–22, a pair of researchers at the University of Toronto, Frederick Banting and Charles Best, led a research project that isolated *insulin*, a hormone that has since saved the lives of millions of diabetics around the world. In 1923, Banting, a temperamental and driven man, was awarded the Nobel Prize for Medicine, along with the project's supervisor, Professor J.J.R. Macleod. Charles Best and another key member of the project, James Collip from the University of Alberta were snubbed. (It was Collip who made one of the key breakthroughs.) Insulin, an elixir of life, remains one of Canada's greatest gifts to the world.

it in the fridge and then wait several hours, it was hoped they might show restraint — that is, "temperance." Of course, all that really happened (and I speak from personal experience here) was that people ended up choking back lukewarm beer at parties and picnics. Sigh.

You'll find more on prohibition and temperance in Canada at `timelinks. merlin.mb.ca/referenc/db0012.htm`.

"Hyenas in petticoats"

Never retract, never explain, never apologize — just get the job done and let them howl.

— personal motto of activist Nellie McClung

In women's education, the greatest strides were made in the Maritimes, where universities opened their doors to women earlier and more readily than any other region. Politically, however, the big breakthroughs would come in Western Canada.

Leading the fight in Manitoba was a firebrand orator named Nellie McClung. "Our Nell" to her supporters and "the Holy Terror" to her opponents, McClung was a best-selling novelist and a leading member of the WCTU. In 1914, Nellie McClung clashed with Manitoba Premier Rodmond Roblin over the issue of granting women the vote. In a face-to-face confrontation, Roblin dismissed McClung and her supporters as a bunch of "hyenas in petticoats."

McClung retaliated with wit. She staged a "Women's Parliament" at a Winnipeg theatre. Playing to a packed house, the satirical play asked the question: Do *men* deserve the vote? In it, the roles were reversed. Parliament was made up of women, and McClung herself appeared as premier. On stage, men entered pushing a wheelbarrow filled with petitions asking that they be allowed to vote. McClung rises and addresses the men in a pompous, patronizing tone, complimenting them on their "splendid appearance" before launching into a hilarious speech. "Man is made for something higher and better than voting," she tells them. "Men were made to support families. . . . Why, if men start to vote, they will vote too much. Politics unsettles men, and unsettled men mean unsettled bills, broken furniture, broken vows, and divorce." Every line was met with gales of laughter.

Roblin went down to defeat in 1915, partly due to the satirical attacks of the suffragists. But it should be noted that not all men were as stodgy as Roblin. Clifford Sifton, for one, had been converted to the cause of women's rights during the war — by his own patriotic speeches, no less. His cousin, Ida Sifton, had asked him how he could crusade for "liberty and freedom," while still denying it to women. Clifton couldn't come up with an answer.

With Roblin's Conservatives out of office, the newly elected Liberal government of Manitoba gave in, and on January 28, 1916, women won the right to vote in provincial elections. But by then, McClung and her family had moved to Alberta, where the crusade had started anew.

Manitoba was quickly joined by Saskatchewan and Alberta, and the following year by B.C. and Ontario. Over the next few years, the Maritime provinces came onboard as well. In Québec, women faced the hardest struggle; the provincial vote wasn't granted there until 1940, and then only after a long-drawn-out campaign spearheaded by broadcaster and activist Thérèse Casgrain. Nationally, Robert Borden granted women a limited vote in 1917. The following year, he extended it, and on May 24, 1918, the Canadian Elections Act was passed, giving women in Canada the right to vote in federal elections. The "hyenas in petticoats" had won.

Women and the vote

John A. Macdonald tried to extend the vote to women and Native Canadians way back in the 1880s, but his quixotic proposal was rejected. Women in Canada were given the vote in the following order:

1916: Manitoba, Saskatchewan, Alberta

1917: B.C., Ontario

1918: Canada (federal elections), Nova Scotia

1919: New Brunswick

1922: P.E.I.

1925: Newfoundland

1940: Québec

The Herstory site has more on political leaders in the Canadian women's movement at library. usask.ca/herstory/politics.html. For more on McClung (with links to other suffragists, including Casgrain), go to www.nlc-bnc.ca/digiproj/women/women99/mcclung-e.htm. For more on Thérèse Casgrain, leader of the Quebec suffragists, visit www.rendezvousfrancophonie.com/english/personnages/carte_v06.html.

Angels or equals?

Although politically radical, the women's suffragist movement was socially very conservative. Suffragists wanted to uphold Christian and British values, and often the same reformers who wanted the vote for white women wanted it denied to Asian men. For many women, winning the vote was seen as simply the first stepping stone toward reforming society as whole; and that including dealing with the corrupting influence of foreigners. Many of these early feminist crusaders stood for women's rights and — in their own words — a "White Canada." In this, they managed to be both progressive and reactionary at the same time.

This approach reveals a fundamental divide among early feminists. Were they fighting for equal rights or for social reforms? What was the real goal? Many of the suffragists supported the "separate spheres" argument. That is, they believed that women had a "special civilizing mission," separate from that of men. They were, in effect, the angels of the home. They needed the vote to fulfill their role. Without political influence, how could they reform labour laws for children? Or introduce prohibition? Or force the foreigners to assimilate?

A number of leading suffragists rejected this "angel argument." For them, women's rights and the vote were matters of principle. In this, the movement was divided into two allied but starkly opposing camps:

- **Maternal feminism** (which saw the women's movement as a means of "civilizing" society and fulfilling their womanly roles).
- **Equal rights feminism** (which sought the vote as an end in itself).

Equal rights feminism eventually won out, and maternal feminism now seems quaint and outdated. But it should also be noted that the predictions of the maternal feminists were borne out to a certain degree. Women voters have had an immense and far-reaching impact on society. In Canada, 1918 marks a shift in government policy away from property rights and toward social reform. Slowly, the perception of government began to change from that of a purely economic tool to that of a social instrument.

Canada's first female federal MP was elected in Ontario in 1921. Agnes Macphail, a member of the United Farmers, was a one-woman crusade. Funny, forceful, and fearless, she helped lead the way on issues such as prison reform, farm programs, and improved health care. As she herself said, "Whenever I don't know whether to fight or not — I always fight." Macphail herself, however, rejected the maternal "angel of the home" argument.

I do not want to be the angel of any home; I want for myself what I want for other women — absolute equality. After that is secured then men and women can take turns at being angels.
— Agnes Macphail, a champion of equal rights feminism

For more on Agnes Macphail, visit `www.nlc-bnc.ca/digiproj/women/women97/emacphai.htm`.

The Persons Case

Also prominent in the suffragist movement was Emily Murphy. Under the persona of "Janey Canuck," she had written several popular travel books, including *Janey Canuck in the West* about her adopted home province of Alberta. (She was originally from Ontario.) In Edmonton, Murphy became involved in the suffragist movement and especially in the campaign to reform homestead laws — which were grossly unfair to women, giving them virtually no protection or title to land that they worked. Appalled at the way women were treated in all-male courtrooms, Murphy petitioned the Alberta government to set up a separate women's court. What came next was a surprise, to say the least. The Alberta attorney general at that time, Charles Cross, agreed — and promptly appointed Murphy as the judge. And so, in 1916, Emily Murphy (a.k.a. Janey Canuck) became the first female magistrate in the Dominion of Canada — or anywhere else in the British Commonwealth.

Others soon followed. Within a year of gaining the vote, women had been elected to the Alberta legislature. Nellie McClung won a seat in Edmonton in 1921, and others were appointed magistrates. There was just one snag. In the BNA Act, only qualified "persons" could hold such positions. British common law, in turn, held that women were not considered legal persons in matters of "rights or privileges."

On Murphy's very first day on the bench, a lawyer challenged her right to hear the case. As a woman, she was not eligible. She was, in fact, presiding illegally. "You are not even a person!" he insisted. Murphy made note of his objection and continued, but the issue refused to die. Lawyers kept bringing it up again and again, and as more women were appointed to the bench, they too had to deal with this challenge to their authority.

Note: These men were not arguing that women weren't human beings. What they were saying was that, under the legal definitions of the time, women were not eligible to hold public office. And technically, they were right. Until a higher court ruled on the matter, women *weren't* "persons." Not legally.

Lizzie Cyr

In Calgary, in the spring of 1917, a prostitute named Lizzie Cyr was hauled before a female magistrate on trumped-up charges of vagrancy. (The man who pressed charges was upset because Lizzie had given him a sexually transmitted disease and had then refused to reimburse him for his medicine.) Police Magistrate Alice Jamieson sentenced Lizzie to six months hard labour. Her publicly appointed defender, a lawyer by the name of McKinley Cameron, was appalled — both at the conviction and at Alice Jamieson's questionable grasp of what constituted a fair trial. Jamieson hadn't even allowed Cameron to present Lizzie's defense.

After the travesty of Lizzie Cyr's conviction, McKinley Cameron petitioned the Alberta Supreme Court to rule on whether Jamieson had the right to hold office. Cameron's argument was a familiar one: As a woman, Jamieson was not legally a "person." Her rulings were not admissible. On June 14, 1917, Justice David Scott of the Supreme Court of Alberta announced the ruling. Alberta had decided that the term "persons" *did* include women. Jamieson, Murphy, and the others had the legal right to sit as magistrates. It was, however, an ambivalent victory for women. After all, in upholding Alice Jamieson's right to hold office, the courts were also upholding Lizzie Cyr's conviction and sentence of six months hard labour. Sadly, the tale of Lizzie Cyr has been all but forgotten — whitewashed, one suspects, by those who would like to portray the female judges as noble heroines and the male lawyers as caricatured bad guys. It wasn't quite that simple, alas.

The Famous Five

The Alberta ruling only applied provincially. Nationally, the issue still wasn't settled. Were women persons? It sounds so silly today, but at the time it had wide ramifications. Emily Murphy noted that under Section 24 of the BNA Act, only "qualified persons" could be appointed to the Senate. So she issued a challenge to Ottawa: Put your money where your mouth is. Prove, once and for all, that women are indeed "persons." Appoint a female senator. Specifically, *her.* That's right. Emily Murphy may have been fighting for women's rights, but she was also fighting for a cushy job in Ottawa. Patronage meets political crusade: how very Canadian.

Murphy was nothing if not persistent. No fewer than four different prime ministers managed to dodge the issue and avoid her request. Along the way, Murphy discovered something else. An obscure rule stated that any five concerned citizens could request a hearing from the Supreme Court of Canada on any point in the BNA Act. So, in 1927, Murphy got together four other leading suffragists, all based in Alberta, and launched a challenge. The women soon became known as the "Famous Five" (though really, it was Murphy's crusade; the other four just lent their names and moral support):

Emily Murphy, police magistrate

Henrietta Edwards, co-founder of the National Council of Women

Nellie McClung, former Alberta MLA

Louise McKinney, former Alberta MLA

Irene Parlby, Alberta MLA and provincial cabinet minister

"Does the word 'person' include women?" On April 24, 1928, the Supreme Court of Canada announced its decision. Women were *not* legally persons. Canada had overruled Alberta.

But the Famous Five were undaunted, and they went over the Supreme Court's head and pursued the issue all the way to the British Privy Council in London. And the following year, they won. On October 18, 1929, Britain ruled against Canada and in favour of Alberta. Women were indeed persons.

> *The exclusion of women from all public offices is a relic of days more barbarous than ours.*
> — Lord Chancellor Sankey of the Privy Council

Emily Murphy was overjoyed. When news reached her in Edmonton of the Privy Council's decision she began dancing about in her nightgown. "We've won!" she cheered. "We've won! We've won!" Sadly, Murphy never did get her much-coveted Senate appointment. The honour of becoming Canada's first female senator went instead to a well-connected Liberal by the name of Cairine Wilson in 1930. (Wilson would also become Canada's first female delegate to the United Nations in 1949.)

The Persons Case is remembered as a great victory for women. There is a statue to the Famous Five in downtown Calgary and another one in Ottawa, and the Governor General's Persons Award, given for work on behalf of women, is named in honour of their victory. But, on a political level, the Persons Case also underlined the fact that Canada was still not a completely independent nation. Britain after all, had overruled a decision made by Canada's highest court. It was a victory for women — absolutely. But it was also a blow to Canadian sovereignty. Ironic, don't you think?

You'll find more on Emily Murphy at www.nlc-bnc.ca/digiproj/women/women99/murphy-e.htm (part of a larger site, with links to other suffragists). There is a Famous Five Foundation Web site at www.canuck.com/famous5/. For Susan Merritt's Her Story site, go to www.niagara.com/~merrwill/.

King the Conciliator

Both the Liberals and the Unionist/Conservative government lost their leaders within a year. Wilfrid Laurier (see Chapters 15 and 16) died in 1919. Robert Borden (see Chapter 16) retired in 1920. They were replaced, in turn, by the following:

- ✔ **William Lyon Mackenzie King:** Grandson of William Lyon Mackenzie, the rebel leader of 1837, King took over as leader of the Liberals on a progressive platform that included unemployment insurance, old age pensions, and mothers' allowances.

- ✔ **Arthur Meighen:** The man who drafted the conscription bill of 1917 and crushed the Winnipeg General Strike in 1919, Meighen became PM after taking over the leadership of the Conservatives from Borden.

The two men could not be more different. Meighen was a man of confrontation; King, of compromise. Indeed, King had earned a reputation as something of a professional labour mediator, negotiating with unions on behalf of such powerful American industrialists as the Rockefellers. He had even written a plodding but surprisingly progressive book, *Industry and Humanity* (1918). Arthur Meighen faced off against King in the House of Commons with undisguised contempt. The two men had debated each other back in their university days, and there was no love lost between them.

> *The most contemptible charlatan ever to darken the annals of Canadian politics.*
> — Meighen's description of King

> *Sarcastic, vitriolic, and the meanest type of politician.*
> — King's description of Meighen

The Antigonish Movement

The message was simple: Practise self-help. Started in the late 1920s by a pair of Catholic priests (Fathers Moses Coady and Jimmy Tompkins), who were working through St. Francis Xavier University in Antigonish, Nova Scotia, the Antigonish Movement focused on study groups, adult education, and economic self-improvement. At a grassroots level, it helped launched small-scale co-operatives — everything from credit unions to fisheries — and over the years, it grew to play an important role in Canada's foreign aid programs. The movement itself has won international acclaim.

For more on the Antigonish Movement, go to wwwdev.cuna.org/data/cu/research/irc/archive3_1.html.

Regional protest parties had been growing stronger for several years. In 1919, the United Farmers of Ontario (UFO) were swept to power provincially, and two years later the United Farmers of Alberta (UFA) did the same. On a federal level, Thomas Crerar founded the National Progressive Party in 1919. It was an unruly, populist party — but one with high standards of integrity.

When Meighen went to the polls in 1921, he was trounced. Even the Progressives beat him, bringing the old two-party system in Canada to a dramatic end. King didn't have a majority, but he did manage to rule for the next four years with the support of the Progressives. In the next election, Meighen's Conservatives did better: They won more seats than King — but *not* enough to form a majority. Rather than step down, King decided to cling to power by courting the Opposition. The Progressives, although greatly reduced, still held the balance of seats under their new leader, Robert Forke—though no one was ever *really* in charge of the Progressives. Trying to get them to agree on anything was like trying to herd mice.

The King–Byng thing

King somehow managed to cobble together an alliance of Liberals and Progressives, along with J.S. Woodsworth and his followers. But in 1926, a scandal erupted involving kickbacks and bootlegged liquor in the Customs Department. Facing an open revolt in the House, King hurried over to Governor General Julian Byng, the former British Commander at Vimy Ridge. What followed has been dubbed the King–Byng Affair — though personally, I prefer "the King–Byng thing." More melodic.

King wanted the Governor General to dissolve the House and call an election. Byng refused. Instead, he invited Meighen to form a government. After all, reasoned Byng, an election had just been held eight months earlier, and anyway, the Conservatives did have more seats than the Liberals. King was aghast. In his mind, the Governor General was there to rubber-stamp requests from the government. Byng did not have the option of saying no. As it was, Arthur Meighen's shaky government lasted all of three days before it fell. In the election that followed, the original Customs scandal was quickly forgotten. Instead, King railed against the "meddling" of the Governor General in Canadian parliamentary procedure, and warned the public that Byng was trying to reduce Canada back to the level of mere colony. The Governor General should be a figurehead. Nothing more.

King also accused Meighen of seizing power "unconstitutionally," and the message hit a responsive chord with the voters, who returned King to power with a working majority — his first ever. Meighen had been humiliated. Lord Byng, a genuine war hero, had been vilified. And Canadian political independence had been reasserted — in a shabby manner, true. But the unofficial rules had now been set. Governors General, and by extension the Royal Family, were to be no more than ornaments. They were *not* to interfere.

Was King right? Or was Byng? Even today, no one can agree. Historians generally sympathize with Byng. But the consensus — as near as I can see — is that although the Governor General had the *constitutional* right to deny King's request, he did not have the *moral* right. Confusing, no?

"Not a single Indian remaining"

Although inroads were being made in the field of workers' rights, social reform, and the women's movements, one group was not included: Canada's forgotten First Nations. The goal of Canada's Indian Act was simple: complete assimilation. That is, the disappearance of Native language, lifestyles, belief systems, and culture, followed by their absorption into mainstream Canadian society. This was called "enfranchisement."

To vote or own property, one first had to relinquish all Native claims. And reflecting older Victorian-era notions of women taking the identity of their husbands, when a male head of a family decided to give up his legal status as an Indian — his entire family was stripped of theirs as well. More notoriously, Native women who married non-Native men automatically lost their status. (Incredibly, the goal of cultural assimilation, and the restrictions on Native women, would remain in effect right up until 1985!)

The King years were a bad time for Native groups in Canada, and the man in charge was a career bureaucrat — and poet — named Duncan Campbell Scott. Scott served as Canada's senior administrator of Indian policy from 1913–32. He was also one of the biggest hypocrites Canada has ever produced. As a poet, he wrote sad, woeful laments about the "vanishing Indian," that "weird and waning race." As a bureaucrat, he didn't hesitate to tighten the screws.

> *The Indian in himself had no title to the soil demanding recognition, nor, in his inferior position as a savage, had he any rights which could become the subject of treaty or negotiation.*
> — Duncan Campbell Scott in an early statement of policy

Scott's goal was to continue until "not a single Indian remained" that was unassimilated. He tried to outlaw "senseless drumming and dancing" and introduced stiff fines for any Native person wearing traditional dress outside of the reserve. In 1927, Scott had the Indian Act amended to outlaw Native political organizations and prohibit them from raising funds without government permission. Frederick Loft, a Mohawk veteran of World War I, tried to fight back by organizing a pan-national League of Indians. Among his demands were that Native Canadians be given the vote, as well as greater control over reserve property and funds. Denounced by the government as "an agitator," Loft was put under police surveillance and his proposed League was effectively outlawed.

Native Canadians would not be allowed to vote in Canada until 1960, more than 40 years after women — *non-Native* women — had won that right.

For a detailed look at Canada's Indian Act, including amendments, go to
`www.bloorstreet.com/200block/sindact.htm`. You'll find a history of the
vote in Canada at `www.civilization.ca/membrs/canhist/elections/`
`el_000_e.html`.

Pier 21

Too many people in Canada forget that people crawl across minefields to
get here.

— Ignat Kaneff, Bulgarian-born Canadian patriot

They called it "the Gateway to Canada." At Pier 21, a large warehouse-like
building in Halifax, refugees and immigrants to Canada were processed, cared
for, fed, assisted, and sometimes even housed by staff members. Between
1928 and 1971, as many as 1.5 million people passed through its doors. The
staff, in turn, was supported by a dedicated team of volunteers who provided
counselling for the newcomers — and often acted as translators and interpreters as well. (In one case, a ship arrived carrying hundreds of passengers
who, between them, spoke 32 different languages.) Canada was indeed
becoming a very different sort of country.

They arrived at Pier 21 in waves. During World War II, thousands of children
arrived, evacuated from Britain. After the war, almost 50,000 "war brides"
arrived (women who had married Canadian servicemen and had now showed
up, bewildered, tired, and exhilarated). My favourite story told by a British
war bride was how, after arriving at Pier 21 and boarding a train bound for
Vancouver, she finally saw the Pacific. The journey had completely exhausted
her. She hadn't imagined any country could be so vast. And here she was at
last, at the end of her trip. "Actually," said the conductor, "that's not the
Pacific Ocean. That's Lake Ontario."

In the late 1950s, a mass exodus of Hungarian refugees fleeing Soviet oppression
poured into Canada. More than 35,000 arrived, and half of these came through
Pier 21. By the 1960s, however, the age of the jet airplane was at hand and
more and more refugees began arriving by air. Fewer ships docked, and those
that did were often half empty. The last large groups to arrive at Pier 21,
ironically, came by plane, flown in to Halifax airport and then bussed out to
the pier for processing.

In 1971, Pier 21 closed down for good. The Gateway to Canada stood empty
and in crumbling disrepair for decades, but in the 1990s it was revamped and
reopened as a slick interpretative centre. Even today, ghostly footsteps are said
to echo through the building: the memory and small epic tales of countless
new Canadians.

You can find out more about Pier 21 at `pier21.ns.ca`.

Part VII
Dark Days
(1929–1959)

By Bob Chambers, 1944. Used by permission of the Chambers family. Image courtesy of National Archives of Canada (C-044300).

Prime Minister Mackenzie King navigates dangerous waters, taking Canada
through the conscription crisis of World War II more or less united.
And — like a true Canadian — he does it in a canoe.

In this part . . .

Disaster. Drought. Poverty. War. Internment camps. The nuclear bomb. The Cold War. And happy suburban households filled with all the latest consumer gadgets. It was a dark time, marked by hardship and heartbreak for many Canadians, but it was also an era of economic rejuvenation. The 1950s were boom years, just as surely as the 1930s were years of financial ruin and poverty.

Chapter 18

The Dirty Thirties

In This Chapter

▶ The stock market crashes

▶ Droughts ravage the Prairie provinces

▶ R.B. Bennett takes over as PM

▶ Several radical new political parties are born

Ten Lost Years

— historian Barry Broadfoot's evocative title describing
a decade of economic despair (1929–39)

*E*ven today, economists and historians can't quite agree on *why* the Great
Depression ever happened. The most common view, perpetuated in college
courses and history texts, is that the Depression was caused by the evils of
unbridled capitalism. That is, the *laissez-faire* (or unregulated) economic
system collapsed under its own weight, only to be rescued by massive
government intervention: "bad" capitalism saved by "good" social programs
and regulations. But it wasn't that simple. In fact, government meddling right
at the start of the crisis seems to have exacerbated the problem. The high
tariff walls that many countries — including Canada — erected cut off the free
exchange of goods and actually *heightened* the effects of the Depression.

In many ways, the prosperity of the 1920s was a colossal house of cards, and
in 1929, it all came tumbling down. Over-extended credit, easy money, heavy
debt, and ineffective financial regulations helped make the Depression
possible. Misguided government intervention and public panic made it worse.
It was World War II, *not* increased spending on social programs, that finally
brought the Depression to an end. (Social programs helped alleviate the
misery — they didn't solve the crisis.)

Still, on a perceptual level, the Depression did signal the end of the glory days
of unfettered capitalism — in much the same way that World War I brought
an end to the allure of European imperialism. After the Great Depression,
nothing was ever the same again. The government was no longer allowed to
be a mere spectator, sitting on the sidelines as market forces ran their course.
Governments were now expected to take an active, interventionist approach.
Public opinion demanded it. If Canadians today tend to look to the government
as both the source — and the solution — of society's problems, the roots of
this lie partly in the "ten lost years" of the Great Depression.

The Great Depression

Stock market prices have reached what looks like a permanently high plateau.

— Yale economist Irving Fisher in 1929, two weeks
before the market collapsed

October 29, 1929. Black Tuesday. The New York Stock Exchange crashed. Investors lost millions. People's life savings were wiped out in an instant. The Toronto Stock Exchange followed, as banks went under and creditors were ruined. The Crash of 1929 wasn't so much the *cause* of the Depression as it was a symptom of deep economic instability. The Depression started much like World War I: a domino effect of crises, one after another.

Panic ensued. Led by the United States, countries retreated behind protectionist tariffs, putting up walls and raising the drawbridge. At a time when increased international trade and open world markets were direly needed, the doors were slammed shut. Canada, as a nation whose economy was built largely upon exports, was one of the worst hit — indeed, some have argued that Canada was in fact *the* worst-hit country in the Western world.

The Prairie provinces suffered the most. A bumper crop flooded the market even as demand dried up, pushing prices down. Then, like a one-two punch, a severe drought began. It devastated southern Saskatchewan and the adjoining corners of Alberta and Manitoba. For seven years, almost no rain fell. The breadbasket had become a dust bowl. Topsoil blew away, towering dirt storms darkened the sky, and a plague of grasshoppers followed, devouring what little remained. It was like something out of the Old Testament. (My father, raised in southern Saskatchewan during the Depression, remembers having to eat stewed ditch-side weeds to survive.)

The grasshoppers came in clouds . . .

— from an eyewitness account of the Great Depression

More than 200,000 people were forced to leave their farms. Saskatchewan's per capita income fell 71 percent in just three years, and two-thirds of the population was forced to go on some sort of public assistance. Alberta's income fell 61 percent. Statistics vary, but wheat prices tumbled from around $2 a bushel in 1928 to just 35 cents in 1932. In Newfoundland (not yet part of Canada) the collapse was so bad that in 1934, the island had to give up self-government in order to receive direct aid from Britain.

Overall, income in Canada fell by almost 50 percent. Imports fell by 55 percent; exports by 25 percent.

Of 10 million Canadians, 2 million were living on relief handouts.

The jobless rate went from 4 percent to a staggering 27 percent. More than one in four Canadians were unemployed.

This, at a time when there was no unemployment insurance or social welfare programs. The destitute had to rely on private charity and government soup kitchens. It was humiliating. Heart-wrenching. And numbing. Scurvy and malnourishment returned. Suicide rates soared.

"Bonfire Bennett" to the rescue!

Prime Minister Mackenzie King, in power when the Depression hit, was just as baffled and unprepared as anyone. There had been economic downturns before, some of them quite severe, but nothing like this. The marketplace was supposed to be self-correcting, but this time the downward spiral seemed unstoppable. No one knew what to do. The federal government tried to pass off responsibility to the provinces. The provinces passed it off to the municipalities. And the municipalities passed it off to church groups and local charities. And they turned their anger back on Ottawa.

Mackenzie King was a master of vague language, but in a rash moment he had declared that he wouldn't give "a five-cent piece" of relief money to any province with a Tory government. The new leader of the Conservative Party, R.B. (Richard Bedford) Bennett pounced on King's threat as an example of how corrupt and uncaring the Liberals had become. Bennett's bombastic style had already earned him the nickname "Bonfire Bennett," and he vowed that if elected, he would end unemployment "or perish in the attempt." He also promised to "blast" Canada's way into the world market.

On July 28, 1930, R.B. Bennett defeated Mackenzie King and was crowned PM. It was the worst thing that could have happened to him — or the country (just as it was King's good fortune to be *out* of power during the worst years of the Great Depression). Bennett certainly had his work cut out for him. Unfortunately, he was the wrong man for the task. A self-made millionaire, he was born of a humble home in New Brunswick, and rose to prominence as a Calgary corporate lawyer and business tycoon. This was a man who believed in capitalism and the free enterprise system.

> *One of the greatest assets any man or woman can have on entering life's struggle is poverty.*
>
> — R.B. Bennett at the height of the Great Depression

Still, Bennett went in swinging. He earmarked $20 million for emergency relief, out of a total federal budget of just $500 million — and over King's shrill cry of "fiscal irresponsibility!" (By 1938, federal relief programs reached $350 million.) Bennett also raised the tariff on imports by nearly 50 percent. True, this did protect domestic industries and helped end the trade deficit. But in the long run it was a disastrous approach, one that eventually cut off Canadian exports to the world. Bennett's protectionist tariffs did more harm than good, and as the Depression deepened, much of the public's anger became focused on Bennett himself. As a scapegoat for frustrated Canadians, his very name became emblematic of a system that had failed. Broken-down, horse-drawn automobiles became known as "Bennett buggies." Hot water and barley became "Bennett tea." Shantytowns became "Bennett-burghs." Abandoned farms, "Bennett barnyards." And so on.

Tiptoeing to independence: Canada and the Commonwealth

Britain's 1931 Statute of Westminster granted Canada independence in matters of foreign affairs. It was an important milestone, but mainly symbolic. After all, by 1931, Canada was already effectively sovereign. The Statute of Westminster wasn't so much a *declaration* of independence as it was a *confirmation*.

✔ In 1922, Britain had tried to pressure Canada into getting involved in yet another overseas conflict, one between Turkey and Greece over a disputed territory known as Chanak. Mackenzie King dodged the request, saying that he would have to ask his Parliament — and his Parliament was on holiday. The Chanak Crisis has passed into the footnotes of history, but it did mark a distinctly Canadian assertion of independence: non-confrontational, vague, and slightly apologetic.

✔ In 1923, Canada signed its very first international treaty, all on its own. The Halibut Treaty with the U.S. helped protect Canada's Pacific fisheries. Admittedly, "*Remember the Halibut Treaty of 1923!*" doesn't have quite the same ring to it as Vimy Ridge or the Battle of Queenston Heights, but it was a proud patriotic moment nonetheless. Really.

✔ At the Imperial Conference of 1926, the Balfour Declaration confirmed what Canada had already won back in World War I (see Chapter 16) by formally recognizing Canada and the other dominions as "autonomous communities within the British Empire, equal in status [and] in no way subordinate."

✔ And on December 11, 1931, King George V signed the Statute of Westminster, creating the British Commonwealth: a trade and military alliance of independent dominions united under the British Crown. This was *not* the Commonwealth of today. With only Canada, Newfoundland, Australia, New Zealand, South Africa, and the Irish Free State having been granted dominion (that is, self-governing) status, the original British Commonwealth was very much an old boys' club of "white" states. It wasn't until 1947, after India and Pakistan had fought their way to independence, that the Commonwealth was reorganized in its current form, as a trading and economic development coalition — with the term "British" dropped from the title.

Still, 1931 did mark Canada's political independence. Kind of. Sort of. It wasn't a complete break. At Ottawa's request, the Judicial Committee of the British Privy Council remained the final court of appeal. And, because Canadians couldn't agree on an amending formula of their own, any future changes to the Canadian Constitution would still have to be passed by the British Parliament first. Sigh.

If you would like to read the Statute of Westminster in its entirety, go to www.fordham.edu/halsall/mod/1936westminster.html. For a history of the Commonwealth, visit www.chogm99.org/what/history1.htm.

Displaced workers began "riding the rods" hopping on rail cars in search of transient employment. An entire semi-nomadic subculture developed, and with the warmer weather on the West Coast, many of the homeless gravitated towards Vancouver. Bennett began deporting any immigrants who were on relief (a hard-line approach that was continued under King as well). As many as 30,000 new Canadians were unceremoniously hustled onto ships and sent back to Europe. *Blame the foreigners!* Always a popular strategy.

On to Ottawa

All those restless, bitter, unemployed men. It was a recipe for insurrection, something Bennett clearly feared. His solution? Government work camps for unmarried men, set up by the Department of National Defence. Working in the bush, the "inmates" were paid all of 20 cents a day (low even by Depression-era standards). They called themselves "the Royal Twenty-Centers," and they soon came to resent the demeaning slave camp atmosphere. In 1935, they went on strike. Led by a radical union activist named Arthur "Slim" Evans, more than 1,000 relief camp workers climbed onboard eastbound freight trains in Vancouver, heading for Ottawa and a showdown with Bennett himself. By the time they reached Regina, their numbers had doubled. They were angry young men with nothing to lose.

Bennett stopped the trek in Regina and sent for Evans. But talks quickly broke down into angry accusations and not-so-veiled threats. Evans returned to Regina more determined than ever, and Bennett called in the RCMP, who seized the strike leaders. On July 1, 1935, riots broke out. Police clashed headlong with the protestors. A Regina constable was killed, dozens of strikers and police officers were injured, and 130 protestors were arrested. The "On to Ottawa" trek was over.

For more on the Great Depression from a labour point of view, go to `www.civilization.ca/membrs/canhist/labour/labv25e.html`.

A deathbed conversion?

Let's face it, R.B. Bennett was not a very likeable man. Historian Michael Bliss describes R.B. as "erratic, emotional, insensitive, conceited, [and] self-obsessed." Still, Bennett did launch several key projects:

- In 1932, he oversaw the creation of the Canadian Radio Broadcasting Commission, forerunner of today's CBC, making him the unofficial "Father of Public Broadcasting in Canada." (The publicly funded National Film Board was created later, in 1939, under King.)

- In 1934, he created the Bank of Canada to regulate currency and monetary policy, and to advise the government on financial matters.

In the U.S., President Roosevelt had promised the people a New Deal, one that would involve a radical restructuring of society. Bennett, with an election fast approaching, decided to offer a New Deal of his own. Without consulting his cabinet, he gave a series of public radio addresses in January 1935. (Radio was the cutting edge of technology at the time; it would be like a PM today going online to address the nation.) The public, and Bennett's own dumb-founded ministers, were amazed at what they heard. Bennett had performed a complete flip-flop. "The old order is gone," he intoned. "It will not return." Bennett, once a die-hard believer in unbridled, unregulated capitalism, was now arguing that the entire system needed to be overhauled. Among Bennett's proposals:

- Unemployment insurance
- Minimum wages (and limits on work hours)
- An extension of federally backed farm credit
- Fair-trade and anti-monopoly legislation
- Farm rehabilitation measures to deal with erosion and water conservation
- A revamped Wheat Board to oversee and control grain prices

Bennett's critics scoffed at his plans, calling it "a deathbed conversion." Even now, historians are divided on whether Bennett's New Deal was a sincere attempt on his part to reform society, consistent with his views, or whether it was just a desperate ploy to win re-election. (Historians such as James Gray and P.B. Waite have presented evidence that Bennett was indeed committed to reform, and had advocated government regulation of the economy long before he was ever elected. Others are less convinced.)

"King or Chaos!"

Bennett tried his best to bring in a New Deal, but by then it was too late. He had, in the words of one commentator, "dug the grave too deep." Bennett's supporters deserted him, and in 1935, under the banner "King or Chaos!" the Liberals were returned to power. Bennett, a bitter and unrepentant man, eventually left Canada altogether. He ended his days in Britain as a member of the House of Lords, and he remains the only one of our prime ministers to be buried outside of Canada. In the words of historian John English, "Bennett never forgave Canada for failing him."

Although Mackenzie King was a more adept administrator than Bennett, he had no real answers either. He dithered and delayed, referring much of Bennett's New Deal to the Supreme Court, where most of it was ruled unconstitutional on the grounds that it infringed on provincial jurisdiction.

"Million Dollar Babies": The Dionne quintuplets

One of the saddest stories to come out of the Depression was that of the Dionne quintuplets: five girls — Annette, Emilie, Yvonne, Cecile, and Marie — born to French-Canadian parents in a farmhouse near North Bay, Ontario, in May 1934. As the first quintuplets to survive infancy, the little girls became an international sensation.

The Ontario government stepped in and removed them from their parents, and built a special hospital/display centre dubbed "Quintland." The girls were turned into a sideshow attraction, a circus act, and the government of Ontario reaped millions as tourists lined up to gawk and grin. Movie rights and advertising spots were sold, and the province made at least $500 million off the girls — about $5 *billion* by today's

standards. The girls' trust fund, $22 million at the height of the Dionne craze, had mysteriously dwindled to just $800,000 by the time they were eligible to receive it at age 21.

By the 1990s, the three remaining sisters — Annette, Yvonne, and Cecile — now in their sixties, were surviving on poverty-level pensions. When they asked for compensation from the province, Ontario Premier Mike Harris — in what just may be the single most misguided political decision ever made — decided to play hardball with the three elderly ladies. He offered them a token allowance, take it or leave it. Harris, who hails from North Bay ironically, faced intense public outrage. His knees quickly buckled, and by 1999, the quints had received $10 million.

Canada's First Nations had faced the brunt of bureaucratic "good intentions." Under King, they now faced government neglect. Hard to say which was worse. As historian Olive Dickason notes, throughout the 1930s, "Indian affairs drifted into a state of flux and ad hoc decisions." This was in marked contrast to the directed policies of earlier years. Any Grand Scheme of civilizing the "inferior savage" was now put on temporary hold. In 1936, the administration of Indian affairs was folded into the Department of Mines and Resources, and the objectives shifted from social programs to economic development of natural resources. (The Inuit of the Far North were even encouraged to return to traditional, subsistence-level hunting and fishing lifestyles, to save the government money in relief payments.)

Political upheaval

Radical political parties reached new heights during the Depression. These parties played an important part in the political future of Canada.

The real "red menace"

Sharing a stint at the Kensington Pen with Tim Buck was the *real* red menace: Norman "Red" Ryan, the nation's most notorious outlaw. Nicknamed "Canada's Jesse James," Ryan led a spectacular career as a bank robber, army deserter, and prison escapee. Captured and sentenced to life, he underwent a miraculous conversion. He became a model prisoner — an altar boy in the prison chapel even — and wrote long repentant letters to the newspapers. Soon journalists and intellectuals had rallied to his cause, and early parole was arranged.

When Ryan was released, Prime Minister Bennett himself travelled to Kingston to congratulate the reformed criminal first-hand. Ryan wrote a series of pious, anti-Communist newspaper articles reassuring readers everywhere that he had learned his lesson: *Crime doesn't pay.* A year later, Red Ryan was gunned down in a battle with police at a liquor store in Sarnia, Ontario, after a botched armed robbery. His dying words: "You've got me, boys. I've had enough."

The red menace

The Communist Party of Canada was founded in June 1921, at a secret meeting in a barn outside of Guelph, Ontario. (I once poked fun at Guelph on national radio, describing it as "the only town in Canada named after the sound a cat makes when it coughs up a furball, *guelllphh*." This would probably be a good time to apologize.) During the Depression, the Communist Party was all but outlawed. In August 1931, the party's leader, Tim Buck, and eight others were arrested in raids on party headquarters. The men were not charged with any crime except that of holding the wrong ideas — they were, in effect, political prisoners. This occurred years before the anti-Communist hysteria of the McCarthy witch hunts in the United States.

R.B. Bennett, meanwhile, had vowed to crush the Communists under an "iron heel." Buck was sentenced to five years' hard labour in the Kingston Penitentiary. That was bad enough, but following a prison strike, guards fired into his cell, trying to kill him. As bullets whizzed past his head, Buck threw himself flat against the floor and survived. A cover-up followed, but news of the assassination attempt eventually broke in the House of Commons. When challenged on it, Canada's minister of justice just shrugged. Sure, shots had been fired at Buck, "but only to frighten him."

The CCF and the Regina Manifesto

Hard to believe, but the city of Calgary was once a hotbed of left-wing radicals. There was One Big Union in 1919 (see Chapter 17), and now this: In August

1932, delegates from farmers' parties and labour unions — including members of the "Ginger Group," a coalition of independent MPs — met in Calgary to create a new political party: the Co-operative Commonwealth Federation (CCF).

The Communists believed in revolution, the overthrow of the existing order, and complete state control. The CCF, in contrast, advocated "democratic socialism." In Regina in 1933, the party adopted a platform penned by a committee headed by University of Toronto history professor Frank Underhill. The Regina Manifesto, as it was known, called for "a new social order." Among other things, it advocated:

- Nationalizing key industries such as banks, mines, and utilities (that is, taking them out of private ownership and into public, state-run management)

- Providing a guaranteed minimum income

- Free health service for all Canadians

- Children's allowances and unemployment insurance

- State-owned farms, which would be leased back to the farmers in lieu of private land ownership (something that didn't go over very well with the CCF's farm supporters, and was later withdrawn)

If there was any doubt about the CCF's mission to create a socialist "Kingdom of God," the final sentence of the manifesto left little doubt:

> *No CCF Government will rest content until it has eradicated capitalism and put into operation [a] full programme of socialized planning . . .*

The new party chose J.S. Woodsworth (I introduce you to him in Chapter 17), an MP since 1921, as their leader, and the party attracted many of the old Social Gospel crowd to its ranks. Among them was a Baptist minister and labour activist named Tommy Douglas, who joined the CCF after witnessing first-hand the hardships and misery of his parishioners in Weyburn, Saskatchewan. Seven CCF MPs were elected in 1935, including Tommy Douglas. Douglas later switched to provincial politics, and in 1944 became the premier of Saskatchewan — and the head of the first socialist government ever elected in North America.

The CCF was born in the dust bowl of the Great Depression. In 1961, it joined unions affiliated with the Canadian Labour Congress (CLC) to form the New Democratic Party (NDP), with Tommy Douglas as its leader. CCF + CLC = NDP.

You can read the original Regina Manifesto at www.saskndp.com/history/manifest.php3.

"Bible Bill"

In Alberta, a radio evangelist named William "Bible Bill" Aberhart was espousing an unorthodox new theory called "social credit." Developed by Major C.H. Douglas, a British engineer, it involved complex, pseudoscientific formulas. But the basic premise was simple enough. According to C.H. Douglas, the problem with the economy was that consumers didn't have enough purchasing power. The solution: Provide them with cash vouchers, called "social dividends"(or credit), to make up for this discrepancy — and to help spur economic revival. The SoCreds didn't reject capitalism. Not by a long shot. They just thought it needed a boost.

Bible Bill ran for premier on the solemn vow that if elected, he would issue payments of $25 a month to every adult in Alberta. As might be expected, the promise of money for votes was a very popular one, and Aberhart won a landslide victory in the 1935 election.

> *Poverty in the midst of plenty!*
> — Aberhart's ringing condemnation of the Depression-era economy

Aberhart was a true reformer. He brought in several key bills, including a freeze on debt collection, the creation of government-sponsored crop insurance, and a complete overhaul of existing labour and welfare programs. Social credit, however, was another matter.

The day after his victory, voters started lining up outside government offices, hands out, waiting for their $25 kickback. Aberhart tried to squirm out of it but his own backbenchers forced his hand, and in 1937, the government of Alberta brought in legislation that would allow them to begin issuing social credit dividends directly to citizens. (Dubbed, "funny money," these prosperity certificates are still around and are valued by collectors.)

Monetary policy, alas, was a *federal* responsibility. Ottawa vetoed Bible Bill's proposed legislation and the Supreme Court declared it "unconstitutional." Provinces could not issue their own currency, nor could they go around unilaterally assuming powers that belonged to the federal government. And that was pretty much the end of social credit as a viable economic theory in Canada. The SoCreds themselves continued as a party. Seventeen SoCred MPs were sent to Ottawa in the 1935 federal election, and the party went on to have long reigns in both Alberta and B.C. (Aberhart's replacement as premier was Ernest Manning, father of another prairie populist, Preston.)

At `www.socialcredit.com/backgrnd.htm` you can find more on the background of social credit theory.

Union Nationale

In Québec, a coalition under Maurice Duplessis swept the Liberals out of office in 1936. Duplessis' party, the Union Nationale, launched a few reforms, mainly in the area of rural credit and extended farm aid, but for the most part they were more conservative and unyielding than the government they had replaced. Duplessis wielded a heavy hand when dealing with dissidents — and especially with unions. (A strike at Dominion Textiles in 1937 was particularly bitter.)

Duplessis pandered to Québec nationalists and railed against Ottawa's "oppressive" Anglo policies, real or imagined. He was also notoriously racist. He aligned himself with the most reactionary elements of society, including the Catholic clergy, but he also marked a definite power shift in Québec, away from the Church and toward the state.

> *The bishops eat out of my hand*
> — Duplessis' boast about how he had "tamed" the clergy

In 1937, Duplessis brought in his infamous "Padlock Act," which allowed the government of Québec to lock up and evict anyone from any location that was even *suspected* of being used by Communists. As well, anyone publishing, printing, or distributing Communist material could be thrown in jail for one year — without appeal. When it was pointed out that the act didn't include a definition of what exactly "Communist behaviour" entailed, Duplessis brushed the objections aside. There was no need to define the terms, he said, because Communism was something "that can be felt."

Duplessis reigned like a tinpot dictator. And until it was finally declared illegal in 1957, he used the Padlock Act like a bludgeon to bully his opponents — or anyone else he didn't particularly like, including Jehovah's Witnesses. Duplessis' death grip on Québec would last, with only one interruption, right up until his death in 1959. Incredible. It was a one-party, one-man rule. Echoing Louis XIV's famous dictum, *L'état, c'est moi* ("I am the state"), Duplessis liked to brag, *"L'Union Nationale, c'est moi."*

Mitch and Duff

Along with the SocCreds in Alberta and the Union Nationale in Québec, Mackenzie King faced serious challenges from his own provincial Liberals as well, most notably from:

- ✔ **Mitchell Hepburn** in Ontario
- ✔ **Thomas "Duff" Pattullo** in British Columbia

Hepburn was elected on a pro-reform, radical platform, but that was just a ruse. Like Duplessis, once he got himself elected Hepburn reverted to a hard-line, autocratic approach. When Canadian workers at a General Motors plant in Oshawa walked off the job in 1937, Hepburn demanded that King send in the RCMP to crack some skulls. King refused. So Hepburn put together his own army of strikebreakers, mainly college thugs and anti-Communist war veterans, who were deputized as special constables and referred to, wryly, as the "Sons of Mitch's." It was American-style vigilante justice on a Canadian scale, and it earned Hepburn the enduring reputation as a hard-ass. The greatest battles Hepburn fought, however, were with Ottawa. He wrangled endlessly with King for increased provincial rights.

Duff Pattullo waged a similar battle against King and the federal government. As Premier of B.C., Pattullo was a swaggering, loud-talking, brash man who exuded confidence. He had crossed the Chilkoot Pass during the Klondike gold rush, and had served as mayor of Prince Rupert before leading the B.C. Liberals to victory in 1933 under the wonderfully oxymoronic banner: *"Socialized Capitalism!"*

Pattullo fought tooth and nail with King to extend provincial powers — and to gain federal backing for his often wild-eyed relief schemes. He liked to refer to B.C. as "an empire," he tried to annex Yukon, and he was especially tough on migrant workers and panhandlers. But overall his record was fairly impressive.

Backed up by growing labour unrest and a string of increasingly violent public sit-ins in Vancouver, Pattullo hammered out a "little New Deal" with Ottawa that was tailored especially for British Columbia. It gave the province what some historians have called "the most progressive system of social services" in Canada. Pattullo left behind a legacy — or at least an attitude — that has lingered in B.C. even today, where social awareness is often at the forefront of any issue, however small. Pattullo even tried to introduce Canada's first public health care system, and was blocked only by the angry resistance of doctors and other medical practitioners. (The honour of launching Canada's first public health care system would go to Saskatchewan instead.)

Federal-provincial relations (yawn)

The tug-of-war between the provinces and Ottawa grew so tense that King appointed a committee to look into the matter and make recommendations. The Royal Commission on Dominion-Provincial Relations was born. (Note: the use of the older term "Dominion" to refer to the national government. Today, it would be "Federal-Provincial Relations.")

It took three years and a whole lot of money, but the Commission eventually reported back in 1940 — after the Depression had ended, natch. Also known as "the Rowell-Sirois Report" (in reference to its chairmen, N.W. Rowell and Joseph Sirois), it recommended an overhaul of federal–provincial relations, especially in the area of taxation — and generally at the expense of the provinces.

Confederation had been designed with the idea of creating a "strong central government." But, as the report noted, the pendulum had now swung too far the other way. Power needed to be shifted *back* to the federal government. Specifically, Rowell-Sirois recommended:

✔ Granting the federal government increased power over taxation

✔ Giving the federal government responsibility for unemployment insurance and pensions

✔ And creating "equalization payments," managed by the federal government, which would transfer funds from the richer provinces to the poorer ones

The report was met with high-pitched, almost hysterical opposition from the provincial premiers, particularly Mitch Hepburn in Ontario. And although Hepburn and the others managed to kill the report, Ottawa implemented many of the proposed changes anyway during the following years, in a typically patchwork Canadian fashion. Indeed, the 1940s and 1950s would prove to be the highwater mark of Canadian centralism.

Perhaps the most important idea to come out of the Rowell-Sirois Report was the proposal for equalization payments, which finally began in 1957. These payments, managed by the federal government with the goal of distributing wealth between the "have" provinces and the "have-nots," are now a hallmark of Canadian federalism. Critics say that equalization payments are unnatural and unfair, and that they interfere with the marketplace by artificially propping up poorer regions at the expense of richer ones. Supporters, however, credit these payments with being the key that has helped Canada avoid the type of stark disparity in regional income that you see in the United States and elsewhere. These payments may blunt wealth, the argument goes, but they also blunt poverty as well. It all depends on where your priorities lie. Do you want more millionaires or fewer poor people? You can't always have both.

Chapter 19

World War II

● ●

In This Chapter

▶ Germany invades Poland, sparking another world war

▶ Canadian troops see battle at Hong Kong, Dieppe, Italy, and Normandy

▶ Conscription threatens to tear Canada apart — again

▶ Japanese Canadians are forced out of the West Coast

● ●

> *[Canadians] live in a fireproof house, far from inflammable materials.*
> *A vast ocean separates us from Europe.*
> — Canadian senator Raoul Dandurand, in an address
> to the League of Nations

*U*nder Mackenzie King, Canada became increasingly isolationist. In Europe, meanwhile, a new breed of dictators appeared, promoting a fascist ideology (fascism being a particularly potent blend of militant nationalism and totalitarianism, which glorifies the state over the individual). Benito Mussolini in Italy, Adolf Hitler in Germany, Francisco Franco in Spain: fascist movements were appearing everywhere, including Canada. As the dictators flexed their muscles, the war-weary democracies of the world adopted a policy of appeasement, granting concession after concession.

When Mussolini prepared to invade and bomb the independent African kingdom of Abyssinia (Ethiopia) in 1935, the League of Nations tried to stop him by introducing punitive trade sanctions against Italy. The Canadian advisory officer at the League, Walter Riddell, pushed to have oil included in the embargo, something that would have made an invasion all but impossible. It was a bold move on Riddell's part, but one made without Ottawa's approval. When King found out he panicked and quickly overruled Riddell's initiative. King claimed he had "saved Europe from war." In fact, all he had done was help render the League of Nations toothless.

The Spanish Civil War (1936–39) erupted when General Franco seized power. Volunteers from around the world rushed to Spain to join the fight against fascism. Much to King's chagrin, the Communist Party of Canada, the socialist CCF and many trade unions helped support the creation of a Mackenzie-Papineau Battalion, or "Mac-Paps" as they were known (named after the rebels

The death — and rebirth — of Norman Bethune

Among the Canadians who fought in Spain was a doctor from Gravenhurst, Ontario, named Norman Bethune. An ardent Communist and champion of causes such as medicare, Bethune worked as a medic on the front lines of the Spanish Civil War, where he developed the world's first mobile blood transfusion units.

Bethune later travelled to China to join the Communist forces under Mao Zedong, who were fighting against a Japanese military invasion. He went to China accompanied by another Canadian, a nurse named Jean Ewen, who had lived in China and spoke the language. (When Bethune first met Mao, Ewen was on hand as an interpreter, but she has since been airbrushed out of history — almost literally. She appears nowhere in the official paintings or photographs.) Ewen eventually left China, but Bethune remained. During an exhausting marathon round of battlefield surgery, Bethune nicked his finger with a scalpel. He contracted blood poisoning

and in the fall of 1939, he died — only to be resurrected as a "Hero of the Revolution," by Chairman Mao, who, in turn, went on to join the ranks of Stalin and Hitler as one of the world's most infamous mass murderers.

While in China, I visited Bethune's grave, several hours south of Beijing by train. I was surprised to discover that as well as being a Communist icon and propaganda hero, Bethune is also credited with introducing modern medicine to China. Statues of him in China seem to emphasize his striking physical resemblance to Lenin, something Mao commented on when he and Bethune first met. In Canada, Bethune's place in history is problematic at best. Once a hero among Canada's left, he has now been critically reassessed and found wanting, especially in light of the atrocious crimes against humanity committed in the name of communist ideology. Hero? Martyr? Communist stooge? It's a tough call.

---

of 1837; see Chapter 11). Some 1,600 Canadians fought in Spain. Only half of them ever returned. Mackenzie King, like most world leaders, preferred to take an "ostrich" approach to the spread of facism: eyes shut and head in sand. Adolf Hitler, however, was about to force the hand of Western democracies. Neutrality would no longer be an option.

On the Battlefield

On September 1, 1939, Hitler rolled his tanks into Poland in a sudden *blitzkrieg* ("lightning war") attack. At the same time, in a secret agreement with the Nazis, the Soviet Union invaded Europe's eastern frontier. On September 3, Britain and France declared war on Germany. World War II (1939–45) had begun. Canada was no longer a colony, and as such did not automatically go to war when Britain did — even though support was strong. With only three MPs dissenting, Canada's Parliament voted in favour of war against Nazi

Germany. King waited a week before the declaration was announced, partly as a symbolic assertion of Canadian sovereignty.

Hitler would eventually turn on his former Soviet allies and invade Russia. The U.S. entered the war in 1941 after the Japanese attacked a naval base in Hawaii. The main players then, in the order they entered the war, were:

- ✔ **The Allies:** Great Britain (along with Australia, New Zealand, and South Africa), France, Canada, Russia, and the United States
- ✔ **The Axis Powers:** Germany, Italy, and Japan

Under King's able and autocratic minister of munitions and supply, C.D. Howe, Canada launched a massive industrial mobilization. A Wartime Prices and Trade Board was set up to curtail inflation and profiteering. And even with gasoline, meat, butter, rubber, and other goods being rationed, Canada's economy boomed.

Canada supported the war effort through a British Commonwealth Air Training Plan. As many as 131,500 airmen from all corners of the Commonwealth were trained at facilities in Canada. More dramatic still was the Battle of the Atlantic, which was waged from 1940 until the end of the war. In an attempt to starve Britain out, German U-boat submarines, travelling in deadly "wolf packs," attacked ships trying to cross the Atlantic. Supplies and men did manage to run the gauntlet, but at great cost. German U-boats even entered the St. Lawrence and eventually sank 23 vessels — frightening King to such an extent that he closed the river to shipping. Canada provided crucial air and sea escorts to supply convoys, with the Royal Canadian Navy growing from just 13 vessels to a fleet of 373 ships. Almost 1,200 Canadians died during the Battle of the Atlantic.

> *The real heroes of the Atlantic war were the civilian seamen. An estimated quarter of them did not survive the war.*
>
> — military historian Desmond Morton

Hong Kong

Following a surprise attack on the U.S. fleet in Pearl Harbor, the Japanese Imperial Army went on a rampage across Southeast Asia. They were soon within range of Hong Kong, Britain's "Gibraltar of the Orient." In fact, Hong Kong was almost impossible to defend, especially against the battle-hardened troops of Japan. Winston Churchill had admitted as much. Still, Britain couldn't exactly surrender it without a fight. At the very least, a "symbolic" defense was required. It was now Canada's turn in the barrel. So, more than 1,900 inexperienced Canadian troops, some of whom had yet to fire a rifle, were sent into eye of the storm, "like lambs to the slaughter."

The attack began on December 18, 1941. Japanese troops swarmed ashore on Hong Kong Island and overran the British, Indian, and Canadian positions. In the midst of the fighting, Sergeant-Major John Osborn of the Winnipeg Grenadiers saved his men by throwing himself on a live grenade. Later that same day, Canadian Brigadier John Lawson radioed his superior officers from inside his pillbox. He was surrounded, he told them, and he was "going outside to fight it out." With a pistol in each hand, Lawson kicked open the door and charged out, guns blazing — to his death.

On Christmas Day, following a final desperate counterattack, the governor of Hong Kong formally surrendered, as the Japanese began bayoneting wounded soldiers and assaulting — and killing — unarmed nurses. The Canadians taken prisoner at Hong Kong faced inhuman conditions in Japan's cruel P.O.W. camps. Many were forced to work as slave labourers in mines and shipyards. More than 550 Canadians died, either in battle or as prisoners of the Japanese, who had a well-deserved reputation for brutality.

Dieppe

The year 1942 was a desperate one for the Allies. France had fallen, the British army had barely managed to escape, German troops were massed along the shores of the English Channel, and on the Eastern Front, more than three million German troops had struck deep into Russian territory. The United States had entered the war, but their troops had yet to play a role in any major action in Europe. Nor had the Canadians, though they were at the front lines of a possible German invasion of Great Britain, guarding the coast from an attack that seemed imminent. Under pressure from Stalin to establish a Second Front and draw German troops away from Russia, British Prime Minister Winston Churchill and his Chief of Combined Operations, Lord Mountbatten, decided to test Hitler's defenses. They chose the French harbour town of Dieppe as their target. No large amphibious assaults had been attempted so far. The standard strategy was to charge in, capture a port, and secure the area. Because surprise was thought to be a key to success, heavy bombardment prior to a major assault was considered counterproductive. The barrage at Dieppe would last barely 10 minutes. The British Command also decided to land tanks directly from the sea, something else that had never been tried before. Still, confidence was high. Intelligence reports suggested that the town was poorly defended. In fact, Dieppe was a fortress.

On August 19, 1942, Operation Jubilee was launched. It was huge. More than 6,000 Allied troops were involved and of these, 5,000 were Canadians, untried in combat and about to receive their "baptism of fire."

Things went wrong right from the start. The ships landed men at the wrong sites, often with tragic results. The Germans, perched atop coastal cliffs, rained lead down upon the Canadians. The tanks arrived, but the beach was not soft shale as the men had been told; rather it was a nightmare of chalky, large rocks piled so thick they jammed the tanks' treads and didn't allow traction. Tanks spun themselves in, and by the time this horrendous error was noticed, it was too late. The few tanks that made it across the beach were confronted by street blockades, and they ended up driving frantically back and forth, looking for an opening that didn't exist.

The battle objectives were ridiculously complicated. Plans ran over 100 pages, and were as complex as they were unrealistic. The Royal Regiment of Canada, for example, was expected to secure a beachhead, eliminate coastal defenses, cross a 12-foot seawall and rows of barbed wire, scale a 200-foot cliff, and take out heavy anti-aircraft batteries and several machine gun nests. They were expected to do all this *before* the main wave of soldiers arrived. And they were given all of 30 minutes to do it.

The raid on Dieppe failed because it could never have succeeded. General J.H. Roberts, the Canadian commander, was just as misinformed as any of his men. At Dieppe, inexperienced, undertrained troops were sent in without cover in broad daylight. The 2nd Canadian Infantry Division was, in effect, caught in a shooting gallery. The battle lasted nine hours. Men who were wounded on the beach lay choking on their own blood. As the tides came in, many of them drowned. Bodies washed in along the shore for days. The first amphibious assault of World War II was over.

Of the 5,000 Canadians who stormed the beaches at Dieppe, there were 3,300 casualties. Of these, more than 900 were killed.

The battle was only the start of their ordeal. As many as 1,900 Canadian soldiers were taken prisoner at Dieppe and marched into German P.O.W. camps. A copy of the British battle plans had fallen into enemy hands, and in it the Germans came across a passage that read: "Whenever possible, the prisoners' hands will be tied to prevent destruction of their documents." Outraged, the German High Command condemned these "wild-west measures," which they considered "a disgrace and lack of respect." It was the Canadian prisoners who would pay the price. In direct retaliation, the Germans tied, and then later manacled, the hands of the soldiers they captured at Dieppe. The Canadians were bound like this *for over a year.*

The Dieppe raid was a disaster. It almost seemed as though it were *designed* to fail, if only to demonstrate the futility of trying to establish a Second Front. Were Canadians used as "cannon fodder" by Churchill to placate Stalin's demands for some kind of action? The controversy over Dieppe continues even today. Certainly, Dieppe provided valuable experience on how *not* to launch a coastal invasion. In many ways, Dieppe was a warm-up for D-Day, the final Allied invasion that came two years later. At Normandy in 1944, the lessons of Dieppe were put to good use. Objectives were simpler, open beaches were chosen as landing points, rather than heavily fortified harbours, and instead of relying on stealth and surprise, the Allies used massive bombardments before the attack. Dieppe made D-Day possible.

The Falcon of Malta

In the middle of the Mediterranean Sea, another siege was underway. Allied forces had managed to cling to the Island of Malta, and the German and Italian planes attacked in waves. A small band of Allied pilots fought them back. It was a desperate defense, but a hero soon emerged: a thin young man from Verdun, Québec, named George Beurling (dubbed "Buzz" by the press).

Fearless, handsome, unruly, lethal: Buzz Beurling had an almost unnatural ability as a pilot. He could spot planes in an empty sky, and would then swoop in for the kill. They called him the Falcon, and his ruthless, almost reckless style made him a legend in his own time. In one 14-day stretch alone, Beurling destroyed 27 enemy airplanes, often against overwhelming odds. By the time the war ended, he had shot down 31 planes and was ranked among the Allies' top ten pilots.

A loner by nature, Beurling often clashed with his superiors, and though haunted by nightmares of the men he had killed, he seemed addicted to the blood sport of aerial warfare. He died in 1948, in a fiery crash in Rome, while en route to fight for the Israeli airforce. Today, Buzz Beurling, the "Falcon of Malta," is all but forgotten.

At www.vac-acc.gc.ca/general/sub.cfm?source=history/secondwar/dieppe (part of a larger WW II site), you'll find more on the Dieppe raid.

The Road to Ortona

Winston Churchill called it "the soft underbelly of Europe," but Italy was anything but. In early July 1943, American, British, and Canadian troops landed on Sicily and fought their way across the island. (Canadians provided an infantry division and a tank brigade.)

Italy surrendered, but Germany seized control of the country and German troops rushed south to battle the Allies as they crossed over from Sicily to the mainland. Inch by inch, the Canadians fought their way up the length of Italy before getting locked into a fierce month-long battle against two crack German divisions near the seaside town of Ortona. In the rubble-strewn streets, tanks and artillery were of limited use, and the Canadian 1st Division had to fight the Germans back house by house. It was an important victory, but it came at a great cost: 502 dead and 1,837 wounded. In Sicily and Italy combined, almost 6,000 Canadians died.

D-Day

Operation Overlord, the final Allied invasion of Northwest Europe, was launched on June 6, 1944. More than 5,000 ships crossed the English Channel, and 107,000 men stormed ashore on the beaches of Normandy. Among them were more than 14,000 Canadians, along with 110 Canadian warships. The flags of three armies were flying that day: Great Britain, the United States, and Canada. The Canadians landed on Juno Beach, a site tougher than most, and fought their way inland, covering more ground that first day than any other Allied division. The Liberation of Europe had begun. The end of the Nazi era was at hand.

Still, the D-Day invasion was only the start. It would take almost a year to finally defeat Germany. The Americans and British provided the main thrust, but Canadians played an important role, too. As the left flank of the Allied advance, Canadian troops cleared the coast and pushed eastward, liberating Holland in the spring of 1945. Even today, Canadian veterans are — arguably — more honoured in Holland than they are in their own country. With the Soviets surrounding Berlin, Adolf Hitler killed himself. A week later, Germany surrendered and was later carved in two, with West Germany democratic and East Germany communist. The war against fascism was over. And the Cold War had begun.

> More than one million Canadians and Newfoundlanders served in World War II (Newfoundland was not a part of Canada at that time).
>
> Of these, 45,000 gave their lives.
>
> Another 55,000 were wounded — often seriously.

For more on the Battle of the Atlantic, Italy, Normandy, and Holland, go to www.vac-acc.gc.ca/general/sub.cfm?source=history/secondwar. For more on Canada and the Commonwealth Air Training Plan, visit the museum in Brandon, Manitoba, at www.airmuseum.mb.ca/. You'll find more on the "Valour and the Horror" of Canada and World War II at www.valourandhorror.com/.

For World War II through Canadian eyes (part of a larger site), go to collections.ic.gc.ca/courage/worldwariiabriefhistory.html. If you'd like to learn more about Canadian war monuments see: www.stemnet.nf.ca/monuments.

See Table 19.1 for a complete timeline of World War II.

Table 19.1		A Timeline of World War II
1939	September 1	German troops invade Poland — two days later, Britain and France declare war on Germany
	September 10	Canada declares war on Germany
1940	May–June	French defenses collapse and British troops flee from Dunkirk in a mass evacuation
	June 22	France surrenders to Germany
	August–September	Battle of Britain — a German air attack is defeated
1941	June	Germany invades its former ally, Russia
	November 16	Canadian troops arrive in Hong Kong
	December 7	Japanese attack U.S. fleet at Pearl Harbor
	December 8	U.S. and Canada declare war on Japan — three days later the U.S. declares war on Germany and Italy as well
	December 18–25	Battle of Hong Kong — in a fierce attack, Japanese overrun British, Indian, and Canadian positions
1942	April 27	Canadians vote three to one to allow conscription
	August 19	Dieppe raid ends in disaster for Canadian troops
1943	July–August	Allies invade Sicily — Canadians suffer especially high casualties
	September 3	British, U.S., and Canadian troops land in Italy
	November	Conscription begins in Canada
	December 21–28	Battle of Ortona — a hard-fought Canadian victory against German troops in Italy
1944	June 6	D-Day: Armies under three flags — Britain, the U.S., and Canada — storm the shores of France
1945	February–March	Canadians push Germans back across the Rhine
	April 22	Russian troops reach the outskirts of Berlin
	May 7	VE Day (Victory in Europe): Germany surrenders
	August 6	U.S. drops an atomic bomb on Hiroshima, Japan — three days later, a second bomb falls on Nagasaki
	August 14	VJ Day (Victory in Japan): Japan surrenders

On the Homefront

In March 1940, King called a snap election and won a huge majority — thanks largely to overwhelming support in Québec, where Ernest Lapointe, King's minister of justice and key "Québec lieutenant," had campaigned vigorously on the promise that the Liberals would *never* introduce conscription.

Conscription crisis (part two)

It was all very familiar. Another war in Europe. Another meat grinder. Another generation of young men sent to their deaths. And, just as inevitably, the issue of conscription (forcing men into military service) once again arose. In World War I, conscription had torn Canada apart along regional, linguistic, and class lines. As I describe in Chapter 16, Borden kept the faith, and Canada paid the price. Mackenzie King, in contrast, was concerned above all with maintaining Canadian unity *and* Liberal rule. In King's mind, the two were inextricably linked. To King, the war was a disruptive sideshow.

What role should Canada play? Churchill had declared, "Give us the tools and we'll finish the job!" And that was the heart of the matter: men or materials, what should Canada be supplying? At home, men were needed to harvest crops, mine ore, and log forests. On the battlefield, soldiers were just as badly needed. In Canada, volunteers dwindled and a cry went up to begin drafting men. King faced relentless, mounting pressure. There was just one snag. The Liberals, remember, had been elected in Québec on an anti-conscription platform.

"If necessary, but not necessarily . . ."

Here's where King's peculiar brand of genius came to the forefront. In 1942, he announced that he would hold a national plebiscite — a referendum, in effect — not on conscription, but on the *possibility* of conscription. That is, Canadians would vote on whether to release the government from its earlier promise *not* to introduce the draft. King wasn't asking for a vote on conscription, heavens no. But only on the *option* of introducing conscription. Pure bafflegab. King himself later summed up his confusing position in one of the most celebrated examples of political doubletalk in Canadian history:

> *Conscription if necessary, but not necessarily conscription.*
> — Mackenzie King, master of evasive action

Historian Michael Bliss, a staunch defender of Mackenzie King, insists that the policy was "precise" and the meaning "clear." But certainly, at the time, King's position was interpreted in wildly different ways. Historian Ramsay Cook called the statement "a masterpiece of calculated ambiguity." The results of the 1942 plebiscite were startling:

- ✔ Québec voted *no* by 73 percent.
- ✔ The rest of Canada, meanwhile, voted *yes* by 80 percent.

Nationally, King had been released from his earlier promise. He was now free to introduce conscription. If necessary. But not necessarily. He managed to drag it out for two more years, against growing hostility from within his own ranks. In a singularly shabby manner, King dumped his hardworking minister of defense, Colonel J.L. Ralston, who had been advocating conscription, and brought in General Andrew McNaughton instead for one last attempt at raising enough volunteers. Alas, McNaughton failed as well, and in 1944 King was finally forced to bring in the draft. Ah, but the PM had one more trick up his sleeve — and it was a doozy.

"Zombies" to the rescue!

Under the National Resources Mobilization Act (NRMA), thousands of men had already either volunteered or been called up — *for home defense*. Why not use the NRMA to fill Canada's overseas commitments? With Canada under no real threat of invasion (though Japanese subs were skulking around the Pacific Coast), the NRMA men had so little to do that they had been dubbed "Zombies." (The name was taken from a recent Hollywood voodoo movie.) True, the NRMA men hadn't signed up to fight overseas, but if you were going to draft people into service, why not draft the Zombies?

Conscription began in November 1944. Riots broke out in Montréal, and nationalist leaders in Québec tried to rally anti-government opposition, but for the most part King was viewed by French Canadians as a man who had tried his best to keep his promise. (Current Québec nationalists are not nearly as kind in their assessment of King.) King had achieved the near impossible; he had taken Canada through the war, more or less united.

The real opposition came from the Zombies themselves. At a remote camp in Terrace, B.C., they mutinied for a week before giving in. Some boarded ships at gunpoint. Of the first 10,000 called up, it was said that over half deserted. Historian Desmond Morton considers many of the tales of NRMA desertions to be "fabrications," but even so, the Saga of the Zombies is not exactly one of Canada's finer moments.

Roughly 13,000 NRMA men were sent abroad. Fewer than 2,500 actually reached the battlefield, and only 69 died in action. From a military point of view, Canadian conscription had hardly been a factor at all. From a political and emotional point of view, it had the potential wallop of dynamite. Mackenzie King, however, managed to weather the controversy, and in 1945, just a year after the conscription crisis came to a head, he was re-elected with a majority — thanks to the full support he received in Québec.

Canada and the Holocaust

World War II was a barbaric era. The Nazi's systematic massacre of Jews, along with Gypsies and homosexuals, was horrific — surpassed in number only by the millions who died under Communist rule in the Soviet Union. Between Hitler and Stalin you have two of the most evil men in history. But they didn't do it alone. They were aided and abetted along the way.

Sadly, just when the Jews of Europe needed sanctuary most, the Western world shuts its doors and bolted the gate. And Canada was the most uncaring of the lot. In the words of historian Irvin Abella, Canada's regulations aimed at keeping out Jews were "probably the most stringent in the world." Consider the following immigration numbers for Jewish refugees during Hitler's reign of terror (1933–45):

- The United States: 200,000
- Great Britain: 195,000 (of which, 125,000 were re-routed to British-held Palestine)
- Argentina: 50,000
- Brazil: 27,000
- Canada: less than 5,000

This scandalously low number was in keeping with the policies of Mackenzie King, who wanted "to keep this part of the continent free from unrest and from too great an intermixture of foreign strains of blood." Especially Jewish blood. Overseeing King's immigration policies was a bureaucrat named Frederick Blair, who set up a veritable "blockade" on refugees fleeing Nazi persecution. Public opinion demanded it. Anti-Semitism, after all, had taken firm root in Canada. And nowhere was this truer than in Québec — the very province that had given King his majority.

Today, Québec nationalists angrily deny charges of past anti-Semitism, but the evidence speaks for itself. The propagandist-priest Abbé Groulx (sometimes described as "the spiritual father of modern Québec") joined the nationalist newspaper *Le Devoir* and the rest of the chorus in denouncing Jews as "a race that refused to be assimilated." Canada's own would-be Hitler, the fascist leader Adrien Arcand, also hailed from Québec. Once the war started, Arcand was thrown in jail, but hostility towards Jews did not abate. Universities such as McGill maintained "quotas" on the number of Jewish students allowed to enter. And that proud bastion of French-Canadian pride, the St. Jean Baptiste Society, presented Ottawa with a petition signed by 127,000 people demanding further restrictions on Jews. In Toronto, Jewish families were assaulted on public beaches.

Canada places greater emphasis upon race than upon citizenship.
— Frederick Blair in a 1941 wartime statement of
immigration policy under Mackenzie King, eerily
echoing Germany's own racial obsessions.

Japanese Canadians and the war

The Asian immigrants who settled on the West Coast faced some of the
worst discrimination Canada has ever meted out. The B.C. Asiatic Exclusion
League incited race riots in Vancouver under the battle cry of "Stand for
White Canada!" Newspapers in Victoria warned of a "yellow menace," and the
Canadian government, having already introduced a special head tax on
Chinese, passed the Immigration Act of 1923, which effectively barred any
further Chinese from entering the country.

When Japan attacked the U.S. base in Pearl Harbor in December 1941, Canada
declared war against the Japanese as well. At home, the anger, fear, and long-
simmering racism became focused on Japanese Canadians. Pressured by
West Coast MPs, Mackenzie King announced that the Canadian government
would begin forcibly evacuating people of Japanese descent from the coast.
Anyone who resisted would be imprisoned.

> *Let our slogan be for British Columbia: "No Japs from the Rockies to
> the sea!"*
> — Ian Mackenzie, King's minister of pensions and health

By September 1942, more than 22,000 men, women, and children had been
forced to move inland. Of these, 75 percent were Canadian-born citizens.
Families were often roused from their sleep in the middle of the night and
given less than 24 hours' notice. An entire ethnic population was dispossessed,
stripped of its belongings, and carted off to relocation camps — all without
trial, charges, or due process. (About 660 Germans were interned during the
war as well, along with 480 Italians.) More than half of the Japanese families
were sent to remote shantytowns deep in the B.C. interior, in what were —
effectively — refugee camps. The weeks turned into months. The months
turned into years.

The evacuation was only the first blow. Homes, businesses, fishing boats, and
family possessions that had been left behind were now confiscated by the
government and auctioned off in a public looting. Often, government agencies
would roll the property over, selling it for profits of 200 percent or more.

Now, you would think that after Japan had surrendered, the relocation
restrictions would end. But no. Even as the war came to a close, Mackenzie
King announced the creation of Stalinist-style "loyalty commissions" that

would interrogate Japanese Canadians and determine who among them were truly faithful to Canada. Those who refused to co-operate would be "deported" to Japan. More than 4,000 Japanese Canadians were eventually hounded out of the country. More than half were Canadian-born citizens and more than a third were children under the age of 16 who didn't even speak Japanese.

Two points are worth noting: (a) Canada's actions contravened the newly formed United Nations Declaration of Human Rights, and (b) deportations based on racial grounds had actually been defined as "a crime against humanity." (It is also worth noting that when the atomic bomb was dropped on Hiroshima, King expressed in his journals his relief that such a weapon was used "on yellow people" and not on the decent white races of Europe.)

To recap: Under the glorious leadership of Mackenzie King, Canada had

- ✔ Relocation camps

- ✔ Racial segregation

- ✔ Government-sponsored looting

- ✔ Deportation orders (during peacetime, no less)

- ✔ Loyalty hearings

- ✔ Forced labour

You can't blame wartime hysteria for this, either. Restrictions against Japanese Canadians lasted until 1949, almost *four years* after the war had ended. An investigation later revealed that the losses suffered by Japanese Canadians during the evacuations and as a result of government-sanctioned confiscations that followed at "not less than $443 million."

The Japanese community in B.C. was destroyed by the war, and the fight for redress and an apology would last 40 years. It was only in 1988 that the Canadian government finally offered a formal apology, along with compensation of $21,000 for each surviving claimant as well as a community fund and a full pardon to those who had been wrongfully convicted.

Two years later, the government issued a similar apology to Canadians of Italian origin who had also been interned during the war.

To find out more on the internment of Japanese Canadians, go to www.lib. washington.edu/subject/Canada/internment/intro.html.

"The socialists are coming! The socialists are coming!"

One of the few political groups to oppose the internment and evacuation of Japanese Canadians was the socialist CCF Party, which denounced the government's actions as "a direct negation of decent, elemental, fundamental democracy." During the war, the CCF had its first big breakthrough when Tommy Douglas won the 1944 provincial election in Saskatchewan, becoming the head of the first socialist government elected anywhere in North America. Tommy Douglas would remain premier for the next 17 years and would later become "the Father of Medicare" in Canada when he introduced public health care in Saskatchewan (see Chapter 21). In Canada, the left wing has always been small — but influential.

Chapter 20

Canada and the Cold War

· ·

In This Chapter

▶ In a world of Cold War confrontations, Canada attempts to follow a middle path

▶ Prime Minister St. Laurent presides over a "golden era" of prosperity

▶ Newfoundland becomes Canada's tenth province

▶ The thunderin' prairie prophet, John Diefenbaker, roars into town

· ·

> *The United States will not sit idly by if Canadian soil is threatened*
> — paraphrase of U.S. President Franklin D. Roosevelt's public
> pronouncement on the eve of WW II. A promise or a threat?

*W*orld War II made Canada and the United States the two richest nations on earth. Canada now had the world's third largest navy and fourth largest air force, with a GNP (Gross National Product) that had more than doubled. But the war also left Europe and much of Asia devastated. Britain and France were on the brink of bankruptcy and facing economic ruin — so give the Americans their due. Under the far-sighted and generous terms of the Marshall Plan, they helped fund the recovery of Western Europe.

During the war, Roosevelt and King had signed several key agreements, which brought the U.S. and Canada ever closer:

✔ **The Ogdensburg Agreement** (1940) established a Permanent Joint Board to integrate North American defenses. For the first time ever, the Canadian and U.S. military were formally linked — and, as the name of the board made amply clear, the relationship was meant to be *permanent*.

✔ **The Hyde Park Declaration** (1941) helped co-ordinate the war effort of the two countries by having them work closely together in production — while also supporting Britain through a "lend-lease" arrangement (with the U.S. providing war materials on credit).

Historian Donald Creighton complains that King acted like "a puppet on a string," dancing to Roosevelt's tune, and there is some truth to this. Even worse, Canada was fast becoming an economic satellite as well. During the post-war years, King's minister of economic reconstruction, C.D. Howe (also active during the war, see Chapter 19), openly courted U.S. investors. He was shameless. American money, he liked to coo, was "always welcome."

The Post-War Years

In Canada, the post-war era was one of turmoil and prosperity. The year 1946 was the worst one for strikes since 1919. Union membership was up, unemployment was down, prices were low, and income was rising. Central authority in Canada reached its greatest heights during the 1940s and '50s, but the regions were growing in strength too. In 1947, in the Leduc Valley south of Edmonton, Imperial Oil hit a gusher and Alberta was transformed almost overnight from a sleepy "have-not" prairie province into an oil-rich economic superpower. By 1959, Alberta was spending more money per capita on health care and education than any other province.

World War II opened doors to women, presenting them with the sort of employment opportunities that they had long been denied. But when the war ended, women were expected to return to their traditional roles and make room for the soldiers who were now re-entering the workplace. It was an attitude that cut across gender lines, with 75 percent of men and 68 percent of women agreeing that women should once again become the angels of the home. The 1950s were a notoriously conservative time.

Don Mills, Ontario — Canada's first "planned" community — marked the beginning of a new suburban, commuter lifestyle, made possible by the automobile. A fundamental shift had occurred. Canada had become a *consumer society,* with an emphasis on consumption, not production. Television, originally promoted as a way to "bring families together," introduced mass pop culture directly into the living rooms of the nation. And with the suburbs came the ubiquitous shopping plaza and the start of that all-Canadian pastime: hangin' out at the mall. The post-war years also saw a surge in the birth rate, as Canada's population increased by 50 percent (from 12 million to 18 million) between 1946 and 1961. The baby boom generation, as it is known, has moved through each demographic stage — from rebellious adolescents to middle-aged consumers — like a "pig in a python," shifting trends and societal focus as it goes. (The boomers practically *invented* modern youth culture — now a multibillion-dollar-a-year industry.)

Keynesian economics

Under Mackenzie King, the government became increasingly involved in the economy, following a policy advocated by British economist John Maynard Keynes, who argued that public leaders should play a stabilizing role in controlling the economic cycle of boom and bust. Prior to the Great Depression of the 1930s, the marketplace was assumed to be self-correcting. Keynes challenged this assumption, urging governments to help lessen market fluctuations by *spending* money during bad times (even at a deficit, if need be) and *cutting back* during good times. Canada was among the first countries in the world to adopt a Keynesian approach. Critics have since argued that this system "meddles" in the marketplace and may actually increase market fluctuations and prolong economic downturns.

"The Man in the Mask"

Mackenzie King remained an isolationist at heart, overly cautious and extremely wary of the outside world and its messy divisive entanglements. But the days of the "fireproof house" (see Chapter 19) were gone forever . . .

On a warm evening in September 1945, Igor Gouzenko, a cipher/decoder clerk at the Soviet Embassy in Ottawa, gathered up more than 100 classified documents and attempted to defect. I say "attempted" because Canada didn't want him. Not at first. The poor man, stalked by Soviet assassins, speaking broken English with a pregnant wife and an infant son in tow, had risked everything — only to be turned away by Canadian authorities. Indeed, King wanted to send Gouzenko right back to the Soviets, and he might have done it too, if it hadn't been for several high-level British intelligence officers who urged King to offer Igor political asylum.

What Gouzenko revealed was alarming. The Soviets had penetrated the highest echelons of Western defense. There was a spy in Canada's Department of External Affairs, another one at the British High Commission (the Commonwealth equivalent of an embassy), and still another planted in a Canadian atomic research laboratory. There was even a Canadian MP on the Soviet payroll: Fred Rose of the Labour-Progressive Party (as the Canadian Communists were now known). Rose, the first and only Communist ever elected to federal office in Canada, was eventually convicted and sentenced to six years on charges of conspiracy. Gouzenko also revealed moles deep in the U.S. State Department and Treasury Board. The Soviets, it became clear, were making preparations for a third world war.

Igor Gouzenko, forced into hiding, lived the rest of his life in seclusion. He testified at government hearings with a cloth sack over his head, and the press dubbed him "the Man in the Mask" — which sounded better than "man with a pillowcase over his head." (Gouzenko later wrote a memoir and a novel, *The Fall of a Titan*, which won the 1954 Governor General's Award.)

Canada was where the Cold War was born. And as the spy scandal broke, Winston Churchill coined the term "Iron Curtain" to describe the ominous wall of silence that had descended between the Communist East and the Democratic West. Make no mistake — the Soviet Union was an extremely aggressive, expansionist state. It crushed democratic movements in Czechoslovakia, Hungary, and elsewhere, and set up puppet regimes throughout Eastern

Europe (in much the same way that the U.S. would set up puppet regimes in Latin America). As early as 1949, the Soviet Union had detonated an atomic test weapon. The United States was no longer the world's sole nuclear power, and a high-stakes game of poker had begun.

The Cold War would last more than 40 years (from 1945 to 1989) and, during the darkest of these days, full-scale nuclear annihilation was a very real possibility. The world was on the edge of the abyss. Panic and hysteria were rife, most notably in the U.S., where public "witch hunts" flushed out possible Soviet sympathizers. Even the democratic socialism of Canada's CCF was deemed suspect, and in 1956 the party toned down the rhetoric of its original Regina Manifesto by issuing a more moderate "Winnipeg Declaration," which emphasized social policy over ideology — to no avail. The Cold War had chilled political plurality and had frozen out debate.

Displaced persons

Canadians had always been, first and foremost, British subjects. But that changed with the Citizenship Act of 1946, which came into effect on January 1, 1947. On that day, Canada became the first country in the Commonwealth to define its people not as British subjects, but as citizens of their own country. For the first time ever, loyalty toward Canada was made the "primary" identity of Canadian citizens. The British connection was relegated to a secondary position, where it soon faded away almost entirely. The historic ties that once bound Canada to Great Britain were eroding. (British citizens, however, continued to enjoy special privileges in Canada, a situation that would last well into the 1980s.)

Nowhere was the changing face of Canada more evident than in the immigrants, exiles, and refugees who arrived following World War II. The war had left millions of people dispossessed, unable or unwilling to return to their ravaged and occupied homelands. Political and economic refugees had become a pressing international concern, but Mackenzie King, forever fretful about social stability, was reluctant to offer sanctuary. In fact, he went so far as to install blatantly discriminatory immigration laws aimed at preserving "the fundamental character" of Canadian society (that is, white and Christian, and preferably of northern European stock). Strict racial and ethnic guidelines were set up to discourage — and even block — blacks, Arabs, Asians, and Jews from entering Canada.

This too is part of the great "Mackenzie King legacy": racial and ethnic barriers that would last until 1962. Even then, King was just responding to the mood of Canadians, who were divided on the issue of immigration and who often felt threatened by the impending "flood" of refugees.

Among the first to arrive after the war were 4,000 Polish war veterans who had fought for the Allies only to see their nation swallowed up by the Soviet juggernaut. Soon after, Dutch farm families began arriving from the Netherlands, where thousands of hectares of valuable land had been flooded by the Nazis who had breached the nation's seawater dikes. In Canada, religious and cultural organizations banded together to form the Canadian Christian Council for the Resettlement of Refugees (CCCRR), which included Catholic, Baptist, Lutheran, and Mennonite sponsors.

For the most part, the "displaced persons" of the post-war years — a term shortened to "DPs" — came to Canada either as sponsored relatives or under government labour schemes that required them to sign contracts guaranteeing Canada two years of manual labour: in mines, fisheries, railways, or — in the case of women — as maids. They were, in essence, the modern equivalent of indentured servants. Our very own serfs. Between 1946 and 1952, more than 160,000 European DPs arrived in Canada.

Much like the "peasants in sheepskin coats" who had arrived under Laurier (see Chapter 15), the DPs helped reshape Canadian society in radically new ways. More than 1.7 million newcomers — DPs, immigrants, and war brides alike — came to Canada during the 1940s and '50s. Despite Mackenzie King's best efforts, Canada was becoming a more mixed and multicultural place.

For more on post-war immigration, including DPs (part of a larger site), go to www.ucalgary.ca/HIST/tutor/canada1946/1frame.html.

The Universal Declaration of Human Rights

The United Nations was founded in April 1945

- ✔ To promote international peace and security
- ✔ To provide a forum for international debate
- ✔ To assist economic, social, and cultural development
- ✔ And to expand basic human freedoms

The UN's Security Council included five permanent members (the United States, the Soviet Union, Britain, France, and China), all of whom were given a veto, which led to constant sabre-rattling standoffs. And though often used as a platform for crass propaganda, the UN itself has managed to survive. This is largely due to the "moral force" under which the United Nations operates, as embodied by its Universal Declaration of Human Rights.

Called "the conscience of humanity," the UN Declaration asserts individual rights as the cornerstone of international law. It seeks to protect people on the basis of race, gender, language, religion, and political beliefs. It also declares that everyone has the right to health care, education, and employment. This dramatic assertion of human worth was drafted by a Canadian: John Humphrey of Hampton, New Brunswick. As Director of the UN's Human Rights Division, Humphrey was the key architect of the declaration, which was proclaimed and adopted on December 10, 1948.

Recognized (if not honoured) by virtually every nation on earth, the declaration has served as the basis of constitutions around the world, as well as for Canada's own 1982 Charter of Rights and Freedoms. The mass deportation and internment of Japanese Canadians and the racially based closed-door immigration policies introduced by Mackenzie King would never have been permitted under the terms of the UN declaration.

> *All human beings are born free and equal in dignity and rights.*
> — from Article 1 of the Universal Declaration of Human Rights

John Humphrey worked for the UN for 20 years, promoting freedom of speech, the status of women, and racial equality. He oversaw the creation of 67 different international conventions and charters, as well as the constitutions of dozens of different countries. Few Canadians have had a greater impact on world events, and yet, in Canada, he is all but forgotten.

You can find the full text of the UN Universal Declaration of Human Rights at www.un.org/Overview/rights.html. For links to more articles on John Humphrey, go to www.historytelevision.ca/humphrey/english/jph.htm.

The King legacy

> *Always to be elusive, always to be anonymous, always to be ambiguous — that was the King political style and strategy.*
> — historian Norman Hillmer

When William Lyon Mackenzie King retired in 1948, he was the longest-reigning prime minister in Canadian history — almost 23 years at the helm — and was, in fact, the longest-reigning elected leader in the history of the English-speaking world. True, Mackenzie King was an odd duck. He dabbled in the occult and held eerie midnight seances in which he sought advice from dead leaders — and comfort from his dear departed mother. He was a spiritualist, a flake, and a lonely mamma's boy. But none of that really matters. What we need to evaluate is his *political* legacy.

The Mackenzie King Redemption Committee, as I like to call it, has been working overtime lately, trying in vain to convince Canadians to embrace King as our "greatest leader ever." A recent poll of history professors anointed King as Canada's "best" prime minister, but the public didn't buy it. King remains — as always — a somewhat plodding, somewhat bland, and somewhat enigmatic figure: the very embodiment of the colour grey. Mackenzie King was, in the words of one of my colleagues, "a Canadian in the *worst* sense of the word."

Even Mackenzie King's supporters end up damning him with faint praise, admitting that, although King was an uninspiring and not especially creative leader, he was still "a very capable administrator." Yawn. In historian Frank Underhill's celebrated phrase, the best thing that could be said of Mackenzie King was that he "divided us least." King's achievements were real enough. He kept Canada more or less united during World War II, he oversaw the start of the post-war economic boom, and he introduced several important social programs:

- Old Age Pension (1926/27)
- Unemployment Insurance (1940)
- Family Allowance (1944)

Although he has been accused of being an American "puppet," King had some serious reservations about Canada's increasingly cozy relationship with Uncle Sam. One of King's final acts while in power was to veto a move within his own party to pursue free trade with the U.S. In this, King was a Canadian nationalist — a cautious, uninspiring nationalist to be sure, but a nationalist nonetheless.

Ultimately though, Mackenzie King is a professor's hero, not a people's hero. If King is admired and relentlessly championed in academia, it is precisely because he exemplifies those very traits that are suited to professors, administrators, and senior bureaucrats alike: he was a very adept manager, politically astute, cautious but firm, who achieved longevity — if not greatness. He was, in a way, the political equivalent of a tenured prof.

> *The height of his ambition was to pile a Parliamentary Committee on a Royal Commission.*
>
> — poet F.R. Scott on Mackenzie King's leadership style — or lack thereof

For more on Mackenzie King, go to `cnet.unb.ca/achn/pme/wlmkcb.htm` (part of a larger prime ministers' Web site).

Canada as a Middle Power

When Mackenzie King finally stepped down, he was replaced by Louis St. Laurent, a former lawyer who had served as King's most trusted "Québec lieutenant." Only our second French-Canadian PM, St. Laurent governed the country during some of its most prosperous, golden years. The press called him "Uncle Louis" in reference to his avuncular and carefully crafted public image, but St. Laurent was anything but folksy. He ran the country as though he were the CEO of a large corporation, and his temper was legendary. And unlike King, St. Laurent was no isolationist. He took Canada's commitments abroad very seriously.

NATO

In 1949, Canada and the United States joined forces with ten European states to create the North Atlantic Treaty Organization (NATO). Earlier, as King's Secretary of State for External Affairs, St. Laurent had been instrumental in the creation of this international alliance of Western states.

During these negotiations, Canada had fought to have a clause added (Article II, also called "the Canadian clause") that would have committed NATO to developing common economic aims and social values. The Americans, muttering all the while about this "typical example of Canadian moralizing," begrudgingly agreed, but the victory was a hollow one. Article II was never put into practise and NATO remained a strictly *military* alliance. It couldn't even be called a coalition of democracies, because its membership included Portugal, which was still a fascist dictatorship.

Was Canada's involvement in NATO necessary? Ill-advised? Unavoidable? Some historians have argued that in joining NATO, Canada had abandoned its traditional principles of tolerance and compromise. Others portrayed NATO as a trap that forced Canada into the quagmire of U.S. militarism. Others cried out that NATO had in fact turned Canadians into lapdogs of "American imperialism." Hindsight, however, is 20-20. Communist expansionism was a very real threat, and one that needed to be checked. Certainly, most Canadians favoured membership in NATO at the time, and the proposal passed with overwhelming support in the House of Commons. Only two MPs stood opposed.

And so, Louis St. Laurent was involved in NATO both at its inception (as a diplomat) and its launch (as PM). Under St. Laurent, Canada sought to position itself as "a middle power," able to influence the superpowers, while still maintaining good relations with all sides. This was later amended even further to "a moderate mediatory middle power." Exciting, no?

Being a "middle power" is like bragging about being a C-student.
— from *Why I Hate Canadians*

Newfoundland joins Canada (or is it the other way around?)

St. Laurent also extended Canadian independence on the homefront.

> ✔ In 1949, the Supreme Court of Canada was made the final court of appeal (replacing the British Privy Council in that regard).

> ✔ In 1952, Vincent Massey became the country's first Canadian-born Governor General.

But the greatest cause for celebration — from an unabashedly federalist viewpoint, at least — was when Newfoundlanders finally came onboard.

In 1949, Britain's oldest colony became Canada's newest province. During the war, Newfoundland's strategic — and vulnerable — geographic position had become clear. American troops had been stationed on the island since 1941, and the U.S. later built army bases there as well, signing on for 99-year leases. In the dawning age of intercontinental bombers, Newfoundland was an ideal military site, jutting out as it did into the North Atlantic. Canada and Britain also established a military presence on the island, and Newfoundland found itself pulled in three directions at once. Its options were as follows:

(a) Remain under direct British administration (something Britain was trying to discourage, if only to be rid of the expense and responsibility).

(b) Declare outright independence and return to a system of responsible government (something that might easily have pulled Newfoundland into the U.S. orbit as an American protectorate).

(c) Join Canada.

Spearheaded by a fast-talking, pig-farmer-turned-political-crusader by the name of Joey Smallwood, the Canadian option eventually won out — but only by the narrowest of margins: 52 percent in favour, 48 percent opposed — a difference of just 4 percent. The Avalon Peninsula, which includes St. John's, had voted heavily *against* Confederation, but the outlying regions helped tip the balance in Canada's favour. (This was actually the *second* referendum on the issue. In the first, Responsible Government had edged out Confederation, with British Rule coming in third. But the results were considered inconclusive, so a follow-up vote was held, and the next time around, Smallwood won.)

Labrador — going once, going twice . . .

Labrador is the harshest, most inhospitable place in Canada south of the Arctic Circle. Mountains plunge into the sea, and only a scattering of coastal fishing villages and a few newly created "Hydro Cities" have taken root. The rest is uninhabited — and uninhabitable. A colony of a colony, Labrador is Newfoundland's own distant outpost — and a source of ongoing friction with the bordering province of Québec. The headwaters of several key Québec hydro projects lie within Labrador's borders, something that causes no end of grumbled threats and gnashed teeth amongst Québec nationalists.

From 1774 to 1809, ownership of Labrador actually bounced back and forth between the two. At first only the shoreline was at stake, but in 1927, the British Privy Council awarded a huge chunk of real estate — the present-day boundary — solely to Newfoundland. And just five years later, Newfoundland offered Labrador up for sale. This wasn't the first time either. Newfoundland tried to sell Labrador's coast twice before, once in 1890 and once in 1923, but there were no takers.

On March 31, 1949, Newfoundland and Labrador joined Confederation as Canada's tenth province. (This date is sometimes given, incorrectly, as April 1, which was the original choice. Smallwood, however, arranged to have the union officially occur at one-minute before midnight, because, as he put it, he didn't want to spend the rest of his life hearing taunts about how Newfoundland joined Canada on April Fool's Day.)

As Newfoundland's first premier, Joey Smallwood ruled the province for more than 20 years, from 1949 to 1972, and along the way earned a reputation as both a strikebreaker and a lip-service socialist. As part of a controversial campaign to modernize the province, Smallwood was also responsible for shutting down several hundred remote outpost communities, forcing the residents to relocate. In his own words, Smallwood was determined to drag Newfoundlanders "kicking and screaming into the twentieth century." He forgot to add "weeping."

> *I know our Newfoundland people. I am one of them. I am blood of their blood, bone of their bone, soul of their soul . . .*
> — Joey Smallwood, Father of Confederation

> *Loved, feared, and hated.*
> — biographer Harold Horwood's summation of Joey Smallwood

For an excellent Newfoundland & Labrador Web site (with Confederation listed under "Government and Politics"), go to www.heritage.nf.ca/home.html. For a biography of Joey Smallwood (part of a larger "Encyclopedia of Newfoundland and Labrador" Web site), go to enl.cuff.com/entry/78/7807.htm.

The Indian Act of 1951

Native Canadians enlisted in proportionately higher numbers during World War II than did any other segment of the general population. Around 6,000 Native men signed up, and this in turn, had an unexpected side effect. When Native war veterans returned to their scattered reserves and sub-standard housing, the inequalities of Canadian society became glaring. Hadn't Canadian soldiers, Native and non-Native alike, fought to free the world from racial exclusion and ethnic oppression? Hadn't they gone to war for democracy? Freedom? Equality? And yet, back home, Native Canadians did not have full citizenship, were not allowed to vote, and still faced restrictions on their movement outside of their designated reserves. Led by church activists and Native war veterans, Canada's First Nations became increasingly politicized and increasingly vocal in their demands.

Faced with these growing protests from Canada's Natives, the government decided to revise the Indian Act — and for the first time *ever*, Native groups were involved in the discussions. The results weren't groundshaking. Native bands were given more control over their own financing and affairs, and some were even allowed to incorporate as municipalities. Overall, though, there were very few changes. Native Canadians were still not allowed to vote (although they could cast ballots in local band council elections), and the stated goal of the Indian Act was still the assimilation and disappearance of Native cultures. What had changed was the *process*. In this sense, the revised Indian Act of 1951 did mark an important shift. It was the first small step toward Native self-government.

Unfortunately, the revised act also enshrined discrimination against Native women, who automatically lost their legal status if they married a non-Native or non-status man. A Native woman who married a white man, for example, was no longer considered a Native. (Native men who married non-Natives, on the other hand, retained their full legal status.) Incredibly, this discriminatory clause was not removed until 1985.

Korea: Canada's forgotten war

At the end of World War II, the Korean peninsula was divided in half at the 38th parallel between the Soviet-backed communist government in the north and the U.S.-backed republic to the south. It was an uneasy truce — and it came crashing to an end on June 25, 1950, when North Korea launched a massive invasion of the south. The UN condemned the communist attack and the United States immediately began mustering support for a counterstrike. As luck would have it, the Soviets were boycotting the UN Security Council at that time and weren't able to veto the American plan for a multinational "police action."

Although 16 countries came to the aid of South Korea, the UN Force itself was, in essence, a U.S. operation. (It was also the first time that Canadians had ever served under U.S. leaders.) Canada supplied three battleships and a Royal Canadian Air Force (RCAF) transport squadron, and later sent in ground troops as well. The Korean War was the first great test of UN resolve. It was also a show of strength by the United States, which had now completely eclipsed Britain as the world's foremost military power. Symbolic of this change was the decision by Canada's armed forces to switch from British to American equipment, tactics, training, and weaponry, a move that had begun in 1947 and that was accelerated by the Korean War.

Things went badly for the UN "police force." American, South Korean, and British troops were pushed back to a final desperate toehold in the south as the Soviet-backed Northern Army steamrolled down the peninsula. But the UN forces under General MacArthur struck back at Inchon, west of Seoul, and succeeded in pushing the communists back, deep into their own territory. At this point, Red China, now under the rule of Mao Zedong, threw its might behind North Korea. Hundreds of thousands of Chinese troops poured in — and that's when it got *really* messy. The war cost more than three million lives, and at one point, the U.S. openly considered using nuclear weapons. At Kap'Yong, Canadian troops turned back a major Chinese advance and — along with Australian units — received a citation from the U.S. government for their bravery under fire.

The seesaw struggle for Korea eventually ended right back where it had started: at the 38th parallel. On July 27, 1953, a ceasefire left the Korean peninsula divided into two opposing armed camps. Since then, the South has become an industrialized democratic state, while the North remains mired in ideology and abject poverty. Of the nearly 30,000 Canadians who served in Korea, there were more than 1,550 casualties. Of these, 516 died.

You'll find more on Canada and the Korean War at www.vac-acc.gc.ca/general/sub.cfm?source=history/KoreaWar.

Missile trackers amid the tundra

Canada is the ham in the Soviet-American sandwich.
— comment made by the Soviet ambassador to Canada at the height of the Cold War

During the Cold War, Canada was caught in the middle. Literally. Modern intercontinental ballistic missiles (ICBMs) could deliver nuclear warheads across the pole in a matter of minutes, and if the U.S. and the Soviet Union ever went head to head, the shootout at the Armageddon Corral would be played out directly over the Great White North. During the 1950s a series of expensive radar lines were built across Canadian territory:

> ✔ **The Pinetree Line:** Running along the 50th parallel, it was completed in 1954. The whopping $450 million price tag was divided between the U.S., who paid two-thirds, and Canada, who paid one-third.
>
> ✔ **The Mid-Canada Line:** Completed in 1957, it ran along the 55th parallel and was built and paid for by Canada. A bargain at $250 million.
>
> ✔ **The Distant Early Warning (DEW) Line:** An engineering and construction marvel of more than 20 sites built along the 70th parallel of Canada's Arctic, it was completed in 1957 and paid for by Uncle Sam.

Was this a good thing, having American bases in Canada's Far North? Did the DEW Line represent a loss of national sovereignty? Or an affirmation? After all, Canada was now under the protection of the U.S. defensive umbrella — and for very little cost or commitment. Critics, however, warned that Canada had made a deal with the devil. We were caught in a crossfire, and when the bullets started to fly, Canadians were the ones who would pay the price.

The United Sates, meanwhile, was now asserting its authority over Canada's northern defenses. Canadian officials were not permitted to approach or enter DEW sites except with prior U.S. approval — even though these sites were, technically, on Canadian territory. Canada's newly forged military independence, having just been asserted during World War II, was now among the first casualties of the Cold War. Mind you, as part of the DEW Line agreement, the Americans formally — and *finally* — accepted Canada's Arctic claims, something that had remained unresolved since the 1880s. (The Northwest Passage, however, remained a bone of contention, with the Americans insisting, with good cause, that the passage was an *international* sea route.)

Keeping the peace: The Suez Crisis

Modern Canadian identity was born, almost by accident, in the Middle East. In 1956, Egyptian President Gamal Nasser seized the Suez Canal, which joined the Mediterranean and Red Seas. The canal was in Egyptian territory, but was managed by French and British moneymen. It was also one of the key supply routes for Arabian oil.

What followed has been described as "the last hurrah" of old-world European imperialism, the sort of gunboat diplomacy that had founded the French and British empires — and that had ended in the ashes of two world wars. Britain and France formed a secret pact with the beleaguered Jewish state of Israel for a joint operation against Egypt. As agreed, Israel attacked first, driving its tanks across the Sinai Desert to within striking distance of the Suez Canal. Britain and France then announced an ultimatum demanding that all armed forces — Egyptian and Israeli alike — withdraw from the region. Israel complied. Egypt refused, and the British and French began bombing the Canal Zone. Their goal was clear: to topple the Nasser government and regain ownership of the crucial supply route.

Britain and France had achieved the impossible: They had united the Soviet Union and the United States in a condemnation of the attack. The Soviets (who were even then in the process of stamping out democracy in Hungary) threatened to bomb Paris and London. The Americans demanded that the Anglo-French occupation forces be withdrawn immediately. And the world teetered on the brink of World War III.

Only Australia and New Zealand stood by Mother Britain's side. In Canada, a request for public support was met with a chilly response from St. Laurent, who made it very clear that Canada's first obligation in international affairs was now to the UN Charter, and not to Britain. During the Boer War in 1899, World War I in 1914, and World War II in 1939, Canada's response had been unequivocal. "Ready, aye ready!" Those days were over. Indeed, historians Norman Hillmer and J.L. Granatstein have described Prime Minister St. Laurent's refusal to support Britain during the Suez Crisis of 1956 as "the de facto end of the British Empire in Canada."

As events spun out of control, Canada's position as a "mediatory middle power" was now put to good use. Lester Pearson, Canada's top diplomat and a former president of the UN General Assembly, came to the rescue. Pearson, a soft-spoken man who spoke with a slight lisp, had once been nicknamed "Mike" by an airforce instructor who felt Lester wasn't "tough enough." Now, addressing the UN General Assembly, Pearson argued for the creation of a UN peacekeeping force.

> *We need action not only to end the fighting but to make the peace.*
> — Lester "Mike" Pearson in his historic UN address

After tireless, endless, persistent lobbying on Pearson's part, the worlds' first international peacekeeping mission was organized. Armed troops would position themselves between warring factions and impose a ceasefire. They would wade in and *make* peace happen. It was bold, heroic, and more than a bit naive. It was very, very Canadian.

General E.L.M. Burns of the Canadian Armed Forces was put in charge of the United Nations Emergency Force (UNEF), but Egypt rejected the use of Canadian soldiers. The reason? The Canadians still wore British-style uniforms and served under a flag that included a prominent Union Jack. The Canadian Queen's Own Rifles even bore a name similar to one of the British units that had invaded the Canal Zone. Canada still bore the stigma of a British colony, in perception if not in fact. (It was something Pearson never forgot. Years later, as PM, he gave Canada a new "distinctly Canadian" flag.) In Egypt, Canada supplied administrative troops instead.

Lester Pearson, the architect of UN peacekeeping, had saved the world from war, and for this he was awarded the 1957 Nobel Peace Prize. Today, Canadians take a certain proprietorial pride in peacekeeping, both in its origins and its ideals. But public opinion at the time was divided. Many Canadians were critical of Pearson's initiative and scornful of St. Laurent for turning his back on Britain and France, Canada's two "founding nations."

Farewell to Uncle Louis

The Liberals had now been in power for 22 years straight. They had grown autocratic and insensitive over the years, but they had also launched several important mega-projects:

- ✔ **Trans-Canada Highway:** started in 1949 and completed in 1962, after the Liberals had left office

- ✔ **St Lawrence Seaway:** started in 1954 and officially opened in 1959, also after the Liberals had left office

- ✔ **TransCanada PipeLines:** incorporated in 1951 and completed in 1958 — again, after the Liberals had left office

The St. Lawrence Seaway, a billion-dollar joint project with the U.S., opened up the interior of the continent to ocean-going freighters. Near Montréal, the seaway cut through the Mohawk territory of Kahnawake. More than 500 hectares of land were taken and dozens of homes lost as the water passage was blasted and bulldozed along the edge of reserve. The Mohawk were now cut off from the great river that had figured so prominently in their history (see Chapter 1). This was called progress.

For more on the history and importance of the St. Lawrence Seaway, go to collections.ic.gc.ca/stlauren/.

But the straw that broke the Liberals' back was the great pipeline debate of 1956. C.D. Howe, now minister of trade and commerce, had worked out a deal with U.S. investors to build a 3,700-kilometre gas pipeline from Western Canada, north of Lake Superior, all the way to Montréal. To meet a deadline, Howe and the Liberals ran roughshod over Parliament, invoking closure (cutting off debate) again and again in order to force the legislation through without amendments. When the 1957 elections rolled around, their arrogance would come back to haunt them.

The Tories, now known by the wonderfully contradictory name of "Progressive Conservatives," (having merged with the members of the Progressive Party in 1942), were led by a firebrand prairie populist from Saskatchewan named John Diefenbaker. And in 1957, Diefenbaker surprised everyone by beating the Liberals and winning the election. It was a slim victory. St. Laurent might have cobbled together a coalition with the CCF or the SoCreds and stayed in power, but his heart was no longer in it.

> *They just got tired of seeing us around.*
> — a disheartened St. Laurent on the Liberal defeat of 1957

Diefenbaker: Renegade in Power

They called him "the Chief," and he shook things up right from the start. John Diefenbaker upped the old age pension, he increased wheat payments to farmers, and he immediately signed a North American Air Defense agreement (NORAD) that integrated U.S. and Canadian systems — although "integrate" is somewhat misleading. With NORAD, Canada's air defenses were pretty much put under U.S. control. The pact was derided by the Liberal Opposition as a rash surrender of Canadian autonomy.

Louis St. Laurent, meanwhile, had stepped down, and the leadership of the Liberal Party now passed to Lester Pearson, the Saviour of Suez and the only Canadian ever to win the Nobel Peace Prize. Surely, that alone would put him over the top? Nope. Faced with Dief's thundering oratory, Pearson seemed awkward and unexciting. Diefenbaker, in the words of one historian, "roasted" Pearson with his rhetoric.

Diefenbaker had taken office just as the post-war boom began to cool. Unemployment was now on the rise, and the German economy had already surpassed Canada's. When Pearson glibly suggested that the minority-government Conservatives hand power back to the "more experienced" Liberals, Diefenbaker pounced on the challenge. He dissolved Parliament and called a snap election.

Dief was a charismatic campaigner, a man of bombast and grand vague visions. "I see a new Canada!" he proclaimed. "A Canada of the North!" Canadians, he assured voters, had "a rendezvous with destiny!" What exactly that meant no one was sure. But it certainly sounded good.

> *Humbug and flapdoodle served up with an evangelistic flourish.*
> — the *Toronto Star*'s evaluation of Dief's grandiose style

It worked. Pearson and the Liberals were absolutely trounced. In 1958, Diefenbaker won what was then the largest landslide in Canadian history. The biggest breakthrough was in Québec, where Maurice Duplessis of the Union Nationale threw his weight behind the Conservatives. Nationally, Diefenbaker won 208 seats to the Liberals' 49 and the CCF's 8. Ironically, Diefenbaker's lopsided victory was probably the worst thing that could have happened to him. It was too much, too soon. He didn't have the experience or the ability to wield that kind of power, let alone deal with what historian P.B. Waite referred to as "the horde of incompetent backbenchers who had ridden into the House of Commons on his bandwagon."

The 15 percent promise

Diefenbaker was all heart and no brains. He saw himself as the political reincarnation of John A. Macdonald. Still sentimentally attached to the ol' British Empire, and deeply suspicious of the Americans, Dief announced soon after becoming PM that henceforth Canada would divert 15 percent of its imports from the U.S. to Great Britain. This percentage, chosen apparently at whim, sounds modest but in fact it represented a massive shift in trade to the amount of $625 million a year — almost doubling total British imports.

The Americans, aghast at Diefenbaker's plans, pointed out that Canada had signed the 1947 General Agreement on Tariffs and Trade (GATT), which had been created specifically to increase world trade and open up international markets — partly as a way of avoiding the sort of self-destructive protectionism that had helped prolong the Great Depression of the 1930s. Under the terms of GATT, one nation could not arbitrarily favour another. The only way around this would be to create a special "free trade zone" between Canada and Britain, something that would have required a complete restructuring of Canadian trade regulations.

Needless to say, Diefenbaker's daft scheme never did get implemented, and all he succeeded in doing was annoying both the Americans *and* the Brits. It was a telling sign of things to come. A great, symbolic, romantic gesture — made without considering its feasibility — the "15 percent promise" summed up the entire Diefenbaker approach to governing.

The Arrow

Ironically, it was one of Dief's few practical decisions that has garnered him the most criticism over the years. Under Louis St. Laurent, the A.V. Roe (Avro) air research company of Malton, Ontario, was given a government contract to develop a state-of-the-art supersonic fighter jet. The CF-105 Arrow was a magnificent craft designed to intercept Soviet bombers over the Arctic. It was also exceedingly expensive. As costs soared and sales abroad failed to materialize, Diefenbaker pulled the plug.

The Avro Arrow contract was cancelled on February 20, 1959, a day still mourned by many as a "Black Friday" for Canadian sovereignty. A.V. Roe fired 14,000 workers, many of them highly trained engineers who packed up and went south in a mass "brain drain."

The prototypes of the Arrow were cut up and scrapped, and the pre-production models destroyed. The Arrow hadn't even been fully test-flown. Why the existing planes were so quickly destroyed remains a mystery, and conspiracy theories abound. There is even a persistent rumour that a single Arrow did survive and has since been kept in secret storage. ("Where it is taken out and flown once a year. By Elvis," as historian Michael Bliss dryly notes.) Avro Canada was also working on a top-secret "flying saucer," code-named Project Y, which — as far as I'm concerned — makes Malton, Ontario, Canada's answer to Roswell. Cue eerie *X-Files* theme music.

Did Diefenbaker make the right choice? Most historians seem to think he did, but Canadian nationalists disagree — vehemently. They argue that Dief didn't kill just an airplane, but rather an entire industry. For all his anti-American posturing, Dief had made Canada *less* independent and *more* tied to U.S. technology than ever before. The Arrow became an emblem of Canadian innovation sold out by unimaginative bureaucrats who kowtowed to the Yanks. The controversy continues, and the tale of the lost Arrow has long since entered the realm of myth, an eternal, tantalizing *"If only . . ."*

Never mind that the Liberals themselves were preparing to cancel the Arrow as well — and certainly would have if they'd won the election. It was Diefenbaker who took the blame. Whether or not he made the right call, Dief certainly bungled the *way* it was handled. He stated (incorrectly) that planes such as the Arrow were now outdated, having been made obsolete by long-range missiles. He then turned around and purchased a bunch of second-hand, second-rate U.S. planes. Dief also declared Canada a "nuclear-free zone." He then brought in American-built Bomarc surface-to-air missiles — which were meant to be armed with nuclear warheads. They ended up being stuffed with sandbags instead. At $685 million, they must rank as the most expensive duds ever produced. By then, Dief's minister of defense had quit in disgust, and Diefenbaker's "reign of error" had begun to crumble.

> The Arrow cancellation was the right choice made the wrong way . . .
> [Diefenbaker] had taken one hard look at the costs of technological
> independence, quailed, and fled.
>
> — historian Desmond Morton

The Canadian Bill of Rights

> I am a Canadian . . . free to speak without fear, free to worship God in my own way, free to stand for what I think right, free to oppose what I believe wrong, free to choose those who shall govern my country.
> — from the pledge of the 1960 Bill of Rights

John Diefenbaker was of German descent, and he was keenly aware of the fact that he was the first PM of neither purely British nor French stock. Dief believed in expanding human rights and in creating a wider, more inclusive nation. In international and economic affairs, he was a bungling and dangerously inept leader. But in terms of social progress, his heart was in the right place. An example of this was his 1960 Canadian Bill of Rights.

The Bill of Rights declared equality of race, religion, and beliefs as the framework for Canadian law. Only problem was, the bill itself was unworkable. As a federal statute, it wasn't enshrined in the Constitution and lacked any authority within provincial courts. As one wag noted, Diefenbaker's Bill of Rights protected all Canadians "except those who lived in provinces." All it did was confuse the issue of individual rights and muddy the waters of federal-provincial jurisdiction. It was a typical Diefenbaker "achievement": one of lofty ideals that was, ultimately, hollow. Still, Dief did make several important inroads while in office:

- ✔ It was Diefenbaker who granted the vote to Native Canadians in 1960.

- ✔ He also appointed Canada's first Native senator, James Gladstone (Akay-na-muka) of the Blood, in 1958.

- ✔ In 1957, he named Hamilton MP Ellen Fairclough as Secretary of State, making her Canada's first female cabinet minister.

- ✔ In 1962, he ended the blatantly discriminatory immigration quotas that had been installed by Mackenzie King.

- ✔ He helped end the Commonwealth's status as "a club for white nations" by supporting the inclusion of Ghana, the Commonwealth's first African member state.

- ✔ He was also instrumental in forcing South Africa out of the Commonwealth for its system of racial *apartheid* (the segregation and restrictions put in place against the country's black majority).

- ✔ He set up a Broadcast Board, which approved Canada's first private television network, making Diefenbaker the unofficial "Father of CTV." (Just as R.B. Bennett had been the "Father of CBC," as I describe in Chapter 18.)

Diefenbaker also helped boost Western Canadian agriculture by arranging wheat sales to Red China. But overall, he was a disaster as PM: vindictive, erratic, indecisive, and tyrannical, with a sense of self-worth that bordered on clinical megalomania. And his regime was about to self-destruct . . .

Farewell to the Chief

In 1962, the Cold War heated up. U.S. President Kennedy pushed the world to the edge of an all-out nuclear war in a showdown with the Soviet Union over missile bases in Cuba. And during one of the tensest moments in human history, Diefenbaker fumbled the ball. Canada was the only U.S. ally who didn't offer a prompt reply to the American request for support. (If Dief had done this as an assertion of Canadian independence — refusing to answer "Ready, aye ready!" to the demands of the American Empire — it might have been one thing. But Dief's response wasn't bold or heroic; it was bumbling and inept, and all it did was heighten the crisis.) Lester Pearson, meanwhile, having gauged public opinion like a true Liberal, performed an impressive flip-flop, reversing his earlier "non-nuclear" policy.

Diefenbaker hated Kennedy. Envious of his youthful vigour — and always suspicious of American intentions — Diefenbaker actually attempted to blackmail the U.S. president at one stage. It's true. During a state visit to Canada, an aide to Kennedy accidentally left behind a private memo outlining U.S. objectives for the meeting. In one of the most bizarre actions ever taken by a Canadian PM, Diefenbaker — rather than return the classified document — attempted instead to use it for political leverage, threatening the White House with its exposure. Kennedy, contemptuous of Dief, considered the prime minister to be "nothing but a platitudinous old bore."

On the homefront, Diefenbaker was just as bad. He clashed headlong with James Coyne, the outspoken governor of the Bank of Canada (responsible for Canadian monetary policy). Coyne, in turn, denounced Diefenbaker as "an evil genius" and angrily resigned in 1961. Soon after, the Canadian dollar was devalued, plummeting to 92.5 cents U.S. *Scandalous!!*

Diefenbaker won a minority government in 1962 and tried to cling to power. But with his nuclear policy and defense plans in utter disarray, and his own ministers deserting him like rats leaving a ship, Dief sputtered and spewed to no avail. His government collapsed, and the following year, the Tories were defeated at the polls. The Diefenbaker Era (1957–63) was over, although Dief himself hung on in Opposition until 1967, tormenting Lester Pearson endlessly and denying the Liberals an outright majority.

> *Everyone is against me except the people.*
> — common Diefenbaker lament

At www.canadianprimeministers.com/biogs.html you'll find more on St. Laurent and Diefenbaker — and all of Canada's prime ministers. For a fascinating tour of the "Diefenbunker," now Canada's Cold War Museum: www.diefenbunker.ca. For a list of links regarding the Avro Arrow, go to diefenbaker.ottawa.com/arrow.htm (part of a larger, extensive, eccentric — and very informative Diefenbaker Web site).

Part VIII

Noisy Evolution

(1960–2000)

The leadership styles of three past Conservative prime ministers:
John A. Macdonald, John Diefenbaker, and Brian Mulroney.

In this part . . .

Lester Pearson guides Canada through the tumultuous years of the mid-1960s before handing over power to Pierre Trudeau. French-Canadian nationalism boils over. Bombs go off. Martial law is declared. A separatist government is elected in Québec and a referendum on sovereignty is held. Trudeau is replaced by Brian Mulroney, and Canada veers sharply to the right and into the American orbit. Separatism in Québec is revived and a *second* referendum is held. This time around it's a squeaker, but the No side wins again. And thus, Canada limps into the 21st century more or less intact . . .

Chapter 21

The Battle for Québec

In This Chapter

▶ Lester Pearson takes office at the height of Québec's Quiet Revolution

▶ Canada's 100th birthday party is marked by Expo 67, a World's Fair in Montréal

▶ Terrorist kidnappings lead to martial law and mass arrests

▶ Pierre Trudeau introduces a program of economic nationalism

*I*t was the best of times, it was the worst of times. It was a time of powerful political crusades and silly "consciousness raising" sessions. It was a time of progress. And a time of unrest. A time of unyielding ideology and self-righteous sincerity. The Age of Aquarius. In a word: the Sixties. Nowhere in Canada did the 1960s hit with quite the force that they did in Québec. The shock waves of that era would last for decades and shake Canada to its very foundations. And the entire chain of events began, domino-like, with a single provincial election.

The Quiet Revolution

In June 1960, the Union Nationale was defeated by Jean Lesage and the Québec Liberal Party. Maurice Duplessis, the autocratic leader of the Union Nationale (I introduce you to him and his party in Chapter 18), had died in office the year before and the party went through two leaders in quick succession before falling to Lesage's Liberals.

It was more than a mere changing of the guards. Lesage's victory marked the start of a stunning transformation of Québec society, one that happened on all fronts: political, social, cultural, and industrial. In his first month alone, Lesage announced a project a day. Education was overhauled, Québec's hydroelectricity industry was nationalized, and the power of the Church was quickly dismantled. They called it the Quiet Revolution. *La révolution tranquille.* Overnight, Québec went from being a sleepy, priest-ridden society — an "anachronism in North America," in one writer's words — to becoming a modern, energetic entity. English Canadians cheered from the sidelines, little realizing that the driving force behind these events was a newly ignited sense of nationalism. It was exhilarating — and explosive.

Maîtres chez nous! (Masters in our own house!)
— battle cry of Québec's Quiet Revolution

The reign of Maurice Duplessis has been portrayed — accurately, I think — as a sort of Dark Ages in Québec history. *La Grande Noirceur* (the "Great Gloom"). And yet, it was Duplessis himself who set the stage, unwittingly, for the radical reforms that followed. It was Duplessis, after all, who first broke the power of the Church in Québec and shifted it to the Office of the Premier. He instilled a fierce sense of pride among the Québécois, and, more importantly, he left behind sizeable budgetary surpluses, which the Liberals used to fund their first wave of projects. If Lesage was the "Father of the Quiet Revolution," Duplessis, the gnarled old tyrant, was the Grandfather.

Jean Lesage, a hard-working, hard-drinking man, blazed a trail across the political map, modernizing Québec's outdated labour laws, introducing a provincial pension scheme, strengthening women's rights and social programs, and modernizing Québec's civil service. As might be expected, he was also confident to the point of cockiness: a man of great ego and appetite.

Jean Lesage is the only person I know who can strut sitting down.
— Prime Minister Diefenbaker

Not only had Québec caught up to Canada, it had roared right past. John Diefenbaker, in power when the Quiet Revolution began, was hopelessly unqualified to deal with the challenge. True, Dief did make some gestures to Québec: He introduced simultaneous translations in the House of Commons, and in 1959 he appointed Canada's first French-Canadian Governor General, Georges Vanier, a distinguished diplomat and hero of World War I. But for the most part, Dief was way, way out of his depth.

Little Louis and the "other" Quiet Revolution

In New Brunswick, a second revolution was underway. In 1960, Louis Robichaud, or "P'tit Louis" as he was affectionately known, became the first Acadian ever to be elected premier. (An Acadian had once held office briefly between leaders, but hadn't actually been voted in.) Although more than a third of New Brunswickers were French-speaking Acadians, they were still largely underrepresented and even marginalized within the province. Robichaud set out to change this, and he did it with energy and verve. He brought in French-language public schools and launched a francophone campus, the University of Moncton. He drafted legislation that would make New Brunswick the country's first — and only — officially bilingual province. He also introduced far-ranging social and labour reforms, something that pitted him against the might of the Irving Empire, an economic force in the Maritimes. In his ten years in power (1960–70) Louis Robichaud helped revitalize both New Brunswick — and Acadia.

Under Lesage, Québec opted out of 29 different federal-provincial cost-sharing projects — mainly as an assertion of provincial rights. But although Lesage often clashed with Ottawa, he was never a separatist. (Lesage preferred something he called "co-operative federalism.") Among his ministers, however, was a rumpled ex-journalist named René Lévesque, who was growing increasingly impatient with Lesage's federalist stance.

Pearson: Peacemaker as PM

Lester Pearson was an internationally respected statesman. As the "inventor" of UN peacekeeping (see Chapter 20), he had helped avert a world war and had been honoured with the Nobel Peace Prize. But nothing had prepared him for the rough-and-tumble of national politics — or Diefenbaker's relentless assaults.

Under Pearson, the Liberals finally managed to dislodge John Diefenbaker in 1963, but they were unable to gain a clear majority of seats in the House. This left Pearson in an extremely precarious position. (A second election two years later had the same results. Pearson never did gain a majority.) During the 1963 campaign, Pearson had promised "60 Days of Decision!" a slogan that would come back to haunt him as his government became mired in false starts and endless *in*decision. Pearson's finance minister, Walter Gordon, was an ardent economic nationalist who attempted to bring in a budget that would have blocked foreign takeovers of Canadian industries, but the scheme was so muddled and unpopular that Pearson was forced to beat a hasty retreat. Not a good start.

The Vietnam War: "You peed on my rug!"

Once he was elected, Pearson quickly patched things up with Kennedy. (During the Diefenbaker years, Canada–U.S. relations had reached an all-time low.) But Kennedy was assassinated just eight months later, and was replaced by a loud-mouthed Texas redneck named Lyndon B. Johnson.

Under Johnson, the Americans increased their military presence in Southeast Asia, pumping money and men into a doomed war of attrition against communist forces in Vietnam. When Pearson was invited to Temple University in Philadelphia in 1965 to accept a prestigious World Peace Award, he used the event to criticize U.S. military policy. When Johnson heard about this, he was livid. In his mind, it was a breach of diplomatic protocol for a head of one state to criticize another "in his own backyard." (An odd gaffe, considering Pearson's background in diplomacy.) When Pearson met up with Johnson later, the president went ballistic. He grabbed the Canadian PM by the shirt and bellowed, "You peed on my rug!" Pearson emerged from the manhandling looking distraught and shaken.

During the Vietnam War, at least 500 Canadian firms supplied war materials to the United States, everything from ammunition to aircraft engines to napalm (a particularly nasty form of "liquid fire"), as well as a deadly herbicide/defoliate known as "Agent Orange," which was tested at a Canadian base in Gagetown, New Brunswick.

Incredibly, more than 10,000 Canadian men went south to the U.S. to volunteer for combat in Vietnam (including the brother of a friend of mine from Moncton, who came back shattered, both physically and otherwise). At the same time, more than 32,000 American draft dodgers and army deserters fled north. My parents were part of an "underground railway" of safe houses that helped funnel draft dodgers into Canada. We were living in a farmhouse south of Regina at the time, not far from the U.S. border, and though I was only four or five years old back then, I remember vividly this procession of scared young men coming through our house.

Redefining Canada

At home, Pearson worked to improve Canada's economic base and broaden the country's social safety net. Among the legislation passed during Pearson's time in office (1963–68) were the following:

- ✔ **The Auto Pact (1965):** an agreement that removed duties on trucks, cars, and automotive parts moving between Canada and the U.S. As an experiment in "one-industry" free trade, the pact was a rip-roaring economic success. (President Johnson often complained that the U.S. "got screwed by Canada" in the Auto Pact.)

- ✔ **Canada Pension Plan (1965):** A mandatory investment fund, the CPP pools money deducted from wages to provide a minimum standard of living for Canada's elderly. (Québec has its own separate pension plan.)

- ✔ **National Medicare (1968):** Saskatchewan's CCF government had already created Canada's very first public health care system in 1962, against strong opposition from the province's doctors, who launched a bitter strike in response. The system itself was a success, and Pearson wanted to create a similar one nationally. After extensive, angry debate, Pearson's Medical Care Act came into effect, with Ottawa paying 50 percent of the cost and the provinces retaining control over administration.

- ✔ **Capital punishment abolished:** Under Pearson, capital punishment was put on "temporary" hold. This, in turn, was made official in 1976 by Pierre Trudeau, who allowed a free vote (that is, not along party lines) on the issue in the House of Commons. It's just as well that Parliament voted to abolish the death penalty. Over the last few years, several high-profile cases have involved people who were wrongly convicted of murder — only to later be set free. If Canada still had capital punishment, they would have been executed.

Pearson managed to do all of this in just five years, without ever having a majority government. Remarkable.

Canada's flag

As PM, Lester Pearson's most enduring legacy was Canada's national flag: that stylized red maple leaf Canadians now sew so proudly on their backpacks. Prior to this, the Red Ensign was used in lieu of a national flag, with a Union Jack in one corner and a coat-of-arms in the other. Pearson, however, wanted to create a flag that was truly and distinctly Canadian, one without imperial baggage or colonial symbolism (in other words, no Union Jacks or fleurs-de-lis). The original proposal was for three green maple leaves bordered by blue. Diefenbaker, an ardent old-school monarchist, was outraged. He wanted the British Empire honoured on Canada's flag and he derided the proposed banner as "the Pearson Pennant." The great flag debates of 1964 were brutal and exhausting. Pearson let it drag on for six long months before finally bringing in closure (shutting down debate and forcing a vote). It ended with the Liberals rising to sing "O Canada" and the Tories, led by Dief, replying with a defiant — and very noisy — rendition of "God Save the Queen!"

Twice before, in 1925 and again in 1946, Mackenzie King had toyed with the idea of giving Canada its own flag — only to back down in the face of opposition. In 1964, historian George F.G. Stanley, working without a ruler, came up with a new design, and a 20-year-old Ottawa seamstress named Joan O'Malley followed his rough sketches to create Canada's first flags — four in all. Stanley's design was inspired by the red-and-white emblem of the Royal Military College in Kingston, where he was one of the deans. (The maple leaf itself is an historic Canadian symbol, used as far back as 1700. By World War I, Canadian soldiers wore maple leaf badges, and in 1960 even the Royal Canadian Legion adopted a red maple leaf as its emblem.)

On February 15, 1965, Canada's national flag, with its single red maple leaf, was raised for the first time above the Peace Tower in Ottawa. In a very real sense, it was a declaration — not of independence — but of identity.

> *The search for a flag was really a search for a country.*
> — John Matheson, MP, who headed the search for a new flag

For a good overview of Canada's national symbols (everything from the coat of arms to the flag to the beaver), go to home.ican.net/~marlatt/craig/symbols.html. At fraser.cc/FlagsCan/toc.html you'll find an extensive and informative look at Canada's flags and symbols, provincial and national. For more on Canada's flag (with links to provincial flags as well), visit www.fotw.stm.it/flags/ca.html. You can find flags of Canada before 1965 at www.fotw.stm.it/flags/ca-1868.html. To look at some of the proposed designs (including the Pearson Pennant) go to www.fotw.stm.it/flags/ca-prop.html. And you'll find John Ross Matheson's own history of the flag debates at collections.ic.gc.ca/flag.

The status of women

During the 1960s, the women's movement became increasingly militant. (See Chapter 17 for information on women seeking the vote in Canada.) In 1966, university activist Laura Sabia sent out a call for a united front, and 32 different women's groups came together to form the Committee for the Equality of Women in Canada. Within a year, the group had forced the Pearson government to launch a Royal Commission on the Status of Women, which was chaired by journalist and broadcaster Florence Bird.

Bird submitted her report three years later, in 1970, after criss-crossing the country and reviewing hundreds of briefs. She made over 160 different recommendations aimed at improving opportunities and equality for women. The recommendations covered everything from education to family law. Ottawa tried to avoid the issue, hoping that it might die down over time, but if anything, the determination of the women's movement grew. And in 1972, the National Action Committee for the Equality of Women (NAC) was formed, bringing together 300 feminist groups from across Canada, and dedicated to seeing the recommendations made in the Bird Report put into practice.

> *A call to revolution.*
>
> — *Toronto Star* description of the Bird Report

1967: The last good year?

It was Canada's centennial year. The 100th anniversary of Confederation! And Canadian nationalism was at an all-time high. The Order of Canada, created by Pearson in 1967 to honour Canadian achievement, exemplified this newly awakened pride. But not everyone was as enamoured with the centennial. Québec separatists certainly saw no cause for celebration, and they adopted the cry *"Cent ans d'injustice!"* ("100 years of injustice!") to mark the anniversary. Still, it was a good time to be Canadian. Optimism was up, the future was bright, and the economy was doing well — so what if there were dark undercurrents lying in wait just below the surface?

Canada's centennial celebrations coincided with the Montréal World's Fair, dubbed Expo 67, which was staged on an artificial island in the St. Lawrence under the heading "Man and his World." Pierre Berton has dubbed 1967 "the last good year," which seems awfully churlish to those of us who weren't born then or, in my case, weren't even in kindergarten yet. (Apparently, I grew up *after* Canada's "best" years. Just my luck.)

Expo 67 was one of Mayor Jean Drapeau's wild schemes. (Much of the dirt used to create the artificial island had, in typical Drapeau fashion, been taken from the earth excavated during the construction of Montréal's new, rubber-wheeled subway system — which was another Drapeau project.) Expo 67 was a great success, with its space-age geodesic dome and its glittering array of world pavilions. Canada was suddenly hip, and Peter C. Newman declared Expo 67 "the greatest thing we have ever done as a nation." Gosh. Greater than the Last Spike or Vimy Ridge or Suez? I guess you had to be there.

If you'd like to know the full story of how they built the Expo 67 site, go to naid.sppsr.ucla.edu/expo67/map-docs/buildingexpo.htm.

"Vive le Québec libre!"

He said it reminded him of Paris after it was liberated from the Nazis. General Charles de Gaulle, president of France, was referring to the cheering crowds that had greeted him in Montréal as he arrived to attend Expo 67. The insult was clear: Québec was an occupied country waiting to be freed from Anglo oppressors. But De Gaulle was only warming up. His attack on Canadian Confederation was about to be taken to a new level.

At a St. Jean Baptiste Day celebration on June 24, 1967, General de Gaulle addressed the crowds from a balcony at Montréal's City Hall. "*Vive le Montréal!*" he cried. "*Vive le Québec!*" And then — the bombshell: "*Vive le Québec libre!*" The crowds roared. It was the slogan of the separatists, and the effect was electrifying. De Gaulle had, in effect, legitimized the radical wing of Québec's nationalist movement, had given the separatists an international stamp of approval. Talk about "peeing on someone's rug." Prime Minister Pearson stated that De Gaulle's actions were "unacceptable" and the French leader's visit was abruptly cut short.

> *Canadians do not need to be liberated. Indeed, many thousands of Canadians gave their lives in two world wars in the liberation of France . . .*
> — Pearson's pointed reply to General de Gaulle

B&B and "the Three Wise Men"

Pearson had taken office at the height of the Quiet Revolution, and he knew the ground was shifting beneath his feet. In 1963, Pearson established the Royal Commission on Bilingualism and Biculturalism to examine the growing crisis in Ottawa–Québec relations and recommend changes. André Laurendeau, editor-in-chief of *Le Devoir*, and A. Davidson Dunton, former head of CBC, were appointed co-chairmen.

In 1965, Pearson recruited three leading Québec activists to join the federal government and help staunch the growth of separatism. The press called them "the three wise men":

- ✔ **Jean Marchand,** labour leader.
- ✔ **Gérard Pelletier,** activist and editor of *La Presse.*
- ✔ **Pierre Elliott Trudeau,** law professor and one of the founders, along with Pelletier, of *Cité libre,* an influential journal of social critique.

Trudeau, the son of a self-made millionaire, was something of an intellectual gadfly. Fluently bilingual and ruthlessly rational, he studied at Harvard, the University of Paris, and the London School of Economics. As a young man, he backpacked and hitchhiked his way around the world, travelling through some of the most dangerous places on the planet and surviving on his wits alone. As an eyewitness to wars and revolutions in China, Israel, India, and Southeast Asia, Trudeau developed a deep and long-lasting distaste for ethnic nationalism — and that included the separatists of Québec.

Tensions between Ottawa and Québec were about to escalate. In 1966, a stunned Jean Lesage was dumped by the voters, but the reforms he helped launch continued, like a runaway horse that throws its rider and races on in full gallop. Jean Lesage's term as premier (1960–66) was over, but the Quiet Revolution was not. Québec's new premier, Daniel Johnson of the Union Nationale, kept Lesage's agenda in tact and in some cases took them even further, particularly in the area of provincial powers. Johnson's slogan, *"Equality or independence!"* was a dark foreshadowing of things to come.

Pierre Trudeau, named minister of justice in 1967, often went head-to-head with Daniel Johnson over Québec's ever-increasing, ever-expanding, never-ending demands. Johnson wanted a constitutional amendment giving Québec — not French Canadians as a people, mind you, but the actual provincial government — distinct status within Confederation as one of Canada's "two founding nations." Trudeau refused.

As minister of justice, Trudeau also brought in several key changes to the Criminal Code. He introduced measures to liberalize divorce laws and end restrictions on homosexuality and access to abortion. Private morality should not, in Trudeau's view of liberalism, be subjected to government legislation.

The state has no business in the bedrooms of the nation.
— Pierre Trudeau

The Philosopher King

In 1968, Lester Pearson retired, and in the hard-fought leadership convention that followed, Trudeau won on the fourth ballot to become the new leader of the Liberal Party and Canada's 15th prime minister. A new era had begun and Canada would never be the same again.

Trudeaumania

Trudeau immediately dissolved Parliament and called an election, and under the enigmatic and somewhat cerebral slogan "the Just Society," he began barnstorming across Canada. Young, suave, and free-spirited, Trudeau seemed to capture the spirit of the age. He was less a public leader than he was a star, and a wave of giddy excitement, at times bordering on hysteria, swept the land. They called it "Trudeaumania."

> *For a few warm spring months in 1968, Pierre Elliott Trudeau synthesized the dreams, achievements, and illusions of the liberation era.*
> — historian Desmond Morton

But beneath the glib, playboy image and the intellectual musings lay a cold and unyielding man. Peter C. Newman described Trudeau as an "existential hero" who had "an icicle for a heart." Trudeau's steely nature became clear early on, at the end of the 1968 election campaign, when Trudeau attended the annual St. Jean Baptiste Day celebrations in Montréal. The PM was in the bandstands with other dignitaries watching the parade when separatist agitators surged forward, hurling bricks and bottles. As the projectiles flew, everyone in the stands fled. Everyone except Pierre Trudeau. He waved away his bodyguard and sat, alone, watching the parade as bottles and rocks whizzed past, some shattering just beside him. Trudeau never flinched. Mayor Drapeau quickly returned as well, having escorted his wife to safety, and together they stared the rioters down. It was a brilliant bit of public theatre. That single moment, as much as anything else, won Pierre Trudeau the respect of Canadians — and the federal election, which was held the very next day.

The Official Languages Act of 1969

Want to know why we have French on the back of Corn Flakes boxes and bilingual federal tax forms that are equally confusing in both official languages? You can thank Pierre Trudeau. Or blame him, depending on your bias. It was Trudeau who brought in official bilingualism in 1969, based largely on preliminary reports submitted by the Royal Commission of Bilingualism and Biculturalism, which had originally been appointed by Lester Pearson.

The point of the Official Languages Act (OLA) was not, as some feared, to "shove French down our throats," but rather to ensure that Canadians, French or English, had access to federal services in their own language. So why the big fuss? Why the whole *"Bilingual today, French tomorrow!"* hysteria? Beats me. The OLA was followed, in turn, by regulations that required bilingual labelling on commercial products. Hence, our all-Canadian Corn Flakes.

The White Paper on Indian Affairs

With Trudeau in power you had to be careful of what you asked for. When Native groups complained that the Indian Act was discriminatory, Trudeau said, "Fine. Get rid of it." In 1969, Trudeau's minister of Indian affairs, a young MP named Jean Chrétien, presented a white paper on Native issues. (Government documents are colour coded; a white paper is an official but non-binding policy proposal.) The White Paper of 1969 was drafted without consulting a single Native group in Canada — and it showed. Among other things, the paper proposed

✔ Abolishing the Indian Act

✔ Getting rid of the Department of Indian Affairs

✔ Transferring most of the responsibility for Native rights to the provinces

✔ Eliminating reserve lands and ending special status for Native Canadians

The ultimate aim was to dismantle the reserve system and bring Natives into mainstream Canadian society (in other words, *equality through assimilation*). Ironically, rather than ending the Native question, the 1969 White Paper had the exact opposite effect. It sparked an angry outcry, which led in turn to a more united front among Native groups. Some, like Native Senator Gladstone and Cree lawyer William Wuttunee, supported the white paper's goal of absolute equality and short-term upheaval for long-term benefit. But the vast majority of Native groups did not. Spearheading opposition to it was the National Indian Brotherhood, which asserted that Native Canadians had prior legal and historic claims that could not be extinguished by an Act of Parliament.

> *If we accept this policy, and in the process lose our rights and our lands, we become willing partners in [our own] cultural genocide. This we cannot do.*
> — statement by the NIB regarding the 1969 White Paper

The Alberta Indian Association countered with a proposal of their own (known as "the Red Paper"), which argued that Native Canadians were, in fact, "citizens plus," with unique and inalienable rights given to them as the descendants of Canada's original inhabitants. In the Far North, meanwhile, Inuit groups organized into a national *tapirisat* ("alliance") in 1971, dedicated to preserving Inuit language and culture, and improving living conditions.

Across Canada, traditional aboriginal elders and angry young activists were joining forces. Native rights had suddenly become a hot political issue, and amid the firestorm of protest, Trudeau was forced to back down — a rare event indeed. The government withdrew the white paper in 1971, and in its stead an Office of Native Claims was created to settle outstanding land issues.

For more on the Assembly of First Nations, visit `www.afn.ca`. You can also find out more about the Inuit Tapirisat of Canada by visiting `www.tapirisat.ca/html/aboutitc_s.html`.

The October Crisis

The Quiet Revolution didn't stay quiet for long. By 1963, a terrorist group calling themselves the *Front de libération du Québec* (FLQ) had begun setting off bombs in Montréal. Calling for an end to "Anglo-Saxon colonization," the FLQ justified the violence with shrill Marxist propaganda and overheated political manifestos. Over the next seven years, the FLQ — a loose coalition of separatists and would-be revolutionaries — staged more than 30 armed robberies and exploded more than 200 bombs. They killed six people and injured more than 40 others, including a small child.

> *In a little while the English, the federalists, the exploiters, the toadies of the occupiers, the lackeys of imperialism — all those who betray the workers and the Québec nation — will fear for their lives!*
> — FLQ communiqué, March 1969

On October 5, 1970, a band of FLQ terrorists burst into the Montréal home of British trade commissioner James Cross and took him prisoner. Canada's separatist crisis was now an international incident.

The FLQ group holding James Cross hostage vowed to kill him unless they received half a million dollars in gold bullion and secured the release of 23 prisoners. As part of the negotiations, the government allowed the latest FLQ manifesto to be read on national television and to be published in newspapers. "We live in a society of terrorized slaves!" cried the FLQ terrorists who were now holding James Cross. The manifesto ended on a familiar, Gaullist note: *Vive le Québec libre!*

On October 10, just two days after the manifesto was broadcast, armed men from another FLQ group abducted Québec's minister of labour and immigration, Pierre Laporte.

As public panic set in, Trudeau ordered the army into Ottawa both as a show of force and to protect government officials. With helicopters landing and armed men taking up position on the streets, Trudeau was confronted by an angry journalist who demanded to know just how far the prime minister was willing to take this. Trudeau replied: "Just watch me."

Democracy first must preserve itself. Within Canada there is ample room for opposition and dissent, but none for intimidation and terror.
— Pierre Trudeau at the height of the 1970 October Crisis

On October 15, Québec Premier Robert Bourassa sent word to Ottawa, asking for federal intervention. Trudeau responded by invoking the War Measures Act, which gave the government sweeping, dictatorial powers. (See Chapter 16 for the origins of the War Measures Act.) Far from being a unilateral imposition by Trudeau, the Act was passed with overwhelming support in the House of Commons: 190 to 16. Only the NDP stood opposed. Canada was now under martial law. Civil liberties were suspended, the FLQ was banned, and the police were allowed to arrest and detain citizens without trial — or even explanation. In a series of pre-dawn raids, police officers rounded up more than 450 people and held them without bail. (All but 25 of them would later be released.)

It was the first time in Canadian history that the War Measures Act had been used during peacetime — and the public wholeheartedly agreed. In fact, the 1970 imposition of the War Measures Act was probably the single most popular pieces of legislation ever passed in Canada. Almost 90 percent of the population supported it, and this support was just as strong among French Canadians as it was among English Canadians.

The FLQ response was quick — and cruel. The day after the War Measures Act was passed, Pierre Laporte was strangled and his body was dumped in the trunk of a car. He was the FLQ's seventh and final victim.

But time was now running out for the FLQ, and by early December, the police had surrounded the hideout where James Cross was being held. The kidnappers released the British trade commissioner in exchange for free passage to Cuba for them and their families. A few weeks later, the police captured Francis Simard and the brothers Jacques and Paul Rose, who had kidnapped and then killed Pierre Laporte. (A fellow FLQ member, Bernard Lortie, had already been captured.) The longest sentence any of them served was 11 years. By the early 1980s, every one of the FLQ members involved in the October Crisis was back on the streets.

To this day, historians are divided over whether the government's actions were justified. Certainly, Trudeau crushed the FLQ. There was never a resurgence of political terrorism in Québec after 1970. But did the ends justify the means? Tommy Douglas, leader of the NDP, said "No." In his memorable description, the government had "used a sledgehammer to crack a peanut." Gérard Pelletier, Secretary of State at the time and the man responsible for signing the War Measures Act into being, replied curtly: "Anyone can play Monday morning quarterback. What would have happened *without* the special measures, no one will ever know. In history, the past conditional tense explains nothing."

Canada and the welfare state

The term "welfare state" was first coined in Britain during World War II. Today, it has come to refer to any industrialized society where the government plays a deliberate role — through policy and administration — in modifying market forces for social reasons (that is, countries where profit alone is not considered the highest good). The welfare state aims to give citizens equal access to services, minimum income, and protection from economic hardships arising from old age, sickness, or unemployment. Because of the negative nuance of the word "welfare," many people now refer instead to "a social safety net."

In Canada, the welfare state was launched by Mackenzie King in the 1940s and reached its highest point under Trudeau in the 1970s. Since then, the government of Canada has pulled back from its role as social guarantor, citing high costs and criticism that the welfare state drains people's initiative, overtaxes the middle class, and may actually prolong the very problems it was designed to prevent.

You can find documents from the October Crisis, including text of the FLQ manifesto, at `members.xoom.com/history_1/his951/docs/october/` `index.htm`.

Multiculturalism: The new ideal?

Canada has an aboriginal past, a bilingual present, and a multicultural future.

— former Manitoba premier Gary Filmon

Pierre Trudeau, the Father of Official Bilingualism, was also, in his way, the Father of Canadian Multiculturalism. In 1971, he brought in a Multicultural Act, which emphasized the equality of all "cultural and ethnic groups" in Canada within the framework of a bilingual country. It also provided for funding to ethnic organizations and for further second-language instruction. This was a significant shift in attitude. Multiculturalism, with all its vitality, variety, and confusion, was now embraced on an official level. It was now something to be proud of. As sociologist Reginald Bibby put it, "Canada has decided to enshrine a demographic reality into a national virtue."

From the 1960s on, Canadian immigration policy moved away from crude quotas on race and ethnic background — and toward an emphasis on education and work skills. At the same time, the criteria for evaluating refugee claims were broadened. (Generally speaking, immigrants are *pulled,* refugees are *pushed*. Immigrants come to Canada because they are seeking better

"Da, da Canada! Nyet, nyet Soviet!"

Want to know the real high-water moment of Canadian nationalism? It took place on ice in 1972, when Team Canada played the Soviets in a first-ever, best-of-eight hockey series. The Canadians, overly confident, were stopped cold by the finesse and speed of the Soviets and had fallen far behind by the time the series moved to Moscow. But Team Canada fought back and managed to tie the series, and on September 28, 1972, the two teams met in one final, heart-stopping game. Back home, the country came to a standstill as the population crowded around radios and TV sets. With the clock counting down into the final minute of play, Paul Henderson — *with just thirty-four seconds remaining* — picked up his own rebound and flipped it into the net. Across Canada, people went wild with joy. "I don't think I've ever felt so intensely proud to be Canadian," said Paul. (For more on the '72 series go to `www.canoe.ca/72Summit/`.)

opportunities for themselves and their children; refugees come because they are fleeing persecution or war. Illegal immigrants often attempt to play on public sympathy by passing themselves off as refugees, and we would do well to keep the distinction between "immigrant" and "refugee" in mind.)

The year 1971 also marked an important milestone in the evolution of present-day Canada: For the first time in Canadian history the majority of immigrants that year were not of European ancestry. It was a watershed moment that signalled the beginning of a newer, more eclectic approach to nationhood. Critics of multiculturalism decry it as a divisive force, but there is no evidence to support this claim. Tensions exist, to be sure. But over the last 30 years, multiculturalism has *not* led to the collapse of national unity, nor has it sparked race riots and widespread chaos. Far from it. The real threat to Canadian unity remains the separatist movement in Quebec. Multiculturalism, on the other hand, has helped revitalize and invigorate Canadian society.

Bill 22

Even as Canada was becoming bilingual on a federal level, Québec was becoming *unilingual* on a provincial level. In 1974, in an effort to outflank the separatists and steal some of their thunder, Premier Robert Bourassa passed Bill 22, which made French the only official language of Québec. Businesses that operated in English — or even French *and* English — faced restrictions. Children who wanted to attend English schools had to pass language tests to prove that they really were "English" enough. And thus, the state began testing the language skills of six-year-olds. *Welcome to the strange world of Québec language laws!* Stay tuned, it just keeps getting better and better.

The PQ in power

Too little, too late.
— René Lévesque's response to English-Canadian concessions

René Lévesque had been one of the stars of the Lesage Liberals and a key strategist of the Quiet Revolution. It was Lévesque who arranged for the provincial government to take over 11 private power companies to form the publicly owned Hydro Québec — a symbol of Québécois pride and potential even now. But Lesage's stubborn federalist beliefs rankled, and Lévesque became disillusioned and left the Liberals entirely. By 1968, he had brought together several smaller separatist groups to form a larger political union known as the Parti Québécois (PQ). On November 15, 1976, in an election that shook the nation, Lévesque defeated Bourassa's Liberals and put the province's first openly separatist government into power.

The Québec independence movement was no longer an angry fringe. It was now in control. Lévesque, the short, rumpled chain-smoker, was about to go head-to-head with Pierre Trudeau, the cold intellectual. It was one of the most fateful personality clashes in modern Canadian history. Lévesque appealed to Québécois' hearts, Trudeau to their heads. Lévesque was warm and welcoming. Trudeau was austere and unyielding. As one cabinet minister noted, they represented two poles of Québec society. "Lévesque is what we are; Trudeau is what we would like to be."

Bill 101

In 1977, the PQ government passed Bill 101, a controversial "Charter of the French Language" that banned English on commercial signs and severely restricted access to English-language education. Now, technically, it didn't ban *English,* but rather "any language other than French." Mind you, my father was working in Montréal at that time, and as he pointed out, the PQ didn't have any problem with the restaurant signs in Chinatown. Bill 101 was never really pro-French. It was anti-English. Still, the point of this wasn't simply to pick on the poor Anglos. Many Québécois had genuine and understandable fears that if they lost their language they would lose everything. Bill 101 was seen as their first, crucial line of defense.

The big owe

The Olympic Games can no more have a deficit than a man can have a baby.
> — Montréal Mayor Jean Drapeau, tempting the gods

In 1976, Montréal hosted the 21st Olympiad. Like Expo 67, the Montréal Olympics were the brainchild of Jean Drapeau, the little mayor with the big dreams. Drapeau believed in grandiose gestures and towering landmarks, and the Summer Games seemed like the ideal way to showcase Montréal for all the world to see. But what about the expense? Drapeau brushed these concerns aside. There could be no deficit. It was impossible. Alas, where Expo 67 was ultimately a success, the Montréal Olympics have gone down as one of the greatest disasters of civic planning ever.

The most enduring example of this is the stadium itself, a giant oval known as the Big O. The design, chosen by Drapeau personally and without public debate, included a futuristic retractable roof and a soaring angular tower. Only problem was, neither the tower nor the roof was finished in time — leaving an embarrassing architectural stump on display during the Games. And then it was discovered that the tower itself couldn't be finished because of a design flaw. It might, um, fall over. The stadium was shoddily constructed, as well. Pieces keep falling off, among them a 55-tonne support beam that came crashing to the ground unexpectedly one day. Then it was discovered that the partially finished tower was starting to list, and extensive — and expensive — renovations were needed. The final tally puts the cost of the Montréal Olympics at $3.5 billion — more than ten times the original estimate of $310 million. *Look, Ma! Dad had a baby!*

The Berger Commission

It seemed like a grand idea at the time: a multibillion-dollar mega-project to build a gas pipeline from Alaska, through the Mackenzie Valley, and down to Alberta. But just to be sure, Trudeau appointed Thomas Berger, a judge of the British Columbia Supreme Court, to look into the matter. If Ottawa was hoping that Berger would simply rubber-stamp the deal, they were sorely disappointed.

The judge took his assignment seriously and made a far-reaching, comprehensive study of the social, environmental, and cultural impact that the pipeline would have. He flew to remote communities, he heard testimony from hundreds of people, and in 1977, he submitted his report. It was a bombshell. The pipeline could not go through as planned. Native land rights had to be settled first, the environmental effects were dire, and a ten-year hold on any construction was urged. The Berger Commission was an important milestone of Canadian history: For the first time *ever* Native people were fully consulted on a proposed development scheme affecting their land. And for the first time ever, the government paid heed.

> *The risk is in Canada. The urgency is in the United States.*
> — Thomas Berger in his report on the Mackenzie Pipeline proposal

Sleeping with the elephant: The rise of economic nationalism

Living next [to the United States] is in some ways like sleeping with an elephant. No matter how friendly and even-tempered the beast, one is affected by every twitch and grunt.
          — Pierre Trudeau in a 1969 address in Washington, D.C.

Like many Canadians during the 1960s and 1970s, Trudeau was becoming increasingly alarmed at the extent of American penetration into the Canadian economy. A 1972 study outlined Canada's options:

(a) Stick with the status quo (and with it, the looming possibility of a slow, piecemeal takeover of the Canadian economy).

(b) Go for continental integration (in other words, free trade and a complete surrender to American influence — and prosperity).

(c) Expand ties to Europe and Britain, and decrease dependence on the U.S.

Trudeau chose the so-called "third option." Now, back in 1958, Diefenbaker had thought he could realign Canada's trade balance simply by decree (I discuss his "15 percent promise" in Chapter 20). Trudeau decided to use government policies instead. Pierre Elliott Trudeau, the great world citizen and implacable foe of "irrational" nationalism, introduced some of the most unabashed examples of economic nationalism in Canadian history since John A. Macdonald and the National Policy (see Chapter 14). Trudeau's attempts at wrestling some control of the Canadian economy away from the U.S. included the following:

- **Foreign Investment Review Agency (FIRA):** Introduced in 1973, FIRA was set up to screen foreign business takeovers to see whether they provided any "significant benefit" to Canada. FIRA sounded like a good idea at the time — but ultimately it proved to be toothless and ill-advised, a "paper tiger" that created all sorts of red tape and expensive studies but achieved very little. To critics of the program, all that FIRA did was discourage investment and stunt economic growth.

- **Petro-Canada:** Canada's national oil company, Petro-Canada was created in 1975 as a Crown corporation (government owned and operated) to help "Canadianize" the nation's petroleum industry, which was, at that time, completely dominated by foreign corporations.

- **National Energy Policy(NEP):** Established in 1980 during the height of a world oil crisis, the NEP was a sweeping government program aimed at (a) increasing Canadian ownership in the oil industry, (b) forcing the Western provinces to give the federal government a bigger cut of the pie, and (c) making Canada more self-sufficient in energy. It was a massive intervention on the government's part and one that was based on the false assumption that oil prices would continue to rise. In fact, by 1982 prices had started to plummet and the government found itself heavily in debt and over-extended. The NEP punished Alberta but did little for Canada, even as the country sank into its worst recession in 40 years.

Trudeau's policies outraged the Americans and angered Western Canadians, especially in Alberta, where Premier Peter Lougheed denounced the NEP as "an assault" on provincial ownership of natural resources. The federal government in turn, felt Alberta was hoarding its wealth at the expense of the country. It was the classic Canadian dilemma: Which should take precedence, national interests or regional? Provincial or federal?

Many of the economic problems Trudeau faced while in office were unavoidable, stemming as they did from the oil crises of the 1970s when the Organization of Petroleum Exporting Countries (OPEC) united to control supply. They sent prices skyrocketing by 160 percent. But much of it was his own doing. Trudeau was notoriously erratic.

When the Progressive Conservatives under Robert Stanfield proposed government-sanctioned wage and price controls in order to fight inflation, Trudeau mocked the policy mercilessly and ran an election campaign on it in 1974. "Zap! You're frozen," he snickered in reference to Stanfield's crazy scheme. Then Trudeau got himself re-elected and, next thing you know, he's introduced wage and price controls. It didn't work, of course, and the experiment was eventually scrapped, but it is indicative of the type of uneven financial policies that marked Trudeau's years in office. By 1979, Canadians had had enough.

Joe Who?

Joe Clark, the kid from High River, Alberta, was only 36 years old when he came out of nowhere to win the 1976 Progressive Conservative leadership convention. The following morning, the headlines asked "Joe Who?" and the nickname stuck. Awkward and uncharismatic, Joe Clark hardly seemed cut out for the role of giant-killer, but just three years later, he defeated Pierre Trudeau to become the youngest prime minister in Canadian history. (Clark was 39 when he won the election and turned 40 the day after he took office, so saying he was PM at 39 is a bit misleading.)

Under Trudeau, the economy had foundered. Inflation was up, the West was alienated, and the country was growing weary of Trudeau's arrogant antics. On May 1979, Pierre was voted out and Joe was voted in. Trudeau duly handed in his resignation as leader of the Liberal Party and prepared to paddle off into the sunset. The Trudeau era was over. Or so it seemed . . .

Chapter 22

A Charter Country

*J*oe Clark defeated Trudeau in 1979, but his was a *minority* government, and as such he needed the support and good will of the other parties to stay in power. No such luck. When Clark and the Tories tried to bring in a tough-minded budget, they were toppled by a vote of non-confidence in the House.

Trudeau had barely announced his retirement when the Clark government fell. The Liberals, now leaderless, pleaded with Trudeau to return, and in the February 1980 election that followed, Joe Clark went down in flames. He had been in office for only seven months, during which time Parliament had sat for just 49 days and had passed exactly one bill: a minor amendment to old-age security. That was it. That was the "Joe Clark legacy" in a nutshell.

Still, during his brief term in office, two important events did unfold, and in both cases, Joe handled himself admirably and with surprising aplomb.

> ✔ **The Vietnam refugees crisis:** In the late 1970s, flotillas of desperate Vietnamese "boat people" fled communist oppression only to be refused entry by one country after the next. Canada, however, opened its doors. The federal government, along with church groups and private organizations, rushed to sponsor refugees, and from 1979 to 1980 nearly 60,000 Indochinese were given sanctuary in communities across the country. Under the direction of Flora MacDonald, Joe Clark's Secretary of State for External Affairs, Canada's contribution was second to none.

> ✔ **"The Canadian caper":** Following an Islamic revolution in Iran, 52 American citizens were held hostage inside the U.S. embassy in Tehran. However, six diplomats managed to elude capture and they sought refuge at the Canadian embassy, where ambassador Ken Taylor arranged to

keep them hidden until they could be smuggled out of the country three months later. They escaped in January 1980, using Canadian passports. Both Taylor and his deputy, John Sheardown, risked their lives by hiding the American fugitives in their homes, and a gush of pro-Canadian sentiment swept the U.S. They called it "the Canadian caper." Ken Taylor was awarded a Congressional Gold Medal for his actions.

Round Two

Welcome to the eighties.
> — a smiling Pierre Trudeau after winning the 1980 election

We thought we said goodbye to Trudeau in 1979, but in February 1980 he was back, with a majority government and a trademark rose in his lapel. True, the roses that Trudeau cultivated had especially prickly thorns, but no matter. The Philosopher King had been given a second lease on life and he planned on making the most of it. As Pierre himself put it, quoting Robert Frost, "I have promises to keep, and miles to go before I sleep."

The 1980 referendum

When the Parti Québécois finally called a referendum, it wasn't on outright independence, but on something they called "sovereignty-association," which was basically divorce with bedroom privileges. That is, under the PQ proposal, Québec would become a separate country but would still be allowed to enjoy all the economic benefits of Confederation. And the PQ honestly believed that the rest of Canada would go along with this cunning plan of theirs. Amazing.

But wait. It gets better. The PQ wasn't even asking for a final decision. Not just yet, anyway. Instead, the 1980 referendum would be about whether to give the PQ permission to *begin* negotiations with Ottawa on a *proposal for* — not separation, remember — but "sovereignty-association." As the PQ's lengthy, convoluted, and thoroughly test-marketed referendum question stressed, a second follow-up poll would be held before any final deal was struck. It was absolutely risk-free. How could the PQ possibly lose?

Alas, the campaign went badly for the separatists right from the start. At a PQ rally, broadcaster Lise Payette shovelled contempt on women who were thinking of voting *Non* in the referendum, dismissing them as nothing but a bunch of "Yvettes." (Yvette was the name of a stereotypical housewife in Québec schoolbooks, traditionally used to demonstrate the "proper" role of women. Calling someone an "Yvette" is an insult.) The backlash against Ms. Payette's comments was immediate. Women joined the *Non* side in protest and even took to calling themselves "Yvettes" as a defiant badge of honour. The PQ had tried to play the feminist card — and had lost.

To make matters worst, Lévesque's own language laws helped undermine much of the separatist appeal. French had reasserted itself and Anglo dominance was now on the run. For the most part, the Québécois had indeed become "masters in their own house," and the francophone re-conquest of Montréal was well underway. So why separate?

Pierre Trudeau and former newspaper editor Claude Ryan spearheaded the federalist forces and they won, handily. On May 20, 1980, 60 percent of Quebeckers voted *Non* to sovereignty association. It was a humiliating defeat for both René Lévesque and the PQ. Against Joe Clark they might have won, but not against Pierre Trudeau. "Separatism," Trudeau declared, "is dead."

The uncertainty of Québec's future under a separatist government took a heavy toll on the province's economy, sparking an exodus of businesses from Montréal — a city that was under "linguistic siege" as one fretful Anglo put it. It was an unprecedented migration. Nearly150 corporate offices packed up and moved west to Toronto, which now outpaced Montréal as Canada's economic powerhouse. Indeed, Québec's separatist movement has been *very* good for Toronto.

For a look at the lead-up to the 1980 referendum from a separatist point of view, go to `uni.ca/newdeal1979.html` and `uni.ca/pq.html`.

The Constitution Act of 1982

Hard to believe, but Canada was still not a fully independent nation. The country was governed under the terms of the British North America Act, first drafted by John A. Macdonald and the others back in 1867 (see Chapter 13). The BNA Act was an act of *British* Parliament, and any changes to it had to be approved by Britain. This had become a mere formality, of course. But it still took time and energy, and — more importantly — it was a mouldy relic of colonial times. Britain would have gladly turned its remaining authority over to Canada, and Canada would have been more than happy to accept. There was just one snag: With Britain removed from the equation, how would future constitutional changes be made? If the Constitution was to come home, an "amending formula" had to be worked out first.

Attempts to patriate (bring home) Canada's Constitution had been made before, most notably during the 1920s and later in 1964, when Pearson had presented a blueprint for future constitutional changes. Dubbed "the Fulton-Favreau Formula" after its two key architects, it was approved by every premier in Canada, including Québec's Jean Lesage. But before the deal could be ratified, Daniel Johnson and the Union Nationale were elected and all bets were off. Canada's Constitution remained in the hands of Britain.

Trudeau had already entered the constitutional fray once before, back in 1971, at a meeting of premiers in Victoria. Several wide-ranging changes had been agreed upon, including a veto for Québec. Premier Bourassa concurred — but soon caved in to criticism from the French-Canadian media that he hadn't gotten enough out of Ottawa. (In fact, Bourassa caved in on the plane ride home, after only hearing *rumours* of dissent back in Québec.) When Bourassa squelched the deal, the Victoria Charter ended up on the scrap pile with all the other constitutional proposals.

Fast forward to 1980. During the referendum campaign, Trudeau promised Québec he "would renew the Constitution." With the separatists now reeling, he decided to make his move. He had three primary goals:

✔ To patriate Canada's Constitution.

✔ To create an effective amending formula for future constitutional changes.

✔ To add a Charter of Rights and Freedoms.

Unlike Diefenbaker's decorative 1960 Bill of Rights, Trudeau's charter would be part of the Constitution itself, giving the charter real impact, both legally and culturally. It would, in fact, outline the moral foundations of Canadian society.

Joe Clark and the Tories hotly contested Trudeau's Constitutional initiative. At one point early on, the Commons came close to breaking into an out-and-out brawl as members crossed the floor to yell in each other's faces. Some MPs even left their seats to plead their case directly to the Speaker of the House, denouncing the Trudeau government as an example of "totalitarianism [on a par with] Hitler." Yup. The Tories compared Trudeau to Hitler. Subtle, eh?

A fatal flaw: The "notwithstanding clause"

Trudeau had his work cut out for him. Negotiations with the various provincial premiers were long, drawn-out, and seemingly endless. Language rights, natural resources, the ownership of offshore oil, control over exports and imports: The provinces and the federal government battled it out, point by point. In the new Constitution, who would get what? And why?

Women's groups lobbied to have a clause added to guarantee equality between sexes. Québec wanted language laws to be solely a provincial right. New Brunswick wanted language laws to be national, with both French and English given equal status. Several provinces were worried that Trudeau's proposed Charter of Rights and Freedoms would encroach on provincial jurisdiction.

As talks bogged down, Trudeau sandbagged the premiers with a sudden ultimatum. Either they quit bickering and come up with an acceptable compromise package, or he would go it alone. He would bring the Constitution home without them. There was an immediate outcry, and the matter was eventually taken to the Supreme Court where it was ruled that — although highly irregular — Ottawa *could* patriate the Constitution unilaterally. Trudeau then isolated Lévesque from the rest of the pack and hammered out a final deal. Why did Trudeau sidestep the premier of Canada's largest province? The answer was simple. No separatist government would ever have agreed to tie Québec to a renewed made-in-Canada Constitution. Trudeau knew this, and Lévesque knew that he knew. And so, in a final night of subterfuge and brinkmanship, an agreement was worked out with the other nine premiers while Lévesque was sleeping.

In exchange for his Charter of Rights, Trudeau accepted a fateful compromise: Section 33, which is better known as the "notwithstanding clause," because it states that several key areas of the Charter are in effect "notwithstanding" those rights reserved by provincial legislatures. What this means — incredibly — is that the provinces can override specific sections of the Charter of Rights and Freedoms anytime they feel that those sections conflict with their own provincial statutes. All the provinces have to do is invoke the clause — and *hey presto!* — the "inalienable" rights of Canadians vanish in a puff of smoke. Only in Canada. Sigh. (It was this loophole that would later allow Québec to override the rights of English Quebeckers with its restrictive language laws. When the Supreme Court ruled that the province's language bills were unconstitutional, Québec simply invoked the notwithstanding clause.)

"Québec" stands alone

René Lévesque, cut out of the loop during the final night of negotiations, was understandably bitter and he refused to endorse the deal. Instead, he complained that Pierre Trudeau and his henchman Jean Chrétien, then minister of justice, had betrayed Québec. Lévesque repeated these claims again and again. So often, in fact, that his version of events has become the accepted one (even in English Canada). Namely, that "Québec" was excluded from the final negotiations and that "Québec" has never accepted the terms of the 1982 Constitution. But this isn't exactly true. *René Lévesque and the Parti Québécois government* have never accepted the 1982 Constitution. And that is a different matter entirely. The Constitution Act was not "forced" on Québec. If anything, Québec "forced" it on the rest of Canada. Consider:

✔ In 1982, the prime minister of Canada was from Québec, the minister of justice was from Québec, and so was a third of the cabinet.

✔ Of Québec's 75 federal MPs, 72 of them supported the deal.

✔ Even with the separatists in power provincially, a full 60 percent of Québec's democratically elected representatives — federal and provincial combined — gave their approval to the 1982 Constitution Act.

By any standard, 60 percent is a majority. But myths die hard, and the "betrayal and humiliation of Québec in 1982" has caused no end of grief — as we will see in Chapter 23. Reaching new heights of hyperbole, historian and broadcaster Laurier LaPierre even went so far as to describe the final deal between Trudeau and the premiers as "the Night of the Long Knives." Who says that only the winners get to write history? In Canada it is the separatist version of events that often becomes the textbook standard.

Native protests

Québec nationalists weren't the only ones upset by the 1982 deal. Native groups were just as shocked to learn that there was no mention whatsoever of Canada's First Nations in the original draft. Only after heavy protests was a clause finally added — but at the insistence of Alberta premier Peter Lougheed, it was limited to "existing" treaty rights. Angry at these limits and the vagueness of the protections being offered, Native leaders travelled all the way to London to make an appeal directly to the British courts. They argued that because the original treaties had been signed in the name of the British Crown, the ultimate responsibility for Native rights still lay with Britain. The Native delegates received sympathy, but no real support.

I have had a long-running argument with friends of mine active in the Native movement who insist that they got screwed by the Constitution Act of 1982, which they feel closed the door to any future claims. But I disagree. Section 35 of the Constitution Act, recognizing as it does "existing aboriginal rights," also *entrenches* these rights in the very bedrock of Canadian society. Native claims are now part of the game plan. They can't be legislated away — or ignored. That seems like a victory to me.

The Constitution comes home

On April 17, 1982, in a simple outdoor ceremony, Queen Elizabeth II proclaimed the Constitution Act of 1982 (which was passed in Britain under the name of the Canada Act). Trudeau and Chrétien were both on hand, beaming away, even as the skies above them darkened. They signed their names as the first few drops of rain began to fall. It was an omen of things to come.

That wet, windy day in April marked Canada's true moment of political independence. It also marked the birth of a dangerous myth. Namely, that Québec has never accepted Canada, that it had been railroaded into a renewed Confederation.

And anyway, is Canada truly independent? The Constitution is no longer under British jurisdiction, true. But the British Crown is still our head of state, something I have always found strange and a bit unsettling. A modern, democratic, multiethnic, pluralistic society with an outdated and archaic Royal Family at the helm? Figurehead or not, doesn't the very concept of inherited social status and pedigreed bloodline go against everything Canada now stands for? Or is it just me?

The Charter of Rights and Freedoms

The 1982 Charter recognizes four fundamental freedoms as the bedrock of Canadian society:

(a) Freedom of conscience and religion.

(b) Freedom of expression, including freedom of the press.

(c) Freedom of peaceful assembly (a little APEC pepper, anyone?).

(d) And freedom of association. (That is, the freedom to avoid "guilt by association." One of my profs called it "the freedom to mingle with the dregs of society — without it ever being held against you.")

There is much more to the Charter than this, though. It also covers the following:

- ✔ The right to life, liberty, and security.

- ✔ The right against unreasonable search and seizure.

- ✔ The right, upon arrest, to have the reasons clearly explained.

- ✔ The right to be presumed innocent until proven guilty.

- ✔ And the right to equal protection under the law, without discrimination on the basis of race, national or ethnic origin, religion, gender, age, or mental or physical disability.

Canadians are united by the Charter in a moral and legal sense, just as surely as they had been untied politically by the original BNA Act.

The impact of the Charter

Positive freedoms are different from negative freedoms, just as individual rights are different from collective rights. *Positive freedoms* include the right to do what you want without interference. *Negative freedoms*, on the other hand, cover the freedom *from* pain, *from* fear, *from* discrimination. The two often clash. For example, my freedom of speech (positive) clashes with your freedom from fear (negative) if I go around espousing violence against your race or gender — or you personally.

Individual and *collective* rights often clash as well. In Québec, for example, the individual rights of shopowners to post signs in any language they choose is curtailed by laws aimed at protecting larger collective rights — in this case, French-speaking Quebeckers as a whole. Now, if the 20th century taught us anything, it is that there is a very real danger in elevating collective rights (especially those of the state) over those of the individual. Fascism and communism, after all, both put collective rights above those of the individual — and we all know where that led.

O Canada(s)

O Canada did not become our official national anthem until 1980 — exactly 100 years after it was first performed. Québec composer Calixa Lavallée wrote the music in 1880, and Judge Adolphe Routhier provided lyrics for it in French. The English version didn't come until much later, when Robert Stanley Weir, another Québec judge, penned them in 1908.

The English rendition of *O Canada* is not a translation from the original French. In fact, the two sets of lyrics express starkly different viewpoints. The French version focuses on history, the English one on geography. The French version is replete with swords and "glorious garlands" and great exploits. The English one tells Canadians to "stand on guard" and describes Canada as a land of hope "for those who toil." Which is to say, the French version is Catholic. The English one, Protestant. (Author Mordecai Richler considered Canada's duelling anthems an example of "our national schizophrenia.") Only the first verse in either language is official.

For a full and fascinating history of Canada's national anthem, including the official lyric(s), earlier versions, and an audio file, go to www.pch.gc.ca/symb/anthm_e.htm#top.

Trudeau firmly believed that his Charter had placed the rights of the individual as the highest good and the final court of appeal (that is, in any conflict, the rights of the individual should be given precedence). Critics, however, argue that Canada's Charter of Rights and Freedoms — by including Native, language, and gender rights — is in fact a tool of "collectives." Others have argued that the Charter has undermined the democratic process itself by replacing the authority of elected lawmakers with that of the courts, making Canada a country "governed by judges." But a study by Osgoode Hall challenges this notion. In Canada, it would seem, judges still give way to legislators and rarely override them. Of 76 recent cases in which laws were challenged on the grounds that they contradicted the Charter, only seven of the laws were actually struck down.

Western alienation, or "that #%@!* Trudeau!"

Canada's East–West rift was at its absolute worst during the Trudeau administration. At the height of the 1970s oil crises, Ottawa complained bitterly about greedy "blue-eyed sheiks" in Alberta. And the West replied with bumperstickers that read: *Let those Eastern bastards freeze in the dark.* Calgary's mayor, Rod Sykes, upset at the callousness of this, replied with a bumper sticker of his own: *That "Eastern bastard" is my brother.*

Trudeau was blunt and insensitive when dealing with Western concerns. "Why should I sell your wheat?" he demanded of farm protestors, ignoring the fact that Canada's Wheat Board (at that time) was a federal agency — and a federal responsibility. When farmers complained about Trudeau's hostile indifference to their problems, Trudeau just shrugged.

> *When there is too much sun, they complain. When there is too much rain, they complain. A farmer is a complainer.*
> — Pierre Trudeau, on the nature of agricultural unrest in Canada

Such sentiments did not win him many fans in the West. I grew up in Alberta during the Trudeau era and I can vouch for the fact that the man was deeply, *profoundly* unpopular. When Trudeau took a train through B.C., protestors at Salmon Arm pelted the coach he and his sons were travelling in with rancid garbage. Trudeau pulled back the blinds and gave them the finger, a gesture that became known in Canada as "the Trudeau salute."

But time heals most wounds — and wounds most heels, as my dad liked to say — and Albertans have slowly come to admire the man they once denounced so vehemently. Indeed, in a recent poll, Albertans chose Pierre Trudeau as Canada's greatest prime minister. The mood in the West now seems to be, "Sure, Trudeau pissed us off, and he ignored us and annoyed us, but he also saved the country. And that's gotta be worth something."

> *I came into politics to keep Québec in Confederation. Someone else will have to save the West.*
> — Pierre Trudeau, following the 1980 referendum

The Trudeau Legacy

On a snowy evening at the end of a leap-year February in 1984, Pierre Elliott Trudeau went for a long walk and looked for signs of destiny in the sky. "But there were no signs," he said wistfully. "There were only snowflakes." The next day he announced his retirement.

Trudeau should have left two years earlier, after the triumph of the Constitution Act and the Charter of Rights and Freedoms. Instead, he lingered on for two more years like an actor who stays on stage after the applause has petered out. In 1984, unemployment was high, the value of the Canadian dollar was in free fall, and the public was growing weary of Trudeau's aloof arrogance. It is highly unlikely he could have won another term.

Still, for the most part, Pierre Trudeau went out a winner. He achieved almost everything he had set out to do. He forced Canada to accept its bilingual reality. He established multiculturalism, not just as a demographic fact, but as a cultural ideal. He brought the Constitution home, and he beat the separatists — beat them black and blue. Pierre Trudeau first went into politics to reconcile Québec's place in Confederation. And he did just that. He is, perhaps, Canada's most admired and popular prime minister — and its most hated. Even now. Certainly, his place in history is secure:

✔ In an Angus Reid poll released in January 2000, Canadians chose Trudeau as "PM of the century." He placed first in every region of Canada with a national rating of 41 percent, far ahead of Lester Pearson who placed second with 13 percent of the votes.

✔ In a Canadian Press survey taken the same year, the country's journalists and broadcasters named Trudeau "the top newsmaker of the century."

Among historians, however, Pierre Trudeau's ranking is not nearly so high. A survey taken of university professors, and repackaged as a book in 1999, ranked Trudeau as fifth, below Louis St. Laurent. (Mackenzie King, ever the professor's hero, was ranked number one.)

With only a brief interruption, Pierre Trudeau was the prime minister of Canada for 15 tumultuous years — third-longest after Mackenzie King and John A. Macdonald. Economically, the Trudeau Era (1968–84) was an erratic time. According to Keynesian theory, economies should alternate between times of high unemployment and high inflation — but not both. Yet across Canada and much of the Western world a new phenomenon was born: "stagflation," a bewildering combination of inflation *and* high unemployment.

During Trudeau's reign, the national debt soared from $16 billion in 1968 to $154 billion in 1984. A string of misguided government programs sputtered and died, and theories of economic nationalism foundered. It was an era strewn with the bodies of doomed experiments, but in spite of this, Trudeau had a major long-term impact. In many ways, he reshaped the very idea of what it means to be Canadian. To recap, under Pierre Trudeau:

✔ Canada redefined itself as a bilingual, multicultural country.

✔ The separatists were defeated — temporarily as it turned out.

✔ The American economic influence was checked (but not halted).

✔ Numerous Crown corporations were created, giving Canada greater control over its natural resources.

✔ Political terrorism in Québec was crushed.

✔ The Constitution was brought home.

✔ And a Charter of Rights and Freedoms was created, establishing the moral and legal underpinnings of modern Canadian society.

Oil and the *Ocean Ranger*

The oil crunch of the 1970s led to greater — and at times frantic — exploration and drilling across Canada. Among them were the following:

✔ The oil sands of northern Alberta, where the boom town of Fort McMurray has developed into a lively outpost of exiled Newfoundland workers.

✔ The Arctic, where Dome Petroleum received heavy government grants to search for oil in the Beaufort Sea.

✔ The underwater Hibernia fields of Newfoundland's Grand Banks.

The Grand Banks are vast sub-ocean plateaus extending more than 600 kilometres east, into the North Atlantic. Once one of the world's richest fisheries, the Grand Banks were where John Cabot first scooped up cod by the bucketful. It was also the site of one of Canada's worst Maritime disasters, when the offshore oil platform, the *Ocean Ranger* — the largest drill rig of its type in the world — capsized in a raging storm on February 15, 1982. The platform was anchored 265 kilometres east of Newfoundland, in open ocean, and all 84 men on board died; 56 of them were native Newfoundlanders. The *Ocean Ranger*, leased by Mobil Oil Canada, was hit by waves cresting 18 metres high and gale force winds that strafed the platform at 145 kilometres an hour. The tragedy underlined both the financial risks and the physical dangers of offshore oil exploration.

Trudeau made many controversial calls. An advocate of disarmament, he slashed Canada's contribution to NATO by half and allowed Canadian ships and planes to rust in neglect. He also brought in the metric system, beginning in 1975, which changed our miles to kilometres and our fractions to decimals.

Autocrat. Democrat. Dilettante. Love him or hate him, Pierre Trudeau's impact on Canadian society has been immense and far-reaching.

> *We are all Trudeau's children — whether we like it or not.*
> — from *Bastards & Boneheads*

Go to www.bloorstreet.com/200block/sconst82.htm for more on the Constitution Act of 1982 (including Canada's Charter of Rights and Freedoms). You'll find a full course in Québec history, including many of the areas covered in this chapter, at members.xoom.com/history_1/his951/index.htm.

Chapter 23

"Yankee Doodle Dandy": The Mulroney Years

*W*hen Pierre Trudeau retired in 1984, he was replaced by John Turner, who had once served as Trudeau's minister of justice and later as minister of finance. Although he retired from Cabinet in 1975, and left political life entirely soon after, John Turner was welcomed back with open arms and adulatory media hype. He lasted all of 80 days.

As PM, John Turner's awkward style and stiff mannerisms paled in comparison to the smooth-talking charisma of the Tories' new leader: Brian Mulroney, a man who "oozed confidence," in the words of one reporter.

On the election day of September 4, 1984, Brian Mulroney mopped the floor with Liberals. The Conservatives won a huge landslide, giving them the largest parliamentary majority in Canadian history — a record that still stands. The Conservatives won 211 seats, to the Liberals' 40, and the NDP's 30. The big breakthrough came in Québec, where the Tories won 59 seats out of 75, breaking the Liberal grip on that province. Brian Mulroney had delivered Québec to the Tories.

I was living in St. Canut, a francophone community in rural Québec, when Mulroney was swept into office in the 1984 election, and I remember the wild excitement that followed. Cars roared up and down the streets, waving the Québec flag and cheering Mulroney's name. A new day had dawned. The Trudeau years were over. The Mulroney era had begun.

> *Give us twenty years and you will not recognize this country.*
> — Brian Mulroney in 1984, on the bright future that awaited Canada

"Canada is open for business!"

> *The years after 1984 marked a decisive shift in Canadian history. For the first time Canada apparently cast its lot wholly with the United States.*
> — historians Norman Hillmer and J.L. Granatstein

Brian Mulroney, the son of an electrician, grew up as an Irish Canadian in the blue-collar French-Canadian town of Baie-Comeau, Québec. It was a company town, and Mulroney was a company man. A corporate lawyer and former president of the Iron Ore Company, he had a knack for high-stakes negotiations. Perhaps he could apply his skills to Canada as a whole?

It needs to be stressed: Brian Mulroney promised us a new era of fiscal responsibility and national unity. When he came to office in 1984, he had two broad goals:

- ✔ to revitalize Canada's stagnant economy (mainly by forging closer ties and better relations with the United States).

- ✔ to "bring Québec into the 1982 Constitution" (that is, to amend the original deal in order to make it acceptable to Québec's provincial government — see Chapter 22 for more on the Constitution Act).

Mulroney made his presence felt right away. He ended the economic nationalism of the Trudeau years by dismantling the National Energy Program (NEP) and overhauling the Foreign Investment Review Agency (FIRA), which had been set up to restrict take-overs of Canadian industries. Under Mulroney, FIRA made a 180-degree turnaround and was renamed "Investment Canada" with a new goal of *encouraging* foreign investment, especially American. (There's more on the NEP and FIRA in Chapter 21.) Gone was the old coy modesty. Canada wanted American cash — and lots of it!

> *Canada is open for business!*
> — Brian Mulroney, shortly after getting elected

Men in motion

I'm not a dreamer. But I do believe in miracles. I have to. Because somewhere the hurting must stop

— Terry Fox

During the 1980s, the journeys of three Canadians helped redefine the concept of heroism. All three were from B.C., and all three achieved remarkable feats in spite of serious physical disabilities.

Terry Fox (Marathon of Hope):

As a teenager, Terry Fox lost his right leg to cancer. Just three years later, he set out on a cross-Canada run to raise money and increase awareness of cancer research. It began in St. John's, Newfoundland, in April 1980 with Fox dipping his artificial leg in the Atlantic Ocean. The haunting image of Terry Fox, running in a painful hop-step rhythm, attempting to cross a landscape as vast as Canada's was at once poignant and heroic. Terry Fox covered two-thirds of the distance before being forced to stop outside of Thunder Bay, Ontario, in September. The cancer had spread to his lungs and the following June he died, just one month short of his 23rd birthday. (A common misconception is that Fox only made it "halfway." In fact, he had covered 5,370 kilometres of a 7,600-kilometre trek, and was about to enter the "straightway" of the Prairies.)

Fox raised $25 million for cancer research and inspired a charitable foundation and an annual fund-raiser run in his honour that has raised an additional $265 million — so far. Go to www. terryfoxrun.org to find out more.

Steve Fonyo (Journey for Lives):

Steve Fonyo was inspired by the saga of Terry Fox and decided to complete the journey. Fonyo had lost his left leg to cancer when he was only 12 and in March 1984, at the age of 19, he began his own cross-Canada run. In was a tough haul, but Fonyo passed Thunder Bay and kept on going. He crossed the Prairies in one of the worst winters in years, often running through blizzard conditions and in temperatures that dropped to –30°C. The following May he reached Victoria and waded into the Pacific. He had covered more than 7,920 kilometres and had raised $13 million. Sadly, controversy surrounded Fonyo both during the run and after. He was later arrested on drunk driving charges and was constantly in financial trouble — but for those who are quick to criticize Fonyo, I urge them to first do what he did: run across Canada on one leg.

Rick Hansen (Man in Motion):

Rick Hansen, a friend of Terry Fox's (they had played on the same wheelchair basketball team), had been injured as a youth in a truck accident that left his legs paralysed. A strong, competitive athlete, Hansen set off in March 1985 to circle the world by wheelchair. Hansen's Man in Motion journey took more than two years and covered more than 34 countries, including Australia, the U.S.S.R., and China — where he rode his wheelchair on the Great Wall itself. He raised $20 million for spinal cord injury research. It also inspired a romance and marriage with his physiotherapist Amanda Reid (a tale described as "one of the great love stories" of Canadian history). For more on Rick Hansen and the Man in Motion world tour, visit www.rickhansen.com.

The 1980s were about more than just big hair and bombastic rock anthems. It was also a time of renewed capitalism and a vigorous right-wing political program as personified by Ronald Reagan in the U.S., Margaret Thatcher in the U.K., and Brian Mulroney in the Great White North.

Under Mulroney, Canada drew closer to the United States than it had ever been before. White House documents released in 1999 under the U.S. Freedom of Information Act (on a request by journalist Lawrence Martin) confirm that the United States was thrilled to pieces by the election of Brian Mulroney. They felt Mulroney was on the same ideological "wave length" as the Reagan administration, and expressed enthusiasm for Mulroney's "pro-U.S. stance."

The Shamrock Summit

Playing on their Irish roots, Brian Mulroney and Ronald Reagan met on St. Patrick's Day in March 1985 in Québec City. Dubbed the "Shamrock Summit," the meeting ended with the Prime Minister of Canada serenading the president with a heart-felt rendition of *When Irish Eyes Are Smiling*.

Now, back when Brian was a wee lad in Baie-Comeau, the wealthy Chicago tycoon Robert McCormick would come in now and then to inspect his mills. And whenever he did, McCormick would send for young Brian (who had a beautiful voice) and have the boy sing to him. The ageing American millionaire would then pay Brian $50. That was a lot of money in the 1940s, especially in a blue-collar company town like Baie-Comeau. Mulroney had recounted this anecdote on several occasions, without ever grasping the distasteful subtext behind it. For many Canadians, seeing their PM up on stage crooning a line from an Irish love song to the U.S. President was excruciatingly embarrassing to watch. "You get the impression," noted commentator Eric Kierans, "that our prime minister invited his boss home for dinner." It certainly set the tone for much of what followed.

Free Trade and the GST

Don't talk to me about free trade. . . . Free trade is a danger to Canadian sovereignty. You'll hear no more of it from me. . . . This country could not survive with a policy of unfettered free trade. . . . This is a separate country, we'd be swamped. It's bad enough as it is.
> — statements made by Brian Mulroney prior to being elected

The Shamrock Summit was only the beginning. Trade negotiations with the United States were soon underway — Brian's early declarations notwithstanding. Opponents pointed out that in 1985 nearly 80 percent of Canadian exports were already going to the United States — an all-time high. What was needed was a boost to Canada's declining exports to the rest of the world.

Others worried that free trade would undermine Canadian autonomy and jeopardize social programs and cultural industries (by curtailing government subsidies). Supporters of free trade, on the other hand, argued that Canada needed to get in "under the umbrella" of the Americans' tariff wall, and that free trade offered Canada crucial access to U.S. markets.

The Free Trade Agreement (FTA), removing tariffs and import duties between the two countries, was negotiated in 1987. Critics of the deal complained that Mulroney had no mandate to launch such a wide-ranging deal, and the Liberal-dominated Senate warned Mulroney that they would not pass the bill unless it was approved by the public in a general election. And thus, the federal election of 1988 became, in essence, a referendum on free trade with the United States. John Turner, the stammering, ineffective leader of the Liberals, played the anti-American card to no avail. Mulroney was returned to power in 1988 with a second straight back-to-back majority — something no Conservative leader had accomplished since John A. Macdonald.

The 1988 election also marked the first time in Canadian history that any federal party had ever successfully campaigned on a platform of closer ties with the U.S. Indeed, free trade was a radical departure from standard Conservative Party policy. Former Tory PMs such as Macdonald, Borden, and Diefenbaker had all been *anti*-free trade (and even anti-*American*).

Historically, free trade was a Liberal platform. Over the years, it had been championed by the Liberal Party on several occasions — and in each case, was quashed:

> ✔ In 1891, Wilfrid Laurier and his Liberals proposed a "commercial union" with the U.S. and were defeated by John A. Macdonald.

> ✔ In 1911, Laurier again ran on a platform of "reciprocity" with the U.S. and was again defeated. The Conservatives under Robert Borden, crying "No Truck nor Trade with the Yankees" were swept into power.

> ✔ In 1948, a Liberal plan to introduce a policy of open, unfettered trade with the U.S. was again blocked — this time by their own leader, Mackenzie King, who vetoed the idea shortly before he retired.

When Brian Mulroney embraced a modern version of "commercial union" with the U.S. (that is, free trade), he rejected the principles of John A. Macdonald and embraced those of Wilfrid Laurier. Indeed, by today's standards, John A. Macdonald would be a Liberal, and Laurier would be a Tory. (The Conservative Party's current anti-free trade fringe — led by mavericks like David Orchard — are in fact closer in spirit to that of John A. than are Brian Mulroney or Joe Clark.)

It was a Liberal-appointed Royal Commission, headed by Donald Macdonald, that urged Canada to take the "leap of faith" required to fully integrate its economy with that of the U.S. The commission, appointed in 1982, reported back after Mulroney had taken office, but their views dovetailed nicely with the pro-business, pro-American beliefs of the new prime minister. In January 1989, the FTA came into effect, removing virtually every commercial trade barrier between the two countries. It was now a wide-open playing field that stacked Canada (population: 27 million) against the U.S. (population: 250 million). Confidential papers from that time, recently released by the White House, describe the proposed Free Trade Agreement with Canada as "a major victory for the United States."

> *The Canadians don't understand what they have signed. In 20 years, they will be sucked into the U.S. economy.*
> — a gleeful Clayton Yeutter, U.S. trade representative

Canada's *Goods and Services Tax (GST)* came into effect on January 1, 1991. (Mulroney had to stock the Senate with extra Tory appointees to get the tax passed by the Liberal-dominated Upper House.) Set at 7 percent, the GST replaced a federal manufacturer's tax of 13.5 percent, and in doing so, shifted the burden from private companies to individual consumers. The GST, in turn, was brought in to compensate for import duties and excise taxes that were now being lost under — you guessed it — free trade. Keep that in mind the next time you cough up your share of the national sales tax: Free trade isn't free.

On a World Stage

If nothing else, during the Mulroney years Canada gained a higher international profile. Examples of this include the following:

- **The Expo 86 World Fair in Vancouver**

- **The 1988 Winter Olympics in Calgary** (which, unlike the disastrous 1976 Montréal Olympics, actually turned a profit)

- **Group of 7 Economic Summit in Toronto, 1988 (Halifax, 1995):** The G7 — now G8 with the inclusion of Russia — is an association of the world's leading economically developed nations, namely: the U.S.A., Japan, Germany, Britain, France, Italy, Canada, and — *ahem* — Russia.

- **La Francophonie:** As the former French Empire crumbled, France scrambled to maintain ties with its former colonies, as well as with countries like Canada that have large francophone populations. By the 1970s an international French-speaking federation had formed, similar to the British Commonwealth. The first summit of *La Francophonie*, as it was known, met in Paris in 1986 with Prime Minister Mulroney invited as one of the speakers. The following year, 1987, Canada hosted a *Francophonie* summit in Québec City. Two of Canada's provinces — Québec and New Brunswick — are also members of the organization.

CSIS: Cloak and daggers

During the 1960s and 1970s, the RCMP dabbled in all sorts of dubious activities. In the interests of "national security," they spied on feminists, social activists, college professors, Québec separatists and homosexual civil servants. The Mounties were involved in more than 400 break-ins. They also planted illegal wiretaps and opened people's mail. The "dirty-tricks" squad of G-Branch even stole membership lists of the Parti Québécois and burned down a barn and blamed it on separatist agitators. All of these unsavoury details, and more, were dragged out in the open during a Royal Commission established in 1977 (*Inquiry into Certain Activities of the RCMP*). The final report recommended disbanding the Mounties' secret service arm entirely and replacing it with a civilian organization. And so, in 1984, the Canadian Security Intelligence Service (CSIS) was born, with many of the original members transferred directly from the RCMP. The goal of CSIS is to monitor and prevent sabotage, terrorism, and foreign espionage. And though they are not police officers, members of CSIS were given broad powers to conduct searches, wiretappings, and other surveillance — as long as they get a warrant first. They even have a secret training camp, a "spy school," so to speak, located at Camp Borden, Ontario. *"The name's Bond, eh?"*

As well, 4,500 Canadians served in the 1991 Gulf War, as part of a UN-backed coalition, led by the United States, which liberated the oil-rich country of Kuwait from Iraqi occupation. (Critics, however, felt that Mulroney had compromised Canada's role as an international peacekeeper.)

Whose passage?

Canada began as an obstacle to the riches of the Far East, and the lure of a Northwest Passage to Asia tantalized and tormented explorers for hundreds of years. The Passage itself wasn't conquered until 1903–6, when the Norwegian navigator Roald Amundsen made it through onboard the *Gjoa.*

The *second* ship to sail through the Northwest Passage, and the first to do it from west to east, was the RCMP schooner *St. Roch,* which travelled from Vancouver to Halifax in 1940–42 under the command of Sgt. Henry Larsen. In 1944, Larsen returned to Vancouver, threading his way through the dangerous ice-ridden archipelago on a quicker, more northern route, and in so doing became the first person to make a "round trip" through the Passage. The voyages of the *St. Roch* were undertaken largely to assert Canadian sovereignty over the region, but the U.S. still insisted that the Northwest Passage was an international sea route, not belonging to any one nation.

In 1985, the U.S. made a point of sending an icebreaker, the *Polar Sea*, through the Northwest Passage without asking Canada's permission first. The Americans did provide details of the route they would follow, and their crew included three official Canadian observers, but it was still an affront to our national pride. Mulroney responded by declaring that the Northwest Passage belonged to Canada "lock, stock and barrel" and quickly announced plans to (a) build a $500 million state-of-the-art icebreaker and (b) purchase a fleet of billion-dollar nuclear-powered submarines to prowl Canada's Arctic waters.

Alas, high costs eventually killed this drum-beating scheme. Mind you, Canada did establish Ellesmere Island National Park in 1988, at the very tip of the Arctic Archipelago, on the most northerly land in North America. The park operates as a nature preserve for muskoxen, caribou, fox and arctic hares. But the real purpose was political — as a display of Canadian sovereignty in the Far North. I love that. From high-tech super-powered nuclear submarines to a herd of caribou. It's so Canadian. *"You back off, mister, or I'll declare another National Park. I'm not foolin'!"*

The last cod

When John Cabot had first arrived off the Grand Banks of Newfoundland in 1497, he claimed his men could scoop up codfish simply by lowering buckets into the water. The cod fishery was thought to be "inexhaustible," but by the 1990s the Grand Banks had been fished to death. Huge ocean-going trawlers had scoured the ocean floor with drag-net fishing, and the cod stocks plummeted. Canada had tried to assert control over the region by extending its fishing limits to 200 nautical miles (roughly 400 kilometres) back in 1977, but the plunder had continued anyway. In 1992, a grim-faced John Crosbie, Minister of Fisheries and a native Newfoundlander, announced that Ottawa was closing down the northern cod fishery. It was hoped the halt would be temporary, but the cod stocks never did recover. The UN described it as "a commercial extinction." Fishermen received $1.9 billion in compensation, but no amount of money could bring back the cod.

For a history of the cod fishery, from Cabot to the present, visit www.stemnet. nf.ca/cod/home1.htm or collections.ic.gc.ca/cod/index.htm.

Native Land Claims

It is only in the last 25 years that outstanding Native land claims have begun to be taken seriously. The government now recognizes two basic types of claims:

- ✔ comprehensive
- ✔ specific

Comprehensive claims involve territory not covered by treaties. That is, areas where aboriginal title was never given up. *Specific claims* deal with outstanding grievances and breaches of specific treaty agreements. (The government also acknowledges "claims of a third kind," which is a sort of catch-all phrase dealing with those that don't fall into either category.)

Comprehensive claims are difficult to evaluate and can drag on for decades. Specific claims — in which the government is both the defendant and the judge — are notorious for being tossed out on the flimsiest of technicalities. In spite of this, hundreds of unresolved land claims are slowly working their way through the system. And it's making a lot of lawyers rich.

James Bay

The first comprehensive land claim settlement was in the James Bay area in 1975. When the St. Lawrence Seaway had been carved through Mohawk land in the 1950s, Native rights were scarcely acknowledged, let alone addressed (for more on this, see Chapter 20). Those days were gone. Now, when the government of Québec wanted to build a huge hydroelectric project in the province's north, they were forced to negotiate terms and conditions with the James Bay Inuit and Cree who lived in the region.

The James Bay and Northern Québec Agreement that followed was the first major settlement since the Numbered Treaties of the 1870s and 1920s (you can read more in Chapter 14). Under the 1975 agreement, Inuit and Cree surrendered their rights to some one million square kilometres of territory — an area the size of British Columbia — and in return were granted the following:

- ✔ self-government within their own communities
- ✔ exclusive hunting, trapping, and fishing rights
- ✔ a trust fund of $225 million, payable over the following 25 years

Further projects by Hydro-Québec, including the proposed flooding of a vast stretch of territory, increased tensions between the provincial government and the Inuit and Cree. In 1994, the northern Cree successfully derailed this $7 billion mega-project, a victory that demonstrated the growing strength and political savvy of Canada's First Nations. (The campaign to block the Hydro-Québec development was led by the militant Grand Chief, Matthew Coon Come, who was just recently elected head of the Assembly of First Nations.)

The Penner Report

Native self-government — control over land, resources, and administration — had become one of the main focuses of Native groups. This was given a major boost in 1983, when the Penner Report on aboriginal issues (named after its chairman, Keith Penner) endorsed greater Native control in the areas of health, education, and band membership. It was a radical departure in the approach to policy. Or, as Inuit delegate Zebedee Nungak later said, "We're here to do constructive damage to the status quo."

The Penner Report also marked the first time an official government report used the term *First Nations* when describing Canada's aboriginal people. This may seem like a minor semantic point, but in fact it represented a profound shift in perception. (There is a vast difference between talking about "Indian tribes" and talking about "First Nations.") Not everyone agrees with this change in terminology. Melvin H. Smith, an outspoken critic of what he calls "the rights industry," argues that the term *First Nations* is inaccurate and intentionally misleading. But is it? The definition of *nation* includes "an ethnic group sharing a common cultural or linguistic background." By this definition, the Acadians and the Québécois are both nations — and so are Canada's aboriginal societies. The Iroquois Confederacy. The Ojibwa trade empire. The Inuit of the High Arctic. The complex cultures of the Pacific Coast. Surely these rank as "nations"?

The Sechelt Band Agreement

In 1987, the Sechelt Inlet Band north of Vancouver became the first Native group in Canada to break away from the authority and terms of the Indian Act. After a ten-year battle, they were granted self-government within their reserve lands, in an arrangement similar to that of a municipal government. As a result, they now deal with the B.C. provincial government directly, with Ottawa removed from the equation. Under the terms of the agreement, the Sechelt Band was given authority over its own zoning, land uses, property taxes, health services, and education.

The Lubicon Cree

Even as concessions were being won, Native groups were growing more and more militant. The Lubicon Cree of northern Alberta, for one, had never signed Treaty 8 (1899), which purported to grant control over the region to the Canadian government. Was this a comprehensive claim or a specific claim? The Lubicon land *is* covered by treaty, but it's not a treaty that *they* have ever signed. And, as it turns out, the ancestral territory of the reserve-less and treaty-less Lubicon Cree is right in the middle of Alberta's lucrative oil patch — just to the south of my hometown, Fort Vermilion. The Lubicon Cree eventually took their case all the way to the United Nations. And in 1988, they began using civil disobedience (non-violent protests) and road blockades to draw attention to their still unresolved claims.

The Constitutional Can of Worms

Brian Mulroney got cozy with the separatists in Québec right from the start. He seems to have believed — naively, as it turned out — that he could some-how *convert* them to federalism. Mulroney's prize catch and proud protegé was Lucien Bouchard, a man who had campaigned on the separatist *Oui* side in the 1980 Referendum. But that didn't stop Mulroney from making Bouchard the Ambassador to France in 1988. (That's right, Brian Mulroney, the prime minister of Canada, sent a card-carrying separatist to represent us in Paris. *"Good call, Brian!"*)

Bouchard and Mulroney were old friends, and when Mulroney spoke of the historic "humiliations" and "collective trauma" that Québec had suffered at the hands of evil English Canadians, those were Bouchard's words — literally. Lucien Bouchard helped write speeches for Mulroney and advised him on issues of Québec sovereignty. It was kind of creepy, like some sort of political séance, with the separatist message being channelled through the body of a national leader.

> *A menacing mix of demagogue and political opportunist.*
> — author Mordecai Richler's assessment of Lucien Bouchard

Economically, Mulroney was the "Father of Free Trade and the GST." But he was also a self-proclaimed prophet of conciliation and compromise, and when the provincial Liberals under Robert Bourassa came to power in Québec in 1985, Mulroney made a bold announcement. He would renegotiate the terms of Canada's Constitution. (The Parti Québécois had never accepted the 1982 Constitution Act, as I describe in Chapter 22.) It was a grave miscalculation on Mulroney's part, and it set in motion a devastating chain of events that took Canada right to the brink of dissolution. Brian Mulroney, the "boy from Baie-Comeau" would ultimately go down in history as the Pandora of Canadian Politics: someone who unwittingly unleashed forces that he could barely comprehend, let alone control.

"A distinct society"

On an invitation from Mulroney, Premier Robert Bourassa presented Ottawa with a list of demands. They were, in Bourassa's words, the "minimum" that Québec would accept in exchange for giving its approval to a revamped Constitution Act. What Bourassa presented was a blueprint for the decentralization of Canadian government, with key powers being handed over to the provincial legislatures. Bourassa also wanted the provinces to be able to opt-out of any federal-provincial plan — but still be compensated for it by Ottawa (that is, Bourassa wanted to be able to say *no* and still receive money from the federal government. This is the "Canada as convenience store" model of Confederation).

Bourassa also asked that Québec and the other provinces be given a veto on any future Constitutional amendments, something that was a recipe for gridlock. But Bourassa's most controversial demand was that Québec be declared "a distinct society" within Canada. Not French Canadians as a whole, mind you. But the actual province of Québec.

The Meech Lake Accord

In May 1987, Mulroney and Canada's ten premiers met at a secluded retreat at Meech Lake in the Gatineau hills of Québec, northwest of Ottawa. With only a few minor revisions, including areas such as Senate reform, the premiers gave their unanimous approval to Bourassa's list of demands. And why not? The provinces were gaining all sorts of new powers at the expense of the national government.

Mulroney came out of the meeting beaming. He declared that the Meech Lake Accord would "enhance Canadian unity" and "strengthen the bonds of Confederation." (How exactly surrendering federal powers to the provinces would "strengthen" the bonds of Confederation, or how giving one province special status would "enhance" national unity, wasn't clear.)

For the Meech Lake Accord to come into effect, it had to be ratified by Ottawa and all ten provinces before June 1990. After that self-imposed deadline passed, the deal would automatically lapse. The clock was ticking, but Mulroney felt confident. After all, he had the support of every single premier, including Québec's. What could possibly go wrong?

Ah, but a lot can happen in three years, especially in the world of politics . . .

Opposition to Meech

Former prime minister Pierre Trudeau strode back onto the public stage like a vengeful Shakespearean ghost and denounced Mulroney as a "weakling" who had rendered the Canadian state "impotent." If the Meech Lake Accord passed, warned Trudeau, "the Canada we know and love will be gone forever." Opposition to the accord grew, and it focused on three areas:

- ✔ the "distinct society" clause
- ✔ the weakening of Canada's national government by granting excessive power and full vetoes to the provincial legislatures
- ✔ and finally, the process itself (the accord was criticized as a "deal worked out behind closed doors by 11 men in suits")

Section 2(b) of the Meech Lake Accord — "Québec constitutes within Canada a distinct society" — caused the most outrage because it enshrined in the Constitution the *deux nations* view of Confederation: that Canada was a pact between two "founding nations." Native groups were also incensed that the accord ignored aboriginal rights. The First Nations wanted special status too. And why not Newfoundland, while we're at it?

Mulroney insisted that proclaiming one province a "distinct society" was merely a symbolic gesture to Québec. But Premier Bourassa himself clearly stated clearly that having his province recognized as separate and distinct within Canada would change the entire way the Constitution was interpreted. And anyway, why would Bourassa insist that a "gesture" be formally entrenched in the Canadian Constitution if he didn't plan on taking full advantage of it?

The final critique is more problematic: the idea that the Meech Lake Accord was invalid because it was worked out behind closed doors. But how should it have been done? Through community bake sales and town hall meetings? Elected heads of states negotiating political amendments: that is exactly how governments are *supposed* to run. Heck, that's why we elect representatives in the first place. There were public discussions on the terms of Meech, but ultimately it was up to Canada's duly elected representatives to hammer out the details and come to a consensus. They did just that at Meech Lake — flawed though the results were. No. It was the *content* of Meech Lake that was the problem, not the process. After all, this isn't a small-scale farming commune in which we are living. It's a huge country with a population fast approaching 30 million with a two-level federal system of government.

Confederation itself was worked out in much the same manner as Meech, back in 1864, and was later revised during similar closed-door meetings in 1982. But where the delegates in the 1860s were hailed as "Fathers of Confederation," the architects of Meech Lake were denounced as "11 men in suits." The times had changed — but not necessarily for the better.

Bill 178

In December 1988, right in the middle of the Meech Lake hullabaloo, the Supreme Court of Canada declared that Québec's restrictive French-only language laws contravened Canada's Charter of Rights and Freedoms. Premier Bourassa responded to this by simply invoking the Constitution's "notwith-standing clause" (covered in Chapter 22) and overriding the Supreme Court ruling. He then introduced Bill 178, which *extended* the ban on English signs in Québec (or rather, "non-French" signs). The Supreme Court of Canada was not so supreme after all. It was also an amazing act of chutzpah on Bourassa's part, considering that at that time he was asking the rest of Canada to accept the terms of the Meech Lake Accord, which would have increased Québec's powers tenfold. Is this what the future held under the auspices of a "distinct society"?

> *Never before in the history of Québec has a government suspended fundamental liberties to protect the French language and culture.*
> — Premier Bourassa, on his use of the "notwithstanding clause" to override Canada's Charter of Rights and Freedoms

No doubt about it, Bill 178 played a key role in turning public opinion against Meech Lake. Years later, Brian Mulroney — still trying in vain to defend his legacy — pointed out, somewhat huffily, that the real problem was not with the Meech Lake Accord but with Trudeau's Constitution Act. It was Trudeau's "notwithstanding clause," after all, which had allowed Québec to ride rough-shod over Canada's Charter. Bourassa was simply using it to his advantage. This is true. But what is less clear is how Mulroney's beloved accord, in declaring Québec a "distinct society," would have fixed the problem. The notwithstanding clause wasn't eliminated by Meech. Far from it. If anything, Québec was being given even greater leeway and an even stronger justification to enact restrictive legislation — in order to protect and preserve its constitutionally guaranteed "distinct" status.

New kids on the block

Brian Mulroney was re-elected in 1988 with two important issues still unresolved: Free Trade (which was ratified soon after) and the Meech Lake Accord, which still hadn't been passed by all ten provincial legislatures. The June 1990 deadline was approaching, and there were dark clouds on the horizon. In three provinces (New Brunswick, Manitoba, and Newfoundland) the old pro-Meech premiers had been defeated and new leaders had been elected in their place. And in each case, the new premiers expressed dissatisfaction with the Meech Lake Accord. They were:

> ✔ **Frank McKenna** (Liberal): elected in New Brunswick in 1987
> ✔ **Gary Filmon** (Conservative): elected in Manitoba in 1988
> ✔ **Clyde Wells** (Liberal): elected in Newfoundland in 1989

New Brunswick premier Frank McKenna soon relented and gave his support to the deal, but Filmon in Manitoba, heading a minority government and facing an angry Liberal Opposition, held back. In Newfoundland, Wells was openly critical of the accord. (An angry Robert Bourassa fumed and said that the time might come when Canada would have to "choose between Québec and Newfoundland.")

As resistance to Meech Lake grew, a Conservative commission headed by Jean Charest recommended making 23 changes to the original Accord. At that point, Lucien Bouchard, now Mulroney's minister of the environment, had had enough. He left the Conservative Party in May 1990, complaining, "This country doesn't work anymore."

A fateful boast

Mulroney called a last-ditch, last-minute meeting with the premiers in early June. It lasted seven exhausting days. With the deadline for Meech looming and the pressure on, Mulroney managed to wring an agreement from the remaining holdouts. Clyde Wells was the last to give in, but he too eventually agreed to bring Meech Lake before his legislature for approval. Everything seemed wrapped up — but then Mulroney's ego got the better of him. In a fateful boast to the *Globe and Mail* he gloated over the fact that he had intentionally increased the pressure on the premiers by holding talks so near the final deadline.

In Mulroney's own words, he had "rolled the dice." It was a telling phrase and one that enraged Canadians and premiers alike. Mulroney appeared to be gambling with Canada's future, and his ill-timed "roll of the dice" comment crippled what little goodwill remained towards the accord, as the public railed against what they considered to be Mulroney's reckless approach. It was the beginning of the end for Meech. (Mulroney later tried to deny he ever made the comment, but the reporters in question produced a tape recording of the interview and offered to play his words back to him.)

"No, Mr. Speaker"

In June 1990, with the deadline fast approaching, Manitoba premier Gary Filmon finally put the Meech Lake Accord to a vote. Or rather, he tried to. Now, in order to bring a bill forward for debate in the Manitoba legislature without public hearings required the unanimous approval of all members.

This should have been a mere formality, but Elijah Harper, a Cree Native and NDP Member of the Manitoba legislature — upset that Meech Lake failed to address aboriginal rights — refused to give his approval. When asked by the Speaker repeatedly and over several days, whether he would give his assent to introduce the bill, Harper, holding an eagle feather, mumbled, "No, Mr. Speaker." And Canada's entire political machinery came grinding to a halt.

The Meech Lake Accord died in the Manitoba legislature, tripped up on a legislative technicality. Ottawa scrambled and attempted to extend the deadline by three months, but by then it was too late. In light of Meech's demise, Newfoundland premier Clyde Wells withdrew the bill as well. On June 23, 1990, the deadline passed and the Meech Lake Accord was dead. It was a one-two combination punch: Manitoba and Newfoundland, Harper and Wells, that ultimately killed the Accord — and with it, Brian Mulroney's career. The failure of Meech Lake set off a domino effect of events that would eventually take Canada to the very edge of the abyss.

The Charlottetown Accord

Bourassa was livid. He threatened to hold a referendum on Québec secession, and Mulroney panicked and quickly patched together a *second* constitutional deal. The Son of Meech, so to speak. Named the *Charlottetown Accord* after the city in which it was drafted, it was a mishmash of concessions and "collective rights." Yessir, the 1992 Accord had something for everyone: full Native self-government, provincial rights (with vetoes), Senate reform, and, of course, "distinct status" for Québec. This time, instead of being taken to the respective provincial legislatures, the agreement would be voted on by *all* Canadians. The matter would be settled, not by "men in suits," but by everybody. Supporters said it was "grassroots decision-making." Opponents said it was a crazy way to run a country. "Democracy gone mad," in the words of one commentator.

Pierre Trudeau, crabby as ever, once again re-emerged from the shadows and denounced the Charlottetown Accord as "a mess that deserves a big *No*." Trudeau said it went too far. Jacques Parizeau, the hardline separatist leader of the Parti Québécois, said it didn't go far enough.

The Charlottetown Accord was backed by the weight of the entire Canadian political establishment: every province, every premier, the prime minister, the leaders of the Opposition, the Assembly of First Nations — all approved the new deal. And they still lost. The final tally of the referendums held on October 26, 1992, saw the Charlottetown Accord rejected by 54 percent of the population. (Only in Atlantic Canada was there a solid majority in favour of it.) In Québec, the results were almost exactly the same as the national average, with 55 percent of Quebeckers voting against the Charlottetown Accord.

The West Wants In and the East Wants Out

History is a chain reaction of cause and effect, and often the *reaction* is just as important as the initial action. Such was the case with Brian Mulroney's term in office. In many ways, Mulroney has had a greater impact in the backlash he inspired than in what he actually attempted to do. Nowhere is this more evident than in the regional protest parties that were created in a direct response to Mulroney's handling of national unity issues. They were:

- **The Reform Party:** formed by breakaway, dissatisfied Conservatives in 1987 with Preston Manning as its founding leader
- **The Bloc Québécois:** a separatist coalition formed in 1990 after the death of Meech Lake by former Conservative and Liberal MPs with Lucien Bouchard chosen as their leader

Under Mulroney, the federal Conservative Party's traditional support in Western Canada began to collapse. Many Westerners felt betrayed by Mulroney and what they perceived to be his constant pandering to Québec. The Reform Party was launched under the banner, "The West Wants In."

> *With us, politics is not a game, but a passion.*
> — explanation of Reform's roots by one of the original party members

The Bloc, meanwhile, was formed in the wake of the Meech Lake Accord. Note: the Parti Québécois is a *provincial* separatist party, formed in 1968 under René Lévesque. The Bloc Québécois is a *federal* coalition of separatist MPs formed in 1990. (PQ=provincial; Bloc=federal.)

21 Days

In 1986, Brian Mulroney slashed Canada's youth budget and cancelled Katimavik, a national volunteer corps that had recently received a commendation by the UN. What followed was one of the most remarkable and controversial political protests in Canadian history. Senator Jacques Hébert, the eccentric and idealistic co-founder of both Katimavik and Canada World Youth (an exchange program with the developing world), went on a three-week hunger strike in the foyer of the Upper House to protest the cuts. Katimavik itself was resurrected in 1994-95 and is still going strong. For more on Katimavik, go to katimavik.org and for Canada World Youth, www.cwy-jcm.org. (I was a participant in both programs, and in spite of their sometimes painfully good intentions, I recommend them highly.)

Although both Reform and the Bloc began as fringe protest parties, they quickly became major players in Canadian politics. Mulroney had managed to alienate both his Québec base and his Western base, and the results were disastrous. With the Bloc taking Québec, Reform taking the West, and the Liberals taking Ontario, the Conservative Party was virtually wiped out in the elections that followed. (Both the Bloc and Reform went on to become Official Opposition as well: the Bloc in 1993; Reform in 1997.)

RCAP and the Shoot-Out at the Oka Corral

It started with a golf course and ended with a gun battle, the death of a police officer, and an armed showdown that captured headlines around the world. In March 1990, Mohawk protestors in the Oka region outside of Montréal occupied forests that were slated to be cut down to make room for an expanded golf course. The forest, and the graveyard nearby, were considered sacred by the Mohawk, who had already seen their land whittled down to 1 percent of what they had originally been granted more than 260 years earlier. When the Mohawk barricaded the roads and refused to leave, the Mayor of Oka sent in the police and a fierce gun battle erupted. Corporal Marcel Lemay, an officer with the Québec provincial police force, was killed. The situation spiraled out of control as a second sympathy barricade was erected across the Mercier Bridge leading into Montréal by the Mohawk in Kahnawake. The army was called in and a tense standoff ensued that lasted well into September. The remaining Mohawk protestors eventually laid down their arms and attempted to walk away, at which point mayhem broke out. No one was ever charged in the death of Corporal Lemay.

The Oka Crisis led directly to the formation of the 1991 Royal Commission on Aboriginal Peoples (RCAP) to examine the relationship between Canada's First Nations and the government, as well as with Canadian society as a whole. The commission reported back in 1996 after an exhaustive five-year study, and the recommendations it made were complex and far-reaching. More than 400 changes were proposed, many of which were very sensible. For example, the commission recommended the creation of an independent tribunal for land claims, separate from any government agency. This made a lot of sense. After all, the Government of Canada had a clear — and advantageous — conflict of interest when it came to resolving Native grievances. As judge, jury, and defendant, the government was evaluating the very claims made against it — something that insured that the cards were always stacked in its favour.

> *The process [of Native land claims] is heavily weighted in favour of the government. A claim may be rejected solely on the legal advice of the Department of Justice. . . . This is a clear conflict of interest.*
> — from an earlier report by the Canadian Human Rights Commission

The Somalia Affair

In 1991, the East African country of Somalia boiled over in anarchy and civil war — followed by drought and widespread famine. When the UN sent a peacekeeping mission to Somalia, the support troops included Canada's elite Airborne Regiment, who arrived in December 1992. The following March, members of the Airborne captured a 16-year-old Somali boy who was attempting to pilfer supplies from the Canadian camp. The boy was bound, burnt, beaten, and tortured to death while under custody of the Airborne. He died pleading with the soldiers in the only word of their language he knew: "Canada... Canada..." The scandal shocked the nation, and the disgraced Airborne Regiment was eventually disbanded. The Somalia Inquiry into the killing dragged on until 1997 before releasing its final report, in which Canadian military command was criticized. The Somalia scandal tarnished the hard work and reputation of Canada's peacekeepers. Thousands of Canadians — from civilian observers to members of the Armed Forces and the RCMP — have worn the "blue beret" of UN peacekeeping, and the vast majority have done so with honour and courage. It's one of the toughest jobs on earth.

For more on Canada's role in international peacekeeping visit www.dnd.ca/menu/legacy/peace_e.htm and for a Canadian peacekeeping veterans site: www.islandnet.com/~duke/cpva.htm.

Far more controversial, however, was RCAP's proposal that Native self-government be taken to a higher level. Rather than simply giving Native communities control over their resources and administration, the commission recommended that a "third order of government" be created, separate from that of the provincial or federal legislatures: an indigenous parliament to be called the House of First Peoples. A segregated government based upon race and ethnic background — is this really what Canadian democracy stood for? Many Canadians balked at the idea. The price tag for the reforms outlined by RCAP were around $30 billion over a 15-year period. And this was at a time when the federal government was trying to trim costs as it wrestled the federal deficit under control. In short, the recommendations of the commission were more a "wish list" than they were a practical blueprint for change.

The Voter Revolt of 1993

Brian Mulroney was probably the most unpopular leader in modern democratic history, falling to around 9 percent support, the lowest level ever recorded for any Canadian prime minister. He retired in June 1993, and was replaced by Kim Campbell, then minister of national defense. ("Don't mess with me," she once joked. "I've got tanks.")

In taking over as party leader, Kim Campbell also became Canada's first female prime minister. But when faced with the wrath of the Canadian voters in the election that followed, Kim was tossed out of office so fast her head spun. She even lost her own seat. On October 25, 1993, the Progressive Conservative Party of Canada was all but destroyed, cut down from a majority of 169 seats to a rump of only *two*: Jean Charest in Québec, and Elsie Wayne in New Brunswick. That was it.

The Tories ended up spending $15 million to elect two MPs — that comes to $7.5 million each. They even lost official party status. Which is to say, technically, the Conservative Party didn't even *exist*. (In the 1997 election, they regained enough seats to have their party status reinstated. Barely.)

A panel of history professors recently declared that Kim Campbell was the "worst prime minister in Canadian history," but this is patently unfair. It was Brian Mulroney who was the real culprit; Kim Campbell was simply the fall guy. Mulroney, however, refused to accept responsibility for the collapse of the Conservatives, choosing instead to blame it on a conspiracy of "left-wing media" and disloyal Western Reformers who refused to play ball. Which is to say, he blames both the left wing *and* the right wing.

The Mulroney Legacy

Brian Mulroney promised a new era of regional conciliation. Instead, he left the country splintered and with separatism in Québec about to boil over. He also promised a new era of "fiscal responsibility" and an end to political cronyism. He left nine years later having run up the largest peacetime debt in our nation's history. (In fact, under Mulroney, Canada incurred *more than half* the total national debt accumulated since Confederation in 1867.)

He was also the undisputed King of Patronage (patronage being a distinctly Canadian art form of awarding jobs and government perks to friends, political cronies, and party hacks). In his first year alone, Mulroney set an all-time record: making an incredible 1,280 patronage appointments, filling the ranks with party insiders, organizers, school chums, old friends, former business associates, regional fundraisers, failed candidates, and backroom organizers. Everybody got a piece of the Tory pie.

> *Let's face it, there's no whore like an old whore.*
> — Brian Mulroney, on the fine art of patronage

Without meaning to, Brian Mulroney helped revive two of Canada's great fears: Québec separatism and the economic "Americanization" of Canada. The poor guy. Even when he *succeeded* he didn't get credit. Certainly, free trade with the United States was a bold move — and it has not been the boogieman that Canadian nationalists portrayed it to be. The country hasn't been "sucked into" the U.S. economy. At least, not yet. The economy is booming and business is humming thanks largely to Canada's close ties to the U.S.

Canucks in outer space

Here's a little known fact: Canada was the third nation in space, after the Soviet Union (1957) and the United States (1958). In a country as far-flung and thinly populated as ours, the interest was never in spy satellites or military defense, but rather in crossing the distance, in transcending geography. The focus was on communications. Here are some of the highlights in Canada's satellite/space program:

Alouette I: Launched in 1962, Alouette's mission was to study the upper atmosphere (and especially the disruptions caused by the Northern Lights) in order to help improve long-distance radio transmissions.

Anik A-1: Launched in 1972, Anik (from the Inuktitut for "brother") was the world's first domestic telecommunications satellite system. By using a geostationary orbit — where the satellite revolves with the earth, keeping a constant position in the sky — Anik was able to provide 24-hour, coast-to-coast telephone and information services.

The Canadarm: A 15-metre-long robotic limb designed and built in Canada, the Canadarm has been used on NASA shuttle flights since 1981. Canadarms help load and unload cargo bays, they capture damaged satellites and launch new ones, and have even been employed to swat away ice chunks that form on liquid-waste vents.

Astronauts: Want to know how a hockey puck ended up in outer space? It wasn't a Mark Messier slapshot that did it. It was Marc Garneau of Quebec City, Canada's first astronaut, who took a puck along with him during his 1984 mission onboard the space shuttle *Challenger*. (A giant stuffed moose head probably would have been out of the question.) Garneau returned to space in 1996 onboard the *Endeavour* and is scheduled for a third voyage as well. Canada's second astronaut in space (and first woman) was Roberta Bondar of Sault Ste. Marie, Ontario, who was part of the *Discovery* crew in 1992. At last count, eight Canadian astronauts have flown on NASA missions, the most recent being Julie Payette of Montreal in 1999.

Today, it is the Internet that is connecting remote regions and shrinking distances, just as surely as the first satellites did in their day. The world is now just a click away. The Canadian Space Agency's official site is at www.space.gc.ca. (For more on Canada's astronauts click on "Human Presence in Space" and then "Canadian Astronaut Office." And while you're there, check out the cool space badges they got to wear, under "Space Missions.") For a history of Canada in space, including satellite programs and the Canadarm, visit pacific-space-centre.bc.ca/SRC/history.htm.

During his nine years in office, Brian Mulroney made some tough choices. In 1992, he abolished federal Family Allowance payments. Two years earlier, he was accused of "shutting down the National Dream" by ending passenger service along the old Canadian Pacific Railway line. It was the CPR that had first bound Canada together, from sea to sea, in 1885 (I discuss this in Chapter 14) and many Canadians still had a romantic attachment to it. However, it should be noted that the Canadian public had long since given up on the CPR by the time Mulroney pulled the plug. It was an economic decision. Cold and simple. (Others insist that the CPR had given up on passengers first: that poor service, screwy schedules, and bad management are what killed the CPR's passenger line.)

Meanwhile, RCMP allegations that Mulroney had accepted kickbacks for arranging a 1988 Air Canada purchase of Airbus jets (a scandal known as "the Airbus Affair") were quashed for good in 1997 when the Liberal government was forced to apologize for allowing the investigation to drag on and were ordered to pay Mulroney's legal costs. It was a bittersweet victory for Mulroney, because — Airbus or no Airbus — his reputation, based on patronage, government debt, and national unity remained in tatters.

> _Brian Mulroney knew how to lead elites — how to get premiers on his side, business groups in his pocket, and unity in his caucus — but when he urged Canadians to go over the top with him, they shot him in the back._
> — historian Michael Bliss's summation of Brian Mulroney's career

Chapter 24

Where Do We Go From Here?

In This Chapter

▶ Québec holds another referendum on sovereignty

▶ The Canada/U.S Free Trade Agreement is expanded to include Mexico

▶ Nunavut, a new northern territory, is created

▶ The Reform Party votes itself out of existence and re-emerges as the Canadian Alliance

*J*ean Chrétien became leader of the Liberal Party in June 1990, on the very day the Meech Lake Accord died. (The accord, a failed attempt at gaining Québec's approval of the Constitution, is described in detail in Chapter 23.) It was an omen of things to come. Chrétien went on to a landslide victory in 1993 and became Canada's 20th prime minister, but the Ghost of Meech Lake stalked him still.

Chrétien ran against Paul Martin for the Liberal leadership. Martin had supported Meech Lake; Chrétien had opposed it (publicly at least; privately he tried to arrange its passage). The Martin/Chrétien camps — still active today — were pitted against each other in a scorched earth policy that peaked with Martin supporters chanting *"Vendu! Vendu!"* ("Sell-out!") at Chrétien for his "betrayal" of Québec. The insult stung and the bad feelings lingered.

In 1993, Jean Chrétien inherited a parliament and a country that was badly splintered and sharply divided along regional and linguistic lines. The separatist movement had been revived and was now simmering just below the surface. Free trade with the United States had drawn Canada ever closer to complete economic integration with the giant to the south, and Native demands for self-government were now coming to a head. Thus, under Jean Chrétien, the Three Great Themes of Canadian History still dominated the national agenda:

   ✔ the tension between French and English Canada

   ✔ the presence and pull of the United States

   ✔ the outstanding grievances and growing demands of the First Nations

The End of Canada?

In Québec, the Parti Québécois was elected in 1994 and a hardline separatist, Jacques Parizeau, became premier. An opponent of Meech Lake and the follow-up Charlottetown Accord, Parizeau was determined to take Québec out of Confederation entirely and he soon set a date for a referendum on sovereignty: October 30, 1995.

The 1995 Referendum

The campaign for the future of Québec officially started at the beginning of October (though both sides had been jockeying for position long before that). The team roster, so to speak, broke down like this:

Leading the pro-Canada *Non* forces:

- **Daniel Johnson**, leader of the Québec Liberal Party and son of the former Union Nationale premier of the same name (Robert Bourassa, dying of skin cancer, had since stepped down)
- **Jean Chrétien**, Prime Minister of Canada

Spearheading the pro-sovereignty *Oui* side:

- **Jacques Parizeau**, Premier of Québec and leader of the Parti Québécois
- **Lucien Bouchard**, head of the federal Bloc Québécois (and also, ironically, Leader of Her Majesty's "Loyal" Opposition)
- **Mario Dumont**, leader of the Action Démocratique Party

Before the campaign began, the federalist *Non* forces were confident to the point of complacency. They were sure the separatists couldn't possibly win, and Chrétien in particular never took the threat seriously — not at first. Instead, he lulled Canada into a false sense of security. His message was basically, "Don't worry, be happy." And it almost cost us the country.

The separatist side started strong but soon appeared to have stalled. Parizeau couldn't seem to break the 50 percent barrier, but when Bouchard entered the fray and took over as the head of the *Oui* campaign, the debate was suddenly energized. Bouchard was a forceful and charismatic speaker, and the momentum quickly shifted to the separatist side. A vote for sovereignty, said Bouchard, would be like "a magic wand" that would change everything. The crowds cheered.

Chrétien had the stunned look of a bunny caught in the glare of approaching headlights. He could see Canada slipping away and at one point he apparently broke down in tears during a Cabinet meeting. In a televised address to the nation, a distraught Chrétien pleaded with Québec voters to search their souls and see if they could come up with "one good reason to destroy Canada."

Only a massive, last-minute pro-Canada rally in Montreal, just three days before the vote, seems to have averted disaster. On October 30, 1995, the *Non* side won by the slimmest, most hair-raising margins imaginable with just 50.6 percent of the vote.

It wasn't so much a "narrow victory" as it was a "near defeat." Not so much a referendum, as a near-death experience. The *Globe and Mail* called it "the worst moment in Mr. Chrétien's career." And they were right.

In the 1995 Referendum, Canada had come within a heartbeat of breaking up. Not that the separatists exited the stage gracefully. No sir. At a *Oui* rally following his defeat, Jacques Parizeau complained bitterly that *real* Québécois (that is, white and French-speaking) had been defeated by "money and the ethnic vote" — a statement that ranks among the nastiest comments ever made by an elected leader in Canada.

> *We will soon have the country we desire — and we will have our revenge . . .*
> — Jacques Parizeau, in the wake of the 1995 Referendum

Parizeau stepped down as premier soon after, still bitter and unrepentant, and was replaced by Lucien Bouchard, who took over as both leader of the Parti Québécois and as premier of Québec.

Jean Chrétien and the Liberals were re-elected in 1997. And the following year, Lucien Bouchard and the Bloc Québécois were also re-elected. Thus, Canada's ongoing Cold War with the provincial government of Québec continued, as Bouchard promised yet *another* referendum — just as soon as "winning conditions" presented themselves. The referendums and the wrenching national debates would never end. It would be, in the words of Bouchard, "like endless trips to the dentist." He was sure that at some point, Canada's resolve would have to crack. In fact, just the opposite happened.

Plan B

After the near-debacle of the 1995 Referendum, Chrétien's resolve hardened. Plan A was one of reconciliation and compromise: one that stressed the benefits of Confederation. Plan B was a hardline approach: one that was more aggressive and unyielding, and which stressed the consequences of separation. Ottawa now switched to Plan B.

Chrétien brought in Stéphane Dion, a law professor from Québec, to strengthen the federalist position. As minister of intergovernmental affairs, Dion quickly made a name for himself with his relentless attacks on the separatist party line, as he shot holes through their assertion that "Canada is divisible, but Québec is not." (Stéphane Dion is sort of like Pierre Trudeau, but without the testosterone.) Ironically, Dion himself had supported Meech Lake and the recognition of Québec as a "distinct society" — but he was just as dogged in his defense of Canadian unity.

The Supreme Court ruling

When it became clear during the 1995 Referendum that the *Oui* side might squeak by with a narrow win, the question immediately arose: would 50 percent plus one (that is, a bare majority) be enough to allow Québec to separate? Chrétien suggested that it would not. Parizeau was incensed at this, and warned Ottawa that if it refused to negotiate a break-up in the wake of a slim *Oui* majority, Québec would make a "unilateral declaration of independence" and immediately sever all ties with Canada. Bouchard, meanwhile, attempted a bit of pre-emptive blackmail of his own, stating that if Ottawa refused to negotiate the terms of Québec sovereignty, Québec might renege on its share of the national debt.

Section 356 of Québec's own Civil Code states very clearly that 50 percent plus one is *not* enough to dissolve a legal entity (such as a political organization or a society or, one assumes, a province). In fact, a two-thirds majority among members is required. As more than one commentator suggested, perhaps it is time that Lucien Bouchard, premier of Québec, actually read the province's Civil Code.

The 1995 Cree and Inuit Referendums

The separatists of Québec have always insisted that they can walk out of Confederation with the province's current borders in tact. But the Inuit and Cree who occupy the northern two-thirds of the province (an area roughly the size of British Columbia) beg to differ. They occupy the heartland of Québec's valuable Hydro-Electric industry and they figure if Québec can separate from Canada, they should be allowed to separate from Québec. Fair's fair, right? And certainly the Cree and Inuit have an older, prior claim to the region than do today's Québécois.

During the divisive 1995 Referendum, the aboriginal people of Québec's north held their own referendums, and the results were sobering for those who feel that Québec is "indivisible." On October 25, 1995, the Cree in Québec voted 96 percent to reject Québec separatism and remain in Canada. The Inuit followed this up with a second referendum a day later. The results? 95 percent voted to stay in Confederation. The message to the rest of Québec was clear: "You can leave if you want, but you aren't taking us with you."

With all the confusion and uncertainty surrounding these issues, Ottawa asked the Supreme Court of Canada to rule on the question: "Can Québec, or any other province, unilaterally secede from Confederation?"

The answer came in August 1998, and the answer was: *no*. Québec could not unilaterally secede, even after a referendum victory. Neither the Canadian Constitution nor international law recognized such a right. (Unilateral declarations of independence are recognized in international law only in cases of severely oppressed minorities, such as those in colonized countries, or groups struggling against foreign military occupation. And the people of Québec are not an "oppressed people," not by any stretch.)

However, the Supreme Court also ruled that if a *clear* question was asked and a *clear* majority voted in favour of independence, then Ottawa would be duty bound to negotiate the terms of secession. What exactly constituted a "clear question" and a "clear majority" the Supreme Court didn't say. It left that up to the government to decide. But the Court did insist that democracy is more than simple majority rule. (It should also be noted that the Court's ruling was outside the realm of the infamous "notwithstanding clause" and thus cannot simply be overruled by a provincial legislature.)

The Clarity Bill

> *If things are clear, we negotiate. If there is no clarity, there is no negotiation.*
> — Stéphane Dion on the government's approach to future referendums

In response to the Supreme Court ruling, Stéphane Dion drafted Bill C-20, better known as "the Clarity Bill," which stuck closely to the terms outlined by the Court. In a way, Dion's bill is simply the "legislative equivalent" of the Supreme Court ruling, putting into law what the Court has already declared: namely, that in any future referendums, the question and the results must be clear. If not, Ottawa is within its rights to boycott the entire process.

It is important to note that the Clarity Bill does *not* dictate the exact wording of the next referendum question, nor does it say what exactly a "clear majority" entails: "We'll fall off that bridge when we get there," so to speak. But it does lay down the general terms and rules of engagement for any future separatist/federalist battles.

> ✔ Québec's borders would indeed be subject to negotiation, and its aboriginal people would indeed have to be consulted. (The Clarity Bill itself makes no direct mention of Québec, but applies to all provinces.)

✔ Referendum questions must be submitted first to the House of Commons for approval. The question must be straightforward and cannot allude to future hypothetical arrangements. (By these criteria, both the 1980 referendum question, which was on the vaguely defined concept of "sovereignty-association," and the 1995 question, which referred to a possible "partnership" with Canada, would be disallowed.)

✔ And, because separation would require a constitutional amendment, negotiations on the break-up of Canada would have to involve all the other provinces as well.

The Clarity Bill imposes conditions and guidelines on future referendums. As such, both the Parti Québécois and the Bloc have vehemently denounced it. The bill has been called "an assault on Québec" and a "crime against history" aimed at "crushing" the spirit of the Québécois. One PQ minister even went on a tirade that ended with him calling the Clarity Bill "an anti-democratic Soviet-style law" on par with Stalin. Gosh.

I'm going to go out on a limb here and make a prediction. Twenty years from now, historians will look back at Stéphane Dion's Clarity Bill as a major victory against separatism. Perhaps *the* major victory. It will be recognized for what it was: a brilliant outflanking manoeuvre that very well may have saved Confederation, if only by making future secession debates less manipulative and more honest. Certainly, the bill itself presents a powerful deterrent to launching yet another tumultuous vote on separation.

Of course, not everyone agrees with me. There has been strong opposition to the Clarity Bill from federalists as well. Some fear that by outlining the terms of separation, the government has, in fact, presented a blueprint for the end of Canada. Joe Clark, resurrected leader of the Conservative Party, denounced the Clarity Bill as "a road map to secession." Alexa McDonough, leader of the NDP, called it "irresponsible." Columnist Peter C. Newman felt that the bill "legitimizes Canada's break-up."

Critics point out that Canada is now one of the only countries on earth that has formally acknowledged it can be dissolved. In fact, of the world's developed nations, only two others have even *allowed* for their own dissolution, let alone provide the ground rules: Austria and Czechoslovakia (and the latter soon broke into two: the Czech Republic and Slovakia). Many countries, such as France and the United States, explicitly *forbid* any attempts at breaking them up, stating that they are "indivisible."

But at this stage, it is far too late for Canada to suddenly declare itself a sacred union that can't be broken. The precedent has already been set. Canadians have allowed two votes on the issue: one in 1980 and another in 1995, and the Supreme Court has ruled that yes, provinces can leave Confederation under certain conditions. In a bilingual, multiethnic, far-flung, regionalized country like Canada, it could hardly be otherwise. As Dion himself said, "This country only makes sense by mutual consent."

In other words, you can't force people to stay in Canada against their will. But you can force them to play fair.

> *"Un Québec indépendant dans un Canada uni!" ("An independent Québec within a united Canada!")*
> — comedian Yvon Deschamps' famous description of what Québec really wants.

(Deschamps' joke was, incredibly, adopted as a working model by Bouchard and Parizeau during the 1995 Referendum. Sigh.)

For a modern manifesto of the Québec separatist movement, check out the hardline 1995 Sovereignty Bill at www.sfu.ca/~aheard/bill1.html. For a look at Canadian unity from a federalist position, surf on over to www.uni.ca/index_e.html and click on "Learn More/Permanent Content" and then on "background" for historical perspectives on the Québec sovereignty debates.

The French-Canadian culture site at about.com, hosted by Johanne Pouliot, covers a wide range of subjects, including history, legends, festivals, geography, and the sovereignty movement.

NAFTA: From Eaton's to Wal-Mart?

Let's see if you can spot the difference:

Jean Chrétien *before* the 1993 election: anti-Free Trade, anti-GST

Jean Chrétien *after* the 1993 election: pro-Free Trade, pro-GST

Notice anything odd? In January 1994, just months after taking office, Jean Chrétien signed an agreement that greatly expanded Brian Mulroney's original Free Trade Agreement with the U.S. The pact now includes Mexico, a country of 98 million people. The new deal, known as NAFTA (North America Free Trade Agreement) removes most of the tariffs and duties between the three countries, creating one large "mega-market," with the U.S. leading the way.

The effects of NAFTA on Canadian retail were immediate. In a move that many took to be a foreshadowing of things to come, the U.S. retail giant Wal-Mart immediately invaded the Canadian market, buying out old Woolco properties and quickly establishing more than 150 Wal-Mart stores across Canada. It was a massive expansion of American investment into the Canadian business sector.

And five years later, Canada's grand dame of retail business, the venerable Eaton's Company, was forced to file for bankruptcy protection. It folded soon after, ending a 130-year Canadian dynasty. For many, the shift from the all-Canadian Eaton's to the warehouse-like stores of Wal-Mart is symptomatic of the increasing Americanization of Canada's consumer society. However, it should also be pointed out that our current and ongoing prosperity depends largely upon open trade with the U.S.A.

> *The Americans are our best friends — whether we like it or not.*
> — Robert Thompson, former leader of the Social Credit Party

Is wealth an end in itself? Opponents of NAFTA fear that Canada's close ties with the U.S. have undermined Canadian independence. Certainly, a recent U.S. study on the effects of NAFTA on Canada/U.S. relations sent shivers down the spines of Canadians when it stated bluntly that the border between the two countries was becoming increasingly "irrelevant."

The study, conducted by the Carnegie Endowment for International Peace, notes that in many key sectors Canada and the U.S. have already attained a greater degree of economic integration than have the members of the European Union. Some 200 million people cross the border every year, and more than US$1 billion in trade crosses it — *every day*. Several analysts have even predicted that the Canada/U.S. border will soon "disappear" entirely; a suggestion that is rejected by the Customs Departments in both countries.

With the explosive U.S./Mexico trade now underway, Canada finds itself caught up in the modern equivalent of the old "triangular trade" that took shape in the colonial days of New France (to find out more, see Chapter 4).

Native Settlements in the 1990s

Canadians like to think of themselves as the Dudley Do-Right of world nations, but in 1999 the United Nations presented a stinging rebuttal to this image. In a scathing report, a UN Human Rights Committee ruled that Canada is in violation of international law in its treatment of aboriginal rights, something the UN panel described as "the most pressing human rights issue facing Canadians."

Certainly, the manner in which Native claims are dealt with in Canada is an absolute mess. There is a huge backlog of hundreds of outstanding land claims and thousands of unresolved lawsuits (everything from disputes over resources to broken treaty promises). The tally runs into the *billions* of dollars, and it has turned into a legal and legislative quagmire, sucking up money to very little effect. The process is ponderously slow.

There is a glimmer of light at the end of the log-jam, however. In Chapter 23, I wrote about the need for a separate, independent board for evaluating and administrating claim settlements (as it is, the federal government sits as judge, jury, and defendant — a clear and confusing conflict of interest). Well, I'm happy to report that plans for an Independent Claims Body are now underway in the hopes of speeding up the process.

The scandal of Canada's residential schools

In the late 1800s, the Canadian government began removing Native children from their homes and placing them in boarding schools to better assimilate them into white society — under the guidance of a proper Christian education, of course. In the standard phrase of the day, the Natives who attended the schools would be "civilized." This was done by stripping the children of their language, religion, customs, and culture.

This assault on Native society, often undertaken with the best intentions, lasted for 200 years. The last residential school in Canada didn't close down until 1996. More than 100,000 Native children were sent to residential schools (around 20 percent of all Natives went through the system). Separated from their families, the children were easy prey for emotional, physical, and sexual abuse. Equally shattering, in the long run, was the loss of cultural identity.

In January 1998, the federal government formally apologized to Native survivors of the residential schools and set up a $350 million community "healing" fund. At present, more than 6,300 Native plaintiffs are suing the Canadian government and the churches involved: Roman Catholic, Anglican, United, and Presbyterian. Indeed, some church groups have been pushed to the brink of bankruptcy by the weight of their past sins.

I remember talking with a Native medical student from Vancouver who said, "I really believe that it was the residential schools, more than anything else, that broke the spirit of Native society in Canada. It wasn't the poverty, it was the abuse. And it was passed on from generation to generation."

The Nisga'a Agreement

There are two basic ways to take territory away from its original inhabitants: (a) you can negotiate terms and treaties with them, or (b) you can go to war and *force* them to formally surrender it to you. Either way is acceptable by the rules of law. The Nisga'a of northwestern B.C., however, never ceded any land in treaties nor have they ever been conquered. By European legal standards, it would seem that their land still belongs to them.

Their outstanding land claim was finally settled in 1999 when Bill C-9, the Nisga'a Final Agreement Act, was passed in the House of Commons (it became law the following year, after being approved by the Senate). It was the first treaty involving B.C. to be signed since 1899. In exchange for abandoning all future claims and giving up their tax-free status (although they are still exempt from paying the GST and many provincial taxes), the Nisga'a were given the following:

- ✔ self-government

- ✔ payments worth roughly $253 million (including cash settlements, transfers, and trust funds)

- ✔ exclusive rights to forest and mineral resources on some 2,000 square kilometres of land (roughly 10 percent of their original territory) in the lower Nass Valley

- ✔ hunting rights and a share of the region's salmon stocks

It seems simple enough, but it is actually a very controversial settlement. It was passed in the House only after a heated, raucous debate that lasted 42 hours straight. Some people complained about the amount of money involved. After all, the Nisga'a population only numbers 5,000. But most of the criticism was directed at the system of government that was introduced. Although non-Nisga'a residents will be consulted on matters that affect them, ultimate authority is reserved for Nisga'a. In the words of opponents, it is "race-based government," something that goes against the basic principles of Canadian democracy. Others called it "a triumph of idealism over common sense."

The Nisga'a will have control over language, culture, property, public safety, and citizenship (that is, deciding who are "true" Nisga'a and who are not), as well as policing, courts, taxes, social and health services, child custody, adoption, and education. They are required to administer these under the terms of Canada's Charter of Rights and Freedoms — though critics argue that the agreement itself, based on racial background, already contravenes Canada's Charter. Retired Supreme Court judge Willard Estey has stated that the Nisga'a Agreement is in fact "unconstitutional," because it creates an independent state inside Canada with the power to effectively overrule both provincial and national laws. Kind of like "sovereignty-association."

For articles and information on the Nisga'a Agreement, including criticisms, visit www.nisgaa.org.

Nunavut

It was the largest and richest aboriginal land settlement ever made in Canada. On April 1, 1999, the new territory of Nunavut ("Our Land"), was carved out of the eastern side of the Northwest Territories in Canada's Arctic. More than twice the size of British Columbia, Nunavut covers two million square kilometres and about one-fifth of Canada's total land mass. The Inuit were allowed to retain ownership of 18 percent of the land — and they chose well. The areas they kept contain 80 percent of Nunavut's known mineral reserves: copper, lead, zinc, gold, and silver.

Under the terms of the Nunavut Land Agreement (first drafted in 1993), the territory was given self-government and a $1 billion cash settlement to be paid out over 14 years. The Inuit also retained their hunting rights. (Even today, more than half of all Inuit families rely on hunting for food.)

Unlike the Nisga'a Agreement, Nunavut does not have a racially based form of government. Instead, it operates along non-partisan lines, without political parties and with each member elected as an independent. That is, instead of being run according to ideology or party platform, Nunavut operates on a consensus-style system of "public" government, something that is closer to traditional Inuit forms of decision-making. The territorial government certainly has some serious social problems to deal with: high unemployment, crime, and drug and alcohol abuse.

Nunavut is also one of the most thinly populated regions on earth. There are just 24,700 people in Nunavut, of whom 83 percent are Inuit. (The working language of government will be Inuktitut.) The capital of Iqaluit, located on Baffin Island, has a population of 4,200. The rest of the people live in 27 other remote communities scattered across the Arctic. Nunavut represents the first time that any single First Nations group will have a majority presence in a provincial or territorial government. (The Dene and Métis of the Western Arctic rejected a similar $500 million offer in 1990 because it required them to surrender all aboriginal title to the land.)

The Nunavut Agreement has attracted international attention, particularly from countries like Australia and the United States, which have large aboriginal populations of their own and are studying the Canadian agreement as a possible model for their own land settlements. (However, Australian prime minister John Howard has recently rejected Canada as a role model for future aboriginal land claims settlements.)

December 6

It was one of the darkest moments in Canadian history. On December 6, 1989, deranged gunman Marc Lépine entered the Université de Montréal's polytechnical school and, in a 20-minute rampage, killed 14 female students with a semi-automatic rifle before turning the gun on himself. He targeted women, yelling, "You are all a bunch of feminists, and I hate feminists!" before he began shooting. The 1989 Montreal Massacre was the worst single-day mass murder in Canadian history and it shook the nation to the core. Heidi Rathjen, a student who had narrowly escaped when Lépine began his killing spree, helped create the Coalition for Gun Control, which led to an overhaul of Canada's gun laws and the introduction of stricter firearms registration under Bill C-68, which was passed in December 1995 (for more information, visit www.guncontrol.ca).

[The creation of Nunavut] is part of Canada's natural evolution — as natural as the birth of Saskatchewan and Alberta in 1905, which were taken out of the old N.W.T. to give residents more control over their lives.
— David F. Pelly, a writer specializing in Arctic issues

An "Information Gateway" to Nunavut can be found at `www.nunavut.com`. For the Nunavut Handbook, an on-line travel guide, go to `www.arctic-travel.com`. And for a quick overview of Nunavut, visit `www.arctic.ca/LUS/Nunavut_info.html` (but note: the population figures are out-of-date).

APEC and the Pepper Spray

In November 1997, leaders from around the Pacific Rim descended upon Vancouver for a summit held at the University of British Columbia. Members of the Asia Pacific Economic Conference (APEC) included dictators such as General Suharto of Indonesia and President Jiang Zemin of Communist China, both of whom were responsible for thousands of deaths.

When protestors gathered, the RCMP was ordered to clear them out. Protest signs were confiscated and students were pepper-sprayed to make way for the APEC motorcade. Several protestors were arrested, hauled away, strip-searched, and detained. Their crime? Questioning Canada's cozy snuggle-fest with Third World dictators.

The accusation, never proven but widely accepted, was that the RCMP actions were ordered by the Prime Minister's Office itself. When confronted at a news conference by guerrilla journalist Nardwuar and asked whether he thought pepper spray was acceptable in a democracy — "Does mace equal freedom?" — Jean Chrétien just laughed it off.

For me, pepper — I put it on my plate.
— the Prime Minister of Canada's oh-so-witty reply on being asked about the pepper-spray tactics of the RCMP

The RCMP's actions seemed to contravene Canada's Charter of Rights and Freedoms. Specifically: freedom of speech, freedom of expression, and freedom of assembly. But in the investigation that followed, the police insisted that they had secret inside information that the student protestors were planning a "serious breach of security." The pepper spray was simply a "pre-emptive strike." In other words, the protestors were nailed not for what they did or what they were doing, but for what they might have *possibly* been *thinking* about doing. Maybe.

Visit `www.nardwuar.com/apec` for the full story on Nardwuar vs. Jean Chrétien.

Hard Right: The Canadian Alliance

The rise of the Reform Party took everyone by surprise. Founded in 1987 with Preston Manning as leader, Reform began as a fringe protest party of Western Conservatives disillusioned with the policies of Brian Mulroney (see Chapter 23 for a full discussion of the Mulroney years). But the new party quickly became a giant killer, toppling the once powerful Conservative Party and replacing it as Canada's right-wing alternative to Liberal rule. Here is a quick snapshot of the rise of Reform.

- ✔ **1988:** In the federal election, the Reform Party fails to win a single seat.

- ✔ **1989:** In a by-election in Alberta, Reform elects its first MP, Deborah Grey. Mulroney and the Conservatives all but jeer.

- ✔ **1993:** Reform leapfrogs from a single MP to 52 seats — just two shy of Official Opposition (the honour of being "Her Majesty's Loyal Opposition" goes instead to the separatist Bloc Québécois). Support for the Conservative Party collapses, and the Tories are left with just two seats.

- ✔ **1997:** Reform surges ahead of the Bloc to win 60 seats and become the Official Opposition.

From zero to Opposition in less than ten years. It sounds like a rousing success story, except for one thing: The Reform Party under Preston Manning failed to elect a single MP east of Manitoba. Reform had stalled. It was a regional party and as such could never hope to form a national government. Manning realized this and decided to pursue a broader right-wing coalition. And thus, in February 2000, the Reform Party of Canada voted itself out of existence and re-emerged as the Canadian Alliance, uniting federal Reformers and provincial Conservatives. (The federal Conservative Party under Joe Clark rejected Manning's overtures.)

It was a bittersweet victory for Preston Manning. He had indeed succeeded in forging a wider, more broad-based conservative alliance, but in doing so, he lost his job. Instead of Manning, the new party chose Stockwell Day, former provincial treasurer of Alberta, to be their leader. Like Manning, Day is an evangelical Christian and a social and fiscal conservative.

- ✔ **Fiscal conservatives** believe in reducing the role of government in people's lives. They advocate cuts to social programs and prefer private enterprise to public projects. Their motto is: balance the books, cut government spending, and slash the deficit. This approach has taken root at a provincial level, most notably in Alberta under Ralph Klein and in Ontario under Mike Harris.

✔ **Social conservatives** are opposed to abortion, gun laws, gay rights, and public spending on multiculturalism. They often support tougher penalties for criminals and a crackdown on illegal immigrants. Stockwell Day is both a social *and* a fiscal conservative, something that has been met with near-hysteria at times. (On the eve of Day's victory as leader of the Canadian Alliance, the cover of *Maclean's* magazine featured a picture of Day with the headline *"How Scary?"* emblazoned across it in huge letters. Not *"Is* he scary?" — but *how* scary. I thought that was ridiculously slanted, and I'm not even a social conservative.)

Lyin' Jean?

Poor ol' Brian Mulroney. Reviled, resented, and treated with scorn by his fellow Canadians, he now has to watch as Uncle Jean and the Liberals go through his policies one by one and pick out the ones they like. Brian Mulroney (PM from 1984 to 1993) has derided the Canadian Alliance as simply "the Reform Party in pantyhose." Well, the same might be said of Jean Chrétien. In terms of economic policies, he is, in many ways, simply "Brian Mulroney in drag."

Chrétien promised to axe the GST and end Free Trade. He did neither. In fact, he has pursued Mulroney's economic policies — everything from low-inflation to NAFTA — with even greater enthusiasm than did Brian. But where Mulroney has had to carry the nickname "Lyin' Brian" for years, Chrétien is treated with an abiding and inexplicable affection by the Canadian electorate. In light of Chrétien's fiscal policies, the GST promise, privatizations, and NAFTA, perhaps, out of fairness, we should be referring to our current PM as "Lyin' Jean."

Still, give the Liberals their due. Under Chrétien and Finance Minister Paul Martin, they have balanced the budget for the first time in 20 years, have ended the annual deficit, and have even begun paying off Canada's bloated national debt. Heck, they have even started to bring in *surpluses*. After the awful excesses of the previous years, this really is an impressive achievement. (Mind you, Mulroney insists that the Liberals are merely basking in the light of his own glory. In Mulroney's words, the Conservatives "planted the garden," and the Liberals "picked the flowers.")

The most common way for economists to evaluate a nation's performance is through the use of a "misery index." The most straightforward example of this would be one that adds (a) the rate of inflation with (b) the rate of unemployment. The higher the number, the worse the economy. Using this standard method of evaluation, Jean Chrétien ranks as far and away the best Canadian prime minister since Lester B. Pearson. Now, a pair of professors at McGill recently juggled the numbers and tried to show that Chrétien is actually our *worst* prime minister since World War II and that Brian Mulroney was our best. But the two professors were using a system they invented themselves, so the results were unconvincing — to say the least.

Canada: Still Number One

Canada has always beaten the odds.

— our unofficial national motto

If our history teaches us anything, it is this: Canada is a success story. This is a country that has, through hard work and a bit of luck, managed to triumph over geography, internal inconsistencies, cultural faultlines, and the constant pressure of living next door to the United States. As I have written elsewhere and repeated often, our history is the tale of the slow triumph of human decency, the narrowing of the gap between the "ideal" and the "real." This is what our history teaches us; warts and all, good and bad.

Don't just take my word for it. In June 2000, the United Nations declared Canada the best country in the world in which to live, for the seventh year straight. We really are "number one."

The UN report (which compares standard of living, education, and longevity) also cautions Canada to improve in areas of poverty, gender equity, and literacy rates. And as I mentioned earlier, the United Nations has criticized Canada's slow handling of outstanding Native claims as well. Economically, Canada ranked 22nd, based on gross national product per capita (Luxembourg ranked #1). But as the UN report itself notes, "income is not the sum total of human lives."

Which is to say, Canada may not be the richest or strongest, but it has a legitimate claim to being the best.

Part IX
The Part of Tens

" - - - And Now We Are Ten!"

When Newfoundland, inappropriately labelled "Newfie" in this old cartoon, finally joined Canada (or was it the other way around?) the provinces were rounded out to 10. Today, with the three northern territories it comes to a lucky 13.

In this part . . .

Key moments. Important leaders. Political firsts for women. This is a final grab bag of interesting items culled from my cluttered files on Canadiana, a checklist of sorts, covering everything from the famous to the obscure. You can use the information that follows to confound your foes and impress your friends. It makes for great cocktail party repartee. *"Did I ever mention that the first time a woman in Canada was elected to a provincial assembly was in 1917?"* Yessir. You'll be the life of the party with these goodies.

Chapter 25

Ten Great Canadian Quotations — Pre- and Post-Confederation

· ·

In This Chapter

▶ Memorable comments, quotes and quips from Canada's past

· ·

Canada's "master gatherer," John Robert Colombo, once wrote an entire history of Canada based on great quotations (*Colombo's All-Time Great Canadian Quotations*). It was a fun approach, so I thought I would give my own personal list of favourite quotes.

Pre-Confederation

Here are ten great quotations from early Canadian history:

"Faux comme un diamant du Canada" ("As fake as a Canadian diamond")

This was an expression popular in France after Jacques Cartier returned from his third voyage to Canada (1541–42) loaded down with what he thought were diamonds and gold. It turned out to be nothing more than quartz and iron pyrites ("fool's gold"). Cartier's voyages are described in detail in Chapter 2.

"We are as near to Heaven by sea as by land!"

These were the last words of the ill-fated English explorer Humphrey Gilbert, just before his ship went down in a squall in the North Atlantic. He was returning from a voyage to the New World, in which he had claimed England's first colony at Newfoundland on August 5, 1583, a date often referred to as "the birth of the British Empire." (For more on the early exploration and settlement of Canada, see Chapter 2.)

"Caesars of the wilderness"

Popular historian Peter C. Newman gave this title to the early fur-trading voyageurs. The phrase comes from a boast made by Pierre-Esprit Radisson, early exponent of a Hudson Bay trade route (which I describe in Chapter 5). In his 1661 journals, Radisson declares: "We were Caesars, being nobody to contradict us."

"I have no reply to make to your general, other than from the mouths of my cannon and muskets."

These were the defiant words of Governor Frontenac in response to English demands that he surrender to an invasion force under William Phips in 1690. For a full account of this dramatic face off, see Chapter 5.

"The paths of glory lead but to the grave."

General James Wolfe underlined this final line in the ninth stanza of Thomas Gray's poem *Elegy Written in a Country Churchyard* before he died in battle on the Plains of Abraham in 1759 (see Chapter 7). Québec was captured, New France was taken, and the history of Canada changed forever.

"They sacrificed everything save honour."

This is the inscription on a cairn in Nova Scotia honouring the United Empire Loyalists. Following the American Revolution (1775–83), 50,000 refugees, still loyal to the British Crown, fled north into what is now Canada. Their story is told in Chapter 9.

"Alexander Mackenzie, from Canada, by land, 22nd July 1793"

Alexander Mackenzie painted this message with a mix of vermilion and grease on a large boulder near the mouth of the Bella Coola River on the Pacific Coast of what would one day be British Columbia. As I note in Chapter 10, Mackenzie was the first person to cross North America overland, north of Mexico.

"The Americans are coming!"

Laura Secord crossed the war-torn Niagara Escarpment with this message to warn British, Canadian, and Native allies of an impending attack during the War of 1812, as described in Chapter 10.

"Up then, brave Canadians! Get ready your rifles, and make short work of it!"

Rebel leader William Lyon Mackenzie used this rallying cry in 1837, urging Canadians to rise up against the British colonial government (see Chapter 11).

"Two nations warring in the bosom of a single state."

This was Lord Durham's famous description of French–English relations in Canada, in his report on the causes and consequences of the Rebellions of 1837. For more on the Durham Report, see Chapter 12.

Post-Confederation

Here are ten more unforgettable quotations (from 1867 to the present):

A Mari Usque Ad Mare (From Sea to Sea)

Canada's national motto, in Latin, was adopted with Confederation in 1867, and was suggested by New Brunswick Premier Leonard Tilley. With Canada now extended to the Arctic Ocean as well, it has been suggested that the motto be changed to "from sea to sea — *to sea.*"

Peace, order, and good government

Canada's "mission statement," the three goals of Confederation as laid out in the British North America (BNA) Act of 1867 (see Chapter 13).

"He shall hang though every dog in Québec bark in his favour."

Prime Minister John A. Macdonald gave this bitter response to the reaction against the death sentence handed down to Métis leader Louis Riel in 1885, as described in Chapter 14.

"The 20th century belongs to Canada!"

Prime Minister Wilfrid Laurier made this prediction in 1904. (What he actually said was "The nineteenth century was the century of the United States. I think we can claim it is Canada that shall fill the twentieth century.") For more on the "sunny ways" of the Laurier days, see Chapter 15.

"Never retract, never explain, never apologize — just get the job done and let them howl."

The motto of activist Nellie McClung, who helped spearhead the campaign to grant women the vote. Manitoba became the first province to do so in 1916, followed closely by Saskatchewan and Alberta. The full story of McClung and the early women's rights crusaders in Canada can be found in Chapter 17.

"Conscription if necessary, but not necessarily conscription."

Prime Minister Mackenzie King made this evasive policy statement during World War II (1939–45) regarding the issue of conscription (forcing men into military service), as I describe in Chapter 19. It is considered a classic of political doubletalk.

"Come near at your peril, Canadian wolf!"

These are lyrics from an anti-Confederate song popular in Newfoundland in the 1860s, when the province first rejected Confederation. The song was revived in the 1940s when union was again proposed. This time, however, the "Canadian wolf" won. Newfoundland joined Canada in 1949 (see Chapter 20).

"The medium is the message."

Edmonton-born communications guru Marshall McLuhan penned this famous aphorism in his 1964 book *Understanding Media*. McLuhan, who also coined the term "global village," recognized that the *way* information is transmitted influences the *content* of the information itself. He has been heralded as the prophet of the Communications Age.

"Just watch me . . ."

Prime Minister Trudeau gave this terse reply on being asked how far he would extend government powers during the October Crisis of 1970. (Separatist terrorists had kidnapped a British trade commissioner; see Chapter 21.)

"Canada is divisible because Canada is not a real country."

Separatist logic at its best. Lucien Bouchard made this provocative statement in the wake of the 1995 Referendum when he explained why Canada is divisible but Québec is not. The details of this ongoing debate can be found in Chapters 24 and 13.

Chapter 26

Five Important English and French Pairs

- -

In This Chapter

▶ Some of the key "pairings" of English and French leaders — enemies and allies alike — who have hurt, helped, and hindered Canada's development

- -

Author Hugh MacLennan once described Canada as a nation of "two solitudes," referring to French and English. He borrowed the phrase from the writings of German poet Rainer Maria Rilke, who spoke of solitudes that "protect and touch and greet each other." But in MacLennan's usage, it is far more melancholy, suggesting as it does parallel lives and separate realities.

But this image isn't accurate, either. Over the years, French and English Canada have collided, co-operated, and clashed headlong. We are, as author John Ralston Saul put it, not so much mere siblings, as Siamese twins — often squabbling, sometimes in harmony, but irretrievably linked. As enemies and allies, friends and foes, leaders from both sides have had an immense impact on the evolution of Canada. Here then are five key historic English–French "pairings" (which adds up nicely to ten):

Wolfe & Montcalm

James Wolfe was the reckless young general sent by the British to capture Québec City in 1759. General Louis-Joseph de Montcalm was the French defender. Both men died from wounds received during the Battle of the Plains of Abraham. Québec fell, and the following year France surrendered Canada to the British. (I tell the whole story of this dramatic moment in Canadian history in Chapter 7.)

Mackenzie & Papineau

In 1837, the colonies of Upper and Lower Canada (which would one day become Ontario and Québec) boiled over in rebellion. The English-Canadian uprising was led by a fiery newspaper editor named William Lyon Mackenzie.

The French rebellions — more widespread and violent — were launched (but not led) by the aristocratic reformer Louis-Joseph Papineau. Although both uprisings were crushed, they did set in motion a series of reforms that led to responsible government and — eventually — Confederation itself. (Though most historians would challenge me on that last point.) See Chapter 11 for more on this quixotic pair of would-be liberators.

Baldwin & LaFontaine

Moderate reformers succeeded where the radical revolutionaries had failed. The fight for greater democratic representation (that is, "responsible government") was led by Robert Baldwin in English Canada, and Louis-Hippolyte LaFontaine in French Canada. The two became close friends and political allies, and together they reshaped the very structure of colonial government in Canada (see Chapter 12). Responsible government was finally won in 1848, first in Nova Scotia under Joseph Howe and then in Canada under Baldwin and LaFontaine.

Macdonald & Cartier

In 1867, Nova Scotia, New Brunswick, and the Province of Canada (Québec and Ontario), joined together to form a new union — one that would eventually stretch from sea to sea. The key architect of Confederation, and father of the country, was John A. Macdonald. Often overlooked, however, was his key French-Canadian ally: George-Étienne Cartier. As I describe in Chapter 13, it was Cartier who brought Québec into Confederation, and it was Cartier who acted as a "co-prime minister" during Macdonald's first eventful years in office. The two men were inseparable. (Macdonald even referred to his old friend as "my second self.")

Mulroney & Bouchard

When Brian Mulroney was elected in 1984, he forged close ties with Québec's separatists, hoping — naively, as it turned out — that he could somehow "convert" them to federalism. Among his Québec lieutenants was Brian's close friend and old chum Lucien Bouchard. But when constitutional talks aimed at bringing Québec into the Constitution began to fall apart in 1990, Bouchard stabbed Mulroney in the back — and twisted the blade, leaving the Tories to form a separatist coalition: the Bloc Québécois. *"Et tu, Lucien?"* (Brian has given instructions that, if he dies before Bouchard—and if Bouchard shows up at the funeral — the service is to be stopped until Bouchard has been shown the door. Only once he has left is the service to resume.) For more on Lucien Bouchard and his infamous betrayal of Brian Mulroney, see Chapter 23.

Chapter 27

Ten Important Aboriginal Leaders

. . . .

In This Chapter

▶ Warriors, diplomats, and politicians: Here are ten influential First Nations leaders from Canadian history

. . . .

*H*ere is a list of important Native leaders in Canadian history. They are covered in more detail elsewhere in this book, and all have played an important role in the long, difficult struggle that Canada's First Nations have had to face. War or peace? Big Bear or Crowfoot? In many ways, these leaders were caught on the horns of a dilemma — how to handle overwhelming problems without falling into despair or defeatism.

Dekanahwidah

A "heavenly messenger" who brought the Great Law of Peace to the warring nations of the southern Iroquois, Dekanahwidah united them in a powerful confederacy (most likely in 1451), as I describe in Chapter 1. Some have even credited the Iroquois Confederacy as being the model for the U.S. Constitution. The Iroquois were the "Romans of the New World," and the key to their strength — and their survival — lay in the united federation first forged by Dekanahwidah.

Membertou

If the settlers in Acadia during the early 1600s were spared the type of blood-shed that the habitants in New France faced at the hands of the Iroquois, much of the credit goes to the Mi'kmaq chief Membertou, who aided the Acadians and promoted friendship with them. For more on the early years of Acadia and the important role that the Mi'kmaq played, see Chapters 3 and 6.

Pontiac

In 1763, the Ottawa war chief Pontiac led a massive Native uprising against the British. The frontier was set ablaze, and every fort west of Niagara was captured (other than Detroit). More than 2,400 soldiers and settlers were killed before a peace treaty was arranged. Pontiac himself was later assassinated. The Pontiac Rebellion is covered in Chapter 8.

Maquinna

When British traders first arrived on the west coast of Vancouver Island in the 1780s, they were met by the wealthy Nootka chief Maquinna, who granted them "diplomatic" status and allowed a trading post to be built — a decision Maquinna would later regret. For more on early European contact along the Pacific Coast, see Chapter 9.

Tecumseh

In the War of 1812, which I cover in Chapter 10, the United States launched a full-scale invasion of Canada. Fortunately, the great Shawnee chief Tecumseh led an alliance of First Nations that helped capture Detroit and push back the American invaders. Tecumseh, one of the "saviours of Canada," died in fierce hand-to-hand combat against U.S. cavalry in a battle in southern Ontario. Tecumseh's friend and ally, the British general Isaac Brock, called him the "most gallant warrior" he had ever seen. Brock too died in battle.

Big Bear

During the Northwest Rebellion of 1885, covered in Chapter 14, a break-away band of Cree under Chief Big Bear (along with another group led by Poundmaker) joined in the uprising, killing settlers and attacking forts. Although he had tried to stop the violence, Big Bear was sent to prison. His spirit and health broken, he died soon after being released. The era of the great Plains Nations was over.

Crowfoot

With the disappearance of the buffalo, the People of the Plains faced starvation and ruin, as an entire way of life came to an end (described in Chapter 14). It was a time ripe for violence, as the Cree under Big Bear had demonstrated. Among the Blackfoot Confederacy, however, Chief Crowfoot kept the peace, urging diplomacy over war. He rejected the call to violence in 1885 and kept his people united during times of incredible hardship.

Frederick Loft

During the 1920s, Loft, a Mohawk veteran of World War I, organized a national League of Indians to fight for Native rights — including the right to vote. Denounced as "an agitator," he was put under police surveillance and his league was effectively outlawed. (See Chapter 17.) Although he was never able to establish his proposed pan-Native alliance, his spirit — and anger — lives on in today's Assembly of First Nations.

Elijah Harper

"No, Mr. Speaker." With these three words, Elijah Harper, a Cree member of the Manitoba legislature, brought the entire Canadian political machinery to a grinding halt. When the Meech Lake Accord was brought forward for debate in 1990, Harper blocked it by refusing to allow it to be introduced. The Accord died, setting off a domino effect of crises that took Canada right to the brink of dissolution. For the full story on how Elijah Harper derailed the best laid plans of Brian Mulroney — with a single, obstinate "no" — see Chapter 23.

John Amagoalik

Inuit leader John Amagoalik was the driving force behind the 1999 creation of Nunavut, a new territory with a population that is over 80 percent Inuit. The Nunavut Agreement also included a final land settlement — the richest and largest such settlement in Canadian history. Amagoalik, the former head of the Inuit Tapirisat ("alliance") spent 20 years fighting for this, and has been hailed as "the Arctic John A." For details on the birth of Nunavut, see Chapter 24.

Chapter 28

Ten Political Firsts for Canadian Women

In This Chapter

▶ Ten women who made Canadian political history

> *Whatever women do, they must do twice as good as men to be thought half so good. . . . Fortunately, this isn't difficult.*
> — Charlotte Whitton, outspoken mayor of Ottawa

Women first won the right to vote in Manitoba in 1916, with Saskatchewan and Alberta following soon after. Two years later, they were allowed to vote in federal elections as well. The early women's movement focused on specific social problems: child labour laws, the "opium trade", temperance (encouraging abstinence in alcohol consumption), and later outright prohibition (banning the sale of alcohol). I cover all this in Chapter 17.

In the 1960s and '70s a second wave of feminism arose (or "third wave" depending on how you're counting), which was more radical and far-reaching. Feminism became an ideology onto itself. And under the slogan "the personal is political," private issues that had once been beyond the realm of government were now the focus of intense public debate. (For more on this era, see Chapter 21.) Pay equity, reformed divorce laws, access to abortion, and equal opportunity programs — criticized by opponents as "reverse discrimination" — were the leading issues of the day. It's been a long, hard road and the following ten women all achieved important political firsts along the way.

Emily Murphy

First female police magistrate

In 1916, Emily Murphy (a.k.a: "Janey Canuck") was appointed to the head of a newly created Women's Court in Edmonton. (In fact, Murphy was the first female judge appointed anywhere in the British Empire.) She later spearheaded the campaign to have women recognized as "persons" in the eyes of the law, a fight that was won in 1929 with a decision by the British Privy Council, which stated that the exclusion of women was "a relic of days more barbarous than ours."

Louise McKinney

First woman elected to a provincial assembly

Elected to the Alberta legislature in 1917, McKinney was the first woman to sit as an elected official anywhere in the British Empire. (Another woman, Roberta MacAdams, was also elected that same year, but was unable to attend the opening day of the legislature, and thus McKinney had the honour of being sworn in first.) As one of the "Famous Five," McKinney lent her support to Emily Murphy's campaign to have women legally recognized as "persons."

Agnes Macphail

First woman elected to the House of Commons

Elected in 1921 in a riding in southwestern Ontario, Agnes Macphail was a one-woman social reform movement, leading the fight for everything from child labour laws to better health care to farm aid. She was especially active in prison reform. (Once, when a warden tried to stop her from entering a prison, telling her, "Jail is no place for a lady," Macphail retorted, "I'm no lady, I'm an MP.")

Cairine Wilson

First woman appointed to the Senate

Canada's first female delegate to the UN

Emily Murphy had wanted to be named Canada's first female senator, but Murphy wasn't a Liberal and in the end Prime Minister Mackenzie King appointed Cairine Wilson instead, a long-time member of the Liberal establishment. Wilson became the first woman in Canada's Upper House in 1930, and in 1949 was a delegate to the United Nations.

Ellen Fairclough

First female federal cabinet minister

Appointed in 1957, as Secretary of State under John Diefenbaker, Fairclough was Canada's first woman to sit in the "inner sanctum" of the Federal Cabinet. The following year she moved to the Department of Citizenship and Immigration and was later made Postmaster General.

Charlotte Whitton

First woman elected mayor of a Canadian city

Mayor of Ottawa, 1951–56 and 1960–64, Whitton's time in office was stormy — at one point she physically assaulted a male colleague for criticizing her. Late in life, looking back at her eventful career, she said, with a smile, "Do you know what I was? I was hell on wheels."(She was referring to the nickname given her by the media and opponents during her days as mayor.) Charlotte Whitton has been called "one of this century's most colourful and controversial women."

Jeanne Sauvé

First woman to be named Speaker of the House of Commons

First woman to be appointed Governor General

A renowned journalist, in paper, radio, and television, Sauvé moved into federal politics in the 1970s and quickly made a name for herself in the areas of science and technology, communications, and the environment. She became Canada's first female Speaker of the House of Commons in 1980, and is credited with completely overhauling the outdated administration of the House. She was appointed Governor General by Pierre Trudeau and served from 1984 to 1990.

Audrey McLaughlin

First woman to lead a national political party

Yukon MP Audrey McLaughlin was chosen as leader of the federal New Democrats in 1989, becoming the first woman to lead a national political party in Canada. McLaughlin stepped down in 1995 and was succeeded by Alexa McDonough, the *second* woman to lead a national Canadian political party. (McLaughlin, meanwhile, went on to be elected president of the Socialist International Women in 1996.)

Rita Johnston

First female provincial premier

In 1990, Rita Johnston was named B.C.'s deputy premier under the Social Credit government of Bill Vander Zalm. When Vander Zalm stepped down in April 1991, Johnston became premier — the first woman to head a provincial government. It was a short-lived tenure, however, and in the October election that followed, the SoCreds were defeated and Johnston herself lost her seat.

Kim Campbell

First female prime minister

Kim Campbell took over leadership of the federal Conservative Party from the deeply unpopular Brian Mulroney in June 1993. In doing so, she automatically became prime minister — the first woman to hold Canada's highest public office. But in the election that followed in October, the Tories were trounced, and Campbell lost her own seat. In 1996, Jean Chrétien (the very man who had defeated her in 1993), named Campbell as Canada's consul general in Los Angeles.

Chapter 29

The Ten Prime Ministers You Need to Know

. . . .

In This Chapter

▶ Ten of Canada's most notable PMs

. . . .

Given a government with a big surplus, and a big majority and a weak opposition, you could debauch a committee of archangels.

— John A. Macdonald on the nature of politics in Canada

*I*n the Cheat Sheet at the front of this book, you will find all 20 of Canada's prime ministers along with the terms they served. It's a long list and one meant mainly for cross-referencing events. The problem with lists like that is they give the impression of equality, as though the items listed are all of similar importance. But many of our PMs served only a few months — at most. And let's face it, no one really needs to know who John Abbott or Mackenzie Bowell or John Turner were. They were hiccups in time, footnotes in history.

So, with that in mind, I present the *short list* of Canadian prime ministers, along with some of the key points you need to know about them. These ten prime ministers, given in order of appearance, are the ones that every Canadian really should be familiar with. These are the ones you *do* need to know.

In the list that follows, the *C* refers to Conservative, and the *L* to Liberal, even though these titles weren't used in every case. (Borden, for one, headed a coalition Union government during World War I, even though he himself was a Tory.)

John A. Macdonald: (C: 1867–73, 1878–91)

Canada's first prime minister, the Father of the Country, and key architect of Confederation, Sir John A. was a true nation-builder who oversaw the creation of a Canada stretching "from sea to sea." Forced out of office in 1873 following the Pacific Scandal, he came roaring back to finish the all-Canadian transcontinental railway: the CPR. During his time as PM, Macdonald championed a protectionist "National Policy" aimed at strengthening Canadian economic independence, and refused to pardon Métis leader Louis Riel after the 1885 North-West Rebellion.

Wilfrid Laurier: (L: 1896–1911)

Canada's first French-Canadian PM, and an eloquent orator, known as "the Knight of the Silver Plume," Laurier sought compromise and conciliation between French and English Canada. He was in office during the Klondike Gold Rush, the settling of the West, and the creation of Alberta and Saskatchewan in 1905. Laurier resisted imperial overtures from Britain to "consolidate the Empire" and launched an extensive, almost reckless, railway program (the forerunner of today's northern transcontinental line, the CNR).

Robert Borden: (C: 1911–20)

As Canada's prime minister during World War I, Borden introduced the contentious conscription bill, allowing the government to draft men into military service. He also gave women the vote, and used Canada's contributions to the war effort to push for greater national autonomy. Considered "the Father of Canadian Political Independence," Borden is probably Canada's single most *underrated* PM.

William Lyon Mackenzie King: (L: 1921–30, 1935–48; with a brief interruption in 1926)

Canada's longest-serving PM (and a perennial favourite of history professors), King was prime minister during World War II, and he managed to keep Canada more or less united during the divisive war years. King oversaw the forced relocation of Japanese Canadians from the West Coast and the bureaucratic "blockade" of Jewish immigrants who were trying to escape the Nazi reign of terror. King also established racially biased immigration quotas that would stay in effect right up until 1962. A grandson of 1837 rebel leader William Lyon Mackenzie, King helped launch Canada's move towards a welfare state by introducing Old Age Pensions, Unemployment Insurance, and Family Allowances.

R.B. Bennett: (C: 1930–35)

A self-made millionaire and PM during the worst years of the Great Depression, Bennett was the wrong man in the wrong place at the wrong time. Even as the economic crisis worsened, Bennett hoped that the market would somehow "self-adjust." When it failed to do so, Bennett tried to bring in a series of wide-ranging reforms, but he was tossed out of office before he could put most of them into practice. Until Mulroney came along, Bennett was the least-liked PM in Canadian history.

Louis St. Laurent: (L: 1948–57)

"Uncle Louis" took over when Mackenzie King retired, and he guided Canada through the golden years of post-war prosperity. As our Cold War prime minister, he promoted Canada's role as a "middle power" and was an early advocate of NATO and other military defense plans. He oversaw construction of the St. Lawrence Seaway and the Trans-Canada Highway, he helped bring Newfoundland into Confederation in 1949, and he supported Canada's involvement in the Korean War.

John Diefenbaker: (C: 1957–63)

"The Chief" was a Prairie populist and an anti-American, pro-British patriot, known for his stirring speeches and soaring rhetoric. Leading the country through a tumultuous, stormy time he scrapped the supersonic Arrow jet, introduced the idealistic — but ineffective — 1960 Bill of Rights, gave Native Canadians the vote, and dismantled King's blatantly discriminatory immigration quotas.

Lester "Mike" Pearson: (L: 1963–68)

Pearson was awarded the Nobel Peace Prize in 1957 for his work in creating the UN's first peacekeeping force. As PM, he laboured under back-to-back minority governments, but still managed to bring in the U.S./Canada Auto Pact, National Medicare, and the Canada Pension Plan. He also gave us our national flag: a stylized red maple leaf. Pearson was PM during Expo 67 and Canada's centennial year birthday celebrations.

Pierre Trudeau: (L: 1968–79, 1980–84)

An intellectual gadfly and rich man's son, Trudeau entered federal politics to (a) secure Québec's place in Confederation, and (b) force English Canada to accept the "French fact." He sparked widespread "Trudeaumania" early on, and later crushed the FLQ terrorist movement by suspending civil liberties under the War Measures Act in 1970. The Father of Official Bilingualism, Trudeau also introduced policies of economic nationalism, including several controversial programs aimed at checking U.S. control of Canadian resources. Trudeau brought home Canada's Constitution in 1982 (against the objections of Québec premier René Lévesque) along with a Charter of Rights and Freedoms.

Brian Mulroney: (C: 1984–93)

The Father of Free Trade and the GST, Mulroney drafted two successive constitutional accords — Meech Lake and Charlottetown — aimed at giving the provinces greater powers and Québec special status. Both attempts failed and separatism in Québec was revived. Following Mulroney's unpopular and highly controversial term as PM, the Conservative Party was all but destroyed in the 1993 federal election.

On-line Resources

Still curious? Want to find out more? Here is a list of recommended on-line Canadiana resources. There's lots to explore. Throughout this book, specific Web sites are listed with the areas that I cover. The list that follows, however, is of broader-based general Canadian sites (with a few fun ones thrown in as well). Almost all of these are "guru" sites that provide access to hundreds and hundreds of other links. Enjoy!

Aboriginal Links (www.bloorstreet.com/300block/aborcan.htm): a comprehensive and wide-ranging list of links to sites dealing with Canada's First Nations.

Bluepete's History Site (www.blupete.com): one of my favourite sites. Click on "History" for an extensive history of Nova Scotia and Acadia, with links to lesser-known, general history sites.

Oh Canada! (www.ualberta.ca/~bleeck/canada): a very patriotic site. It contains everything that every proud Canadian should know.

Canada's Digital Collection (collections.ic.gc.ca): this is the one! An ever-expanding collection of links, this site provides access to a wide range of Canadiana. This should be your first stop any time you're doing research—or simply surfing for fun. Click on "Alphabetical Listing" and scroll down.

Canada History (www.canadahistory.com): a complete history of Canada, with timelines, images, and excellent overviews. (Click on "Contents" first to see the full range of topics covered.)

Canada Information Office (www.infocan.gc.ca): click on "About Canada" and explore.

CanadaInfo (home.ican.net/~marlatt/craig/index.html#home): a good overview of Canadian topics, easy to navigate, with links. (Check out the fascinating "Canadian Personalities" section!)

Canada Rocks the World (www.geocities.com/SouthBeach/1708/Canada_eh.html): a rollicking good Web site with lots of fun links.

Canadiana Quick Reference (part of the National Library on-line) (www.nlc-bnc.ca/services/quickref/ecqrmenu.htm)

Canadiana Resource Page (www.cs.cmu.edu/Unofficial/Canadiana): an extensive and wide-ranging list of links—it's like having access to an entire on-line reference library.

Canadian Heritage Gallery (www.canadianheritage.org): an extensive on-line collection of Canadiana (images, pictures, paintings, and documents).

Canadian History on the Web (members.home.net/dneylan/index.html): another one of my all-time favourite sites. This should be one of your first stops when surfing for Canadiana. Click on "content-based" for links to specific topics. Short summaries beside links are especially useful.

Canadian Inventions (www.stc.carleton.ca/inventor.html): it's a long list!

Canadian Research Links (spider.georgetowncollege.edu/htallant/ courses/his318/318links.htm): links to Canadian history sites, from a U.S.-based Canadian Studies Program.

Canadian Studies: Guide to Sources (www.iccs-ciec.ca/blackwell.html): an extensive bibliographical essay, including print sources and on-line links.

Canadian Studies Program (www.pch.gc.ca/csp-pec): an eclectic site with a wide range of articles, run by the Department of Canadian Heritage.

Canadian World Domination (www.standonguard.com): hilarious! One of my favourite sites. And you thought Canadians were timid.

Dave's Truly Canadian Dictionary (www.luther.bc.ca/~dave7cnv/ cdnspelling/cdnspelling.html): a site that includes comparisons of Canadian, British, and American usage.

Dominion Institute (www.schoolnet.ca/greatquestions/e/about_di. html): this site includes a tie-in with the Great Canadian Questions series and has quizzes to test your new-found Canadian knowledge.

Heritage Project (www.heritageproject.ca): home of the all-Canadian "Heritage Minutes."

The History of Canada (www.linksnorth.com/canada-history): an on-line history of Canada, it provides a good overview.

Important Moments in Canadian History (www.arts.ouc.bc.ca/fiar/ his_home.html): timelines that cover all the major events in Canada's past.

Mysteries of Canada (www.mysteriesofcanada.com): a forum for gathering tales of Canadian folklore. Lots of fun.

National Archives of Canada (www.archives.ca)

National Atlas of Canada Online (atlas.gc.ca): more than just maps! This site has all kinds of links and fun facts.

National History Society of Canada (www.historysociety.ca): with a link to *The Beaver*, Canada's national history magazine. (*The Beaver* is an excellent publication. Check it out.)

National Library of Canada (www.nlc-bnc.ca/ehome.htm)

Parks Canada (parkscanada.pch.gc.ca): a wonderful site for armchair travel, as well as for background on Canadian historical sites.

Prime Ministers of Canada (cnet.unb.ca/achn/pm): bios, background, anecdotes—everything you need to know about Canada's PMs.

United Nations World Heritage Sites (www.unesco.org/whc/heritage.htm): a complete list, with links to Canada's own World Heritage Sites: from the Viking settlement at L'Anse aux Meadows, Newfoundland, to Head-Smashed-In-Buffalo Jump, Alberta.

Virtual Museums (www.civilization.ca): provides access to the Canadian Museum of Civilization, the Canadian War Museum, and the excellent—and highly recommended—Virtual Museum of New France.

This Week in History (parkscanada.pch.gc.ca/library/stories/ stories_e.cfm): a site run by Parks Canada, with lots of stories. Great for dipping into.

Women in Canadian History (www.niagara.com/~merrwill): from Susan Merritt, author of the popular Her Story series of books.

Note: all sites listed above were active as of August 2000.

Index

●●●

• C •

• O •

• P •

• S •

Discover Dummies Online!

The Dummies Web Site is your fun and friendly online resource for the latest information about *For Dummies*® books and your favorite topics. The Web site is the place to communicate with us, exchange ideas with other *For Dummies* readers, chat with authors, and have fun!

Ten Fun and Useful Things You Can Do at www.dummies.com

1. Win free *For Dummies* books and more!

2. Register your book and be entered in a prize drawing.

3. Meet your favorite authors through the IDG Books Worldwide Author Chat Series.

4. Exchange helpful information with other *For Dummies* readers.

5. Discover other great *For Dummies* books you must have!

6. Purchase Dummieswear™ exclusively from our Web site.

7. Buy *For Dummies* books online.

8. Talk to us. Make comments, ask questions, get answers!

9. Download free software.

10. Find additional useful resources from authors.

Link directly to these ten fun and useful things at
http://www.dummies.com/10useful

For other technology titles from IDG Books Worldwide, go to
www.idgbooks.com

Not on the Web yet? It's easy to get started with *Dummies 101*®: *The Internet For Windows*® *98* or *The Internet For Dummies*® at local retailers everywhere.

Find other *For Dummies* books on these topics:

Business • Career • Databases • Food & Beverage • Games • Gardening • Graphics • Hardware
Health & Fitness • Internet and the World Wide Web • Networking • Office Suites
Operating Systems • Personal Finance • Pets • Programming • Recreation • Sports
Spreadsheets • Teacher Resources • Test Prep • Word Processing

IDG BOOKS WORLDWIDE
BOOK REGISTRATION

Register This Book and Win!

We want to hear from you!

Visit **http://my2cents.dummies.com** to register this book and tell us how you liked it!

✔ Get entered in our monthly prize giveaway.

✔ Give us feedback about this book — tell us what you like best, what you like least, or maybe what you'd like to ask the author and us to change!

✔ Let us know any other *For Dummies®* topics that interest you.

Your feedback helps us determine what books to publish, tells us what coverage to add as we revise our books, and lets us know whether we're meeting your needs as a *For Dummies* reader. You're our most valuable resource, and what you have to say is important to us!

Not on the Web yet? It's easy to get started with *Dummies 101®: The Internet For Windows® 98* or *The Internet For Dummies®* at local retailers everywhere.

Or let us know what you think by sending us a letter at the following address:

For Dummies Book Registration
Dummies Press
10475 Crosspoint Blvd.
Indianapolis, IN 46256

...FOR DUMMIES™

BESTSELLING BOOK SERIES